Liberalizing Foreign Trade

Volume 5

Liberalizing Foreign Trade

Edited by
*Demetris Papageorgiou, Michael Michaely, and
Armeane M. Choksi*

Volume 5

The Experience of Indonesia, Pakistan, and Sri Lanka

INDONESIA　*Mark M. Pitt*

PAKISTAN　*Stephen Guisinger and Gerald Scully*

SRI LANKA　*Andrew G. Cuthbertson and Premachandra Athukorala*

Basil Blackwell

First published 1991

HF
1411
· L497
1989
v. 5

Basil Blackwell, Inc.
3 Cambridge Center
Cambridge, Massachusetts 02142, USA

Basil Blackwell Ltd
108 Cowley Road, Oxford, OX4 1JF, UK

British Library Cataloguing in Publication Data
A CIP catalogue record for this book is available from the British Library.

Library of Congress Cataloging in Publication Data

Liberalizing foreign trade/edited Demetris Papageorgiou, Michael Michaely, and Armeane M. Choksi.
p. cm.
Includes index.
Contents: v. 1. Liberalizing Foreign Trade: The Experience of Argentina, Chile, and Uruguay — v. 2. Liberalizing Foreign Trade: The Experience of Korea, the Philippines, and Singapore — v. 3. Liberalizing Foreign Trade: The Experience of Israel and Yugoslavia — v. 4. Liberalizing Foreign Trade: The Experience of Brazil, Colombia, and Perú — v. 5. Liberalizing Foreign Trade: The Experience of Indonesia, Pakistan, and Sri Lanka — v. 6. Liberalizing Foreign Trade: The Experience of New Zealand, Spain, and Turkey — v. 7. Liberalizing Foreign Trade: Lessons of Experience in the Developing World
ISBN 0–631–16666–1 (v. 1). ISBN 0–631–16671–8 (v.5)
ISBN 0–631–17595–4 (7–volume set)
1. Commercial policy. 2. Free trade. 3. International trade.
I. Papageorgiou, Demetris, 1938–. II Michaely, Michael, 1928–. III. Choksi, Armeane M., 1944–.
HF 1411.L497 1989
382'.3—dc19   88–37455
                                                                                  CIP

Typeset in 10 on 12pt Times
by TecSet Ltd
Printed in Great Britain by T. J. Press Ltd, Padstow

Contents

About the Editors

Demetris Papageorgiou is the Chief of the Country Operations Division in the Brazil Department of the World Bank. He has served as a senior economist in the Country Policy Department and as an economist at the Industry Division of the Development Economics Department.

Michael Michaely is the Lead Economist in the Brazil Department of the World Bank. Previously he was the Aron and Michael Chilewich Professor of International Trade and Dean of the Faculty of Social Sciences at the Hebrew University of Jerusalem. He has published numerous books and articles on international economics.

Armeane M. Choksi is Director of the Brazil Department in the Latin American and Caribbean Region of the World Bank. He is co-editor with Demetris Papageorgiou of *Economic Liberalization in Developing Countries*, and has written on industrial and trade policy.

Editors' Preface

The General Objective

"Protection," said the British statesman Benjamin Disraeli in 1845, "is not a principle, but an expedient," and this pronouncement can serve very well as the text for our study of *trade liberalization*. The benefits of open trading have by now been sufficiently demonstrated and described by economic historians and analysts. In this study, we take them for granted and turn our minds from the "whether" to the "how."

The Delectable Mountains of open trading confront the pilgrim with formidable obstacles and there are many paths to the top. The direct route seldom turns out to be the best in practice. It may bring on rapid exhaustion and early collapse, while a more devious approach, skirting areas of excessive transition costs, may offer the best prospects of long-term survival.

Given the sharp diversity of economic background and experience between different countries, and indeed, between different periods in the same country, we should not expect the most favorable route to turn out the same for each country, except perhaps by accident. There are, however, fundamental principles underlying the diversities and it is our thesis that a survey and analysis of a sufficiently broad spectrum of countries over sufficiently long development periods may serve to uncover them.

With this object in view, we set out to study as many liberalization experiences as possible and aimed at including all liberalizations in developing countries in the post-world war period. However, the actual scope of this study had three limitations. First, we restricted the study to market-based economies. Second, experiences with highly inadequate data had to be excluded. Third, to be an appropriate object of study, an experience had to be of some minimum duration. Applying these criteria, we were left with the study of liberalization experiences in the 19 countries listed at the end of this preface. This volume deals with three of these countries (Indonesia, Pakistan, and Sri Lanka). Five other volumes contain the rest of the country studies, and the seventh volume presents the synthesis of the country analyses.

Definitions

"Trade liberalization" implies any change which leads a country's trade system toward neutrality in the sense of bringing its economy closer to the situation which would prevail if there were no governmental interference in the trade system. Put in words, the new trade system confers no discernible incentives to either the importable or the exportable activities of the economy.

By "episode" we mean a period long enough to accommodate a significant run of liberalization acts terminating either in a swing away from liberalization or in a period where policy changes one way or another cease to be apparent.

The "episode of liberalization" thus defined is the unit of observation and analysis employed in each of our country studies.

Identification of Liberalization Episodes

There are three main indicators of a move in the direction of neutrality: (a) a change in the price system; (b) a change in the form of intervention; (c) changes in the foreign exchange rate.

Price system

The prices in question are nominal protection rates determining consumption patterns and, more importantly, effective protection rates affecting production activities. Any change which lowered the average level and distribution of rates of protection would count as a move toward neutrality. Typically, such a change would arise from a general reduction in tariffs, but it might also be indicated by the introduction, rather than the removal, of instruments of government intervention, or even, indeed, by the raising rather than the lowering of the incidence of government intervention. An instance of this might be the introduction of export subsidies in a protective regime previously biased against exports and favoring import substitution. Another instance might be the introduction or increase of tariffs on imported raw materials and capital goods in a regime where tariffs have previously escalated over the whole field, with the zero and lower rates applying on these imports.

Form of Intervention

The form of intervention may be affected by a change in the quantitative restriction (QR) system itself or by replacing QRs with tariffs. Although the actual changes might be assigned price *equivalents*, it is not feasible to assign price equivalents to their comprehensive effects. Moreover, the reactions they induce are so different from responses to price signals that they are better treated as a separate category.

The Exchange Rate

A change in the level of a *uniform* rate of exchange, since it does not discriminate between one tradeable activity and another, is not of itself an instrument of intervention. A move from a *multiple* to a uniform rate would, however, be equivalent to a change in intervention through commercial policy instruments; changes in the rate would modify the effect of commercial policy instruments already in being, for example, where QR systems are operated through the exchange control mechanism itself or where tariffs effective at an existing rate become redundant at a higher rate. Failing detailed studies of the impact of exchange rate changes on QRs or tariffs we take as a general rule that a formal and real *devaluation* constitutes a step towards liberalization.

Policies and Results

We do not take the actual degree of openness of the economy as an indicator in itself of a liberalization episode. Liberalization policies may commonly be expected to lead to an increase in the share of external trade but this is not an inevitable result. For instance, if, starting from a state of disequilibrium, liberalization is associated with a formal devaluation imports may actually fall. Therefore attempts to detect liberalization by reference to trade ratios rather than to policy *intentions* would be misleading. Exceptionally, however, the authors of the country studies have used trade performance as an indication of liberalization, particularly where actual changes in imports can be used to measure the degree of relaxation, or otherwise, of QRs.

Measurement of Degrees of Liberalization

In each country study we have attempted to indicate the degree of liberalization progressively attained by assigning to each year a mark for performance on a scale ranging from 1 to 20. A mark of 20 would indicate virtually free trade, or perfect neutrality, a mark of 1 would indicate the highest possible degree of intervention. These indices are subjective and peculiar to each country studied and in no way comparable between countries. They are a rough and ready measure of the progress, or otherwise, of liberalization as perceived by the authors of the country study in question. They reflect, for instance, assessments of nominal and effective rates of protection, the restrictiveness of QRs, and the gap between the formal exchange rate and its equilibrium level.

Analysis of Successful Liberalization Exercises

To arrive at criteria of what makes for success in applying liberalization policies, the following questions might be asked in our studies.

1   What is the appropriate speed and intensity of liberalization?
2   Is it desirable to have a separate policy stage of replacement of nonprice forms of trade restrictions by price measures?
3   Is it desirable to treat productive activities during the process of trade liberalization uniformly or differentially?
4   If uniform treatment is indicated, how should it be formulated?
5   On what pattern of performance of the economy is the fate of liberalization likely to hinge?
6   Is it desirable to have a stage of export promotion? If so, what should its timing be in relationship to import liberalization?
7   What are the appropriate circumstances for the introduction of a liberalization policy?
8   How important are exogenous developments in deciding the sustainability of liberalization?
9   Finally, what *other* policy measures are important, either in their existence or absence, for a successful policy of trade liberalization?

Lurking behind many of these issues are the (potential) probable costs of adjustment of a liberalization policy and, in particular, its possible impact on the employment of labor.

Scope and Intention of our Study

The general purpose of our analysis is to throw up some practical guidance for policymakers and, in particular, for policymakers in developing countries where the economic (and political) climate tends to present the greatest obstacles to successful reform. It is for this reason that (as already explained) we have based our studies on the experience of a wide spread of countries throughout the developing world. All country studies have followed a common pattern of inquiry, with the particular analytical techniques left to the discretion of the individual authors. This approach should yield inferences on the questions raised above in two different ways; via the conclusions reached in the country studies themselves, and via the synthesis of the comparative experience of trade liberalization in these countries.

The presence of a common pattern of inquiry in no way implies that all country studies cover the same questions in a uniform manner. Not all questions are of equal importance in each country and the same quantity and quality of data were not available in all countries. Naturally, the country studies differ on the issues they cover, in the form of the analysis, and in the structure of their presentation.

The country studies are self-contained. Beyond addressing the questions of the project, each study contains sufficient background material on the country's attributes and history of trade policy to be of interest to the general reader.

The 19 countries studied, classified within three major regions, are as follows.

Latin America

Argentina	by Domingo Cavallo and Joaquín Cottani
Brazil	by Donald V. Coes
Chile	by Sergio de la Cuadra and Dominique Hachette
Colombia	by Jorge García García
Peru	by Julio J. Nogués
Uruguay	by Edgardo Favaro and Pablo T. Spiller

Asia and the Pacific

Indonesia	by Mark M. Pitt
Korea	by Kwang Suk Kim
New Zealand	by Anthony C. Rayner and Ralph Lattimore
Pakistan	by Stephen Guisinger and Gerald Scully
Philippines	by Florian Alburo and Geoffrey Shepherd
Singapore	by Bee-Yan Aw
Sri Lanka	by Andrew G. Cuthbertson and Premachandra Athukorala

The Mediterranean

| Greece | by George C. Kottis |
| Israel | by Nadav Halevi and Joseph Baruh |

Portugal	by Jorge B. de Macedo, Cristina Corado, and
	Manuel L. Porto
Spain	by Guillermo de la Dehesa, José Juan Ruiz, and
	Angel Torres
Turkey	by Tercan Baysan and Charles Blitzer
Yugoslavia	by Oli Havrylyshyn

Coordination of the Project

Demetris Papageorgiou, Michael Michaely, and Armeane M. Choksi of the World Bank's Latin America and Caribbean Region are the directors of this research project. Participants in the project met frequently to exchange views. Before the country studies were launched, the common framework of the study was discussed extensively at a plenary conference. Another plenary conference was held to discuss early versions of the completed country studies, as well as some emerging general inferences. In between, three regional meetings in each region were held to review phases of the work under way. An external Review Board consisting of Robert Baldwin (University of Wisconsin), Mario Blejer (International Monetary Fund), Jacob Frenkel (University of Chicago and Director of Research, International Monetary Fund), Arnold Harberger (University of Chicago and University of California–Los Angeles), Richard Snape (Monash University), Martin Wolf (Chief Economic Leader Writer, Financial Times) contributed in the reviewing process of the country studies and the synthesis volume.

The Series

Indonesia, Pakistan, and Sri Lanka are presented in this volume. The series' other publications are the following:

Volume 1: Liberalizing Foreign Trade. The Experience of Argentina, Chile, and Uruguay;

Volume 2: Liberalizing Foreign Trade. The Experience of Korea, the Philippines, and Singapore;

Volume 3: Liberalizing Foreign Trade. The Experience of Israel and Yugoslavia;

Volume 4: Liberalizing Foreign Trade. The Experience of Brazil, Colombia, and Perú;

Volume 6: Liberalizing Foreign Trade. The Experience of New Zealand, Spain, and Turkey;

Volume 7: Liberalizing Foreign Trade. Lessons of Experience in the Developing World.

Part I

Indonesia

Mark M. Pitt

Contents

List of Figures

List of Tables

Acknowledgments

The author is indebted to all project members for their many helpful comments and suggestions and to the Biro Pusat Statistik for making unpublished data available. I also wish to express my gratitude to Diane Bloomfield for her excellent research assistance and to Delma Burns and Lisa Janowiec for assembling tables and typing the manuscript. I retain sole responsibility for errors.

1

A Guide to Economic Policymaking in Indonesia

Introduction

Indonesia's trade regime has been one of the most complex and volatile in the world. Even Indonesians have found it difficult to keep track of the multitude of trade restrictions that change with every shift in the political wind and have come to rely on a proliferation of commercial newsletters and consulting services in order to understand it. Analysis of the motivation for trade restriction and liberalization, and of the reasons for their success or failure, can thus easily become lost in the elucidation of their anatomy. Consequently, in this introductory chapter we set the stage for the analysis with a summary view of the politics and history of post-war economic policymaking in Indonesia leading up to the major liberalization attempt of 1966–71, and the motivations of the various groups involved.

Five periods in the progress of Indonesian economic policy since World War II are distinguished in subsequent chapters. The first three, addressed in chapters 2, 3, and 4, concern respectively the Dutch Indies trade regime, which ended in late 1949; the 1950–7 period of constitutional democracy, embodying three liberalization attempts; and the "Guided Economy" of 1958–65. The second half of the study focuses on the 1966–71 liberalization, often considered among the most dramatic and far reaching experienced by any developing country. The greater concentration on this episode than on the equally dramatic earlier liberalization stems from the relative durability of the attempt and the continuing liberality of the trade regime in its aftermath. The course of the liberalization and its sources, background, and accompanying policies are described in chapters 5 and 6; its results and developments in the post-liberalization period are discussed in chapters 7 and 8. The results of an econometric analysis of the liberalization are presented in chapter 9. The study concludes with some thoughts on the implications for designing trade liberalization of the Indonesian experience as a whole.

The policy pattern is summarized by an index of liberalization presented graphically in figure 1.1. The index is ordinal and is represented by a

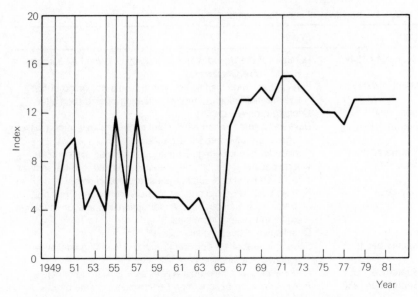

Figure 1.1 Index of liberalization (liberalization periods are between line pairs)

numerical scale ranging from 1, the least liberal trade regime, to 20, the most liberal. There are too few consistently measured or continuously available quantitative data to construct an objective index or to justify explicitly a subjective index. The index presented thus represents the author's judgment, based on the nature of controls and a combination of anecdotal and quantitative information on the severity of their imposition. As an aid to the reader, table 1.1 provides a chronology of important events.

The Pattern of Post-war Economic Policy

The Colonial Legacy

The trade regime inherited from the Dutch by the newly independent nation in 1949 was highly restrictive. Tariffs were low but all goods were regulated by quota – not just separate quotas for individual goods, but quotas on the basis of the ethnicity or the nationality of the importer and the origin of the commodity. Manufacturing firms were grouped into cooperative organizations which regulated their own quotas and allocated licenses among members of the organization. Investment was licensed, there were pervasive price controls, and in the period after World War II smuggling and black markets were widespread, particularly for exports. A

Table 1.1 Chronology of important events

Date	Event
December 1949	Republic of the United States of Indonesia formed as outcome of Round Table Conference
March 1950	Foreign Exchange Certificate system marks beginning of first liberalization attempt; free-list importing begins soon after
April 1950	*Benteng* program begins
August 1950	*Bukti Indusemen* import entitlement scheme allows import without regard to quota; free list expanded
February 1952	Rupiah devalued; Foreign Exchange Certificate system ends
April 1952	Wilopo cabinet forms; import licensing intensifies, to be partially replaced by import surcharges and prepayments
July 1953	First Ali Sastroamidjojo cabinet formed; monopoly importing, "parallel transactions" follow; corruption in operation of foreign exchange system increases
May 1954	Quantitative restrictions intensified
September 1955	Second liberalization episode (Sumitro reforms); quantitative restrictions abandoned
September 1955	National elections held (four weeks after Sumitro reforms)
September 1956	*Bukti Pendorong Ekspor* import entitlement scheme begins during second Ali cabinet; liberalization ends
February 1957	Sukarno unveils his *Konsepsi* of Guided Democracy and Guided Economy
June 1957	*Bukti Ekspor* (BE) system; the third liberalization episode
April 1958	*Bonus Ekspor* price fixed; liberalization ends; quantitative restrictions return
February 1959	Dutch enterprises nationalized
August 1959	Rupiah devalued and BE system ends
August 1960	Limited return to free-list importing
March 1962	SIVA import entitlement certificate system begins
March 1963	Sukarno makes "Economic Declaration" (DEKON)
May 1963	Implementation of DEKON begins
September 1963	Confrontation with Malaysia begins
April 1964	SPP import entitlement certificate system begins
October 1965	Coup attempt fails
December 1965	Official devaluation (Rp 45 to Rp 10,000)
February 1966	Inauguration of BE import entitlement system
May 1966	Increase in BE percentages; BE made negotiable; export procedures simplified
October 1966	Removal of quantitative restrictions; increase in BE percentages
December 1966	Moratorium on external debt agreed upon
April 1967	Foreign Investment Law enacted
July 1967	End of rupiah payments to exporters; all exports receive negotiable BE certificates or DP exchange; import lists by type of exchange are published
April 1970	BE and DP markets merged; overprice (DP) abolished as are export BEs; export receipts surrendered at last DP rate of Rp 326
December 1970	Aid-BE abolished
August 1971	Official devaluation to Rp 415

set of negotiable foreign exchange certificates, linking export and import, was also in existence.

After Independence: 1949–1957

Nationalism, not unnaturally, was a dominant influence on policy in the years immediately following independence. This potent force was increasingly associated with interventionism and antiliberalism in the economic arena, because in practice the economic system created by the Round Table Agreement (under which the Netherlands recognized Indonesia's independence in 1949) left the private sector of the economy under foreign control. As a result, the cabinets of 1949–58 faced the problem of devising economic policy which, if liberal in nature, would be attacked by an increasingly radical and nationalist electorate as benefiting the structures of the colonialists and neo-imperialists.

Socialism Indonesia-style and Indonesianisasi

In this anticolonialist climate, most discussions of Indonesia's economic goals during its first two decades as an independent nation were couched in terms of a uniquely indigenous brand of socialism, based upon the principle of *gotong royong* (mutual assistance) which traditionally regulated the performance of certain agricultural tasks among communities. This idea was set forth in the Constitution, which stated that "The economy shall be organized as a joint endeavor based on the principle of family relationship." The cooperative was widely taken to be the "joint endeavor" envisaged. Government attempts to foster voluntary cooperatives, however, were mostly unsuccessful; these organizations prospered only when valuable privileges such as import and investment licenses became attainable exclusively through membership of a cooperative.

The chauvinism that governed direction of trade policy in the immediate post-colonial years included Indo-Chinese enterprise in the category of "alien capital," even though the Chinese in question were generally second- or third-generation residents of Indonesia. During the 1950s strong anti-Dutch and anti-Chinese feelings led to the process of *Indonesianisasi* (Indonesianization), which entailed official racial discrimination in the allocation of import rights and eventually led to a prohibition of all Chinese trading outside urban areas. A new group of indigenous Indonesian importers and traders was established as a result of these policies. These *Benteng* importers earned substantial rents from their privileged status and became a powerful lobby for quantitative restrictions in trade, as they disproportionately earned the import premiums that resulted. In time, the new importing class became attached to Sukarno's political party, the Partai Nasional Indonesia (PNI), which more than any other was willing to protect and foster their interests. In return, this new class became a major source of income to ministers and parliamentarians, and corruption, always a problem in the administration of the Indonesian economy, increased markedly. To many, the "national" in the term "national importer" no longer referred to ethnicity but rather to one who was a member of or contributed financially to the PNI.

Attempts to Liberalize: 1950–1951, 1955, 1957
In a political environment such as that described above it is hardly surprising that the post-colonial years saw Indonesia moving steadily toward increasing state control of trade, prices, and production. Economic liberalism was identified, irrationally but obstinately, with foreign and colonial interests; the term "free-fight liberalism" was used as an expletive. Nevertheless, three attempts to move trade policy in a more liberal direction were made in the eight years following the Round Table Agreement.

The three episodes can be seen as fairly superficial interruptions of the steady progress toward a controlled economy. The first attempt, initiated by a minority of "economically minded" politicians (Higgins, 1957) in the very first cabinet after independence, was briefly acceptable because it replaced most of the quotas imposed by the Dutch with a free-list importing system, and as such was seen as a means of reducing Dutch power. However, liberal policies had little hope of survival in a political climate where extreme nationalism was the keynote and economic liberalism was equated with support for alien vested interest; liberalization collapsed with the end of the coalition government in 1952, and the progress toward restriction resumed with increased momentum.

The second attempt at liberalization, introduced by a caretaker government in 1955, suffered a similar fate. Its reforms, put together in three weeks and introduced in a single day, were sweeping: the entire quota system that had been reintroduced, together with monopoly importing, was abolished. The reason for haste was the coalition's desire to impress its economic philosophy on the electorate before the national elections scheduled to take place in three weeks' time. The electorate was unimpressed; the elections were lost and the restrictive regime returned with renewed vigor.

Like the first two, the third episode was both initiated and ultimately reversed for predominantly noneconomic reasons, though this liberalization had a firmer base of popular support in the interests of the traditional export regions outside Java, particularly Sulawesi (Celebes) and Sumatra. The import-biased trade regime, and the *Benteng* system in whose benefits they did not share, led these export regions to boycott the foreign exchange surrender regulations in 1957 and to threaten secession. The liberalization episode of 1957–8, launched to placate the regions and forestall secession, failed to prevent civil war and ultimately foundered in the suppression of the regions' attempt to secede in 1958.

Guided Democracy: 1958–1965

The government's victory led to the centralization of power in the hands of President Sukarno and the end of constitutional democracy. On a popular platform of destroying the last remnants of capitalism and leading the economy toward the social goals of the Indonesian Revolution, Sukarno propounded the notion of Guided Economy to justify the direct state control of production and trade. Dutch enterprises were nationalized as part of the conflict over the status of New Guinea (Irian), and state enterprises took over the role that voluntary cooperatives had failed to perform.

With the nationalization of Dutch property putting the state suddenly in control of a large share of the economy and with political opposition stifled after the regional secession was crushed, President Sukarno was able to move the economy quickly into one of almost total state control. The palpably corrupt apparatus for issuing import licenses and other government privileges, denounced as an offshoot of "Western democracy," capitalism, and economic liberalism by both Sukarno and the increasingly powerful Partai Kommunis Indonesia (PKI), was in fact adopted wholesale by the new regime. The rents that once were sought by indigenous importers were now sought by the new state trading firms, but the beneficiaries of the import premiums came from the same political circles as before: rent seeking and quota seeking were now a part of the official state apparatus.

In the ensuing years of Guided Democracy and Guided Economy corruption and black-marketeering were rampant and mismanagement was staggering; the economy disintegrated. Foreign exchange reserves were negative, price inflation exceeded 1,000 percent, and service on the debt exceeded foreign exchange revenues. The fiscal deficit in 1965 was 163 percent of revenue, whereas in the first half of 1966 it was seven times revenue; the terms of trade were at a historically low level. Much of the debt was incurred for costly military adventures, including a confrontation with Malaysia, and showcase projects such as the building of monuments which still litter the capital Jakarta, a nuclear bomb project, and a project to launch a man in space. Per capita gross domestic product (GDP) in 1965 was 9 percent lower than it was in 1958. Capacity utilization in manufacturing was 20 percent or even lower and there were significant food shortages in many parts of the islands.

By 1965 "Socialism à la Indonesia" had been completely discredited, and the adherents of the system were swept away in the violent political and economic turmoil of 1965–6. The details of the coup attempt that precipitated the crisis are still subject to dispute: its immediate results were that hundreds of thousands died, and for quite a long time there was almost no government. The "New Order" that eventually emerged from the chaos was virtually untrammelled by any effective opposition. Its first actions, impelled by the urgent need to seek aid from the West, were to move quickly towards the liberalization that is the principal focus of this study.

2

The Colonial Legacy of Exchange Control

The new Republic of Indonesia inherited a foreign trade regime from the Dutch that was far from liberal. Many of the institutions of trade control established by the Dutch during the 1930s and in the period just after World War II were inherited by the new Indonesian republic with only the names changed.

An examination of the evolution of economic policy in the years before the foundation of the Republic of Indonesia is useful for understanding the methods of state intervention, since their terminology and justification were carried forward almost intact into the post-colonial period. The instruments, though not the motivation for foreign exchange control, remained virtually unchanged. Ironically, independent Indonesia, dedicated to wiping out all vestiges of a Dutch colonial economy seen as unfairly benefiting the few, adopted its economic instruments to similar effect.

Trade and Tariffs during the Colonial Era

Early in the colonial period, the Dutch – through the Netherlands East India Company – enforced monopoly control over all the external trade of the East Indies. During the period of British rule (September 1811 through August 1816), when Holland was a French province, trade was greatly liberalized as part of the sweeping reforms instigated by the interim Governor-General, Lieutenant-General Raffles. Conflict between the British and Dutch over trade and territorial issues resulted in the Treaty of London, signed in 1824. The Treaty swapped Dutch settlements in India and Malaya for British settlements in Sumatra. It also stipulated that both signatories would enjoy preferential treatment in trading with their Asian colonies. One nation, in its Asiatic ports, could not levy import duties on the ships of the other at more than double the rate assessed on its own ships. If it levied no duty, the rate charged by the other nation could not exceed 6 percent. The signatories were bound not to enter into other treaties granting preferential duties and to ensure "free trade" – that is, unimpeded access to ports by each party, with certain well-defined exceptions.[1]

The Treaty of London did not put an end to the rivalry between the two colonial powers. The Netherlands East India Company, through various ploys such as the secret refunding of duties paid on imports of Dutch origin (Furnivall, 1939, p. 144), enacted almost prohibitive duties on English textiles, which violated the spirit if not strictly the letter of the Treaty. Continuing friction led to the Sumatra Treaty of 1871 and the associated tariff reforms which ended preferential tariff treatment and, along with other reforms, ushered in an economic regime known as the Liberal System. Tariff rates were fairly low, with most imports entering duty free or with a 6 percent duty in 1874. Partly in response, imports of cotton goods, which in 1870 were little above the level of 1840, rose threefold by 1875 (Furnivall, 1939, p. 215). Rates crept up over the ensuing decades, but the top rate never exceeded 12 percent.[2] Foreshadowing what all agree to be a distinguishing characteristic of modern Indonesian tariff regulation, the Indies tariff was constantly amended and became increasingly complex and difficult to comprehend. The report of the Englishman J. R. Root in 1906 would be an accurate description of the situation for most of the period since:

> The framework of the tariff is now something like twenty years old, and during the interval that has elapsed many minor changes have been introduced, and administrative orders issued, varying methods of levying the duties, and not infrequently amending previous amendments. The result, as may be imagined, is a considerable tangle. (Quoted by van der Waals, 1926)

The Quota System of the Depression Era

Even before the Great Depression there was active lobbying by the Society for an Active Commercial Policy in the Netherlands for the reimposition of some type of preferential trading arrangement. The idea of a customs union between the East Indies and the Netherlands was debated. The dislocation of the Great Depression and increasing protectionism in other countries added to the pressure on the Netherlands government to act. The early 1930s saw increasing Japanese import penetration in the Netherlands

[1] The British were particularly concerned with gaining access to the ports of Aceh (on the northern tip of Sumatra, opposite the Malay peninsula) and denying access to American traders whose activities in that area were viewed as a threat in the case of war (de Klerck, 1978, vol. 2, p. 114).

[2] On the course of the Indies tariff during this period see van der Waals (1926, especially appendix A).

East Indies, competing primarily with imports from the Netherlands but also, though much less, with local manufacturing. In early 1932, the Netherlands textile industry centered around Twente petitioned the Minister of Colonies and the Governor-General of the Indies for the restriction of foreign cottons into the Indies.

Support for trade restrictions also came from the representatives of the established channels of trade and distribution in the East Indies themselves. Much of the Japanese import was handled not by the large established European import houses – the Big Five – but by an integrated Japanese distribution system that functioned all the way down to wholesale and retail levels, penetrating all corners of the archipelago. Chinese, Indians, and even a few Indonesians constituted the new class of traders benefiting from connections with the Japanese. Perhaps even more frightening to the established commercial apparatus and the government-sanctioned export cartels[3] was the purchasing of native produce by this new distribution system. Japanese success in usurping the established Dutch channels of selling simple manufactures, particularly textiles, to the native population was argued by some, using much the same arguments as are currently in vogue, to be the result of unfair trading practices:

> As far as Japan is concerned the price level, on the strength of which her manufactured goods forced their way into various countries, was not exclusively the result of efficiency and low costs of production. There were in it elements of currency debasement [the devaluation of the yen in December 1931], and a measure and forms of government support, to which the rest of the world was as yet unaccustomed. (de Wilde and Moll, 1936, p. 58)

Pressure from the Big Five Indo-Dutch import houses and from the Netherlands government led to the passage of the Crisis Import Ordinance of 1933 and succeeding acts, which for the first time established direct control of imports. Although tariffs did rise during the early 1930s, their effectiveness as an instrument of protection was restricted by the long-standing Anglo–Dutch treaties limiting the level of tariffs and country-specific tariff discrimination. The system of quotas put into effect in 1933 established a precedent for the use of quantitative restrictions in import trade, and these were to remain an important part of commercial policy in Indonesia almost continually until 1966. More importantly, the quota system marked a dramatic and publicly declared shift in the orientation of

---

[3] During the 1920s and 1930s the colonial government became an active participant in international attempts to form cartels for major exports. Export and/or production restriction schemes were enacted for cinchona (quinine), kapok, tea, coffee, sugar, rubber, and tin. These schemes involved the establishment of production licensing (e.g. estate rubber), export quotas (e.g. tea), export duties (e.g. native rubber), and government purchasing monopolies (e.g. kapok).

the state from the *laissez-faire* of the Liberal System to one of direct intervention in the marketplace through the control of prices, investment, and trade.

Three types of quantitative import control were distinguished. "Free quotas" (*goederencontingentering*) were standard import quotas which set limits on either the quantity or the volume of import flows. Goods covered included automobile tires, unbleached cotton textiles, frying pans, bicycles, ironware, and glassware. "National quotas" (*landedencontingent-ering*) were country-specific quotas, intended primarily to enlarge and protect the share of imports from the Netherlands and secondarily as leverage in bilateral trade arrangements. Boeke (1946) claims that these quotas were responsible for the employment of 7,000 wage earners in the Netherlands. Commodities subject to national quotas included woven piece goods, cement, beer, bleached cottons, and electric bulbs. "License regulations" (*invoerlicentieering*), like free quotas, were (nominally) not country specific; instead, they allocated quota rights to established import houses and distribution channels. The intention was to block the growth of the Japanese distribution system by denying access to quota rights. Firms that obtained quota rights through the license regulation were subject to price controls and could be forced to hold stocks whose timing and price of sale were set by the price control office. In addition, regulations were adopted that required license holders to carry certain proportions of their imports and inter-island trade in vessels under the Dutch flag. By 1936, all coastal trade was reserved for Dutch shipping, dominated by the government-subsidized Royal Packet Navigation Company (the KPM). According to Boeke (1946, p. 90), the share of Indies imports that were under license, free quota, national quota, and unrestricted (for a date unspecified) were 9.29 percent, 17.66 percent, 13.82 percent, and 59.23 percent respectively.

These quantitative restrictions were effective in their aim. The value of imports from the Netherlands of those commodities subject to quota rose by 381 percent between 1933 and 1937, while other imports from the Netherlands, aided only by the licensing regulations, rose by 80 percent (Broek, 1942, p. 109). The share of imports from Japan fell from 31 percent in 1933 to 15 percent five years later (Broek, 1942, p. 124). This quota system must have afforded substantially greater protection to Netherlands East Indies manufacturing than the protection before 1933, which had been derived only from a fairly low tariff schedule. For some key items, such as cotton sarongs, the quota quickly became redundant in the face of increased Indies output. Under pressure from the Netherlands, the tariff on this item was cut in half twice and was reduced for many other items (Shepard, 1941, p. 61); apparently trade restrictions that resulted in the substitution of Dutch for Japanese imports were desirable, but the substitution of East Indian production for Netherlands imports was seen as detrimental to the proper relations between the colony and its mother country.

A 1938 report of the Commission for Economic Collaboration within the Kingdom of the Netherlands (Commissie van Advies voor Economische Samenwerking tusschen Nederland en Nederlandsch Indie) recommended no change in the Netherlands' often exclusive quota in the Indies market, but rather further cuts in the Indies tariffs, particularly for those Dutch manufacturing sectors in greater distress, with the claim that "a sound evolution of the Netherlands Indies industry can succeed only if there exists competition with kindred imported products" (Broek, 1942, p. 111)! Indeed, some members of this commission favored outright restriction on the output of Netherlands East Indian manufacturing in the interests of the mother country. Although this view was not followed absolutely, constraints on manufacturing capacity (described below) were enacted in part to prevent the redundancy of the import quotas assigned to the Netherlands.

It was recognized that the quotas, which affected primarily the inexpensive manufactures consumed by the native population, disproportionately reduced the purchasing power of the poorer segments of the population. The government of the Netherlands stated in their "principles of action" that "within certain limits this rise in prices has to be accepted in the interest of industry in the Netherlands and of the needs of the Empire . . ." (Boeke, 1946, p. 102). In partial compensation, the Netherlands granted 25 million guilders to the Indies to provide for the welfare of those in need. The Netherlands did not reciprocate in trade matters: Java tea paid a lower duty in England than in the Netherlands (where it was 300 percent or more), and the Dutch levied a 900 percent duty on Javanese sugar to protect the sugar beet industry. According to de Klerck (1978, vol. 2, p. 592), "Little attention however, was paid to the actual interests of the overseas dominions, and this is the weakness which . . . has run like a continuous thread through the economic relations between the two parts of the Kingdom."

Manufacturing and Regulation of Investment

The newly established protective regime resulted in a significant upsurge in industrial activity in the Indies. The textile industry, for which quota restrictions were greatest, grew phenomenally during the 1930s. Duty-free import of yarns and capital equipment was initially provided as an additional incentive to those industries, but by 1935 capacity licensing restrictions were imposed. Other sectors – cigarette manufacturing, cement, tires, and brewing – grew considerably behind the quota barriers. In addition, small manufacturing enterprises operated by native Indonesians (and Indo-Chinese) were given some special considerations. The handrolling of cigarettes was protected from competition from Western-owned firms producing machine-rolled cigarettes by legislation that set minimum prices for machine-rolled cigarettes. Small weaving enterprises relying on handlooms were initially exempted from investment and capacity controls. The capacity of modern enterprises directly competing with handloomed products was restricted.

As small enterprises mushroomed, industrial control was eventually expanded to cover firms with as few as five handlooms. The clandestine manufacture and sale of sarongs became widespread as a result. Nevertheless, the government had set an important precedent for discrimination in licensing and control of firms on the basis of the ethnicity of their ownership or the technology of production. The Director of Economic Affairs remarked in 1937 that it was the role of the state "to help economically weaker groups become stronger; and to this end it will occasionally have to hold in check the activities of other groups if the general public interest demands it . . . " (quoted by Boeke, 1953, pp. 233–4). Although there is scant evidence of any net assistance to these groups, as we will see, the assistance of "economically weaker" groups became a focus of policy in independent Indonesia.

A year after the Crisis Import Ordinance, the Netherlands East Indian government invested itself with sweeping control of the industrial sector with the enactment of the Ordinance for the Regulation of Industries (BRO). The stated object, as for the Crisis Import Ordinance, was to protect established industrial enterprises from "excessive competition." The ordinance allowed the government to restrict the number of enterprises in each field, to control their level of output, license new investment, prescribe the method of production, and even set minimum prices. As well as providing monopoly rents to domestic firms operating behind quotas, the ordinance ensured that the Netherlands national quota was not frustrated by the expansion of domestic firms (particularly in the textile sector) and further impeded Japanese penetration into the Netherlands Indian economy.

Foreign Exchange Control, 1945–1949

The occupation of Holland in 1940 led to a comprehensive program of foreign exchange and price control and the creation of a Netherlands Indies Foreign Exchange Institute (NIDI). After the war, foreign exchange control by the Dutch East Indies government remained almost as comprehensive as it had been during the occupation. All imports required a foreign exchange permit issued by NIDI and an import declaration from the Bureau of Goods Supply (BGV). To obtain a permit to import a particular commodity, an importer first had to be accredited with a "Covenant" – an association of importers of that commodity. Covenant membership was dominated by the large import houses and others that had historically imported the commodity in question. These Covenants often had Sub-Covenants below them that allocated import licenses for more finely detailed goods. Goods considered essential were imported by the government's General Import Organization (AIO). The Covenant and the Bureau of Goods Supply decided the volume of import for each item and obtained a "mother" foreign exchange permit for the amount. Another organization, the Institute for Import Assignments (SIPET), distributed this mother foreign exchange permit (*Moedercontract*) among importers on the basis of "historical rights" (*historisch beland percentage*). The precise allocation was determined according to the interfirm distribution of each commodity's import in the pre-war period. Allocations for "newcomers" were to come from the pre-war shares of Japanese and German traders. As we will see, a foreign exchange allocation system based on commodity-specific import associations and mother foreign exchange permits was established in independent Indonesia in the early 1960s.[4]

As a result of the distribution of import licenses on the basis of historical rights, foreign exchange apportioned to new, mostly indigenous, import firms was very limited. In 1948, a special office (Kantoor voor Indonesische Aangelgenheden) was established to allocate import foreign exchange to Indonesian concerns. Sutter (1959, p. 591) estimates that Indonesian firms received not more than 10 percent of import foreign exchange at any time. Furthermore, returned Dutch trading firms evicted Indonesian traders who had moved into their abandoned premises at the time of the Japanese occupation. Finally, in an effort to limit import premiums, price control was more pervasive in this period than before World War II. Tradeables, including important foodstuffs as well as locally produced manufactures, were subject to price control under sweeping ordinances imposed in 1948 (*Prijsbeheeringsordonnatie* and *Prijsbeheeringsverordening*). In the free (black) market, imported goods fetched three to six times their controlled prices.

Import duties were those set by the Indies Tariff Act of 1933. This tariff, set by Dutch law, was not under the control of the colonial government. Duty rates were fairly low, with rates of 6 percent, 12 percent, and 20 percent levied against goods characterized as capital goods or semi-manufactures, ordinary consumer goods, and luxuries respectively. A 50 percent surtax was added to these rates in the late 1940s. Exemption from duty was available for raw materials for use in agriculture and in the metal and weaving industries, and for goods used in transport and medicine. In 1948, these exemptions were extended to all capital goods

---

[4] The operation of the foreign exchange licensing system during this period is described more fully by Panglaykim (1963) and Wirodihardjo (1957).

and intermediate inputs imported by new manufacturing firms. Other capital goods imports were exempted from the tariff surtax. At the beginning of 1949, these tariff benefits were revoked and NIDI stopped allocating foreign exchange for most imports of capital goods that would extend industrial output beyond the level of December 1948. For purposes of foreign exchange allocation, industries were divided into two groups, with the high priority import substitution and "essential" goods sectors obtaining a large and increasing share of import licenses. Capacity utilization in manufacturing was 50–60 percent, primarily as a result of raw material shortages (Java Bank, 1950–1, p. 115), and production was only half that of 1940 (Java Bank, 1949–50, p. 119).

Ad valorem export taxes were levied on a wide range of commodities, with rates varying from 20 percent on odoriferous wood down to 3 percent on most spices. Specific duties were levied on rubber, but although estate rubber had the same specific duty as native rubber it was exempt from the 6 percent *ad valorem* export duty. In addition, in an effort to curb smuggling, export of native products to Singapore and Hong Kong could take place under special "barter" regulations that allowed the exporter to retain part of the foreign exchange earned for the import of a limited set of goods from those export destinations.

The First Inducement System

In addition to foreign exchange control, the Dutch East Indies government began a program of "inducements" (*indusemen*) to export that became an enduring feature of Indonesian trade policy. The first inducements began in West Borneo, where illegal trade in copra and rubber was rife because of the overvalued exchange rate and the area's proximity to Singapore and Malaya. In mid-1946 the Coprafonds, the state copra marketing enterprise, experienced difficulty in purchasing copra for legal export. In addition to cash, the Coprafonds began offering textiles at low controlled prices to smallholders who sold to them. This inducement package was later enlarged to include rice and foreign exchange for imports. The value of these inducements exceeded the cash copra purchase price in West Borneo and added 15 percent in East Indonesia where foreign exchange retention was not offered. Copra purchases by the Coprafonds increased by 258 percent in West Borneo from 1947 to 1948, and by over 70 percent in East Indonesia.

Beginning in February 1947, rubber sold to the Dutch East Indies government in West Borneo entitled the smallholder to receive a chit for 50 kg of price-controlled rice per ton of rubber export. The free-market value of this rice was triple the controlled price. By May 1947, the inducement was expanded to include 100 kg of rice, a chit for 70 yards of price-controlled textiles, a subsidy of Fl 100, and an import foreign exchange right of Straits $100.[5] This foreign exchange right, known as a *Surat Bukti Indusemen* or just *Bukti Indusemen* (Proof of Inducement Letter), was negotiable and was worth four times the official rate of exchange. The free-market value of the textiles was also four times their controlled price when purchased with the chit. As a result, smallholders received Fl 300 per ton of rubber in cash and almost Fl 1,100 in inducement benefits.

By 1949 this inducement scheme had been extended to other parts of the Netherlands East Indies and to most other smallholder exports. In the case of rattan, the rate of inducement was positively associated with the graded quality of the product. Peanut exports hit all-time highs immediately after their inclusion in the inducement scheme. Inducements consisted primarily of a foreign exchange retention right of between 10 and 83.5 percent of the export proceeds, the actual rate varying by commodity, quality, area of export, and country of destination. The foreign exchange retention took the form of a freely negotiable right (*Bukti Indusemen*) to purchase Singapore or Hong Kong dollars at the official rate of exchange for the import of certain nonluxury commodities. The Java Bank, the central bank of Netherlands East Indies, claimed that this inducement system was responsible for the redirection of smuggling trade into legal channels. The Java Bank estimated that illegal export of smallholder rubber fell from 48.9 percent of total smallholder rubber export in 1948 to only 12 percent in 1949 (Java Bank, 1950–1, p. 96).

Summary

Dutch colonial trade policy set precedents that had a major influence on the pattern of policy in independent Indonesia. The Dutch established a pervasive system of import and production quotas whose level and distribution were controlled or influenced by associations of affected trading firms and manufacturing enterprises. Price control was widespread. Official discrimination against the "economically strong group" – meaning Indo-Chinese – was first enacted. The discontent of the export regions of the islands outside Java was manifested in widespread illegal trade. This was countered with various inducements taking the form of negotiable certificates linking export and import rights. These same measures characterized the pattern of policy during the first two decades of Indonesia's independence. In the chapters that follow, we will see that those forces

[5] The florin (or guilder) was the Dutch colonial currency and the Straits dollar was the currency of Singapore. In 1947, the florin was worth about US$0.38 and the Straits dollar was worth US$0.47. Both the florin and the Straits dollar were devalued by equal proportions on September 9, 1949, with their values becoming US$0.26 and US$0.34 respectively.

who proclaimed most loudly the need to destroy the remnants of the Dutch colonial economy were those who adopted its methods of economic control.

3

The Period of Constitutional Democracy

The Liberalization of 1950–1951 and its Aftermath

On December 27, 1949, under the terms of the Round Table Agreement with the Netherlands, the United States of Indonesia came into existence. Three months earlier, the Netherlands Indies guilder had been devalued along with most European currencies. The devaluation was 30 percent versus the US dollar, the same as for the Dutch guilder, leaving the official rate of the Netherlands guilder to the Indies guilder at one.

The new government's freedom to make economic policy was sharply limited by the conditions of the Round Table Agreement. The Java Bank, the central bank of the Netherlands Indies, was to retain its powers and yet remain an independent private corporation in the hands of Dutch owners.[1] Property rights of foreigners, including licenses, were to remain inviolate. Private banking was largely in the hands of foreigners, as were inter-island shipping, electricity generation and distribution, and other vital services. The new Republic of the United States of Indonesia (RUSI) was required to consult with the Netherlands in financial areas that affected Dutch interests, such as money supply and exchange rate policy. Indonesia agreed to accept the Netherlands Indies debt of 4,300 million guilders, of which 1,291 million guilders (US$399 million) was external debt to be repaid in foreign currency. This concession was particularly irksome since much of the debt had been incurred by the colonial regime to finance its military actions against Republican forces.

The sentiment among the Indonesian people was that "the Dutch lion is dead, but his claws are still embedded in the body of Indonesia" (Java Bank, 1951–2, p. 26). There was a general feeling that the Revolution would not be complete until foreign economic domination was eliminated.

---

[1] It was stipulated that (a) no change in the law affecting the Java Bank would be made without prior consultation with the Netherlands, (b) the Netherlands government would be consulted before any change was made in the membership of the bank's board of directors, and (c) the Netherlands would be consulted on the extension of credits by the bank to the government of Indonesia (Schmitt, 1959, p. 42).

In one writer's view, the problem facing the new government of President Sukarno and Prime Minister Hatta was to devise policy for a foreign-dominated and privately owned economy "which if successful, would benefit the interests of their ideological enemies at least as much as their allies, and anticipating the general elections, to attempt to gain the support of the politically sensitive part of the electorate – a group more radically inclined than they" (Glassburner, 1971, p. 80). Surprisingly, the government's first economic initiative was an attempt at trade liberalization.

The Political and Economic Climate at the Time of the Liberalization of 1950–1951

The problems faced by the first cabinet of the new Republic were formidable. The country had suffered through three and a half years of Japanese occupation and then a bitter revolutionary struggle that had resulted in widespread devastation. The linchpins of the economy – plantations, transport, the financial sector, and industrial capital – were in the hands of foreigners.

In addition, the government was saddled with a huge bureaucracy resulting from the fusion of the pre-federal government, the Republican government, and the governments of the pre-federal Dutch-sponsored puppet states. Despite President Sukarno's expressed hope, in February 1950, that the number of civil servants – then about 420,000 – could be reduced by more than half in six months (Feith, 1962, p. 83), the bureaucracy grew even further to 600,000 in the early 1950s, four times the pre-war figure (Kahin, 1963, p. 580). The pre-federal government had run substantial budget deficits, and the same pattern was predicted for the new government, which not only had the enlarged bureaucracy to support but also was burdened with the costs of fighting regional insurgencies and undertaking war reconstruction. Monetary instruments of various kinds had been issued as a means of state finance by a range of authorities during the Revolution, fueling fears of inflation. Smuggling was rampant because of both the unrealistic exchange rate and the government's lack of authority in many regions. Strikes by industrial, dock, and estate workers were common as unions were organized, political parties jockeyed for support, and workers made demands on their Dutch bosses.

Benjamin Higgins (1957) has characterized the attitudes of Indonesians toward economic issues in the immediate post-revolution era as being either "economics minded" or "history minded." Those who were history minded were radical nationalists for whom "completing the revolution" was paramount – that is, eliminating foreign capital and influence, and creating a socialist interventionist state. This group was consistently vague on economic matters – Feith (1962, p. 118) labeled them "solidarity makers," concerned with "fashioning symbols and enacting ritual." The economics-minded group, like the history-minded group, couched their economic philosophy in socialist–Marxist terms, but gave precedence to developing the economy even if this entailed tolerating capitalism and foreign capital for some time. They saw their role as solving economic problems in a legal and orderly way rather than totally reshaping the structure of the economy. To Feith they were the "administrators" whose claim to power derived from their technical skills, Western training, and intellectual culture. Prime Minister Hatta, trained as an economist, and Sjafruddin Prawiranegara, the Minister of Finance, were foremost among this group, and it was they who promulgated the liberalization of 1950–1.

Reflecting the dominance of its prime minister, the Hatta cabinet (December 1949–August 1950) was a strong one, composed to a man of "administrators." Hatta was at the peak of his political power – surpassing even that of Sukarno (Feith, 1962, p. 50) – at the time that the cabinet was formed. During the period of revolution Hatta was the chief negotiator and policymaker, and it was customary to speak of Sukarno–Hatta as one political force. His greater prestige was due to his role in negotiating the Round Table Agreement and in crushing the Communist rebellion (the "Madiun affair") in 1948, and the recent forced exile of Sukarno. The cabinet was a *zaken-kabinet* or business cabinet rather than a political coalition. Four of its members (including Hatta) were without party affiliation and all were considered men of great ability who were not chosen because of party representations but because of their competence.

Neither the economics-minded group nor any other political group, however, had a clearly defined economic program of which this liberalization was a part. Throughout the 1950s, politicians relied mostly on stock phrases and generalizations when discussing economic issues. Mintz (1965, p. 119) explains:

> In a large measure, the general lack of interest in economic doctrine reflects the fairly widespread agreement among all Indonesian parties about the kind of economy they want . . . anti-imperialist and anti-capitalist. Those groups and individuals harboring more precise ideas about the total pattern of the economy have, for reasons of practical politics, refrained on the whole from publicly spelling out their plans in detail.

An exception was Sumitro Djojohadikusumo, Minister of Finance in the Natsir cabinet (September 1950–April 1951) responsible for expanding the liberalization begun by the Hatta cabinet, a leading figure in the subsequent cabinets of Wilopo and Harahap, and author of the sweeping and rapid liberalization that transpired during the short tenure of the latter cabinet. Mintz (1965, pp. 119–20) suggests that Sumitro is "the prime example of what happens to a man who expresses home truths about the realities of the Indonesian economy" who as a result "was one of the most thoroughly disliked men in Indonesian politics."

Part of the problem faced by the pro-liberalization group was the unusual nature of government and the political elite in newly independent Indonesia. The role of government, already extensive under the colonial regime,[2] became even more dominant after the revolution. The government employed almost all educated Indonesians, conferred almost all prestigious social positions, and eventually bestowed almost all the lucrative commercial opportunities as well.

The absence of politically influential groups lobbying for liberalization reflected the strong popular resentment of the ubiquitous Dutch presence in the economy. The economic system that the Dutch had bequeathed and still largely controlled was, incredibly, identified as "liberalism," even though Dutch economic interests could not possibly have preferred a liberal trade regime to the restrictive trade cartel from which they currently derived their extraordinary economic power. Chinese-Indonesians, who controlled much of the wholesale and retail trade and small manufacturing, and were trying to compete in international trading, would be important beneficiaries of a liberal trade regime, but were also much resented and had no political influence. Initially, there was virtually no class of indigenous businessmen, and that which developed during the 1950s was a force against liberalism since, with few exceptions, they owed their fortune and success to the largess and favors doled out by the political parties. As a result the parties did not draw their power from organized economic interest groups, or any other interest groups for that matter. As Feith concluded:

> Hence the actually implemented decisions of government resulted in part from the pressures of parties – pressures coming through party representatives inside the bureaucracy as often as through the formally responsible cabinet minister – and in smaller part from purely intra-bureaucratic pressures. They were rarely a response to pressure from a class or an organized interest. (Feith, 1962, p. 107)

The reforms of the new cabinet came under sharp attack by the radical nationalists. This attack was not aimed specifically at the trade liberalization but rather, as Feith explains,

> represented protest against the readiness of the leaders of the revolutionary movement to allow the movement to lose its momentum and its mystique and integrative capacity. They expressed a resentment for the cabinet's concern for order and legality, which seemed to turn its back on the spirit of the Revolution, and hence to resemble a restored Dutch regime. (Feith, 1962, p. 89)

[2] Furnivall (1939, p. 389) characterized the effect of the Dutch "ethical programme" that began after the turn of the century as "coddling" to such an extent that "the villager cannot even scratch his head, unless an expert shows him how to do it and the Subdistrict Officer gives him permission."

In no way can the trade liberalization begun by the Hatta cabinet and continued by the succeeding Natsir cabinet be seen as acquiescence to the economic power of the Dutch. On the contrary, its immediate effect was to dismantle the comprehensive system of import licensing and interfirm allocation operated by the Covenants, a system which undoubtedly provided significant rents to the large trading houses that controlled them and which prevented new entry because of the reliance on the pre-war pattern of import ("historical percentage") in the interfirm allocation of import licenses. Free-list importing and other innovations (described below) must have reduced import premiums, while the reservation of certain goods for import only by Indonesian importers encouraged new entry. To be sure, the initial lack of alternative trading establishments meant that the Big Five remained the largest importers for some time, but their direct control over the allocation of import licenses, established during the Depression and intensified during the immediate post-war period, was finally broken.

The Foreign Exchange Certificate System and Free-list Importing

The liberalization came in stages, but its inception and introduction came before the beginning of the commodity price boom brought on by the Korean hostilities. On March 13, 1950, a foreign exchange retention system was announced that went far beyond the *Bukti Indusemen* system inherited from the Dutch colonial government. Under the Foreign Exchange Certificate system (*Sertipikat Devisen*) exporters were required to surrender all their export proceeds in exchange for rupiahs at the official rate of Rp 3.80 per US dollar plus a Foreign Exchange Certificate with a face value of 50 percent of the foreign exchange surrendered.[3] These certificates were purchased by importers who were required to submit them in an amount equal to the value of their imports. Certificates were freely negotiable and valid for 30 days. Their price (and thus the price of foreign exchange) was to be determined in a free market after a short period of fixed prices considered necessary to avoid "speculation" and uncertainty.[4] The price was initially set at $199\frac{3}{8}$ percent of the official rate, resulting in effective import and export rates of Rp 11.4 and Rp 7.6 respectively to the US dollar, exclusive of any other taxes, tariffs, or inducements.

Possession of a Foreign Exchange Certificate did not entitle the holder to purchase its foreign exchange equivalent at the official rate. For most commodities – those in the annual import plan – an import license from

[3] Although the name of the Indonesian currency was not officially changed to the rupiah until September 27, 1951, we will refer to Indonesian (as opposed to colonial) currency as rupiahs throughout the text in order to avoid confusion.
[4] There is some dispute over whether the government really intended the value of the certificates to be determined in a free market; Schmitt's (1959) review of the evidence suggests that this was their intention.

the Central Office for Import Matters (Kantor Pusat Urusan Impor, KPUI) was required. The import plan set quantitative limits on imports by commodity. In addition, KPUI enforced price controls on licensed imports, as had its Dutch colonial counterpart. However, soon after Foreign Exchange Certificates were introduced, a free-list import system was created. Commodities on the free list were not restricted by quota but still required approval of price, quality, and terms by KPUI. In June, free-list import was further liberalized and foreign exchange was to be allocated immediately upon request. Price control and an excess profits tax on free-list imports enacted in April were also discontinued in June in the stated belief that competition would preclude the making of "surplus profits."

Export receipts began to grow rapidly in mid-1950 in response to the Korean War commodity price boom and the large devaluation of the effective export exchange rate. Imports lagged more than expected, owing to the novelty of the new certificate system and changes in the system of allocating foreign exchange among firms. The Hatta cabinet was determined both to liberalize trade and to reduce the domination of the large Dutch import houses by further increasing the import free list, by relying more on competition (the "free-fight" system) in allocating import licenses, and by reserving the import of certain commodities for indigenous Indonesians (the *Benteng* system). In July, the free list was enlarged dramatically and included many key textiles, a wide range of finished consumer goods, and important raw materials such as yarns and cloves. In November, the list was enlarged again, and import with Foreign Exchange Certificates was liberalized by shifting their payment date from the date on which the import credit was opened abroad to the date on which the foreign exchange credit was settled. This change eliminated the implicit prepayment requirement of two thirds of the rupiah cost of imports obtained with Foreign Exchange Certificates.

Removal of Quotas: the Revised Bukti Indusemen Scheme

The Hatta cabinet ended on August 17, 1950, with the creation of the new unitary Republic of Indonesia formed by merging the set of Dutch-established political entities that were part of the RUSI into the Republic. The first cabinet of this new Republic, formed by Mohammad Natsir, contained many of the same men who had served under Hatta and was still very much an administrators' cabinet. The two principal economic posts were held by the two names most associated with economic liberality during the decade – Sjafruddin Prawiranegara as Minister of Finance and Sumitro Djojohadikusumo as Minister of Trade and Industry. Not surprisingly, the liberalization begun under Hatta was continued and expanded during this cabinet's tenure.

The central bank proclaimed the free list as the first "step on the road to the complete liberalization of imports" (Java Bank, 1950–1, p. 64). In August 1950 and March 1951 regulations were enacted that permitted the import of almost any commodity without regard to quota and without the need to purchase an import permit. These new regulations, an extension of the (*Surat*) *Bukti Indusemen* scheme begun by the colonial government in 1946–7, supplemented the Foreign Exchange Certificate system during its first year of operation. At the inception of the Foreign Exchange Certificate system, the rate of foreign exchange retention of the *Bukti Indusemen* had been reduced for many goods and now ranged from 5 to 10 percent of the value of export. In August 1950 restrictions on the use of *Bukti Indusemen* certificates were substantially liberalized.

Previously, only Hong Kong and Singapore dollars had been made available with these certificates, and import had to be from those origins and only into the harbor of the export that earned the certificates. The new regulations permitted holders of *Bukti Indusemen* certificates to obtain any foreign currency and import from any destination and into any port. In addition, these importers could bypass the time-consuming procedures for obtaining permits that other imports were required to follow. Indeed, one did not even have to be a recognized importer to import with *Bukti Indusemen* foreign exchange, as was required for other categories of import. Perhaps the most important advantage of certificates was that they could be used to import goods whose quotas were otherwise filled, as well as luxury items which did not appear at all in the import plan or on the free list. The certificates sold briskly on the free market, and their price apparently fluctuated substantially.

With the principal exports benefiting from the Korean War commodity price boom and the Foreign Exchange Certificate system, the government decided that it could afford to capture for itself some of the import premiums that the liberalized *Bukti Indusemen* scheme provided for exporters. It did this in March 1951 by selling its own certificates, called *Bukti Indusemen* new style, which had all the same rights as the *Bukti Indusemen* awarded to exports of certain commodities in proportion to their value, while simultaneously withdrawing *Bukti Indusemen* old style from principal native exports: rubber, coffee, pepper, tea, and tobacco. The *Bukti Indusemen* old style were retained only for minor exports: spices (except pepper), gums, resins, rattan, and shells. The government now fixed the price of the new-style certificates – and thus the old-style certificates as well – at 200 percent of the official exchange rate. It is clear that *Bukti Indusemen* foreign exchange would not be used for import from the free list but rather to import goods with binding quotas (including zero quota). The volume of *Bukti Indusemen* new style issued by the government was sufficient to lead the central bank to proclaim that "in 1951, all connection between planning of essential goods [the quota system] and the issue of licenses was discontinued" (Java Bank, 1951–2, p. 57). The import of goods beyond the quota required the surrender of both Foreign Exchange Certificates and *Bukti Indusemen* certificates, resulting in an effective exchange rate of five times the official rate. The innovation had the effect of capping potential import premiums at 200 percent.

Allocation of Import Licenses among Firms

The way in which import licenses were distributed was altered dramatically in 1950 and 1951. Although the allocation of foreign exchange among importers on the basis of pre-war "historical rights" was discontinued in 1951, other measures were introduced with the purpose of discriminating among importers. The measure that aroused the most political passion and that led to the greatest abuse was the *Benteng* (literally, fortress) system of importing, which was meant to reserve a share of import foreign exchange for ethnic Indonesians. At the time that the Hatta cabinet was installed in December 1949, only 10 percent of imports were handled by the nearly 100 ethnic Indonesian importers. In April 1950, the government announced that these importers were to be given special government protection in the form of a list of commodities which only they would be eligible to import – the *Benteng* list. To qualify as a *Benteng* importer one needed a minimum level of working capital, an office large enough for "several full-time employees," and some prior business experience. Furthermore, at least 70 percent of the capital had to be indigenous Indonesian. It was clear that nonindigenous Indonesians, particularly Indonesians of Chinese descent, did not qualify. Minister of Prosperity Djuanda explained to Parliament that although the government "does not practice racial discrimination, it has full right to make regulations to protect economically weak groups. As is known, indigenous Indonesian nationals as a group are included in the economically weak group [while] nationals in this country who are not indigenous Indonesians form the economically strong group" (quoted by Sutter, 1959, p. 1019).

Initially the *Benteng* list consisted mostly of a range of final consumer goods of low unit value. It included, among other things, paper fasteners, pen nibs, drawing pens, bathtowels, cigarette paper in booklets, matches, pajamas, shirts, and prayer rugs; compared with the free list, it was very unimportant. Nevertheless, *Benteng* importers became increasingly numerous. By the end of 1950 there were 250 *Benteng* importers, and in 1951 the number grew to 751, partly because limitations on the number allowed in each port were lifted. Other importers – mostly Chinese – numbered 3,119 (Sutter, 1959, pp. 1020–1).

Each *Benteng* importer was initially allocated a certain quantity of a specified good to import. Beginning in April 1951, a single allocation was made for all *Benteng* importers, and allocation among importers was made on the basis of competitive tenders. The Bank Negara Indonesia, the bank of issue in republican-held areas during the struggle with the Dutch, was allocated Rp 100 million to lend to *Benteng* importers. As most lacked evidence of creditworthiness, the Bank had to waive its usual standards. Losses to the Bank were enormous, and its President complained that debtors were likely to brand it "colonial" if it insisted on repayment (Schmitt, 1959, p. 87). Nevertheless, the government replenished its credit allocation to *Benteng* importers because they had rapidly become a potent political force, symbolizing the anticolonialist and antiforeign (including anti-Chinese) aspirations of the populace. Any government initiative that reduced import premiums or increased the cost of importing evoked protests from this new class of importers and the politicians who spoke for them.

Imports listed in the annual import plan, and thus subject to quota, were initially allocated according to the "historical rights" system of the colonial period. In 1951, an attempt was made to allow competition to determine interfirm allocations through what was known as the "free-fight" system. Importers were invited through circulars to submit offers for the import of items in the import plan or those required by the public sector directly. The KPUI was to judge these bids on the basis of price and quality in allocating exchange, and was to enforce price controls on those imports that entered the market. Evidence shows that the large import houses that dominated trade before 1950 captured the lion's share of these imports.[5]

Official racial discrimination extended to other areas subject to government control such as investment licensing and banking. Capacity in important industrial sectors was still under state control under colonial ordinances (the BRO described in chapter 2) enacted before the war. In response to special incentives, new industrial enterprises were begun by indigenous Indonesians, some of whom could count on a sympathetic response for additional assistance (sometimes in the form of special dispensations in exchange controls) if their enterprises encountered financial difficulty. Table 3.1 demonstrates the relatively rapid rise in the number of enterprises controlled by the "economically weak group" during the early 1950s. Much of the increase in the total number of enterprises controlled by the "economically strong group" is attributable to a change in the BRO that broadened its geographic coverage of rice mills. Excluding rice mills, the number of enterprises controlled by the "economically weak group" rose by 34 percent and those controlled by the "economically strong group" rose by only 7 percent.

---

[5] There was another small special class of importers known as "middle-class" dealers. These were shopkeepers who retailed imports direct to consumers. They were allocated foreign exchange directly to purchase merchandise in limited amounts and for a limited set of commodities. Indonesian "middle-class" dealers were distinguished from aliens for purposes of exchange allocation.

Table 3.1 Ownership of capacity-regulated (BRO) enterprises, 1941–1955

Enterprises		1941	1950	1951	1952	1953	1954	1955
Spinning	Weak[a]	n.a.	0	1	1	1	1	3
	Strong	n.a.	6	5	5	5	5	10
Weaving	Weak	1,347	1,767	1,731	1,716	1,701	1,834	1,959
	Strong	519	768	752	749	737	720	719
Knitting	Weak	n.a.	2	3	4	9	10	66
	Strong	n.a.	13	19	19	27	29	52
Printing	Weak	107	125	168	208	283	320	398
	Strong	336	399	408	434	449	442	444
Cigarette	Weak	n.a.	1	2	2	4	4	8
	Strong	9	16	21	26	39	45	46
Ice	Weak	n.a.	14	16	22	55	69	70
	Strong	n.a.	224	213	209	237	241	250
Frying pans	Weak	n.a.	0	2	6	5	7	10
	Strong	n.a.	14	14	14	17	16	16
Rice mills	Weak	57	75	87	208	313	364	370
	Strong	589	592	547	720	748	747	751
Rubber remilling	Weak	n.a.	0	29	24	28	30	37
	Strong	n.a.	64	64	66	62	63	65

n.a., not available.
[a] "Weak" enterprises are those owned by indigenous Indonesians; "strong" enterprises are those owned by all others including Indo-Chinese.
Source: Kraal, 1957, pp. 302–3

Retreat from Liberalization: the Devaluation of 1952 and the End of the Foreign Exchange Certificate System

The Natsir cabinet of "administrators" fell in March 1951 in response to a parliamentary motion asking the government to revoke regulations it had established to create regional legislative councils. This was merely the last of a succession of repeated acrimonious disputes which this cabinet had had with parliament. These disputes were symptomatic of the rising power of radical nationalism that had been building up since the Hatta cabinet was formed in December 1949. Feith (1962, p. 92) indicates the speed with which the political environment facing policymakers changed:

> In December 1949 it seemed that government leadership and political leadership were largely coterminous. By August 1950 government and politics stood in open opposition to one another. There was a quick decline in the unity of the political elite and in the power of the government over the political forces in society.

The Natsir cabinet's increasing political difficulties reflected these new political facts of life. President Sukarno, the symbol of revolutionary ardor, was growing in power and popularity relative to Hatta. The PNI, the party of the history minded, was for the first time not represented in a cabinet – in a country in which the prestige of a cabinet minister was extraordinarily high. Sukarno began actively to support PNI efforts to sabotage the program of the cabinet. Other parties were dissatisfied with the lack of patronage and the fiscal restraint of Sjafruddin Prawiranegara. It was only its close relationship with the army that kept the cabinet from falling earlier.

The new cabinet formed in April 1951 by Sukiman Wirjosandjojo, primarily with PNI and Masjumi members, was less influenced by "administrators" than its predecessor. The two main coalition parties disagreed on many issues and the cabinet was nearly paralyzed by interparty squabbling. Reaping the benefits of the Korean War commodity boom, it was generous to the civil service, open to patronage appointments, and provided credit to firms connected with certain political parties. Sumitro, who had served as an advisor to the cabinet, resigned in protest of its economic policies. By early 1952, however, it was clear that the economic situation was changing in a way that required some response. Rubber prices on the Singapore market in February 1952 were nearly half their February 1951 level. The total value of exports was beginning to fall off while the flow of imports in the first quarter of 1952 was nearly double that of the previous year and still rising. Prospects for a poor rice harvest led to sharply higher prices and complaints in parliament.

On February 4, 1952, the government finally acted, but not in an altogether forceful way. The Foreign Exchange Certificate system was abolished and the rupiah was officially devalued from Rp 3.80 to Rp 11.40 versus the US dollar – the effect of which was to leave the effective import exchange rate unchanged. The devaluation of the export exchange rate was tempered by an increase in export duties meant to compensate for the revenue lost from the Foreign Exchange Certificate system. In addition, there were changes in the *Bukti Indusemen* scheme, and the introduction of yet another, though more limited, certificate system.[6]

The new export duties, referred to as Additional Export Duties, were meant to be temporary and supplemental to the normal export duties, which averaged 8 percent. The new duties were 25 percent on rubber and copra and 15 percent on palm oil, palm kernels, tin and tin ore, petroleum, pepper, and coffee. The inducement certificates for certain weak exports, left over from 1947, were abolished. In partial compensation, the weak exports damar and rattan had their normal export duty reduced from 8 to

---

[6] The end of the Foreign Exchange Certificate system was strongly recommended by Dr Hjalmar Schacht, a German financial expert, who had been engaged by Sumitro Djojohadikusumo to prepare a report on the economy of Indonesia. To replace the state revenues that had been generated by the Foreign Exchange Certificate system he advocated raising import duties, particularly on luxury goods. He also strongly recommended abolishing the import-licensing system. The latter recommendation went unheeded; on the contrary, over the next three years the quantitative restriction of trade was intensified.

3 percent. With prices falling steadily with the end of the Korean War commodity price boom, the government began reducing the Additional Export Duties within a few months. On January 23, 1953, all remaining Additional Export Duties were abandoned.

Bukti Ekspor Dollar

A precipitous decline in Indonesian dollar holdings since 1951 prompted the government to link import denominated in US and Canadian dollars to export denominated in these currencies through the *Bukti Ekspor* dollar (BED) (proof of dollar export) scheme. Sellers of dollars earned in commodity export received BED certificates having a face value of 70 percent of their export in addition to rupiahs at the official rate of exchange. Importers (with some exceptions) were required to surrender BED certificates for 100 percent of the face value of their dollar imports. The 30 percent differentials between dollar exports and imports was to be used for rice import, which was exempt from the BED requirement, and to increase dollar exchange reserves.

The BED certificates were originally freely negotiable and valid for 60 days. Immediately after their introduction they sold for Rp 1.50 per US dollar, thereby adding 13 percent to the cost of dollar imports and 9 percent to the return from dollar exports exclusive of duties. The value of the certificates soon rose above Rp 1.70 and then began to fluctuate sharply in the free market. In March, the Java Bank established an exchange equalization fund in order to intervene in the BED market, and in May began to fix and progressively lower the BED price until the system was abolished on January 1, 1954.

In the last four months of its existence, the BED scheme added only 2 percent to the import exchange rate and 1.5 percent to the export exchange rate exclusive of duties and surcharges. Nevertheless, exports to dollar areas more than tripled in 1952 over 1951, mostly at the expense of Singapore and Malaya, and dollar assets of the Foreign Exchange Fund on March 31, 1953, were nearly triple those of the previous March.

Import Surcharges

Although the package announced on February 4, 1952 included the abolition of *Bukti Indusemen* old style issued to minor exports, the government continued to issue the *Bukti Indusemen* new style on its own account, as it had since March 1951. The new regulations required that importers of nonessential goods on an inducement list acquire inducement certificates having 70 percent of the value of import. As a result, the effective import rate for luxury imports was now 510 percent of the old official exchange rate compared with 500 percent previously, exclusive of duties. The right of the holder of *Bukti Indusemen* certificates to import beyond the normal quota limit was no longer operative, since only the government could sell certificates and they were not available on demand as before. The *Bukti Indusemen* scheme had thus become indistinguishable from a 70 percent import duty. The inducement list included cosmetics, perfume, automobiles, household appliances, confectionery, beverages, preserved food, cigarettes, and photographic equipment among other items. The list was reduced on June 3, 1952, when a subset of 25 items, including expensive automobiles and air conditioners, were ruled ineligible for import. Items on the *Benteng* list no longer qualified for import with inducement certificates.

The Sukiman cabinet fell on February 23, 1951, over the signing of a pact with the United States under the Mutual Security Act – the details of which were made public on the same day as the devaluation and the abolition of the Foreign Exchange Certificate system. There is no evidence that these two revelations were connected – indeed, most cabinet members were probably unaware of the pact. A new cabinet formed by Wilopo (Masjumi party) in April was once again a coalition principally of the PNI and Masjumi parties. However, this cabinet differed greatly from its predecessor. Different wings of these parties were involved – cabinet members from both parties were drawn from the less history-minded younger generation. The chief economics post, the Minister of Finance, was filled by the liberal-minded Sumitro[7] – a member of the small but influential Partai Sosialis Indonesia (PSI). Wilopo put heavy emphasis on economic matters in the cabinet program, realizing very well that the declining terms of trade and expenditure commitments of the Sukiman cabinet meant that some measure of austerity was required.

In response to a continuing worsening in Indonesia's trade balance, a package of measures aimed at further restricting imports was put in place on August 28, 1952. Foremost among them was the extension of inducement certificates to a much wider range of imports. Goods were broken up into four groups: group A consisted of goods considered essential and were free of inducements, group B consisted of less essential goods and required

---

[7] Sumitro's economic liberality may seem clear in the context of policymaking in 1950s Indonesia, but his writings do not identify him as an economic liberal in the absolute sense. In a public lecture delivered to the University of Indonesia and republished in its economics journal (Sumitro, 1953) he stated his belief that the governments of developing countries must control foreign trade and foreign exchange absolutely and that "such control can be exerted indirectly through a system of licenses or in some specific cases by directly organizing government agencies as single buyer and/or single seller" (p. 177). He used both methods during the tenure of the Wilopo cabinet. He differs from most of his contemporaries in that rent seeking and political patronage were not his motivation for the selective use of quantitative control, but rather were seen by him as their major drawbacks. His economic philosophy is elaborated further in his monograph on development economics (Sumitro, 1955).

inducement certificates having 100 percent of the value of the import, group C were permitted luxury goods which required inducement certificates of 200 percent of the import value, and group D consisted of goods for which foreign exchange was no longer available. In addition, 40 percent of the cost, insurance, and freight (c.i.f.) import value had to be prepaid before an import and foreign exchange license was applied for. If *Indusemen* or BED certificates were required for an import, they had to be prepaid in full.

These price measures were apparently not enough to reduce imports to the desired levels, perhaps because 86 percent of imports consisted of group A commodities, which were free of inducement (12 percent of imports were from the B list). In September an overall limit on the quantity of foreign exchange to be made available for imports during the succeeding four months was decided upon, and as a result sharper restrictions on import and foreign exchange licensing were in effect for the remainder of the year. According to one observer (Takens, 1954, p. 510) "as from roundabout Oct. 1952, the doors of the Kantor Pusat Urusan Import [the import licensing agency] were practically closed, only to be set ajar several months later, while finally they were thrown wide open in the scope of the 'Lebaran injection' of April [1953]." Indeed, in the first quarter of 1953, the KPUI issued only half the value of import licenses that were issued in the relatively restrictive last quarter of 1952.

In order to reduce import premiums arising from the tightened quantitative restrictions, goods were shifted from the A list to the B list, and the B list was divided into two subgroups. Furthermore, the misnomer "inducement" for import duties was abandoned and replaced by *Tambahan Pembajaran Impor* (TPI) (Additional Import Duty). The A list was reduced to include 51 percent of imports. The B list was broken up into a B1 list and a B2 list. The B1 list, with a TPI of $33\frac{1}{3}$ percent, consisted mostly of goods that were formerly on the A list, and included about 37 percent of imports. The B2 list, covering 11 percent of imports, consisted of goods deemed "semiluxuries" and had a 100 percent TPI. The C list had a 200 percent TPI and contributed only 2 percent of imports. Goods on the D list, as before, were not importable with foreign exchange from the Foreign Exchange Fund but could be imported by foreign nationals after payment of a 200 percent TPI. This shifting of commodities between lists increased the average TPI from 16 percent to 27 percent of import value. Compared with the relatively liberal year of 1951, the composition of imports among these four groups was more skewed toward "nonessentials" in the first half of 1953, despite the TPI import surcharge system.

The advance deposit requirement for imports was stiffened from April 1, 1953. A prepayment of 75 percent of the specific import value plus 100 percent of TPI (and BED if necessary) was required before an import and foreign exchange license was applied for. Furthermore, banks were instructed not to increase credit to importers above the March 31 level. Even special pleas by the *Benteng* importers failed to soften these measures. In October, the prepayment requirement for industrial raw materials and machinery was reduced to 50 percent.

The Beginning of Monopoly Importers: the Jajasans

The system for allocating foreign exchange licenses among importers also changed significantly during this period. Importers of commodities on the free list were no longer able to import these goods in unlimited amounts. The free list remained, but was subject to the same licensing requirements (import planning) as other goods. The list had only an administrative purpose since registered free-list importers were allowed to import from this list only.

Import of two of the most important goods on the original free list – when as such it was not quantitatively restricted – was turned over to quasi-private monopoly import organizations. The import of cloves, an essential ingredient in the Indonesian *kretek* cigarette, was turned over to a private firm owned by an association of cigarette factories. The cloves monopoly was established to halt the closures of smaller indigenous Indonesian *kretek* factories in the face of the growing market share of a single Chinese-owned *kretek* concern which accounted for nearly three quarters of the *kretek* output of Kudus, Java, the center of the *kretek* industry. By 1952, 140 of the 200 *kretek* factories in East Java had closed (Sutter, 1959, p. 1049).

Similarly, the closing of small batik factories in Java led to the formation of a quasi-private firm with sole rights to import and distribute cambrics, the major material in batik production. Cambrics, imported for Rp 60, were sold by the monopolies for Rp 90 and fetched Rp 160 on the black market. Firms found it more profitable to sell their allocations of raw materials on the free market than to use them in their normal operations.

Bukti Indusemen Restored: 1953–1955

The Wilopo cabinet fell in June 1953 over the violence that occurred while a scheme to remove squatters from estate lands in Sumatra was being enforced. The cabinet had some success in reducing the budget deficit, introducing budgetary planning, curbing patronage, halting the growth of the *Benteng* program, and rationalizing the army and civil service. Its reliance on import surcharges and prepayments to curb imports and reduce the budget deficit was resented by the emerging class of urban elites and national importers. The PNI, reacting to the pleas of the bureaucrats and especially the new class of importers, attacked Sumitro – who, in addition to being Minister of Finance, was the (Dutch-trained) Dean of the Faculty of Economics at the University of Indonesia – for "using the theories he had learned in school to make financial experiments" (quoted by Schmitt, 1959, p. 145). In May 1953 a parliamentary motion was passed requiring specific legislation before any new economic measures could be implemented – an important defeat for the government and a clear signal of the political strength of the forces opposing liberalization.[8]

The new cabinet was formed by Ali Sastroamidjojo of the PNI and excluded both the Masjumi and the PSI but had the support of the PKI. Many of its members were history-minded radical nationalists and had close ties with President Sukarno. The Ali cabinet was firmly committed to serving the interests represented by the PNI. The *Benteng* program was expanded ("openly perverted" in the words of Glassburner (1960, p. 313), the money issue was increased, the central bank debt tripled, and foreign exchange reserves were eliminated as a result of its efforts to further the Indonesianization of the economy and the interests of the importing class – now among the most powerful and generous supporters of the PNI.

The cabinet's first crisis was a fully fledged rebellion in the Aceh region of north Sumatra beginning in September 1953. This strongly Islamic area (and Masjumi stronghold) had traditionally traded directly with Malaya – just across the Straits of Malacca – and was aggrieved that this was no longer permitted, particularly in light of the import bias of the trade regime. The Ali cabinet responded militarily to the revolt and, to head off rising discontent in the other export regions, it resurrected foreign exchange inducement certificates for some smallholder exports in October 1953. As before, these *Bukti Indusemen* certificates were provided to exporters in addition to rupiahs at the official rate. The *Bukti Indusemen* rates of 5–10 percent were structured to encourage the export of higher qualities of the commodities involved.

Bukti Indusemen certificates represented a freely negotiable claim to foreign exchange for the import of certain goods from categories B2 and C. Certain other goods (included in an inducement list) could only be imported by providing *Bukti Indusemen* equal to the full c.i.f. value of their import. The latter goods were mostly beverages and provisions. The certificates, which were valid for 60 days, were freely traded at between Rp 0.80 and Rp 1.20 per inducement rupiah during 1953 and rose to Rp 1.70 by the end of 1954. With rubber prices rising in late 1954 and early 1955, the *Bukti Indusemen* scheme for rubber was suspended on February 11, 1955, and replaced by an Additional Export Duty of 10 percent. This latest

[8] Feith (1958) sees the Wilopo cabinet as marking a turning point in post-revolutionary Indonesia in that it saw the "decisive victory of mass leader forces over political forces led by intellectuals" (p. 211). The ascendency of these "mass leader forces" – labor and veterans' associations and the PKI – changed political alignments, brought the PNI and PKI closer together, and increased the involvement of President Sukarno in PNI politics.

reincarnation of the inducement system was revoked effective June 1, 1955.

Attempts to improve the quality of and returns from export went beyond the structuring of *Bukti Indusemen* rates. In July 1953 the export of high grades of rubber and estate rubber and tea to Singapore was prohibited in the belief that higher proceeds would result from the elimination of entrepôt trade. Similarly, exports of copra to the Netherlands were banned in May 1954. To encourage domestic remilling, which had previously been performed in Singapore, the export of rubber slabs of thickness 3 cm or more was prohibited on September 16, 1953; the government instigated a new corporation, N. V. Karet, to act as sole buyer of rubber slabs and remill them for export. Since enforcement of these prohibitions was impossible, it is likely that they failed to achieve their object.

Quantitative Restrictions Intensified: 1954–1955

The balance-of-payments situation deteriorated sharply in early 1954. In May 1954 import licensing was cut back drastically. A foreign exchange quota of Rp 50 million per week was set. Soon after, the international reserves of the Bank Indonesia fell below the statutory level of 20 percent. As prices of imports began to rise as a result of burgeoning import premiums, the government frantically sought to control prices, reduce premiums, and increase exports through a bewildering array of stopgap measures. It created a new agency, the Jajasan Perbekalan dan Persediaan (JPP) (Central Foundation for Stores and Supplies) to manage the import and supply of textiles, cloves, and other essentials. Beginning on October 8, all textile importers were to sell their imports to the JPP which would then deliver them to assigned wholesalers. Traders' margins were set by decree. These regulations failed to prevent massive diversions to the black market. Another agency, the Jajasan Motor, was placed in control of imports of automobile spare parts and accessories.

In July advance deposit requirements increased from 75 to 100 percent for most goods, and from 50 to 75 percent for industrial raw materials and machinery. In August, the Foreign Exchange Fund (LAAPLN) no longer made foreign exchange available for insurance on import shipments. To increase the supply of some goods considered essential, there was a very limited return to free-list-style importing, first for wheat flour in November 1954, and then for cement, fertilizers, salted fish, and a few other commodities in 1955.

Evasion of price control was pervasive and high textile prices, always politically sensitive, remained a problem. Hoping to reduce textile prices, the government ended the JPP's monopoly control of the import and distribution of textiles in February 1955 and returned the import of textiles to private firms. In an explicitly stated attempt to "have the Treasury benefit to a large extent from the enormously increased margin between landed cost and retail price" (Bank Indonesia, 1954–5, p. 102) the government decided for the first time to sell import licenses at auction. Import licenses for textiles, known as *Bukti Impor Tekstil* (BIT), were auctioned through a tender system. The JPP, exempted from the BIT requirement, continued to import textiles as well and to sell them on the wholesale market. What it accomplished by doing this, apart from earning enormous profit, is unclear.

To reduce the import premiums on other goods, a new import certificate, the *Bukti Impor Sementara* (BIS), was required for purchase of all goods except some essentials and textiles covered by the BIT scheme. The BIS was just another import surcharge ranging from 25 percent for capital goods in import category A and 50 percent for other category A goods up to 100 percent for category C imports. The BIS surcharge, begun on July 21, 1955, was in place little more than a month before it was revoked after the fall of the Ali Sastroamidjojo cabinet. Nevertheless, all indications are that at no time since the May 1954 crackdown on import licenses were quantitative restrictions not the binding constraint on almost all importing.

Parallel Transactions and Hong Kong Barters

In 1953 regulations severely limiting imports from the entrepôt centers of Singapore and Hong Kong were effected in the belief that substantial savings could be achieved by importing directly from the country of origin. In September of that year new regulations permitted traders to import from Hong Kong in an amount equal to the value of their export to Hong Kong. This system was known as Hong Kong barters and was the first in a series of country-specific import–export link schemes that provided enormous opportunities for earning import premiums.

Parallel transactions, like Hong Kong barters, were a link between import rights and export. The scheme, which began on October 25, 1954, originally provided 100 percent counter-import rights for export to certain Eastern bloc countries.

Exports to Eastern Europe, in particular Poland and Czechoslovakia, demonstrated large increases as a result of this scheme. In January 1955 changes in the scheme made it more characteristic of an export inducement scheme of the kind reintroduced in October 1953 and described above. Exporters of certain weak products obtained a counter-import right varying from 10 to 30 percent of their export proceeds. Exporters were no longer required to import from the country of export destination; import from any country was permitted.

Import premiums were large during late 1954 and early 1955, so that parallel transactions and Hong Kong barters provided traders with tremendous incentives to export goods to those destinations which yielded import rights. The Eastern bloc countries were in a position to capture some of these premiums by reducing the value of the goods they would barter for Indonesian exports to below the bartered export's world market value. Many of the Indonesian products so acquired were resold by the Eastern bloc countries in Western Europe (Sumitro, 1956, p. 43). The premiums accruing to Indonesian traders were high enough to encourage them to purchase counter-import eligible goods on the Indonesian market in such quantity that the domestic rupiah price of these goods rose above the level that made export to other (non-counter-import) destinations profitable.

Corruption

Corruption, always a problem in the administration of the Indonesian economy, increased markedly during the tenure of the first Ali Sastroamidjojo cabinet. The Prime Minister early declared his intention to change the existing "colonial economy" into a "national economy." A greatly enlarged list of commodities whose import could be undertaken solely by indigenous ("national") importers was issued by KPUI in September 1953 without proper legal authority, and was withdrawn under pressure from the president of the Bank Indonesia, Sjafruddin Prawiranegara. Under the direction of the Minister of Economic Affairs, Ishaq Tjokroadisurjo, the cabinet achieved its objectives for the allocation of foreign exchange in any case, but it soon became clear that a national importer was more narrowly defined as a member of or contributor to the PNI.

A new type of import and export "licensing" developed, euphemistically referred to as *Lisensi Istimewa* (special licenses). *Lisensi Istimewa* were issued to certain favored traders for the export of (otherwise banned) slab rubber with counter-import rights. Others were granted export licenses for rubber export in which the rubber was invoiced at prices considerably lower than world market values. According to Schmitt (1959, p. 168) "a congenial merchant, in return for a contribution to the party, was permitted to understate the value of an export consignment and keep the difference in actual proceeds abroad."

To accommodate further those who held foreign exchange abroad, the Ali cabinet legalized "free of foreign exchange" importing. Under this arrangement, traders could import outside quota limits as long as they did not require foreign exchange from the Foreign Exchange Fund. This kind of importing, which had existed in the period of colonial administration after World War II and was not revoked by the Indonesian government until August 1950, was supposedly restricted to "essential" goods and required that 100 percent of the rupiah value of the import (at the official exchange rate) be paid to the Bank Indonesia in advance. Sumitro (1956, p. 44) claimed that "foreign exchange free" imports were actually "consumer goods of the most luxurious kind such as Cadillac, Mercedes-Benz, etc." Opposition party newspapers often referred to the Ali cabinet as the *Kabinet Mercedes-Benz*. Feith (1962) reports that speculative investment in luxury durables became rife, and that new Plymouth or Dodge automobiles often sold for Rp 400,000 – in excess of US$35,000 at official rates of exchange and US$10,000 at black-market rates. Perhaps as a result of these policies, there was an increasing problem of "nonrealized" exports beginning in late 1954; that is, traders claimed that exports that were licensed were not actually realized and thus no foreign exchange was surrendered. Beginning in November 1954, penalties were assessed on nonrealized exports and were further extended in May 1955.

The number of national importers grew immensely, from 750 to perhaps 6,000–8,000, during the tenure of the Ali cabinet. According to the head of the KPUI, only 50 of these establishments were bona fide and another 200 were only marginally so (Amstutz, quoted by Feith, 1962, p. 375). The new national importers, known as "newcomers," received a disproportionate share of foreign exchange for imports at the expense of the established *Benteng* importers ("oldcomers") and foreign and Indo-Chinese trading houses. Within weeks of the installation of the Ali cabinet national importers as a group were receiving 76.2 percent of import foreign exchange (Sutter, 1959, p. 1033). In the 14 months of Minister Ishaq's tenure, national importers received 80–90 percent of import foreign exchange compared with 37.9 percent in the first four months of 1953 (Feith, 1962, p. 374). Important among the new national importers was a group known as "briefcase importers" who either resold their licenses or acted as frontmen for Indo-Chinese importers (these were referred to as Ali-Baba importers – "Ali" for the Indonesian and "Baba" for the Chinese) and foreign importers ("strawmen importers"). It has been asserted that 10 percent of the value of these licenses was required as a donation to an election campaign fund (Sutter, 1959, p. 1072). A parliamentary investigation summarized by Sutter (p. 1082) found that

> Corruption at the Central Office of Import Affairs was found to be rife. From the doorman on through virtually all the desks concerned with issuing an import license it was necessary to pay bribes to speed up handling of applications or even to get any service. As a consequence persons entitled to receive licenses did not get them, those not qualified did get them, and thus license-selling with commissions up to 200 percent had become common.

The Trade Liberalization of 1950–1951: a Summary

The liberalization begun in March 1950 was an attempt by the economics-minded cabinets of Hatta and Natsir to break the Dutch colonial system of quantitative control of trade and the allocation of import premiums to the large Dutch-owned trading houses. Its stated intentions was gradually to eliminate quantitative restrictions in favor of free-list importing and it made significant progress in this direction.

The momentum of liberalization may initially have been sustained by the concurrent (but unrelated) behavior of rubber prices. As table 3.2 demonstrates, the international price of rubber, Indonesia's most important export, did not begin its upward course in response to the outbreak of hostilities in Korea until the liberalization was announced in mid-March 1950. By the end of the year, rubber prices in New York had increased by a factor of 3.5. Both the Jakarta wholesale price and the New York spot

Table 3.2 External and internal prices, 1949–1954

Year (quarter)	New York spot price of rubber (RSS I)[a] (US$ per lb)	Non-oil exports (million US$)	Total exports (million US$)	Total imports (million US$)	Wholesale price index of 44 manufactures (1938 = 100)	Wholesale price of rubber in Jakarta (Rp per 100 kg)
1949						
I	19.1	65.3	86.3	73.7	670	102
II	16.4	62.9	94.5	96.3	779	92
III	17.6	67.1	95.8	113.4	915	115
IV	17.5	85.8	112.4	131.3	1,189	133
1950						
I	19.9	68.9	97.6	63.4	1,294	275
II	30.9	115.5	152.1	83.7	1,935	475
III	56.0	183.2	226.6	103.4	1,937	826
IV	71.2	265.0	301.8	181.0	2,077	979
1951						
I	72.1	281.8	305.3	110.5	2,491	1,219
II	66.0	307.6	363.2	153.7	2,450	791
III	52.0	221.8	261.3	295.5	2,418	846
IV	52.0	281.8	324.7	246.6	2,384	770
1952						
I	50.5	209.9	246.5	200.5	2,358	750
II	38.0	168.5	211.3	212.2	2,255	640
III	27.4	163.7	213.6	252.7	2,322	561
IV	31.3	189.7	241.3	248.7	2,245	688
1953						
I	26.6	148.9	188.4	162.3	2,510	551
II	24.5	142.6	194.9	194.7	2,509	504
III	23.1	164.5	220.9	211.9	2,483	502
IV	20.9	158.8	211.5	180.4	2,416	519
1954						
I	20.2	134.6	189.8	167.8	2,500	474
II	23.0	141.3	191.0	156.6	2,664	663
III	24.0	173.2	231.3	143.4	2,820	640
IV	29.9	178.9	242.4	115.0	3,006	787

[a] RSS I, rubber smoked sheet I.

Sources: Second column, International Rubber Study Group, Rubber Statistical Bulletin, various issues; remainder, Biro Pusat Statistik, Statistik Konjunktur, various issues

price peaked in the first quarter of 1951 before retreating. As the table shows, exports responded quickly and substantially. No doubt this good fortune speeded up the pace of liberalization.

Why then was the liberalization reversed? An obvious explanation lies in the continuing deterioration of the terms of trade during the period 1951–3.[9] The international price of rubber fell 71 percent between the first quarter of 1951 and the last quarter of 1953 – a fall dramatic enough to evoke a significant response from any nation. Nevertheless, just as the Korean War commodity price boom was not the impetus to liberalization, the boom's end was probably not the major factor in its demise. The shifting political dynamics of the period – the direction of which was only marginally influenced by international price movements – would probably have led to the liberalization's reversal. The power of radical nationalists was growing and increasing political polarization made it more and more difficult for coalitions to govern. Furthermore, the government was unable to contain, let alone reverse, the accelerating expansion of the bureaucracy. Meanwhile, numerous new government initiatives requiring significant expenditure had begun and were politically difficult to rein in. Important among them was the *Benteng* program which generated increasing demands on the government for credit and foreign exchange. The two cabinets that succeeded that of Natsir were too weak and divided to introduce effective remedies: the Sukiman cabinet (April 1951–April 1952) was characterized by factional infighting and increasing corruption, while the Wilopo cabinet that followed (April 1952–June 1953) was at odds with parliament and vacillated in its attempt to deal with the deteriorating economic situation – initially increasing quantitative restrictions and then trying to replace them with the TPI import surcharge system.

The fall of the economics-minded Wilopo cabinet and its replacement with the history-minded cabinet of Ali Sastroamidjojo ended any hope of reviving the liberalization process begun in 1950. Indonesianization was the stated goal of economic policy, while the power of the cabinet and the parties represented was the true object. Economic policy was based on the need to fill the coffers of the parties in power in anticipation of the coming election, to line the pockets of politicians, and to cater to the public desire for symbols of revolutionary ardor and national independence – Indonesianization and an active foreign policy – rather than to respond to the objective needs of the economy and its changing terms of trade. This was the period of "special licenses," parallel transactions, massive corruption, and strident nationalism. The entire trading process became chaotic as import licenses were given mostly to those willing to contribute to the PNI and exporters failed to surrender their foreign exchange. None of this seemed to faze the electorate which was concerned only with symbols

[9] Table 5.2 surveys annual data on the terms of trade from 1938 to 1976.

rather than performance – as evidenced by the results of the 1955 election (see below). Ultimately neither external factors, such as the terms of trade, nor internal economic factors resulted in the extinction of the liberalization begun in 1950. The direction of the trade regime in 1953–5 was determined primarily by rent seeking and the desire of the politically active for militant and assertive initiatives by the state.

The Sumitro Reforms: the Second Liberalization Attempt

The first Ali Sastroamidjojo cabinet fell after a conflict with the army over the appointment of the Army Chief of Staff and was replaced on August 12, 1955, by a cabinet headed by Burhanuddin Harahap. This was a caretaker cabinet pending the outcome of the parliamentary elections tentatively scheduled for the end of September and the Constituent Assembly elections scheduled for later in the year. Although this cabinet, in particular its economics portfolio, was firmly in the hands of economics-minded individuals – the PNI was unrepresented – it had to make policy with an eye to the coming elections. In the cabinet's view, the Ali cabinet had made something of a mess of the economy – rising inflation, corruption, budget deficits, and a loss of international confidence. They needed to demonstrate to the electorate, rapidly and unmistakably, that they were on a very different course. Within a few hours of the cabinet's installation, the Minister of Justice of the previous cabinet was arrested on charges of corruption. Other arrests followed, as well as the temporary exile of former Economics Minister Ishaq Tjokroadisurjo, under summons from the chief public prosecutor.[10]

While the anticorruption drive gained the coalition much publicity in its campaign against the PNI, the cabinet introduced another policy initiative intended to increase its popularity with the voters. The Minister of Finance, Sumitro, who had earlier served in the cabinets of Natsir and Wilopo, initiated a dramatic and far-reaching trade liberalization on September 1, 1955.

All quantitative restrictions were abandoned so as to redirect the massive import premiums to the government's treasury. The parallel transactions and Hong Kong barter schemes were revoked. "Foreign-exchange-free" import was halted, as was the issuance of export licenses which legally underinvoiced exports. The JPP was put into liquidation and its import functions were placed in the hands of private traders, and the Jajasan Motor had its powers revoked. The corrupt import-licensing agency KPUI was abolished and replaced with a new agency – the Biro Devisen Perdagangan (BDP) (Bureau of Trade and Foreign Exchange).

[10] Ishaq was brought to trial in 1959 and again in 1960 for his activities during the Ali cabinet and was convicted and sentenced to five months' imprisonment (Feith, 1962, p. 423).

New incentives, neutral with respect to destination, were provided for exports.[11]

Quotas for imports were replaced with increased import surcharges and more costly import prepayment requirements. Commodities were grouped into four categories with TPI (import surcharges) ranging from 50 percent for goods designated "essential" to 400 percent for "superluxuries."

The TPI rates for goods designated nonessential were originally meant to be temporary, to be replaced by an auction system for foreign exchange. In the event the system was never established. The import of rice, yarn, raw cotton, airplane fuel, and textbooks was exempt from all TPI upon application to the Monetary Board, which oversaw foreign exchange regulation.

Prepayment requirements differed between national importers and others. National importers were required to prepay 100 percent of the value of their imports, including TPI, at the time of application for foreign exchange. Previously, prepayment had been required at the time that a foreign exchange application was granted. Beginning on November 16, 1955, the import of industrial raw materials required only half the usual prepayment. In an effort to reduce the number of importers, nonnational importers were required to deposit a minimum of Rp 5 million with a foreign exchange bank in order to be eligible to import. They could draw on this deposit to meet prepayment requirements when filling an actual foreign exchange application. Beginning in February 1956 national importers were also required to make deposits, but of only Rp 500,000. Importers, both national and nonnational, were no longer tied to lists of goods they could import, and in the near absence of import monopolies (the Jajasans) and quotas it was hoped that "briefcase" importing and license selling would cease. Indeed, the number of importers fell from between 6,000 and 8,000 to 3,684 national importers and only 46 foreign importers. Many of the 1,695 foreign importers who were registered before these regulations took effect found it preferable to import through a national importer paid by commission in order to avoid the large import deposit required of them (Panglaykim, 1963, p. 29).

The opportunity for illegal transactions was greatly reduced by the absence of quotas, and was even further reduced by the structure of the foreign exchange application procedure. Importers did not apply directly to the BDP but rather to an authorized foreign exchange bank which forwarded their application. At no point was there to be direct contact

[11] Sumitro was vociferous in publicly refuting the claim of his critics that this policy package was a "liberalization" or that Indonesia now had a "liberal" import policy. This reflected the strong negative reaction which the term "liberalization" evoked. The phrase "free-fight liberalism" was used as an expletive and even as late as 1968 one observer (Oei, 1968, p. 135) noted that "the term liberalization has an unsavory connotation in Indonesia and is generally avoided."

between importers and the BDP. Instead of names, foreign exchange applications contained code numbers whose meaning was to be known only to a select few. Three different individuals were to review each application separately, to check the accuracy of price and quality information (to prevent mis-invoicing), and to determine the appropriate TPI category. The whole procedure took an average of three weeks whereas under the previous system foreign exchange applications often required four to six months (Sumitro, 1956, p. 48).

Price control was also greatly reduced and simplified as part of the Sumitro reforms. The previous confusing and broad-based system gave way to one encompassing a relatively limited number of traded goods: rice, petroleum products, medicines, electric light bulbs, automobile tires, cigarettes and tobacco, sugar, coal, books, newsprint, coconut oil and fats, and soap. However, with an eye to the elections, the price of gasoline was brought down from Rp 1.80 per liter to Rp 1.04 per liter on the same day that the liberalization was announced.

The Harahap cabinet sought to promote exports through a limited subsidy system known as Export Premiums and through the general reduction of export duties. Beginning on October 24, 1955, a subsidy in rupiahs ranging from 5 to 10 percent of export value was given to exporters of certain weak export products. Exports not considered weak included rubber, copra, palm oil and kernels, petroleum, tin, leaf tobacco, and sugar. The Additional Export Duty on rubber was abolished along with all other Additional Export Duties. In addition, normal export duties as well as a statistical tax, ostensibly an administrative charge of 1 percent, were reduced or abolished for some commodities.

As table 3.3 demonstrates, the liberalization had rapid and substantial effects on relative prices. A wholesale price index for imported textiles fell 23 percent in the first month of the liberalization and was 41 percent lower in June 1956 than in August 1955. The retail prices of some import-competing goods fell even more dramatically. Between August and December 1955, the retail price of white jean cloth fell by more than half, and there were significant falls in the prices of condensed milk and razor blades. The nominal black-market exchange rate fell as well, dropping by 30 percent between August 1955 and April 1956.

Trade flows and the terms of trade around the time of the Sumitro reforms are presented in table 3.4. The quarterly flow of imports increased by almost 50 percent between 1955, quarter III, and 1956, quarter II. The quarterly flow of import of "consumption" commodities more than doubled over the same period. The Sumitro reforms coincided with a mini-boom in natural rubber prices. The New York spot price of rubber smoked sheet I (RSS I) rose by two thirds between March and September 1955 and then fell back to below its previous levels by June 1956. The fall in international prices and the reduced return to illegal transactions as a result

Table 3.3 Price effects of the Sumitro reforms

Date	(1)	(2)	(3)	(4)	(5)	(6)	(7)
1954							
Aug	3,257	3.92	6.20	2.58	28.25	588	62.97
1955							
Aug	5,433	11.00	12.00	7.12	43.50	1,406	79.92
Sep	4,186	5.75	10.16	6.97	35.50	1,230	84.12
Oct	3,921	5.76	8.07	6.81	36.25	1,044	81.94
Nov	3,787	5.55	8.00	5.50	35.00	1,255	83.55
Dec	3,699	5.05	7.78	4.07	33.25	1,339	82.78
1956							
Jan	3,645	4.92	7.56	3.51	34.12	1,119	85.11
Feb	3,509	5.08	7.56	3.22	34.12	916	87.97
Mar	3,452	5.00	7.33	3.26	35.50	839	89.34
Apr	3,364	4.78	6.90	3.26	30.50	785	82.90
May	3,277	4.50	6.68	3.23	31.00	693	82.35
Jun	3,215	4.41	6.30	3.22	32.00	762	81.90

(1) Wholesale price index of ten imported textiles in Jakarta (1938 = 100).
(2) Retail price of white jeans (28 in) in Jakarta (Rp per m).
(3) Retail price of condensed milk ("Nona" brand) in Jakarta (Rp per 14 oz tin).
(4) Retail price of razor blades ("Nacet" brand) in Jakarta (Rp per ten-blade pack).
(5) Black-market exchange in Jakarta (Rp per US$).
(6) Wholesale price of rubber (RSS I) in Jakarta (Rp per 100 kg).
(7) Cost of living index, Jakarta (March 1957 to February 1958 = 100).
Sources: Columns 1–6, Biro Pusat Statistik, *Statistik Konjunktur*, various issues; column 7, Biro Pusat Statistik, unpublished

of the fall in the black-market exchange rate resulted in a sharp fall in the domestic rubber price (table 3.3). Nonetheless, these movements in international prices had nothing to do with the timing or sequencing of the Sumitro reforms – which were wholly determined by the political events described above – but may have hastened their overthrow by the succeeding cabinet.

The surprisingly poor election performance of the parties that made up the coalition cabinet was the proximate cause of the end of this bold liberalization attempt. Only four weeks separated the announcement of the liberalization and the parliamentary elections, so that its direction but not its effects may possibly have influenced the electorate. Much to the disappointment of the coalition partners, economic policy was not a major issue in the election. Although voter intimidation was widespread, Feith (1962) considered the elections to be relatively "free," with the majority of voters registering meaningful choices: "meaningful not as judgments on the performance of particular governments but as ideological identifications" (p. 434).

Table 3.4 Trade flows and the terms of trade at the time of the Sumitro reforms

Year (quarter)	(1)	(2)	(3)	(4)	(5)	(6)	(7)
1955							
I	1,504	440	2,286	94	106	89	63.5
II	1,571	498	2,379	95	106	90	75.8
III	1,745	484	2,663	101	109	93	106.1
IV	2,051	711	3,322	107	114	94	93.0
1956							
I	2,407	1,098	2,189	106	119	89	69.9
II	2,600	1,078	2,464	91	111	82	60.0
III	2,336	939	2,568	90	107	84	66.4
IV	2,095	939	2,827	89	112	79	80.9

(1) Imports (million Rp; Rp 11.40 = US$1).
(2) Imports of consumption goods (million Rp).
(3) Exports (million Rp).
(4) Export price index free on board (f.o.b.) (1950 = 100).
(5) Import price index c.i.f. (1950 = 100).
(6) Terms of trade (1950 = 100).
(7) Rubber (RSS I) spot price, New York (per lb).
Sources: Columns (1)–(6), Biro Pusat Statistik, *Statistik Konjunktur*, various issues; column (7), International Rubber Study Group, *Rubber Statistical Bulletin*, various issues

Reversal of the Sumitro Reforms: the Bukti Pendorong Ekspor System

A new cabinet once again headed by Ali Sastroamidjojo was installed on March 26, 1956, with Jusuf Wibisono as Minister of Finance. Wibisono had earlier held the same position in the cabinet headed by Sukiman Wirjo-sandjojo (April 1951–February 1952). For the first few months, there were few overt changes in economic policy. However, the anticorruption drive, which had implicated members of the first Ali cabinet, was abandoned. The parties dominating the coalition, bolstered by their showing in the national elections held the previous September, returned to the ways of the first Ali cabinet. Indeed, the army created an uproar by trying to arrest the Minister of Foreign Affairs, Roeslan Abdulgani, on corruption charges as he was about to leave the country for an international conference. The cabinet was otherwise known as a "do nothing cabinet" (Schmitt, 1959, p. 203) until the deteriorating international payments position became acute.

On August 5, 1956, the day after Indonesia officially abrogated its substantial debt to the Netherlands, the BDP announced that it would no longer accept applications for import foreign exchange until new import regulations were formulated. The next day, the Export Premium scheme established by the previous Harahap cabinet was abolished and replaced with yet another system of inducement certificates. These new certificates, called *Bukti Pendorong Ekspor* (BPE) (Proof of Export Promotion), were granted to exporters for various proportions of export by commodity in addition to rupiahs at the official rate of exchange. The BPE system differed from previous inducement certificate systems in that the certificates covered a broad range of goods – only sugar, tin, and petroleum were excluded – and did not differentiate between smallholder (native) and estate-produced exports.

BPEs were required for the import of certain commodities and were freely negotiable. How useful they would be was not known until September 3 when the BDP reopened and the new import regulations, which included a return to quantitative restrictions, were announced. Traders had some advance information on the value of BPEs, since the government had guaranteed to buy them back at 125 percent of par if they went unsold. Import commodities were broken down into nine groups, ranging from group I, "highly essential," on which no TPI was levied, which included rice, newsprint, cotton piece goods, school and religious books, raw cotton, powdered milk for babies, and airplane fuel, to group IX, "superluxuries" (also the description for group VIII), on which the TPI was as high as 400 percent. The rate of TPI import surcharge levied against any good in a group was lower if its import required BPE. Goods requiring BPE were drawn from groups III–IX. Luxury automobiles were explicitly included in the list of BPE imports.

The BPE as originally issued required the importer to surrender rupiahs at the official rate in addition to BPE and TPI. Beginning on September 3 a new kind of BPE, known as BPE new style, was issued which did not require rupiahs at the official rate. In August, exports jumped sharply with the introduction of BPE certificates, but then fell back sharply as exporters held stocks in anticipation of further changes. In October the government extended the validity of BPEs to four months and set a floor price of 190 percent of par for new-style certificates. Prices fluctuated considerably (Kraal, 1956).

Several other changes were made, aimed at providing greater protection to domestic manufacturing. Before the BPE system was introduced, the second Ali cabinet reduced the prepayment requirements on the import of capital goods and raw materials used by industry, as long as the importer was national. In addition, a list of commodities which could only be imported by registered national importers (the *Benteng* list) was reintroduced. On January 1, 1957, a list of goods whose import was to be prohibited to protect domestic firms was published. The list included some important textiles such as sarongs, beer, matches, various kitchen utensils, dry cell batteries, and cigarette paper among other items. In order to help state-owned spinning enterprises reduce unsold stocks of cotton yarns, it was declared that foreign exchange applications for the import yarns would only be granted on condition that the importer purchase of an amount of yarn from the national spinning mills equal to 20 percent of the import requested.

The *Bukti Ekspor* System: the Third Liberalization Attempt

In early 1957, the exchange reserve position of Indonesia became critical: on February 2 the exchange reserves of the Bank Indonesia fell below the statutory 20 percent of short-term liabilities. On February 20 the issuance of import licenses for seven important import items was suspended. Licensing was further restricted in March, and on April 29 the issuance of licenses for almost all imports was suspended. Import of goods under the US surplus agreement, wheat flour from Australia, and commodities imported with BPEs was permitted. On June 1, import of raw materials and capital goods for industrial enterprises was permitted if they obtained a Certificate of Urgency from the Ministry overseeing their field of operation. As reserves continued to fall, reserve requirements of the Bank Indonesia were lifted for a six-month period.

This situation was largely due to what the Bank Indonesia euphemistically referred to as the rampant growth of "barter" trade. This "barter" trade originated in the dissident regions of central Sumatra and north Sulawesi, both leading centers of export which were completely ignoring the foreign exchange regulations of the central government in Jakarta and spoiling for confrontation.[12] Foreign exchange earnings from these regions were no longer being surrendered to Jakarta but were used to finance imports back into the areas of export origin. With this situation, the government decided on June 20 to allow the rupiah to find its own value in a free market, effecting the greatest devaluation of the decade, with the hope that "bartering" would cease and the dissident regions would return to the fold. The vehicle for this new floating exchange rate system was the *Bukti Ekspor* (Proof of Export) or BE certificate.

Exporters received BEs, denominated in rupiahs, equal to the value of their exports at the official rate of exchange. BEs differed from previous certificates in that they were not supplemental to payments in rupiahs but replaced them. Export duties were abolished for most products and were replaced with a 20 percent tax on the sale of BE certificates (*Pembajaran Bukti Ekspor*) (PBE). BEs were required for all imports and traded at the

[12] This "barter" trade is not to be confused with special legal barter trade provisions that these regions had enjoyed since 1950. Institutionalized in 1956, these barter trade provisions allowed agricultural products originating from named ports to be exchanged for certain classes of imports in Malaya or Singapore by the exporter as long as the bartered imports entered Indonesia in the port of origin of the exports. Under the most common arrangement, known as 70/30 percent barter, the exporter was permitted to "barter" 30 percent of his export value for imports. In 1962, almost 8 percent of non-oil exports were traded under this barter arrangement.

daily BE call market in Jakarta, where transactions were handled exclusively by foreign exchange banks. Dealing outside this market was not allowed. Prices were quoted in terms of percentage of the official rate of exchange. Within two weeks of their introduction BEs sold for 220 percent of the official rate of exchange, effecting a 48 percent increase in returns to exporters over the previous effective exchange rate consisting of the official rate plus the market price of BPE.

Commodity imports were broken down into six categories (previously there had been eight) carrying TPI (import surcharge) rates of 0–175 percent. All imports, even those of the government, required BEs. Import quotas were abolished for most goods on the TPI list; however, a special license was required to import any good not on the list. Since quotas were not a significant restriction on trade in the first months after BEs were introduced, the introduction of BE certificates and the associated changes in import regulation, together known as the BE system, constituted a trade liberalization of nearly the same magnitude as the Sumitro reforms of September 1955.

Even though most quotas were abolished, importers were still required to obtain import and foreign exchange licenses for their transactions. In addition, at the time of application, importers were required to make a guarantee deposit (*uang djaminan*) of 20 percent of the value of the requested foreign exchange converted at the official rate of exchange. These regulations replaced the much stiffer import prepayment requirements that existed before the BE system.

The BE rate, which was quoted at an average of 214 percent of par during July 1957, rose to an average of 250 percent in October and remained near that level for the rest of 1957. It hit 268 percent in January 1958 and on February 10 its daily increase was limited to 2 percentage points. The rate surpassed the limit at every trading session until, on March 27, the limit was reduced to one point each day and finally, on April 19, the price of BEs was permanently fixed at the previous day's closing price of 332 percent. Apparently the BE price that would allow the market to determine the value of the rupiah was higher than the government was willing to accept. The major objective of the liberalization – halting the expansion of "barter" and preventing the formation of a revolutionary government in the dissident export regions – was not achieved. The PERMESTA rebellion could not be bought off with the higher export returns brought by the BEs and was to be crushed only through military force. The experiment with a floating exchange rate ended just ten months after it began, once its goal of keeping Indonesia whole had been achieved by other means.[13]

[13] The violent end of the rebellion terminated the political roles of all the major political figures who had fought for a more liberal economy, and drastically reduced the power of the two political parties most associated with trade liberalization – Masjumi and the Socialists

4

Trade Policy during the Period of Guided Democracy and Guided Economy: 1958–1965

The end of parliamentary democracy came in stages, beginning with the nonparty "business cabinet" appointed in February 1957 and President Sukarno's announcement of his concept of "Guided Democracy." Various elected bodies were usurped by new councils appointed by the President or by military commands. The elected parliament was dissolved by decree and replaced by an appointed parliament in 1960. The concept of "Guided Economy," based on an aversion to the market mechanism and foreign capital, followed soon after. Dutch enterprises were nationalized as part of Indonesia's campaign to acquire control of West New Guinea (West Irian) from the Netherlands. Retail trading by ethnic Chinese was forbidden outside large urban areas. State trading corporations quickly came to dominate the foreign sector.

The nationalized Dutch trading houses were transformed into state trading enterprises (*Bhaktis*) which became sole importers of many key commodities. According to one study (Panglaykim and Palmer, 1969), the corruption and inefficiency of the *Bhaktis* led to "staggering" wastage. The import of other important goods, especially raw materials like cambrics and cloves, became the exclusive domain of Jajasans.

The allocation of foreign exchange among industrial firms became the domain of a new state apparatus. State-owned firms received first priority

---

(PSI). The Prime Minister of the ill-fated Revolutionary Republic of Indonesia (PRRI) was none other than Sjafruddin Prawiranegara, Governor of the Bank of Indonesia and architect of the 1950–1 liberalization. Other important leaders of the Masjumi party joined him – Mohammad Natsir and Burhanuddin Harahap, prime minister during the Sumitro reforms. All of them fled Jakarta after suffering threats and physical intimidation from political youth groups and were without protection from the police or army. There were rumors that some were to be arrested on charges of corruption and even attempted assassination. Sumitro of the PSI also fled to Sumatra and became a vociferous spokesman for the rebel cause. His pamphlet *Searchlight on Indonesia* (Sumitro, 1959) presents a scathing attack on the economic policies of Sukarno and Djuanda.

in foreign exchange allocation. Certain raw materials, such as weaving yarns, were distributed at highly subsidized prices. Since raw material was allocated among firms according to their productive capacity, one result was that capacity expanded while at the same time being underused. Manufacturing as a whole operated at only 30–40 percent of capacity in 1960 and at only 20–30 percent of capacity in 1965, while textile mills operated at only 5–10 percent of capacity, because this sector more than others sought import premiums through expanding capacity.

Although the period 1958–65 was generally one of quantitative restrictions on imports, price controls, black markets, and smuggling, it was also one, like the 1949–57 period, in which short-lived (but less sweeping) liberalizations were attempted without success. Although they lacked the breadth of the liberalization attempts of 1950–1, 1955, and 1957, they do indicate the government's continued recognition, despite the radical nationalist rhetoric, that the market mechanism afforded some relief from the enormous inefficiency of nonmarket allocation. In addition; just like the liberalizations of the 1949–57 period, these liberalizations were centered on the introduction of negotiable certificates that linked export to claims on foreign exchange for import.

The Return of Quantitative Restrictions

The fixing of the BE rate brought back the quantitative allocation of foreign exchange. The guarantee payment was increased from 100 percent of the par value of import foreign exchange to $133\frac{1}{3}$ percent effective January 2, 1959, and again to 230 percent on April 15. Institutional machinery was put in motion to establish the most comprehensive quantitative control of foreign exchange yet. The import of cloves and 40 percent of yarns was put into the hands of the Jajasan Persediaan Bahan Perindustrian (JBP) (Foundation for Raw Material Stocks) in February 1958. In June, the Ministries of Industry and Trade began a registration of industrial firms and other enterprises so as to gather data for comprehensive foreign exchange allocation. The Foreign Exchange Fund (LAAPLN), falling behind in undertaking its newly expanded responsibilities, cleared the backlog by declaring that all foreign exchange applications submitted in 1958 which had not been approved by December 31 should be considered refused.

Direct government control of trade and distribution increased markedly with the nationalization of Dutch enterprises in late 1958. The large Dutch import houses became state trading enterprises and on April 9, 1959, the import of nine important commodity categories was turned over to them as sole importers. The nine categories were raw cotton, weaving yarns, textiles, paper, cement, reinforced concrete iron and iron wire, tinplate, gunny/jute, and wheat flour. Imports of state trading enterprises consti-tuted 60 percent of total import in 1959. Goods whose import was carried out by other monopoly importers (the Jajasans), such as cloves, cambrics, rice, and fertilizer, made up an additional 20 percent of imports in that year. Thus only 20 percent of imports remained in the hands of private traders, and this was subject to comprehensive regulation. Indeed, for much of their importing, private firms merely acted as agents of the state.

The allocation of foreign exchange among industrial subsectors and firms became the province of two ministries, created in early 1959 by dividing the Ministry of Industry into the Ministry of Basic Industries and Mining and the Ministry of People's Industry. These Ministries were to control the import and oversee the production, sales, and investment of the subsectors in their domain. Expansion of industries which required substantial levels of imported raw materials was to be discouraged. Which subsectors were to be controlled by which of these Ministries was the source of considerable bureaucratic dispute. In a system reminiscent of the Dutch colonial covenants and mother foreign exchange allocations, firms were grouped into industrial associations (Gabungan Sedjenis Industri) for which a quarterly foreign exchange allocation (*djatah*) was made.

The level of imports realized in 1959 fell Rp 3 million below the level of foreign exchange allocated. This was not a deliberate further restriction on importing, but reflected the difficulty that the new state apparatus had with carrying out its new responsibilities. Quarterly foreign exchange alloca-tions were made so late that they could not be realized within the year. The various agencies empowered to allocate foreign exchange fought among themselves. So many permits were needed, from the foreign exchange allocation stage to distribution and price control, that import license applications became hopelessly backlogged. Imports of consumer goods not under the direct control of the state trading enterprises fell to a trickle and few new licenses were granted.

After the suppression of the rebellion in Sumatra and Sulawesi, legal exporting rebounded dramatically. Exports of smallholder rubber, coffee, pepper, and copra were up 234 percent, 297 percent, 428 percent, and 286 percent respectively by weight in the last half of 1958 compared with the first half year. To encourage legal exports from the regions further, beginning in July 1958 the central government permitted provincial governments to retain 10 percent of the tax on BEs (PBE) and on September 3, 1958, authorized the Bank Indonesia to issue *Bukti Ekspor Administrasi Daerah* (BEAD) (Regional Administrative BEs) which car-ried the same import rights as BEs. BEADs were supported by the purchase of BEs by the Bank Indonesia at the Jakarta BE call market and were allocated to the provinces on the basis of total export proceeds excluding oil. The BDP opened branch offices in provincial capitals with the power to issue foreign exchange licenses. As a result the regions were guaranteed some minimum share of imports and no longer had to purchase their BEs or obtain import licenses in Jakarta.

The Devaluation of 1959 and the End of the *Bukti Ekspor* System

On August 25, 1959, the BE system was abolished. The rupiah was officially devalued from Rp 11.40 to Rp 45.00 per US dollar. The tax on BEs (PBE) was replaced with a 20 percent export tax known as *Pungutan Ekspor* (PUEKS) (export levies). As with the PBE, 10 percent of the proceeds from PUEKS could be retained by provincial governments. The TPI import surcharge was replaced by *Pungutan Impor* (PUIM) (import levies), which were assessed at rates varying from zero to 175 percent on six categories of import commodities, differing slightly in composition from the six categories used under the BE system. Advance deposit require- ments were abolished. All import license applications in the BDP backlog were declared automatically rejected and 90 percent of all guarantee deposits, which were 230 percent of the par value of import applications, were kept as a forced loan.

In December 1959 the Ministry of People's Industry divided industrial enterprises into three groups for the purposes of allocating foreign exchange. Group I enterprises consisted of *sandang-pangan* (food and clothing) firms, firms which were net earners of foreign exchange, and government-owned enterprises. These firms were to receive foreign exchange sufficient to operate at 100 percent capacity. Group II en- terprises consisted of processors of domestically produced raw materials, firms in which the government owned 51 percent of the shares, and other firms saving foreign exchange. These enterprises were not to receive sufficient foreign exchange to operate at 100 percent capacity initially, but would do so in the future. Group III enterprises consisted of all other industries. They had no guarantee of foreign exchange at all and might at best be provided exchange to keep them in "running condition." In practice, foreign exchange allocations for materials and spare parts were so inadequate and poorly distributed that even group I enterprises had trouble just remaining in running condition.

There were significant changes in the distribution system in 1959. By government order, all foreign trading establishments except those in large cities were to close. The thousands of predominantly Chinese shopkeepers who dominated retail trade and were wholesalers for export products were forced to close down. In their place cooperative organizations were to spring up under the guidance of various state agencies. These cooperative organizations were to receive allocations of imported and domestically produced goods from the state trading enterprises. The number of private importers was to be reduced to 400 through "re-registration." The provision of *sandang-pangan* became top priority, and *sandang-pangan* shops were established to sell food and clothing at controlled prices. A new agency, the Badan Urusan Bahan Pakaian (BUBP) (Clothing Logistics Board) was established to stock imported and domestically produced clothing for distribution to these shops.

The low level of imports in 1959 and higher export prices in early 1960 led the government to increase import allocations beginning in August 1960. On August 24, 1960, both PUEKS (the 20 percent export tax) and PUIM (the import surcharges) were replaced by a more complicated system, whose stated purpose was to simplify the import system and reduce import duties in general.

Ordinary tariffs, set by the Indies Tariff Act and basically unchanged since 1934, were altered and combined with statistical duties and a customs tax based on the weight of cargo into a single import duty system. Two major groups of commodities were distinguished:

group I – commodities essential to the Indonesian economy;
group II – other commodities needed, but not essential.

Under group II were two subgroups of "prohibited commodities:"

list IIA – goods already produced in sufficient quantities domestically; import of these commodities required permission of the Minister of Trade, and were importable at an exchange rate set by him;
list IIB – goods characterized as luxuries; import of these goods needed the permission of the Minister of Finance and were importable at an exchange rate set by him.

All goods not in group I or on list IIA or IIB were considered to be free-list commodities. They could be imported without restriction but with an exchange rate of Rp 200 per US dollar. Group I commodities were imported at the official rate of Rp 45 per US dollar, and were subject to quota, price control, and an additional import tax known as *Komponen Harga* (price components). Price components were meant to be a temporary bar on any windfall profits that might result from the lower landed price of group I commodities caused by the prospective reduction in import duties. They were to be gradually reduced to zero as quantitative restrictions on these goods were loosened. Neither event was to occur. The import system in effect in August 1960 is summarized in table 4.1.

The rebirth of free-list importing was of course a liberalizing act but of limited importance and duration. Bank financing of free-list importing was forbidden, but the government clearly stated that criminal authorities would not be allowed to investigate how importers actually financed free-list import. Free-list goods were also exempt from all price control. Passenger automobiles, a popular item of illegal import, were specifically included among free-list commodities. Although only 23 automobile

Table 4.1 Import system in August 1960

Group	Exchange rate	Price component		Import duties (%)
I	Rp 45 = US$1	Ex-PUIM group I	= 0%	List A: 0
		Ex-PUIM group II	= 25%	List B: 20
		Ex-PUIM groups III–VI	= 60%	
II				
Free list	Rp 200 = US$1			List C: 30[a]
List IIA	Set by Ministers of			List D: 100
and IIB	Trade and			
	Finance			

[a] Even though free-list commodities were imported at the special exchange rate of Rp 200 per US dollar, their import duty was calculated on the basis of the basic rate of Rp 45 per US dollar.

Source: Commercial Advisory Foundation in Indonesia, 1960, p. 7

makes were allowed, the inclusion of Peugeot, Opel, and Mercedes-Benz guaranteed that most illegal import of automobiles would now be diverted into free-list import.

Import "free of foreign exchange," which had been abolished as part of the Sumitro reforms, was also reinstituted as part of the August 1960 reforms. These imports had to be paid for out of exchange already held abroad. Again, the government promised not to investigate the source of these funds. The system was regularized in October 1961 with the introduction of Special Import Licenses (SIIC) by which unregistered foreign exchange could be used for legal importing with a promise of immunity from prosecution. Several thousand motor vehicles were imported under this program until it was discontinued the following year.

In April 1961 many goods from lists A and B (see table 4.1) were shuffled to the free list, and from the free list to the prohibited list D. The government, having observed the size of import premiums on list A and B goods, sought to capture some of the revenues for the Treasury through this realignment of lists.

Legal exports had declined sharply in response to the expulsion of Chinese traders from rural areas and worsening terms of trade. The ratio of the black-market exchange rate to the legal effective exchange rate increased markedly in 1960; the black-market rate rose as high as 11 times the effective export rate in response to the flight of Chinese capital. This created an enormous incentive for illegal trade and significant amounts of exports were diverted into smuggling. One result of this was that the domestic wholesale price of exports such as rubber far exceeded the return on their legal export. This phenomenon, known as "price disparity," is discussed at length in chapter 5 and by Pitt (1981b). In response to the fall in legal exports the issuance of free-list licenses was slowed, beginning in mid-year, and from early September these imports were virtually suspended.

Legal Underinvoicing of Exports

In export regulations, a significant development was the setting of surrender prices for exports on June 1, 1961. The Ministry of Trade set the prices for all export products. Exporters were required to surrender foreign exchange only up to the surrender price (later called the "check price"). Export receipts in excess of the surrender price ("overprice") could legally be retained abroad or used for import "free from foreign exchange." This legalization of export underinvoicing, along with free-list importing and import free from foreign exchange, represented a decided attempt to reduce "price disparity" by legalizing what would otherwise be an illegal transaction in international trade.

The SIVA Certificate System

In March 1962 a new foreign exchange certificate system that allowed exporters to retain even more of their foreign exchange earnings was introduced. These import entitlement certificates, known as *Surat Izin Valuta Asing* (SIVA) were introduced to counter the growing pattern of export smuggling, reflected in domestic export prices that were triple those of legal export returns for certain commodities. Exporters were required to surrender 85 percent of their export proceeds for rupiahs at the official rate of exchange and received the remaining 15 percent in the form of SIVA. It was required that at least half the SIVA received by exporters be used to import into the region where the exports originated. SIVA earned by an exporter could be sold once or used by the exporter to import a restricted set of "nonessential" commodities (those on lists A, B, and C with certain exceptions). In August 1962 imports were reclassified into five groups, with SIVA-financed imports regularly permitted in four of them. The less "essential" the commodity, the greater the value of SIVA required to obtain a dollar's worth of foreign exchange for its import. Commodities deemed essential (groups I and II) did not require SIVA and could be imported at the low official rate of exchange. However, import of these goods at this rate was subject to quota. Import beyond the quota could be accomplished if SIVA were used to pay for the foreign exchange.

Thus, like the *Bukti Indusemen* scheme of 1951, the price of SIVA acted as a cap on the import premiums of a wide range of imported goods. SIVA prices (and hence potential premiums) were quite high relative to the official price of foreign exchange. By the end of May they reached 15 times the official rate of exchange, 25 times nominal by the end of June, and 30 times nominal by the time the system was abolished in May 1963. The share of SIVA designated for region-specific import sold at a slight discount on the market.

DEKON: the Liberalization that Never Was

President Sukarno, during his visit to Washington in April 1961, accepted President Kennedy's offer that an American team of economists visit Indonesia to make recommendations on how the United States could assist in the economic development of Indonesia. The team, headed by Don D. Humphrey, arrived in August of 1961 and published their report in 1962. The Americans and an International Monetary Fund (IMF) mission that visited in November 1962 proposed a liberalization and stabilization plan to be financed with American aid and IMF loans.

President Sukarno was under great pressure from the PKI, other leftist groups, and its Soviet creditors to form a "NASAKOM cabinet." NASA-KOM, an acronym for Nationalism–Religion–Communism, was a term that came to denote PKI participation in government. Such a cabinet would have precluded American aid and hence the liberalization–stabilization program as structured. After some wavering, Sukarno chose not to include the PKI in his cabinet and to prepare the ground for economic liberalization. According to Mortimer (1974, pp. 264–5),

> In the conflict between pro-Western and pro-Communist policies, the likelihood that the Americans would be prepared to lay out greater sums than the Russians, who were now very cautious about further aid to Indonesia, and the opposition of influential groups in both the government and the army to greater dependence on the Communists, decided the day.

Sukarno's "Economic Declaration" (DEKON) was made on March 28, 1963. Although couched in very general terms so as not to unduly upset his allies on the left, it called for greater emphasis on the price mechanism, praised private entrepreneurs, suggested that foreign aid need not mean a loss of independence, and called for economic decentralization and deconcentration. On May 27 a set of 14 regulations implementing the DEKON program were announced, just after Sukarno left on a trip to Japan. The regulations dismantled price controls, increased charges for public utilities and services, promised government budget austerity leading to a balanced budget in 1964, doubled the salaries of civil servants, and introduced new foreign exchange regulations and a crash program of imports to obtain the spare parts and raw materials that were keeping industrial capacity utilization at low rates.

The new foreign exchange regulations replaced the SIVA system with a new system of export incentives. Ninety-five percent of export proceeds were surrendered at the official rate of Rp 45 per US dollar plus an additional Rp 270 per dollar known as *Perangsang Ekspor* (PE) or Export Incentive. The remaining 5 percent of the foreign exchange export proceeds were retained by the exporter and could be used for the import of certain luxury goods subject to special regulation by the Ministry of Trade. This 5 percent foreign exchange retention, known as *Perangsang Tambahan* (PET) or Additional Export Incentive, was paralleled by a *Perangsang Eksport Istimewa* (PEI) or Special Export Incentive which took the form of a nontransferable foreign exchange allocation that could be used to import goods from the two most essential import categories. Exporters received a PEI allocation of 10 percent of their free-on-board (f.o.b.) receipts and exporter–producers received a 15 percent allocation. These allocations could be used only after payments at the usual import rates. Finally, export duties which were as high as 10 percent on certain commodities were abolished.

Imports were broken down into three categories. The exchange rate that applied to "essential" goods (category I) was the official rate plus an additional Rp 270 per US dollar, which was known as *Hasil Perdagangan Negara* (HPN) or State Trade Proceeds. For category II commodities, an additional HPN (HPN *Tambahan*) of Rp 225 was added to the category I rate. A greater HPN *Tambahan* of Rp 495 per dollar applied to category III commodities, which could also be financed with the 5 percent exchange retention (PET). Special import duties of zero, 50 percent, and 100 percent applied to category I, II, and III imports respectively. Normal tariffs (General Agreement on Tariffs and Trade (GATT) tariffs) of zero, 20, and 30 percent also applied to imported commodities. Although there was no return to free-list importing, foreign aid and credits permitted a large increase in the quantities of foreign exchange available for importing.

The liberalization scheme was very unpopular with many groups. Speculators holding stocks of imports took losses as the prices of many imports fell. However, many prices rose sharply, leading to protest from other quarters. Postal and telephone rates rose fourfold, railway fares rose by factors of 1.5–5. "Essential" import prices no longer benefited from as preferential an exchange rate, causing substantial price increases for some politically sensitive goods. The price of yarns, for example, rose by a factor of 5.5. Imports and certain industrialists were particularly hurt. In concert with the PKI and other left-wing parties, a storm of opposition arose against DEKON. To protect Sukarno from blame for "liberal" sins, the PKI argued that he had admitted his ignorance of economics and therefore could not be blamed for the mistakes of his advisors. Not that DEKON was anywhere near as dramatic a liberalization attempt as the Sumitro reforms or the BE system: in one observer's view (Mackie, 1967, p. 38) "to describe it baldly as 'liberal in tone' is an exaggeration."

In the end, however, it was not dramatic opposition but an unrelated political event that killed the liberalization in its infancy (although its opponents may well have succeeded in time). The end of DEKON came with Indonesia's objection to the formation of the state of Malaysia – a campaign known as *Konfrontasi*. In mid-September 1963, unruly demonstrations broke out over the impending formation of Malaysia, which was seen as a creation of British imperialism. The British Embassy was burned to the ground, British properties were taken over, and relations with Malaysia were severed. In response, the IMF suspended standby credits. Radical nationalism returned as the sole determinant of policymaking, and the new economic slogan became *Berdikari* – standing on one's own feet. The United States was told to "go to hell with your aid."

The SPP System

The other certificate system of this period began in April 1964 and continued until the commencement of the 1966–71 liberalization episode. Exporters were provided with a Production Incentive Certificate (SPP) with a face value of 20 percent of export receipts in addition to rupiahs. SPPs, like SIVA before them, gave their holder the right to import beyond the quota on imports financed with licensed foreign exchange. According to Mackie (1967, p. 41), the SPP system "represented the same despairing admission that since inflation could not be checked, exporters must be reimbursed by a market-determined rate of exchange through an inducement certificate." The official rate remained at Rp 45 per US dollar but, aside from the imports of the state trading corporations, no transactions occurred at this rate. The transactions rate was set at Rp 250 per US dollar which was the rate paid on f.o.b. export proceeds. SPPs were originally valid for two months, were negotiable, and could be used to import from categories I, I, and III. The SPP rate was originally set at Rp 1,350 or 5.4 times the transaction rate, which was also the import retribution per dollar added to the transaction rate for most imports.

Altogether three varieties of SPP were issued: the SPP *Umum* (described above), the SPP *Chusus* (sold by the Bank Indonesia and applicable to a more restricted group of import commodities), and lastly the SPP *Tambahan*, which was actually an SPP *Umum* for an additional 10 percent of export proceeds. This SPP *Tambahan* applied only to exports from areas across the Straits of Malacca from Malaysia, and was meant to compensate for the loss of barter privileges arising from Sukarno's policy of *Konfrontasi* with Malaysia.

In addition to SPPs, national exporters and producers received a nontransferable foreign exchange allocation (*Alokasi Devisa* (AD)), amounting to 5 percent of their export proceeds. This allocation could be used for imports under special regulations set by the Minister of Trade and the Bank Indonesia.

Imports were classified into five categories. The transactions rate applied only to category I imports which consisted of rice, fertilizers, medicines, and certain other "essential" goods. Categories II–V bought foreign exchange at the transactions rate plus the import retribution of Rp 1,350 per US dollar. Category V goods also needed special approval from the Minister of Trade. "Essential" goods entered free of duty; import duties of 50 percent, 100 percent, 300 percent, or 800 percent applied to all other goods. Licensed foreign exchange was sold at a low fixed "transactions" rate of exchange. In fact, aside from the imports of the state trading corporations, very little of this low price foreign exchange was made available, so that imports using SPP dominated the import of most goods not subject to monopoly control.

SPP *Umum* rates rose steadily from their initial rate of 5.4 times the transactions rate of exchange to close at 44.6 times this rate at the last market call before the system was abolished in December 1965. As the transactions rate of Rp 250 per US dollar was over 5.5 times the official rate of Rp 45, the cost of foreign exchange for import, excluding import duties which ranged to well above 1,000 percent, was 248 times the official rate of exchange.

5

The Liberalization of 1966

Political Circumstances

By 1965, President Sukarno's *Konsepsi* of Guided Democracy and Guided Economy were well on the way to fulfillment. He was *de facto* monarch – President-for-Life. He had solidified his position *vis-à-vis* opposition political parties and the army, perhaps the institution with the greatest potential for opposition during the period, banned important political parties, dissolved the elected parliament, sought and received the vociferous backing of the PKI, and fashioned new symbols of state, new ideological themes, and new slogans with which he captivated the masses. The emphasis shifted from solving the practical problems of a newly independent state to creating images of revolutionary ardor and national prestige. Eventually ideological themes became costly military adventures – confrontation with Malaysia – and absurd gestures of national pride – the Indonesian program to put a man in space and develop nuclear weapons.[1]

Beginning with the nationalization of British properties in late 1963 in response to *Konfrontasi* with Malaysia, all other foreign properties had been nationalized by 1965. Even the People's Republic of China handed over the Jakarta premises of the Bank of China. A new class of ill-trained managers, many drawn from the army, took over the management of these properties, as they had those of the Dutch in 1957–8. Denoted "bureaucratic capitalists" by the PKI, they became the new economic and political elite. They earned enormous rents from their control of foreign and domestic trade. Huge profits were made in the state sector. So many of the items subject to price control were diverted into the black market that few transactions actually took place at legally designated prices. Those reaping these returns were denoted the *orang kaya baru* (OKB) (newly rich) and

[1] In 1965, Indonesia announced that it planned to test its first atomic bomb in 1966 after the second Afro-Asian Conference. In the same year an animal was to be put into space, and the first astronaut (who was already named and in training) was to be launched in 1968.

even *orang kaya mendadak* (OKM) (suddenly rich) (Castles, 1965, p. 25). It was claimed that Jakarta had more luxury automobiles than any comparable city in Asia. The effect of corruption and mismanagement in the state sector was summarized by a cabinet minister in 1965:

> There is now no efficiency any more. The competence of the workers has declined markedly and bureaucracy rages. Work discipline and a sense of responsibility are virtually non-existent. (Quoted by Castles, 1965, p. 25)

The Ali-Baba firms of the 1950s period of Indonesianization (where a Chinese entrepreneur adopted an indigenous "strawman") were replaced by Baba-Ali firms by 1965, where OKM bureaucrats adopted Chinese entrepreneurs to invest their newly acquired fortunes. The army, now heavily engaged in commercial activities, lined up with other groups in favoring a state-controlled economy. Among the groups associated with the regime, only the PKI took exception to the course of events. According to Mortimer (1974, pp. 251–2),

> None of the groups associated with the regime, with the partial exception of the PKI, had any very definite ideas on priorities in economic decision-making. Moreover, in the years since independence, the government and its apparatus had come to be viewed as vehicles for the realization of clique and personal advantage rather than the advancement of broad social interests. The groups brought together under the banner of Guided Democracy expected and demanded tangible rewards in the form of patronage and access to spoils in return for their concurrence in the new dispensation.

Aidit, the PKI's leader, claimed that the "bureaucratic capitalists" exploited the workers by stealing the surplus value that they generated. He went so far as to claim that state enterprises might not be a good thing. The PKI began a campaign against "the parasites, the large-scale corrupters, the bureaucratic capitalists" (Aidit, 1964; translated extract in Feith and Castles, 1970.

In mid-1965 the economic situation worsened. Prospects for the rice harvest were poor. The price of rice in rural Java more than quadrupled between June and October. The Jakarta cost of living index rose by a factor of 2.2 over the same period. Between June and September the black-market price of the US dollar more than doubled. The PKI brought its campaign against the bureaucratic capitalists to a climax, naming economic "criminals" and demanding public executions. According to Mortimer (1974, p. 387),

> Foreign observers in Indonesia at this time were struck by the atmosphere of crisis, bordering on hysteria, that prevailed. The hypocrisy with which many officials and politicians had formerly espoused the idea of NASAKOM unity

was wearing thin, and little coaxing was required to reveal the violently polarized attitudes of the politicized segments of the population. Javanese soothsayers, traditional harbingers of crisis and dynastic change, were announcing imminent cataclysm.

The event that precipitated the downfall of the Old Order of Guided Democracy was the GESTAPU coup d'état attempt of September 30, 1965. GESTAPU – an acronym for Gerakan September Tiga Puluh, literally Movement of September 30 – was presumably organized by the PKI and its front organizations with the collusion of important elements of the air force and other segments of the military.[2] Sukarno's role in the coup remains subject to dispute. The collapse of the coup was largely due to the efforts of Major-General Suharto, commander of the army's strategic reserve. Suharto regrouped the army and moved on Jakarta and the plotters' headquarters at Halim Aerodrome. Sukarno, who had arrived at Halim on the first morning of the coup ostensibly because of the safety the airfield offered, left at the demand of Suharto before his troops moved to capture it. The coup was effectively crushed in little more than a day, although effective control of certain areas of central Java was not established for weeks.

Soon after the coup a massive bloodbath ensued, with Communists and ethnic Chinese being the primary targets. The PKI was effectively crushed. Nevertheless, initially it seemed that Sukarno had survived the coup unscathed: "he acted as if nothing had happened" observed Palmier (1973, p. 249). It was the students of Jakarta who broke the political paralysis of the first months after GESTAPU. Organized into KAMI (Action Command of Indonesian Students), students organized a huge rally in January 1966 in which they listed three demands – banning of the PKI, purge of the cabinet, and control of inflation. Assisted by the Faculty of Economics at the University of Indonesia, they organized an economic policy seminar in which major political leaders opposed to Sukarno participated. Sukarno banned KAMI and closed the University of Indonesia in response, actions which, according to Palmier, were eventually to cost him his presidency. On March 11, under direct army pressure, Sukarno signed away most of his power, but remained as president. In that month the PKI was banned. The DWIKORA cabinet of March 1966 consisted of an equal mixture of new members and old. The cabinet was reshuffled in July 1966 (the AMPERA cabinet) to reflect the growing power of the New Order forces, and was to last until June 1968. Suharto was named Acting President in March 1967, but it was not until July of that year that the last of President Sukarno's titles was revoked.

---

[2] The circumstances of the coup have been the subject of considerable debate, particularly with respect to the role of the PKI. The interpretation given here represents more or less the official version of events. The interested reader is referred to Mortimer (1974, appendices A and B) for a review of events from other perspectives.

Thus it would seem that at the time that the liberalization was initiated (1966) the government was not strong, as the still formidable powers of President Sukarno and his loyalists stood in opposition. Important segments of the government still spouted the buzz words of recent years – NASAKOM and NEKOLIM (neocolonialism) – in many of their proclamations. President Sukarno, in his Independence Day speech of August 17, 1966 (aptly titled "Never Leave History"), proposed a return to the economic and political principles and policies of Guided Democracy and refused to accept responsibility for Indonesia's economic dilemma. The speech led to a resurgence of pro-Sukarno demonstrations, some of them violent.

The Sultan of Yogyakarta, Hamengko Buwono, was nominally in charge of reforming the chaotic economy in his role as Vice Prime Minister in charge of Economy, Finance, and Development. Untrained in economics, the Sultan sought counsel from a group of five economics faculty members from the University of Indonesia, all of whom had PhDs from American universities. The five became an economic advisory team to General Suharto and soon four of them became cabinet members. Variously dubbed "technocrats" and the "Berkeley Mafia" – three of them had PhDs from the University of California at Berkeley – they undoubtedly had a significant impact on economic policy and on devising the liberalization strategy in particular. Nevertheless, these economists had no political power base of their own, and the power they had to formulate and implement economic policy has often been overestimated. One knowledgeable observer (Glassburner, 1978, p. 34) has stressed that the University of Indonesia economists could only rely on "their expertise and their persuasiveness" in their rivalry with competing sources of economic policy advice such as the military and the entrenched bureaucracy.

Economic Circumstances

In early 1966, two respected observers of the Indonesian scene (Panglaykim and Arndt, 1966, p.1) reported that "a picture of breakdown has been revealed to the Indonesian people and to the world which can have few parallels in a great nation in modern times except in the immediate aftermath of war or revolution." The Bank Indonesia was unable to pay even on cash letters of credit in late 1965; the foreign debt was almost US$2.4 billion and its servicing in 1966 exceeded the total of anticipated export earnings. A significant share of the debt had been incurred to procure military hardware. Between July 1965 and January 1966 the price level more than quintupled. The government deficit was 163 percent of government revenues in 1965, with much expenditure devoted to funding *Konfrontasi* with Malaysia and grand showcase projects such as monuments in Jakarta – the planned Sukarno Tower and National Theatre – as well as the huge Conference of the New Emerging Forces (CONEFO) complex under construction in Jakarta; the latter project tied up as much as 70 percent of the rolling stock of Java.

Indonesia's angry departure from the IMF and the World Bank in 1965 precluded the immediate assistance of these organizations in dealing with its debt problems. Rejoining the organizations would first require sufficient political support to overcome President Sukarno's continued objection, based on his reiterated view that they represented the powers of neocolonialism and imperialism.

Total gold and foreign exchange holdings of the Bank Indonesia and the Foreign Exchange Fund (including bank balance abroad) fell from US$280 million in 1961 to a low of minus US$48 million in March of 1966 (Pitt, 1988, appendix table 5.1). Table 5.1 presents the Indonesian balance of payments for 1960–5. There were deficits on the current account in each year from 1960 through 1965, which were due almost entirely to the services deficit.

Table 5.1 Balance of payments, 1960–1965 (million US dollars)

Components	1960	1961	1962	1963	1964	1965
A *Goods and services*						
Exports f.o.b.	881	766	711	616	632	634
(Exports of foreign-owned oil companies)	(280)	(239)	(241)	(204)	(206)	(210)
Imports f.o.b.	749	1,058	737	562	590	610
(Imports of foreign-owned oil companies)	(85)	(47)	(55)	(70)	(59)	(60)
Balance of trade	132	− 292[a]	− 26	54	42	24
Services (net)	− 216	− 231	− 222	− 282	− 272	− 272
Balance of payments on account	− 84	− 523	− 248	− 228	− 230	− 248
B *Capital movements*						
Government (net)	186	367	97	112	103	30
Private (net)	− 3	− 13	23	11	25	18
Total capital inflow	183	354	120	123	128	48
C *Changes in international reserves*						
IMF position	− 19	34	21	20	—	—
Other	− 77	134	147	122	88	235
Total changes in international reserves	− 96	168	168	142	88	235
D *Errors and omissions* (net)	− 3	1	− 40	− 37	14	− 35

—, not applicable.
[a] The minus sign indicates an increase.
Source: Bulletin of Indonesian Economic Studies, October 1968, p. 117

Table 5.2 provides index number time series on export and import values and volumes and the associated terms-of-trade series for the period 1950–76, as well as some pre-World War II years. In 1965, export volume reached its highest level ever (though this level was not much higher than levels achieved during the 1950s). These data ignore illegal exporting, which is known to have been substantial over much of this period. In contrast with exports, import volume in 1965 was at an all-time post-Independence low, down significantly from the levels of the early 1960s. (The caveat on illegal trade above applies equally to imports.) As table 5.2 reveals, the commodity and income terms of trade were at their lowest levels since Independence. The commodity terms of trade in 1965 were 14 percent lower than in 1964, and only 58 percent of the 1960 value. Much of

Table 5.2 Summary indices of exports, imports, and the terms of trade, 1938–1976 (1971 = 100)

	Exports			Imports			Terms of trade	
	Value	Volume	Unit value	Value	Volume	Unit value	Commodity	Income
1938	28.6	39.3	61.9	22.1	45.5	46.7	127.3	58.8
1939	31.7	42.0	61.5	21.4	41.9	44.6	120.4	62.0
1940	38.0	42.3	69.1	19.4	35.2	48.6	125.4	69.0
1950	60.7	46.0	140.6	37.1	43.4	85.9	164.4	71.0
1951	98.1	53.8	185.3	73.5	59.4	111.2	149.8	71.0
1952	71.2	51.7	141.3	79.8	71.1	115.3	125.9	63.5
1953	64.0	51.5	120.7	64.4	60.0	113.9	112.5	59.6
1954	66.0	55.3	114.3	53.2	63.5	98.8	136.4	78.8
1955	76.5	50.0	137.5	53.3	57.2	95.9	147.5	82.1
1956	74.1	52.4	126.1	80.6	77.1	91.4	120.7	70.9
1957	75.0	54.9	120.6	67.6	74.3	94.7	132.5	82.4
1958	67.6	53.1	113.0	48.6	60.0	86.5	139.5	83.5
1959	77.3	53.6	131.7	43.7	55.5	83.5	167.3	98.2
1960	71.1	50.6	131.0	48.1	60.5	81.5	164.8	89.4
1961	68.1	55.2	113.9	70.3	83.2	80.1	134.8	80.6
1962	61.6	58.1	110.5	59.3	67.1	76.8	125.0	69.7
1963	62.4	50.6	110.6	50.8	54.8	94.5	119.3	67.3
1964	67.4	57.6	113.1	56.5	56.3	104.2	112.6	67.1
1965	66.8	59.3	106.6	50.2	45.4	110.9	96.4	60.4
1966	62.3	57.6	101.5	45.0	43.2	105.8	97.4	59.8
1967	64.6	65.1	93.5	61.2	50.7	112.0	77.5	53.5
1968	65.7	72.3	90.6	63.0	71.1	107.9	102.3	74.2
1969	82.6	82.9	98.2	72.2	77.2	100.1	105.0	88.3
1970	88.8	92.3	99.3	95.7	102.5	101.2	106.3	95.1
1971	100.0	100.0	100.0	100.0	100.0	100.0	100.0	100.0
1972	139.4	121.5	111.6	139.9	125.3	112.4	99.9	124.8
1973	269.2	146.3	177.8	229.8	169.7	133.6	131.3	198.8
1974	601.8	142.3	406.1	314.4	168.2	176.7	217.3	322.0
1975	575.6	126.3	411.0	390.3	179.5	229.1	189.1	264.8
1976	692.6	141.6	436.9	464.2	204.3	233.6	192.3	304.8

Source: Rosendale, 1975, p. 73; 1981, p. 167

this deterioration was due to the falling price of Indonesia's largest export, natural rubber.

The nation's productive capacity was a shambles. Per capita output (GDP) was lower than it was in 1958 in each of the seven years before the liberalization attempt; in 1965, it was more than 9 percent lower than its 1958 level. Capacity utilization in manufacturing was estimated at only 20 percent (mostly as a result of insufficient foreign exchange for spare parts and imported inputs). The output of the state-run tin mining industry had fallen by half in less than ten years. Transportation and communications infrastructure were run down and operating only intermittently. There were serious shortages of rice in many areas. Per capita rice availability had fallen owing to an oppressive food price policy and the neglect of the irrigation system, coupled with an end to rice imports as part

Table 5.3 Price inflation before liberalization (Jakarta 62-item cost of living index, March 1957 to February 1958 = 100)

Year (month)	Cost of living index	Rate of growth (annual %)	Rate of growth (monthly %)
Dec 1960	215	29.6	—
Dec 1961	380	76.7	—
Dec 1962	976	156.8	—
Dec 1963	2,226	128.1	—
Dec 1964	5,234	135.1	—
1965			
Jan	6,968	183.4	33.1
Feb	8,012	177.7	15.0
Mar	7,444	127.8	− 7.1
Apr	7,593	189.9	2.0
May	7,938	199.6	4.5
Jun	8,492	212.6	7.0
Jul	10,141	260.9	19.4
Aug	11,823	286.0	16.6
Sep	14,371	290.0	21.6
Oct	18,804	374.3	30.8
Nov	22,651	433.4	20.5
Dec	36,347	594.4	60.5
1966			
Jan	56,020	704.0	54.1
Feb	67,312	740.1	20.2
Mar	87,704	1,078.2	30.3
Apr	96,030	1,164.7	9.5
May	102,509	1,191.4	6.7
Jun	137,894	1,523.7	34.5
Dec	267,279	635.4	3.0

—, not applicable.
Source: provided by Biro Pusat Statistik

of President Sukarno's policy of *Berdikari* (standing on one's own feet) following the end of the DEKON liberalization attempt.

Inflation accelerated dramatically in the months before liberalization. Over the period 1950–9 price inflation as measured by the 62-item cost of living index averaged 20.4 percent per year (table 5.3). The rate of inflation grew quickly during the early 1960s, reaching triple-digit levels by 1962, and 594 percent in 1965. The rate exceeded 1,000 percent by the first half of 1966. The price level in June 1966, when the liberalization and stabilization package was being hammered out, was more than 16 times the level of the previous June.

Corruption, although by no means unique to this period, was particularly pervasive just before the liberalization. For example, the Minister of Central Bank Affairs, Jusuf Muda Dalam, was convicted of illegally issuing import licenses totaling US$270 million (almost half a year's total imports) during 1964–6 under special deferred payment terms and of "manipulating" hundreds of millions of rupiahs of state funds. Sundhaussen (1982, p. 245) relates that at Jusuf's trial in 1966 it was alleged that he operated a "Revolutionary Fund" on orders from President Sukarno. This fund was financed by the "contributions" of importers applying for foreign exchange licenses. One importer, who happened to be a beautiful actress, received US$2 million foreign exchange credit directly from Sukarno. Proceeds from the "Revolutionary Fund" were allocated to Jusuf's relatives, wives (he had six), and companies in which he had an interest.

Corruption was not limited to higher officials and Sukarno's cronies. The problem was pervasive at all levels of the state apparatus. Salaries of government civil servants were so low that it is inconceivable that they could survive without graft.[3] As Panglaykim and Arndt (1966, p. 35) noted:

[3] The commercial newsletter *Business News*, published in Jakarta, reported in its September 12, 1966, edition the results of a wage survey carried out by the magazine *Statistik* in June and July of that year. That survey reported the following daily incomes (in new rupiahs, see note 7) for nine occupations:

1 auto mechanic	Rp 70
2 child newspaper vendor	Rp 20
3 cigarette vendor	Rp 35
4 automobile guard	Rp 55
5 civil servant: (a) class E II	Rp 4
(b) class FV	Rp 17
6 bricklayer	Rp 100
7 black-market ticket seller	Rp 125
8 barber	Rp 40
9 doctor	Rp 300

It is striking that a large class of civil servants earned only one fourth as much as a child newspaper vendor, and even the higher class of civil servants earned less. Converted at the free-market exchange rate, these civil servants were earning roughly $3\frac{1}{2}$ cents and $15\frac{1}{2}$ cents per day.

The old regime has left behind a legacy of moral disorder – of graft and corruption, of breakdown of law enforcement and decline in respect for the law – which can have few precedents in modern history.

The Liberality of the Black-market Economy

It is conceivable that the chaos and corruption that characterized the last half of 1965 resulted in something akin to a liberal trade regime because of the magnitude of transactions that took place illegally. Obviously, if all quantitative restrictions and distortionary taxes are ignored by all economic agents with impunity (that is, without cost), then all the resulting prices and resource allocations are those that would exist in a free-trade economy. The Indonesian situation in 1965 was one in which there were significant free (but typically black) markets for most commodities whether or not they were subject to quota or price control, and it was the prices established in these markets that were used by most economic agents in allocating resources. Support for this hypothesis comes from observations on the disparity between the legal prices of traded goods and the prices that actually prevailed in domestic markets, and is discussed below.

Relative prices for tradeables differed from international relative prices as a result of the additional costs incurred by illegal transactions through the risks of penalty and confiscation and the additional costs, real resource costs and otherwise, that might be associated with illegal trade. The risk of penalty and confiscation must have been small in 1965.[4] Real resource costs of illegal trade were probably small as well since there is evidence that most smuggling used customs-administered ports and the same ocean-going vessels as legal trade. This simply reflects the fact that most smuggling represented the mis-invoicing of legally declared trade rather than "ships in the night." The other cost of illegal trade is the bribes paid to customs officials or the import-licensing agency. These are not real costs to the economy, merely transfers. It might be suspected that bribes would not have to be very large since it would not be very difficult to trade illegally even without the connivance of the authorities.[5]

---

[4] Ingrid Palmer (1972) discusses price control and distribution of yarns during this period. She laments her "unfortunate knack of arriving for appointments with OPS officials [the textile 'cooperative' in charge of importing and distributing yarns to textile manufacturers] just after they had been arrested" (p. 169). In addition, seven of the 11 members of the handweavers cooperative (KOPTEKSI) were arrested in January 1965. She reports that there had been prosecutions for corrupt practices but that *none* had been successful, and furthermore that the official price of yarn was closer to the free-market price than regulations would suggest (p. 157).

[5] Not surprisingly, quantitative data on the *ad valorem* costs of bribes are mostly unavailable. Adiratma (1969) notes that smuggling channels were well developed for the inter-regional smuggling of rice in the mid-1960s. The total cost of bribes (*uang rokok*) through the nine checkpoints from the village of Rengasdenglok in Krawang, West Java, to Jakarta was only 3 percent of the value of the rice transported.

In any case, corruption was so rampant that those officials of the state with authority over potentially profit-making activities would compete away much of the rents (in the form of bribes) associated with that authority. Indeed, in 1965 very little foreign exchange that could be allocated at the discretion of authorities was available. Export flows were reduced by smuggling, and legal export earned rights to foreign exchange from the freely negotiable SPP system. The latter accounted for much more import in 1965 (perhaps three times more) than official allocations under the "import plan."

Producers of exports benefited from the existence of illegal trade even if they merely resold their produce to middlemen. The domestic price of some exportables was double or possibly triple the return from their legal export – and yet legal export took place. This phenomenon, known as price disparity, was the result of the competition among those engaged in mis-invoicing exports to purchase goods in the domestic market for export. The smuggled portion of export could then be resold at the higher black-market exchange rate. Smuggling, price disparity, and the black market for foreign exchange are discussed at greater length in the appendix. It is important to note that the existence of price disparity implies that there should not have been any "honest" exporters in all Indonesia. An honest trader, one who obeyed foreign exchange regulations, would have had to buy goods for export in the legal domestic wholesale market at high price-disparity-inclusive prices and export them for a substantial loss since domestic prices far exceeded the legal return to export. Any firm that wished to operate in accordance with the law would simply be driven from the market. It is likely that price disparity also existed for imports subject to high duties. Under competitive smuggling, the price at which some imports were sold in the domestic market was less than the cost of importing them legally. To summarize, in regimes dominated by quantitative controls in which illegal trade is pervasive with competitive (black) markets, firms in sectors subject to control which seek to act legally will be driven from the market – only by joining in illegal behavior can a firm compete.

Black-market sales of price-controlled commodities were rampant, with state trading enterprises, favored manufacturing firms, and *sandang-pangan* shops competing for rents from the illegal sale of the goods with which they were endowed by the state. If profit-maximizing economics agents valued goods at unique (black-market) prices, allocations would be technically efficient. As controlled prices became absurdly out of line as the price index rose at triple-digit rates, it is inconceivable that many establishments would trade at legal prices. Thus Indonesia in 1965 was an economy of quantitatively unrestricted (black) markets where goods were subject to certain "implicit taxes" (and possibly subsidies) that were used to provide (illegal) transfers to certain segments of the population.

The Anatomy of Liberalization

The period 1966–71 saw sweeping changes in the regulation and organization of the foreign trade sector. There was a dramatic shift from the direct control of almost all aspects of the modern economy toward heavy reliance on market signals and price incentives. This period saw the end of most direct allocations of foreign exchange, the elimination of most price controls, an opening to foreign investment, and the acceptance of the private sector as the primary source of economic growth. The important distinction between this liberalization attempt and its numerous predecessors is that it encompassed not merely liberalizing acts but also the destruction of important antiliberal forces – replacing a strongly antiliberal state ideology with one that was nominally liberal, virtually eliminating powerful antiliberal political parties, and dismantling some important institutions of state control.

The nature and targets of this new economic regime were initially formulated piecemeal in the political and economic turmoil that followed the suppression of the PKI and other left-wing parties in the period after the coup attempt of September 30, 1965. Indonesia's newly emerging forces were only slowly able to capture political power in the months after October 1965.

Signals as to the direction of economic policy were at first mixed. In a Presidential Decree of November 22, 1965, the state extended its almost complete control of the economy even further by monopolizing all importing of textiles, as well as their distribution. However, it was announced that state enterprises were no longer to be subsidized: the prices of controlled commodities would rise to cover costs and the budget was to be balanced. The latter declaration could not be taken seriously in view of the continued commitment to completing prestige projects which, it was claimed, were important for "nation and character building."

The first official statements on the direction of economic policy were those of Sultan Hamengko Buwono IX, the newly appointed Vice Prime Minister of Economy, Finance, and Development. In his statement of April 12, 1966, he stressed the importance of the private sector, and that it should "be given an opportunity to develop itself so as to assist in the rehabilitation and stabilization of the economy." The government would henceforth "abandon the attitude that large and medium scale enterprises are the enemies of the State and People."

The first indication of the scope of the liberalization program under consideration came early in 1966 and was made explicit later in that year. Panglaykim and Arndt (1966, p. 18) reported in June 1966 that there was "unofficial" discussion of moving toward a free exchange rate and leaving the allocation of foreign exchange "openly and completely to the price mechanism." A public declaration of the direction of economic policy came with Decision XXIII of the MPRS (Provisional People's Consultative Assembly) of July 5, 1966. The declaration stressed that the new economic program should exclude the following:

a. "free fight liberalism" of the period 1950–7;
b. etatism – where the state and its economic apparatus fully dominate the economy and tend to push out and to stifle the potential creative powers of those economic units which operate outside the government sector;
c. monopolies which are harmful to the people. (Translated by Panglaykim and Thomas, 1967, p. 80)

The MPRS also formally named Suharto as interim head of government, banned Marxism, and forbade Sukarno to govern by Presidential Decrees and Decisions. Suharto's success with the MPRS, an appointed body which had some years earlier anointed Sukarno President-for-Life, had much to do with disenchantment with the state of the economy as well as with *Konfrontasi*. The latter was quickly ended – on August 11 relations with Malaysia were "normalized." Reforming the economy would, of course, be a lengthier process. What the New Order forces did was to bring the economy to the forefront – it became the major objective of the new AMPERA cabinet (formed July 25, 1966).[6] It was this radical reordering of political priorities – placing economic recovery over ideological campaigns – that gained the new government the support that it needed during its fledgling period. As Sundhaussen (1982, p. 240) explains:

> much of the tacit support Soeharto received in the MPRS had been forthcoming because of the priority he wished to give to economic problems, and to some considerable extent the legitimacy of his role as chief policy maker was seen to depend on his ability to improve economic conditions.

The government economic program was drawn up in August and September 1966 with the advice of an IMF mission and was summarized in General Suharto's statement to a meeting of Indonesia's non-Communist creditors in Tokyo in September 1966 to discuss a moratorium on its debt:

> For some months now a reshaping of our political structure has taken place. A new order has emerged with a pragmatic rather than doctrinaire approach in solving our nation's problems.
> The creation of the right social and monetary condition being uppermost in our mind, the Government has planned to introduce to this end measures which in broad outline are as follows:

[6] One knowledgeable observer, O. G. Roeder, correspondent for the *Far Eastern Economic Review*, marks the beginning of the New Order's economic policy initiative with the formation of the AMPERA cabinet (Roeder, 1966, p. 679).

(a) by rendering a more proper role to market forces, create a wider and equal opportunity for participation in the development of our economy by all creative efforts, state and private, domestic and foreign alike;
(b) the achievement of a balanced State Budget;
(c) pursuance of a rigid yet well-directed credit policy of the banking system;
(d) establishment of a proper link between the domestic and the international economy through a realistic exchange rate, and thus creating stimuli to reverse the downward trend of balance of payments.

In December 1966 the government announced that it would balance the budget in 1967, and stated that the control of inflation was to be the first priority of their economic stabilization program. There were no official statements, however, during the first year of the liberalization indicating either an intended sequence or specific targets of policy aside from a balanced budget.

Bonus Ekspor and Devisa Pelangkap Exchange Rate System

Bonus Ekspor
The successful liberalization episode of 1966–71 began, as had many of the earlier liberalization attempts, with the introduction of a certificate linking export with import. Even the acronym of the new *Bonus Ekspor* system – BE – had been used before. Although this certificate system became a major instrument in the liberalization program, it could not at the time be seen as a harbinger of the liberalization to come since it was merely the newest of many certificate systems that had been introduced since Independence. Indeed, the last such system, the SPP system, had been abolished just two months earlier, and at its inception had been every bit as liberal as the *Bonus Ekspor* system.

In this latest incarnation, exports were divided into three groups and exporters were granted a certain proportion of their surrendered export receipts in the form of BE certificates. The remainder of surrendered export receipts were exchanged at the Rp 10 rate,[7] composed of the Rp 0.25 transactions rate plus an export premium of Rp 9.75. The BE certificate represented a nonnegotiable right to foreign exchange for the import of certain goods on the BE list. The export categories and BE percentages are given in table 5.4

On May 24, 1966, the government raised BE percentages, shifted some commodities among categories, and made the BE certificates negotiable for one sale. The new BE percentages are given in table 5.5.

Another stipulation of the May regulations required that half of the BE be used for import into the province of the export's origin. Such regionally

[7] All rupiah prices which follow refer to the "new rupiah." In December 1965, 1,000 "old rupiah" were replaced by 1 "new rupiah."

Table 5.4 Export categories and *Bonus Ekspor* percentages, February 1966

Category	BE percentages	Commodities
I	10	Rubber, copra, tobacco, tea, pepper, palm oil and kernels, coffee, and sisal
II	15	Cocoa, quinine, cloves, nutmeg, cassia, kapok, and sugar
III	50	Vanilla, green tea, foodstuffs, other oilseeds, essential oils, minerals, rattan, damar and other forest products, handicrafts, animals, pearls, and other minor exports

Table 5.5 Export categories and *Bonus Ekspor* percentages, May 1966

Category	BE percentage	Approximate share of total exports	Changes from February classification
I	20	90	Removed: coffee, sisal, cut tobacco
II	60	8	Added from I: see above Added from III: vanilla, green tea, foodstuffs, other oilseeds, essential oils, most minerals, rattan, damar and other forest products, batik, animals, and pearls
III	100	2	Removed: see above

tied BEs were known as *Bonus Ekspor Daerah* (BED) or Regional Export Certificates. The intention was to give the export-oriented regions outside Java an incentive to act against export smuggling and to provide them with an assured share of imports. The latter was in keeping with the tradition begun with the *Bukti Ekspor* system of 1957–9, which had tied foreign exchange receipts and expenditures regionally to forestall rebellion. Exporters were intended to receive the free-market price for the half of their BE that was regionally tied, but it has been suggested that this might not always have happened. Provincial authorities may have compelled their sale at a lower price so as to augment local revenues through resale to private importers.

One hindrance to export that the government had to contend with in the initial phases of the trade liberalization was the bureaucratic tangle to be cleared before exports could be shipped. Before May 1966 an exporter needed no fewer than 60 signatures for each export shipment. Obtaining these signatures was not only time consuming but often involved the payment of "unofficial" charges. The May 1966 reforms, which raised BE percentages, also set forth simplified procedures for executing export. Nevertheless, it was reported that, in early 1967, 39 signatures were still required for each export shipment. Furthermore, provincial and local authorities attempted to collect unauthorized export taxes in the harbors they controlled that were sometimes as large as the foreign exchange tax levied by the central government. Often, exporters had to bargain with local tax departments to determine the tax levied. Jakarta found it difficult to impose its authority in the independent-minded regions, and these nominally illegal levies persisted throughout the period. In addition, sales tax was levied on most export sales even though they were specifically exempted by law.

The May 1966 regulations were intended to return an average of 25 percent of export receipts to exporters in the form of BEs. The other 75 percent of export receipts were surrendered in return for rupiahs at the transactions rate of exchange of Rp 10. In May 1966 BE certificates sold for Rp 110 for each US dollar of face value, or 11 times the official transactions rate of exchange. The BE price fell to Rp 75 per US dollar in early June before recovering to Rp 90 later in that month. With this large gap between the transactions rate and the BE rate, devaluation of the effective exchange rate for exports could proceed by changing the percentage of export receipts surrendered for BEs. This was the announced intention of the government.

In October 1966, at the time that the import-licensing system was abolished (see below), BE percentages were again increased as the government moved toward its goal of a free-floating exchange rate. The new BE percentages were 50 percent, 75 percent, and 90 percent for categories I, II, and III respectively. BEs were now made freely negotiable – rather than limited to a single sale – and the regionally tied BEDs were abolished. In place of BEDs, the central government directly allocated 10 percent of the declared value of exports to the regions of origin of the exports. This allocation of foreign exchange, known as ADO, was sold to provincial governments at the price of Aid-BEs (see below) whose price was fixed below that of regular BEs. Exporters nominally received the Rp 10 transactions rate for the 10 percent of their receipts designated as ADO. Thus the central government earned as net revenue on ADO the difference between the transactions rate and the Aid-BE rate, while provincial governments earned the difference between the Aid-BE rate and the price of foreign exchange on the free market, where they were free to sell any or all of their ADO exchange.

Devisa Pelangkap

The use of "overprice" in further liberalizing the exchange rate became increasingly important in the early stages of the liberalization episode. Overprice is the foreign exchange retained when actual export receipts are in excess of the stated surrender price or checkprice. This foreign exchange could legally be retained and was known as *Devisa Pelangkap* (Complementary Foreign Exchange) or DP exchange.

The setting of surrender prices began in 1961 and the legal retention of overprice was first recognized in 1964. Regulations in effect in 1966 allowed exporters to retain DP exchange earned as overprice for use in importing or to sell it once. Sale of DP exchange could legally be accomplished only through foreign exchange banks at agreed prices. Imports using DP exchange did not require an import license (which was otherwise required for imports financed with non-DP exchange prior to October 1966), but were subject to additional import duties. Exporters were required to keep their DP exchange in a DP "A" account at an authorized foreign exchange bank. After the permitted single sale, this exchange was to be held in a DP "B" account to distinguish it from unsold DP. Because of restrictions on its sale and use in 1966, only a small part of overprice was actually turned into DP "A" account certificates. Unreported overprice was kept as cash abroad or used to finance import smuggling. In 1967 the distinction between DP "A" and DP "B" was abolished, and restrictions on the use and sale of DP exchange were loosened. A DP market was established in Jakarta alongside the BE market.

Since the price of DP exchange was higher than that of BE exchange, the enlargement of overprice margins devalued the effective exchange rate for exports more than an equal increase in the BE percentage. The process of export liberalization consisted of both a step-by-step replacement of BEs for rupiah payment at an overvalued transactions exchange rate and the replacement of overprice – that is, less restrictive and higher-valued DP exchange – for BEs.

With the prospect of a debt moratorium (see below) and having received assurances of new grants and credits of US$174 million from the United States, West Germany, Japan, and other nations, Indonesia initiated its first import liberalization measures in October 1966 at the same time that the BE percentages for export were enlarged. Import license restrictions were almost entirely swept away in a single day (October 3) without pre-announcement. Direct foreign allocations to manufacturing firms were ended. Importers were free to buy almost any good they wished.[8]

---

[8] October 3 not only saw the landmark event of the liberalization, but marked a turn in the relationship between the army and student demonstrators. On that day, soldiers fired on students demonstrating against President Sukarno, wounding 62 and killing one. According to Sundhaussen (1982, p. 245) "3 October marked the end of the political independence the

Imports were classified into five categories.

Category I: essential commodities including rice, fertilizers, textbooks, and pharmaceuticals

Category II: raw materials and auxiliary goods, semifinished products, and capital goods which are foreign exchange earning or saving

Category III: raw materials, auxiliary goods, and semifinished products intended for domestic consumption

Category IV: other goods, mostly finished consumer goods

Category V: a prohibited list, mostly goods deemed "luxuries;" very few goods included with protective intent

The differing types of exchange were restricted to the import of commodities from certain import categories as outlined in table 5.6. Aid-BEs were foreign credits and grants sold by the government to importers in the form of BE certificates; this system of distributing aid monies is discussed at greater length below.

The government continued to import certain goods on its own account. Some goods deemed very essential, such as rice, cotton, fertilizers, and medicine, were imported on behalf of the government at the Rp 10 transactions rate, effecting a substantial subsidy to the import of those goods compared with the cost of imports financed with BEs. Ready-made clothes for sale during the Lebaran holiday period were imported at a special Rp 45 rate. Certain state enterprises, such as the electricity generating authority, also continued to import at the Rp 10 rate. In 1967, it was ruled that government agencies would be required to obtain their

Table 5.6 Types of exchange for various import categories

Types of exchange	Eligible import commodities
BE certificates	Commodities from the BE list (composed of a restricted set of commodities)
Provincial foreign exchange allocations (ADO)	I, II, and III
DP (Complementary Foreign Exchange)	I, II, III, and IV
Foreign exchange from the Foreign Exchange Fund	Subject to license
Aid-BE certificates	Commodities from Aid-BE lists, usually more restrictive than the ordinary BE list

students had obtained by their actions [in opposing Sukarno] in the first quarter of the year, and for the rest of the campaign against Sukarno they accepted the 'guidance' of the Army Headquarters."

foreign exchange on the BE and DP markets in the same manner as private importers.

In July 1967 the BE list was revised, and ADO imports were restricted to commodities on this list. A DP list was formulated which itemized all goods importable with DP exchange but which were not on the BE list. Aid-BE lists remained for each donor country. The relative importance of these types of import financing is demonstrated in table 5.7.

In July 1967 the government also ceased all payment in rupiahs to exporters. In effect, this meant the end to a fixed official exchange rate. For their surrendered foreign exchange, exporters received only BEs. Exports were reclassified into two categories. Category A consisted of rubber, copra, leaf tobacco, coffee, pepper, palm oil and kernels, diamonds, and tin, which together accounted for about 80 percent of total non-oil export. In addition to the 10 percent ADO tax (now without rupiah compensation), category A exports were subject to a 15 percent foreign exchange tax. The remainder, 75 percent of surrendered proceeds, was paid with BEs. Category B exports consisted of all other commodities except gold and silver and paid only the 10 percent ADO tax, receiving 90 percent of surrendered proceeds as BEs. While the increased BE percentages had a devaluing effect, the concurrent reduction in overprice margins for category A exports provided a limited counterbalance. Initially, the overprice margin for category A exports was reduced to nearly zero, but pressure from exporters and an increasing gap between the

Table 5.7 Total import financing, 1966–July 1972 (million US dollars)

Financing	1966	1967	1968	1969	1970–1[a]	1971–2[a]
Export BEs and general						
foreign exchange	340	384	416	475	419	361
Aid-BEs	128	238	240	285	346	393
Program aid	(96)	(145)	(103)	(101)	(125)	(139)
Food aid	–	(6)	(30)	(32)	(39)	(40)
PL 480	(32)	(25)	(89)	(90)	(105)	(111)
Project aid	–	(62)	(18)	(62)	(77)	(103)
DP and free foreign						
exchange	68	114	94	125	32	42
Direct investment	–	1	1	21	65	121
Merchants' L/C[b]	0	0	0	0	146	238
Subtotal	536	737	751	906	1,008	1,155
Imports of oil companies	68	68	80	87	94	132
Total	604	805	831	993	1,102	1,287

–, negligible.
[a] Fiscal year.
[b] L/C, letter of credit.
Source: Bank Indonesia, *Annual Report*, various years

market prices for BE and DP exchange which induced illegal transactions led to a gradual increase in overprice.

The Marketing of Foreign Grants and Credits

Indonesia's method of distributing foreign grants and credits was in keeping with its decision to use market mechanisms to distribute all foreign exchange. Foreign exchange obtained as aid or credits from abroad presented particular problems for Indonesia, because not only was its use typically tied to imports from donor countries, but also commodity imports were limited to lists of eligible commodities and often had to be used within certain periods of time. As restrictions and hence the attractiveness of each country's aid varied, so would the free-market price. To keep from offending those countries who might be embarrassed to find their aid priced lower than that of other donor countries, while at the same time avoiding adding more exchange rates to an already complex multiple exchange rate system, Indonesia tried to fix a common price for all aid foreign exchange which would lead to the free-market sale of all donor country credits. The result was substantially greater demand for some kinds of foreign credits, such as Japanese and Dutch, than others, such as Indian and American.

The credits, in the form of Aid-BEs, were sold at much lower prices than exporter BEs because their use was restricted to imports from donor countries, lists of commodities eligible for import were usually more restrictive, and delivery lags were longer. The Aid-BE rate was constantly readjusted by the government in response to changes in the market for import foreign exchange and to changes in aid flows. Not only had Aid-BEs a price advantage over exporter BEs, but also the terms of importing were altered constantly in an attempt to keep them competitive with exporter BEs and to maintain a balance between the market value of one country's AID-BEs and another's. For example, prepayment requirements were less for import financed with Aid-BEs than with other types of foreign exchange, and in the early 1970s "rebates" on imports with Aid-BEs were offered, with the rate of rebate varying by donor country.

Government Intervention in the Foreign Exchange Market

The government attempted to intervene significantly in the newly formed foreign exchange markets in late 1967 and early 1968. A poor rice harvest and inadequate stocks had precipitated a large rise in prices in the last quarter of 1967. In that quarter alone, the Jakarta cost of living index rose 27.5 percent. Prices of both BE and DP exchange began to rise rapidly. The free-market price of the US dollar leapt from Rp 122.86 on November 11, 1967, to Rp 300 three months later, an increase of 144 percent. In an effort to reverse this trend, the government intervened heavily in the BE market by selling substantial quantities of exchange and by reducing the validity period of BE certificates from three months to three weeks. Expired BE certificates were redeemable at Rp 240 per US dollar, which was the newly adjusted Aid-BE rate. Unsatisfied with the results of these changes, the government further reduced the validity period of BEs to ten days in April to reduce their price and to force imports onto the market. In May, the entire sales procedure was revised. Previously, exporters had been free to sell their BEs directly to importers or to retain them for their own use until the end of the validity period. Sales were accomplished through a call system at the Foreign Exchange Bourse in Jakarta. The new regulations required that all BEs be sold to a foreign exchange bank. On the market day following the submission of their BEs, banks paid exporters the market rate that prevailed the previous day.

The changes were instituted in order to discourage traders from holding inventories in anticipation of a government response to the crisis that would further devalue the effective exchange rate. The government justified these measures as a means of countering the "speculation" that it claimed had fueled the crisis. However, it was clear that the roots of the crisis did not lie in the mostly free foreign exchange market, which merely responded to expectations formed from past experience with government intervention in crises, but rather with the performance of government import and distribution monopolies, which failed to arrange adequately for the import of rice and other basic necessities under their control.

Regulations enacted in May 1968 abolished the special Aid-BE rate. All foreign exchange from foreign grants and credits was now to be sold through the general BE system and would be indistinguishable from ordinary BEs. However, special credit facilities were made available to imports financed with Aid-BEs to encourage their use.

In July, to encourage the use of the still slow-moving Aid-BEs, the government halted the sale of exporters' BEs – the major source of foreign exchange for import. The result was a rush for DP exchange by importers seeking commodities not eligible for import with Aid-BEs and by traders committed to pay for imports from Singapore, Hong Kong, and other non-aid-donor countries. The DP rate quickly jumped from 117 percent of the BE rate in late June to nearly 147 percent in mid-July. On July 31, three weeks after exporter BE sales were halted, they were resumed. Nevertheless, the US$30 million of Aid-BE sales in the month of July equaled the cumulative sales over the first six months of the year.

Although the DP rate fell with the resumption of exporter BE sales, the large gap between the BE and DP rates of July was sufficient incentive for large-scale illegal transactions. A massive fraud was uncovered involving a group of traders who had purchased BEs and opened letters of credit in Singapore and Hong Kong. Forged shipping documents were used to obtain dollars from Hong Kong banks which the traders then retained or resold at the DP rate for a 40 percent profit. The perpetrators earned an estimated US$35 million in foreign exchange and taught the government a lesson about the practical limits to which multiple exchange rates can diverge. The use of BE exchange to import from Hong Kong and Singapore was temporarily halted, and was subject to strict control when eventually resumed. Later in the year, the Bank Indonesia entered the newly organized call market for DP exchange to bring down the DP–BE spread by purchasing exchange on the BE market and reselling it on the DP market.

Protective Pressures

As well as intervening in foreign exchange markets, the government, under increasing pressure from the manufacturing sector, was persuaded to institute some protectionist measures in the form of tariff revision.

Manufacturing had continued to be depressed throughout the first two years of liberalization, even though in the absence of quotas and the raw material allocation system there could be no raw material shortage, the primary cause of unused capacity before liberalization. From the perspective of manufacturers and their workers, the cheap import policy of the government was the cause of their malaise. For example, in its efforts to stabilize the economy and its political position, the government imported large quantities of textiles at a special exchange rate of Rp 45 per US dollar. Nominal textile prices actually fell during some periods. This, coupled with the end of direct foreign exchange allocations to firms at favorable prices, from which import premiums could be earned, led to massive dislocation in the textile sector. The rate of capacity utilization in industry, which had been as low as 20 percent in 1965, fell even lower in 1966 and early 1967. Most estimates put capacity utilization in all manufacturing at less than 20 percent in early 1967 and just 15 percent in the important textile sector.

Under some pressure, the government announced in 1967 that it was going to switch emphasis from "checking inflation" to "stimulating production." There was no dramatic change in policy except moderate increases in tariff protection for import-competing sectors, initially through changes in the exchange rate used in valuing imports for customs duty purposes. In April 1967, a 20 percent increase in nominal protection was achieved by raising the exchange rate for calculating duties from Rp 75 to Rp 90 per US dollar. In July, it was raised again to Rp 130 and in January 1968 to Rp 240 per US dollar. These changes did not differ much from relative changes in the BE and DP exchange rates, except that they were less gradual.

Table 5.8 summarizes measures of the tariff schedule in effect before April 24, 1968, and after the tariff revision of that date. This was the first

Table 5.8 Changes in the tariff schedule on April 24, 1968

		Unweighted average			Median tariff rate	
Commodity category	Number of items	Before April 24, 1968	After April 24, 1968	Percentage change	Before April 24, 1968	After April 24, 1968
A *Consumer goods*						
Luxury	421	121.2	136.0	+ 12.2	125	125
Nonessential	176	52.6	61.4	+ 16.7	50	50
Essential	43	27.3	25.6	− 6.2	5	5
B *Raw materials*						
For agriculture	13	20.0	23.2	+ 16.0	5	5
For textiles	51	30.8	28.2	− 8.4	15	15
For other consumer goods	176	38.1	40.5	+ 6.3	30	30
For investment use	264	25.4	26.3	+ 3.5	15	15
C *Investment goods*	232	17.8	18.3	+ 2.8	5	5
Total	1,376	57.6	64.8	+ 12.5	50	50

Source: World Bank, 1968, p. 74

tariff revision since liberalization. Previously, surcharges of 50 and 100 percent had been levied on a wide range of products, as well as excess profits taxes on yarns, textiles, dry batteries, and other goods. Import prepayment requirements were widespread. The commodity categories in table 5.8 are based on those given in the tariff schedule; table 5.9 provides the distribution of tariff rates in the April 1968 tariff schedule classified by the types of financing permitted. In general, goods importable with Aid-BE had lower average rates of duty than those importable with general (exporter) BE which in turn had lower rates than goods importable with DP exchange. Interestingly, some goods which required expensive DP

Table 5.9 Items of the customs tariff classified by import lists and tariff brackets

	Import lists				
Tariff rate (%)	BE-A Very essential commodities	BE-B Essential commodities	BE-C Less essential commodities	DP, FX Nonessential commodities	Total
0–10	26	268	12	33	339
11–20	2	114	5	33	154
21–40	0	88	16	88	192
41–60	0	15	15	136	166
61–100	0	2	6	190	198
101–150	0	0	4	144	148
151–250	0	1	2	158	161
250+	0	0	0	18	18
Total	28	488	60	800	1,376

Source: World Bank, 1968, p. 80

exchange came in duty free while others which could be financed with any type of exchange paid nonzero duty. Table 5.10 provides the time series on the distribution of tariff rates from 1969 through 1977. The number of commodity classifications with rates above 100 percent declined sharply, and in the last period there was a decline in the number of rates above 60 percent.

Tariff rates for 57 separate commodities for the seven dates between 1964 and 1971 on which significant revision of the tariff schedule occurred are given by Pitt (1988, appendix table 5.2). These tariff rates include the so-called GATT tariff, import surcharges, and excess profits tax but do not include import sales taxes. The rates of the latter are provided separately by Pitt (1988, appendix table 5.2). Some duty rates are in terms of rupiahs per US dollar of import so that the *ad valorem* tariff equivalent varied with the exchange rate set by customs for valuing imports.

Manufactured consumer goods had the highest duty rates throughout the period. In our sample of goods, the highest duty rate in July 1971 was 300 percent levied against imports of drinking glasses. The rate on drinking glasses and many other consumer goods was 800 percent in 1964. These high rates were abolished in December 1965, before the liberalization but at a time when the state made absolutely no foreign exchange available for these kinds of imports. Tariff rates were not changed again until 1968, at

Table 5.10 Distribution of tariff rates, 1968–1977 (percent)

Tariff rate (%)	Time periods[a]							
	1	2	3	4	5	6	7	8
0	8.6	8.7	8.8	8.8	8.7	7.6	7.6	2.6
1–5	4.9	5.1	5.1	5.1	5.1	5.2	5.3	7.9
6–10	10.4	10.9	10.8	12.2	12.2	12.6	12.4	15.0
11–15	1.0	0.8	0.8	0.9	1.0	1.0	1.0	6.1
16–20	10.0	9.3	9.1	9.7	9.6	9.8	10.4	15.3
21–30	7.2	7.7	8.4	8.3	9.1	8.7	10.4	10.6
31–40	7.5	7.0	6.8	6.9	6.8	6.5	7.8	13.4
41–50	2.6	3.2	3.3	4.6	5.3	6.0	8.9	9.6
51–60	9.3	8.7	8.8	7.6	6.7	7.1	10.3	12.1
61–70	0.2	0.4	0.5	1.7	3.4	10.2	16.1	3.6
71–80	4.9	4.9	5.1	4.6	4.8	6.5	4.1	2.2
81–90	2.2	1.8	1.8	1.6	1.6	2.0	2.8	0.2
91–100	7.1	6.6	6.5	6.6	7.7	7.9	1.1	0.5
101–150	10.1	11.9	15.3	14.9	12.1	7.1	1.2	0.7
151–200	4.9	7.4	4.4	3.3	2.9	0.6	0.3	0.1
201–400	9.0	5.5	4.4	3.4	3.0	1.3	0.3	0.4

[a] Time periods 1, ending March 1969; 2, ending September 1969; 3, ending January 1970; 4, ending October 1970; 5, ending June 1971; 6, ending September 1971; 7, ending January 1973; 8, to 1977.
Source: Rosendale, 1978, p. 276

which time most rates were increased. However, after October 1966, almost all these goods were importable with DP exchange and quite a few of them with cheaper BE exchange.

Given all the other policies affecting the cost of imports in addition to listed tariffs, strong conclusions on the magnitude and direction of effective protection cannot be drawn from these data.[9] The important fact is that there was no reversion to the widespread use of quantitative restrictions as protective devices. Over the ensuing years, the desire to protect certain manufacturing subsectors became an increasingly important aspect of policymaking – increasing protection was seen as production "stimulating." Nevertheless, the government did not basically alter its commitment to a relatively free foreign exchange market – one without pervasive import licensing and quotas.

Exchange Rate Unification

On April 17, 1970, the dual exchange rate system was ended. The BE and DP markets were merged at a rate set by the last DP rate of Rp 376 per US dollar. Exporter BEs were abolished. Aid-BE was traded at a preferential rate of Rp 326, the last exporter BE rate. While these exchange rates were nominally floating, the Bank Indonesia intervened in the market in order to support them.

The checkprice–overprice system was abolished and exporters were required to surrender 100 percent of their receipts. Checkprices continued to be posted as indicator prices to act as guidelines at customs, but all foreign exchange in excess of the checkprice was to be surrendered. The 5 percent tax on foreign exchange for category A (major) exports and the 10 percent ADO tax were replaced wth a single 10 percent export tax. The provincial foreign exchange allocations from the ADO tax were replaced by direct rupiah subsidies to provincial governments; the subsidy was initially set at 105 percent of the ADO earnings of each province in the previous year.

The devaluing effects of the new regulations were greater for category A exports than for other more minor exports because a larger share of their export receipts was derived from BE and a smaller share from overprice. In addition, the 5 percent exchange tax levied only on category A exports ended. The net result was a substantial reduction in the variance of commodity-specific effective exchange rates for export.

For imports, the exchange rate unification meant that the "essential" commodities that made up the BE list would no longer enjoy the more favorable exchange rate provided by the use of relatively inexpensive BE exchange. Nevertheless, credit restrictions made importing with BE

[9] The earliest effective protection estimates published are by Pitt (1981a) for 1971. He estimated average effective protection in import-competing manufacturing as 46 percent.

exchange as opposed to DP exchange much less advantageous than posted exchange rates would indicate. Imports with DP exchange could obtain financing abroad at much lower costs than BE imports which were restricted to local sources of credit. As a result, at one time half the value of imports financed with DP exchange were commodities on the BE list.

In December 1970 the last vestige of the multiple exchange rate system disappeared with the elimination of the preferential rate for credit exchange, now referred to as DK exchange (*Devisa Kredit* or Credit Foreign Exchange). To encourage its use, imports with DK exchange were provided with special credit facilities.

Perhaps the concluding act of the liberalization program begun in 1966 was the devaluation of the rupiah on August 23, 1971, from Rp 378 to Rp 415 per US dollar in response to the floating of the US dollar. Again, although nominally a floating rate, the government intervened in the foreign exchange market to keep it stable. Since DK exchange was still moving too slowly, a package of rebates was introduced, with the size of the rebate varying by donor country.

Effective Exchange Rates: an Appraisal

Export Exchange Rates

Two export exchange rate series, labeled "major export rate" and "minor export rate," are introduced in table 5.11. Both rates exclude the value of any overprice – defined earlier as the foreign exchange retained by an exporter as a result of the legal underinvoicing of exports – because the variance of overprice margins by commodity and over time makes their inclusion in the calculation of effective exchange rates too cumbersome. For comparative purposes, the free- or black-market rate of exchange in Jakarta is also presented. This rate represents the exchange rate pertaining to illegally retained foreign exchange (smuggling). All these exchange rates are end-of-period rates and have been deflated by the end-of-quarter values of the Jakarta 62-item cost of living index.

Note that the major export rate in table 5.11 peaked in 1967, quarter IV. This is slightly misleading since it was at this time that overprice margins were at their lowest level – at least until overprice was eliminated in 1970. The minor export rate received a hefty boost from the BE system – its price-level-deflated effective exchange rate rose fourfold between 1965, quarter IV, and 1966, quarter I.

To calculate the effective exchange rate (EER) for exports inclusive of overprice, the percentage difference between realized and declared export values must be calculated. In table 5.12 the overprice for natural rubber sheets (RSS I) has been calculated quarterly for the period 1965 through

Table 5.11 Quarterly price-level-deflated effective exchange rates
(1965, quarter I = 100)

Year (quarter)	Major exports	Minor exports	Major imports	Other imports	Free rate
1965					
I	100.00	100.00	100.00	100.00	100.00
II	95.46	95.46	87.65	99.29	79.69
III	88.76	88.76	51.80	81.19	99.48
IV	55.68	55.68	20.48	40.69	109.48
1966					
I	85.52	96.13	1,459.88	63.39	87.19
II	106.33	237.20	1,943.41	85.12	107.97
III	89.95	213.64	1,781.10	81.91	96.48
IV	100.22	178.29	946.94	48.54	61.78
1967					
I	83.43	131.77	798.66	38.61	45.85
II	103.81	154.97	1,096.26	49.44	56.69
III	140.71	168.60	990.59	45.82	52.02
IV	175.02	209.83	1,233.92	56.65	69.21
1968					
I	126.29	151.55	890.21	43.03	46.22
II	139.60	168.01	984.95	47.50	53.37
III	137.30	164.65	965.62	55.92	62.21
IV	148.82	157.41	924.74	48.73	56.73
1969					
I	140.23	148.33	871.36	42.37	46.90
II	149.31	157.94	927.84	44.76	49.48
III	142.77	151.02	887.17	42.80	47.50
IV	135.42	143.25	841.53	40.59	47.15
1970					
I	126.73	134.05	787.52	37.94	42.06
II	156.40	173.87	918.06	38.09	42.39
III	159.19	176.98	934.44	38.77	42.81
IV	152.67	169.74	896.20	37.19	41.06
1971					
I	144.33	160.46	847.23	35.15	38.92
II	152.77	169.84	896.77	37.21	41.19
III	169.81	188.68	996.22	41.34	45.50
IV	163.67	181.86	960.22	39.84	43.96

Sources: free rate, Biro Pusat Statistik, *Warta BPS*, various issues, and
Indikator Ekonomi, various issues

Table 5.12 Checkprice–overprice system for rubber, 1965–1970

Year (quarter)	1 Average checkprice of rubber (per lb)	2 Average New York spot price of rubber (per lb)	3 Overprice[a] (legal under-invoicing) (per lb)	4 Overprice margin[b] (%)	5 Overprice earnings as percentage of EER for rubber
1965					
I	18.02	26.05	5.83	24.4	50.4
II	20.45	27.57	4.92	19.4	42.5
III	21.83	24.97	0.94	4.1	11.2
IV	19.37	24.17	2.60	11.8	36.3
1966					
I	20.00	25.37	3.17	13.7	36.2
II	18.92	23.93	2.81	12.9	38.0
III	18.21	22.90	2.49	12.0	28.3
IV	17.25	22.07	2.62	13.2	23.3
1967					
I	15.45	21.10	3.45	18.3	31.9
II	13.97	21.20	5.03	26.5	42.1
III	14.86	19.27	2.21	12.9	19.9
IV	14.42	18.07	1.45	9.1	12.9
1968					
I	13.53	17.10	1.37	9.2	12.9
II	13.88	19.27	3.19	18.7	26.0
III	13.12	20.63	5.31	28.8	37.8
IV	13.17	22.37	7.00	34.7	45.5
1969					
I	13.58	23.70	7.92	36.8	45.4
II	14.33	26.60	10.07	41.3	49.1
III	15.00	24.27	12.07	44.4	52.2
IV	15.38	25.10	7.52	32.8	40.0
1970					
I	13.88	24.30	8.22	37.2	44.7

Calculations are for RSS I.
[a] Calculated as (column 2 minus 2.2 cents per lb) minus column 1 (deduction of 2.2 cents per lb corrects New York spot price to f.o.b. net).
[b] Calculated as column 3 divided by (column 2 minus 2.2).
Source: Pitt, 1981a, p. 197

the first quarter of 1970. The margin varied widely over the period. After a severe reduction in mid-1967, the overprice was restored in 1968 and remained at a comparatively high level until the system was terminated in April 1970. After April 1970, illegal invoicing may have continued, but there was only a small incentive to do this.

Overprice margins for less important exports (categories II and III) were significantly larger than those for rubber. These commodities benefited from a 1968 regulation that allowed exporters themselves to set checkprices for their commodities. It has been estimated that on average these checkprices were set at about half the realized prices.

The importance of overprice in exporter receipts is demonstrated by the large share of overprice earnings in the effective exchange rate. At the time the system was terminated, overprice accounted for nearly half the rupiah earnings per dollar of rubber export. For example, the Bank Indonesia officially estimated that in the fiscal year 1969–70 the overprice margin on non-oil exports was 26.4 percent (Pitt, 1988, appendix table 5.3). The variance of these overprice margins over time and commodities largely depended on the administrative ability of the Ministry of Trade to reset checkprices in line with world price movements. The use of this checkprice system meant that export data at the commodity level were undervalued for the years when the system operated (1965–70) since exports were recorded at the checkprices rather than at their realized prices.

To determine the effects of this complicated succession of foreign exchange policies on returns from exporting, the effective exchange rate for rubber exports has been calculated. Although there were periods when literally dozens of effective exchange rates existed, the rubber exchange rate is an adequate proxy for the average effective exchange rate weighted by the value of exports. One reason that this is true is that rubber would carry an enormous weight in such an average calculation. From 1950 to 1969, rubber exports made up on average 57 percent of all nonmineral exports. In addition, rubber's effective exchange rate over that period usually lay somewhere near the middle of a ranking of the effective exchange rate of major agricultural exports. Minor (category B) exports such as pepper, rattan, and kapok had somewhat higher effective exchange rates, while other major exports such as coffee and copra often had lower effective exchange rates.

The effective exchange rates presented in table 5.13 were calculated by summing the values of all trade policy instruments, including such things as the value of import entitlement certificates (such as *Bukti Ekspor* and *Bonus Ekspor*), foreign exchange retention (including overprice) and export taxes and premiums. The effective exchange rate for exports (EER_x) thus calculated may differ, however, from the rate actually realized, because of illegal transactions.

Such was the importance of export incentive schemes that changes in the official registered exchange rates did not significantly alter the effective exchange rate for exports. For example, the official exchange rate was devalued by 200 percent in 1952 from Rp 3.80 to Rp 11.40 per US dollar, but the effective exchange rate was devalued by only 12.5 percent. This occurred because changes in export incentive schemes made at the same time as the official devaluation offset most of the effects of the devaluation.

Table 5.13 Exchange rates, variously defined and adjusted (annual averages), 1950–1972

	1	2	3	4	5	6	7	8
Year	EERx for rubber (Rp per US$)	Cost of living index (1953 = 100)	Index of PLD-EERx (1971 = 100)	Free exchange rate (Rp per US$)	Price disparity for rubber (%)	Price disparity EERx (Rp per US$)	Index of PLD-REERx (1971 = 100)	Index of PLD-NPm (1971 = 100)
1950	7.08	60	77.4	24.65	20.34	8.52	96.24	244.6
1951	7.60	85	58.7	16.17	11.31	8.46	67.46	119.5
1952	9.41	92	67.1	19.63	13.71	10.70	79.06	102.2
1953	11.60	100	76.1	27.32	2.33	11.87	80.48	123.3
1954	12.52	103	79.7	31.98	13.10	14.16	93.21	158.5
1955	11.07	127	57.2	39.13	42.01	15.72	83.94	203.7
1956	11.84	142	54.7	33.33	21.71	14.41	68.82	140.8
1957	17.33	159	71.5	43.65	16.96	20.27	86.47	142.4
1958	29.55	225	86.1	71.74	27.24	37.60	113.33	170.6
1959	32.21	280	75.5	130.82	49.92	48.29	116.95	250.6
1960	37.52	367	67.1	285.17	100.21	75.12	107.40	270.4
1961	40.50	487	54.6	186.67	58.59	64.23	89.44	199.2
1962	136.50	1,324	67.6	760.42	32.75	181.21	92.81	217.6
1963	320.55	2,927	71.8	1,456.00	30.42	418.05	96.85	201.2
1964	788.35	6,106	84.7	3,004.00	18.29	932.52	103.57	205.4
1965	2,638.00	24,715	71.3	14,083.00	33.85	3,591.18	98.54	256.9
1966	36.00	283,166	82.8	105.67	− 4.66	34.32	82.20	182.7
1967	103.38	763,222	88.9	172.25	− 12.17	90.80	80.68	132.6
1968	269.03	1,719,762	102.6	386.67	0.04	270.12	106.51	133.8
1969	318.23	2,020,089	92.3	408.42	2.80	327.13	109.81	131.9
1970	333.65	2,262,000	98.6	388.59	0.54	335.44	100.56	113.6
1971	353.88	2,321,500	100.0	397.33	− 3.26	342.34	100.00	100.0
1972	373.50	2,562,600	95.6	418.00	− 0.02	372.89	98.68	86.6

Source: Pitt, 1981a, p. 201

Indeed, for most of the period covered in table 5.13 the official exchange rate played only a minor part in the calculation of the effective exchange rate. For example, devaluations of the official exchange rate (gross devaluations) of 294 percent, 22,000 percent, 16 percent, and 10 percent in 1959, 1965, 1970, and 1971 resulted in devaluations of the effective exchange rate (net devaluations) of 19 percent, 300 percent, 8 percent, and 10 percent respectively.

Table 5.13 also presents an index of the price-level-deflated effective exchange rate for natural rubber (PLD-EER$_x$). The deflator is the Jakarta cost of living index linked to a 19-item food price index. The tremendous variation in the PLD-EER$_x$ index shows the effects of a consistently rapid rise in domestic prices countered from time to time by devaluation.

Smuggling, Price Disparity, and the Effective Exchange Rate

It is well known that smuggling of agricultural exports – rubber and copra in particular – was widespread. Because smuggling constitutes a significant share of export trade, the calculations of the effective exchange rate for rubber exports that have been presented may not be good measures of the return from export trade; logically, smuggled rubber would be expected to earn more rupiahs per US dollar of exports than legally exported rubber. There is strong evidence that smuggling increased the return to exports beyond that indicated by the effective exchange rates for legal export. One outcome of smuggling for Indonesian trade was the prevalence of price disparity. Export price disparity is the positive difference between the domestic price and the world price of an exported commodity converted at the legal effective exchange rate. In practice, price disparity meant that the Indonesian wholesale price of rubber and other exports often greatly exceeded the legal receipts from their export. Paradoxically, legal exporting took place even though domestic prices exceeded the legal export price – that is, legal exports incurred an apparent loss.

Consideration of the nature of large-scale smuggling explains the paradox. A large share of smuggling takes the form of mis-invoiced misgraded, and misweighed legal trade. Obviously, in order to under-invoice an export or import, it is necessary to declare some positive value. Furthermore, it is logical to assume that success in avoiding detection is inversely related to the degree of underinvoicing. For example, one would have greater success fooling a customs official into believing that 1,000 tons of rubber weighs 900 tons than into believing that the same quantity weighs only 100 tons. Alternatively, grade I rubber may be declared as grade II or, with greater risk of detection, as grade V. In these cases the declared value of a shipment is legal trade, while smuggling is the difference between actual and declared values. The point is that the risk of detection, and hence the cost of smuggling, is decreasing with the ratio of declared value to actual value. Price disparity exists because traders will bid the price of the smuggled commodity above its legal trade return as long as profit can be made from the combined smuggling–legal trade. With competitive smuggling, price disparity passes back to producers the benefits of evading trade taxes. This concept of smuggling is formally set forth by Pitt (1981b) and, more briefly, in the appendix.

Annual estimates of price disparity caused by rubber smuggling are presented in table 5.13, with price disparity measured as a percentage:

$$\frac{P - (\text{EER} \times W)}{\text{EER} \times W} \times 100$$

where P is the domestic price of rubber in rupiahs at Jakarta, EER is the legal effective exchange rate for rubber, and W is the international trade price of rubber (here based on the f.o.b. price of rubber at Singapore less transportation costs).

The effect of smuggling on the domestic price of rubber over much of the 1950s and 1960s is demonstrated by these calculations. During the period 1959–65, smuggling increased the domestic price of rubber, on average, by more than 46 percent beyond the price that would have existed in its absence. In the year 1960 the domestic price was approximately double the legal trade price. An independent estimate for September 1965 (Thomas, 1966) is that price disparity for rubber exceeded 160 percent. After the liberalization measures of 1966, price disparity fell markedly, as can be seen from table 5.13, column 5. Indeed, in some years the domestic price was slightly below the world price.

It is clear that over a number of years smuggling, working through the mechanism of price disparity, counterbalanced a significant amount of the price-distorting effects of government trade policy. The effective exchange rate REERx realized for all exports, legal and illegal, is calculated as the legal effective exchange rate plus the absolute price disparity (EERx (1 + rate of price disparity)). The REERx for rubber presented in table 5.13 indicates a level of price distortion considerably less than is implied by the effective exchange rate for exports. Table 5.13 also displayed an index of the price-level deflated realized effective exchange rate for rubber exports, PLD-REERx. These calculations suggest that, during 1958–65 (regarded as the period of greatest government intervention in the trade sector), the average realized rupiah return on a dollar's worth of rubber export was, surprisingly, slightly greater in real terms than it was at the end of the liberalization period in 1971.

Table 5.14 provides quarterly detail on the effective exchange rate for rubber over the period 1950–74. Table 5.15 deflates the data of table 5.14 by the Jakarta cost of living index linked to an earlier 19-item food price

Table 5.14 Effective exchange rate for rubber, 1950–1974
(rupiahs per US dollar)

Year	Quarter I	II	III	IV	Average
1950	5.50	7.60	7.60	7.60	7.08
1951	7.60	7.60	7.60	7.60	7.60
1952	8.20	8.93	10.26	10.26	9.41
1953	11.40	11.40	11.40	12.20	11.60
1954	12.28	12.44	12.60	12.76	12.52
1955	11.64	10.40	10.83	11.40	11.07
1956	11.40	11.40	12.24	12.31	11.84
1957	12.31	12.31	21.89	22.80	17.33
1958	27.36	30.28	30.28	30.28	29.55
1959	30.28	30.28	32.28	36.00	32.21
1960	36.00	36.00	37.59	40.50	37.52
1961	40.50	40.50	40.50	40.50	40.50
1962	60.00	139.50	173.25	173.25	136.50
1963	240.75	279.85	374.40	387.20	320.55
1964	410.70	736.50	866.10	1,140.00	788.35
1965	2,140.00	2,206.00	2,193.00	4,199.00	2,683.00
1966	17.00	30.00	39.00	57.00	36.00
1967	66.60	86.90	105.00	155.00	103.38
1968	206.40	243.10	295.50	331.10	269.03
1969	320.60	319.60	322.30	310.40	318.23
1970	314.60	340.00	340.00	340.00	333.65
1971	340.00	340.00	362.00	373.50	353.88
1972	373.50	373.50	373.50	373.50	373.50
1973	373.50	373.50	373.50	373.50	373.50
1974	373.50	373.50	373.50	373.50	373.50

New rupiah = 1,000 old rupiah, beginning 1966.

index. These data are averages for the quarters rather than end-of-quarter values. Note in table 5.15 the strong effect that the beginning of the BE system had on the price level deflated effective exchange rate; it rose by almost two thirds between 1965, quarter IV, and 1966, quarter I, even though the BE system was in effect for only part of the quarter. It then peaked in the second quarter of 1966 before falling back, dropping as low as 67.4 in 1968, quarter I, as a result of the cutback in overprice margins. The restoration of the overprice margin later in that year resulted in a 58 percent increase in the index by the last quarter of the year.

Table 5.16 provides quarterly averages of the ratio of the black-market exchange rate to the effective exchange rate for rubber, which can be

Table 5.15 Index of quarterly price-level-deflated effective exchange rates for rubber exports, 1950–1972 (1971 = 100)

Year	Quarter			
	I	II	III	IV
1950	79.1	97.8	104.0	96.9
1951	64.3	69.1	60.2	53.0
1952	57.1	69.3	81.7	80.3
1953	84.0	81.5	80.9	86.1
1954	84.1	85.7	86.0	81.6
1955	66.2	55.1	54.4	51.6
1956	47.3	52.4	56.5	54.9
1957	56.4	55.7	88.9	75.3
1958	77.1	96.0	82.2	75.9
1959	71.0	72.3	72.1	80.8
1960	70.9	66.9	67.7	74.7
1961	66.6	63.3	59.9	40.6
1962	33.4	75.3	82.9	73.0
1963	68.6	68.3	82.6	63.6
1964	45.8	94.7	95.5	84.6
1965	87.7	86.1	60.4	49.1
1966	80.2	91.9	85.7	82.0
1967	67.7	80.0	74.3	86.7
1968	67.4	83.4	93.7	106.4
1969	98.8	106.6	105.9	93.2
1970	87.7	98.2	101.1	100.2
1971	91.6	95.5	107.1	106.5
1972	100.2	101.4	102.5	82.1

The deflator is the index of the prices of 19 food articles in Jakarta.
Source: price deflator, Biro Pusat Statistik, *Statistical Pocketbook of Indonesia*, various issues

viewed as an indicator of the incentive to smuggle. Note the immediate fall in this ratio with the start of the BE system in 1966, quarter I, and the further fall later in the year when the import-licensing system was abolished, thus relieving demand-side pressure on the black-market exchange rate.

Although the discussion above has focussed on the smuggling of exports and the price disparity of export commodities, there is reason to believe that import smuggling was perhaps equally pervasive. Although there is much anecdotal evidence of import smuggling during the 1950s and 1960s, there are no price disparity data for imports to confirm this supposition or to suggest magnitude. However, such data are available for the early 1970s, when the only incentive for smuggling was evasion of tariffs. Comparisons of domestic prices, foreign prices, and the legal effective exchange rate clearly show (Cooper, 1974) that the domestic price of many

Table 5.16 Ratio of free- or black-market exchange rate to the effective exchange rate for rubber exports, 1950–1971

Year	Quarter I	II	III	IV	Annual average
1950	5.30	3.68	3.00	2.44	3.48
1951	1.93	1.96	2.31	2.30	2.13
1952	2.29	2.16	1.89	2.05	2.09
1953	2.10	2.43	2.56	2.33	2.35
1954	2.37	2.39	2.52	2.93	2.55
1955	3.24	4.17	3.81	3.00	3.54
1956	3.15	2.79	2.65	2.69	2.82
1957	2.89	3.55	2.27	2.00	2.52
1958	1.86	2.03	2.79	2.97	2.43
1959	3.13	3.66	3.78	5.44	4.06
1960	10.83	7.84	6.83	5.23	7.60
1961	4.73	4.90	4.07	4.73	4.61
1962	5.61	5.20	6.25	5.18	5.57
1963	5.33	5.30	3.76	4.26	4.54
1964	5.07	3.51	3.66	3.67	3.81
1965	4.13	4.38	5.47	6.15	5.25
1966	3.51	3.62	2.97	2.42	2.96
1967	2.06	1.71	1.73	1.43	1.67
1968	1.35	1.42	1.47	1.48	1.44
1969	1.40	1.27	1.22	1.24	1.28
1970	1.22	1.14	1.16	1.15	1.16
1971	1.13	1.14	1.12	1.11	1.12

Source: Black-market rates, *Picks Currency Yearbook*

imports subject to duty was below the legal cost of importing – that is, price disparity existed for imports. Furthermore, the rate of this price disparity was increasing with the rate of duty levied. This would be predicted by our theory – the higher the rate of duty is, the greater is the level of smuggling attempted and the greater is the price disparity.

Import Exchange Rates

Calculating effective exchange rates for imports over time in Indonesia is immensely complicated by the incessant and widely varied trade interventions that affected them. Furthermore, no single commodity exists, as rubber does for exports, which could usefully proxy effective exchange rate movements for the broad range of imports. In addition, even if data on effective exchange rates for a wide range of imports were available, they would be of limited use for two reasons. First, smuggling of imports undoubtedly resulted in large differences between legal and realized effective exchange rates. Second, for most of the 1950s and 1960s, quantitative restrictions were the binding constraint on trade and import premiums were probably substantial. Thus calculations of effective exchange rates would be poor measures of the bias of the trade regime, since they exclude the large implicit tariffs arising from quotas. Two types of import exchange rate are presented below: standard effective exchange rates which exclude the effects of smuggling and quantitative restrictions on the domestic price of importables, and an index of the relative price of domestic goods to foreign imports.

The major import rate, presented in table 5.11, is the rate pertaining to "essential" commodities which were imported with exporter BE beginning 1966 and with foreign exchange from the Foreign Exchange Fund before that. It does not reflect trade carried out by the state under the special exchange rates described above, and it does not apply to imports such as rice, cloves, and fertilizers still monopolized by the state in the late 1960s. The other import rate is the exchange charged for "nonessential" commodities which could be freely imported with DP exchange after 1966 or with SPPs obtained in the free market during 1965. It does not include any tariff, excess profits tax, or other charges levied against "nonessential" goods. Like the export rates and the free rate, these are end-of-quarter rates deflated by the Jakarta 62-item cost of living index.

The major price-level-deflated exchange rate for imports rose 71-fold between 1965, quarter IV, and 1966, quarter I, even as the price level more than doubled. This huge increase gives some indication of the enormous subsidy (and import premium) associated with import using stage foreign exchange during 1965. To be sure, not much of this import took place. Most state foreign exchange was devoted to the import of monopolized goods and many of the remaining imports, even "essentials," were imported with SPPs. The other import rate pertains to imports not subject to quota. Nonquota imports of this type required SPPs during 1965 and the use of DP exchange in the following years. This price-level-deflated effective exchange rate did not undergo the huge swings that the major import rate experienced and had a much smaller real devaluation. Table 5.17 provides quarterly time series of exchange rate ratios. The ratio of the major import rate to the major export rate is of some interest. It fell almost continuously from the end of the import-licensing system in 1966, quarter III, until the end of the liberalization period.

The nominal protection index PLD-NPm presented in table 5.13 is calculated by comparing domestic and international import price indices and by deflating by the increase in the domestic price level. Keeping in mind the potential error in such a calculation owing to aggregation, note that the PLD-NPm was at its highest level in 1959–65, when the total value

Table 5.17 Ratios of effective exchange rates (percent)

Year (quarter)	Ratio of free rate to rate of				Ratio of major imports rate to major exports rate
	Major exports	Minor exports	Major imports	Other imports	
1965					
I	416.67	416.67	2,200.00	91.29	18.94
II	347.83	347.83	2,000.00	73.26	17.39
III	466.98	466.98	4,225.00	111.85	11.05
IV	819.28	819.28	11,760.00	245.61	6.97
1966					
I	424.81	377.93	131.40	125.56	323.31
II	423.08	189.66	122.22	115.79	346.15
III	446.88	188.16	119.17	107.52	375.00
IV	256.84	144.38	143.53	116.19	178.95
1967					
I	228.97	144.97	126.29	108.41	181.31
II	227.54	152.43	113.77	104.67	200.00
III	154.05	128.57	115.54	103.64	133.33
IV	164.77	137.44	123.40	111.54	133.52
1968					
I	152.50	127.08	114.23	98.07	133.50
II	159.29	132.35	119.21	102.56	133.63
III	188.80	157.44	141.74	101.56	133.20
IV	158.84	150.17	134.97	106.28	117.69
1969					
I	139.35	131.74	118.40	101.05	117.69
II	138.09	130.55	117.33	100.92	117.69
III	138.63	131.06	117.79	101.32	117.69
IV	138.99	131.40	118.10	101.58	117.69
1970					
I	138.27	130.72	117.48	101.19	117.69
II	112.94	101.59	101.59	101.59	111.18
III	112.06	100.79	100.79	100.79	111.18
IV	112.06	100.79	100.79	100.79	111.18
1971					
I	112.35	101.06	101.06	101.06	111.18
II	112.35	101.06	101.06	101.06	111.18
III	111.65	100.48	100.48	100.48	111.11
IV	111.91	100.72	100.72	100.72	111.11

Sources: free rate, Biro Pusat Statistik, *Warta BPS*, various issues and *Indikator Ekonomi*, various issues

of imports was lowest and subject to the greatest quantitative restrictions. It was low in 1951–3, reflecting the relatively liberal import system in the aftermath of the Korean War commodity price boom, but it leapt in 1955 when foreign exchange allotments for consumer goods were sharply curtailed. The effect of the Sumitro trade liberalization of late 1955 is evident in the value of the PLD-NPm for 1956. As the trade regime was liberalized after 1965, the PLD-NPm fell sharply, dropping by nearly two thirds between 1965 and 1972. Thus the estimated PLD-NPm seem to have followed the shifts in the nature of the trade regime.

Comparing price indices composed of differing bundles of commodities introduces errors of unknown magnitude. In addition, it provides no information on how effective exchange rates for various classes of goods fared during the liberalization period. Table 5.18 presents price-level-deflated indices of the ratio of Indonesian to Japanese prices for 41 well-defined commodities. The Indonesian prices were obtained from commercial newsletters (primarily *Business News*, published in Jakarta) and from unpublished data provided by the Indonesian Central Bureau of Statistics. Care was taken that prices apply to consistently defined commodities throughout the 1965–70 period – attention was paid to commodity specifications, brand names, and model numbers when this information was available. Japanese prices were indices of yen export prices at the commodity level published by the Bank of Japan in various issues of *Price Indexes Annual*. The ratios of Indonesian to Japanese export prices, computed every second month beginning with January 1965, were deflated by the deseasonalized Jakarta 62-item cost of living index for the relevant month. These series are provided as index numbers with base September 1966 = 100, which was just before the end of the quota system on October 3, 1966.

In most instances it is wise to examine the overall pattern of prices rather than the performance of any single price. Individual price series are not always informative, particularly because there may be a lot of noise in the data as nominal prices were increasing at triple-digit rates and weekly nominal prices for individual commodities did not always increase smoothly. Indonesian prices pertain to the same week of each month whenever possible. Tariff rates for all commodities are given by Pitt (1988, appendix table 5.2). Groups of related commodities are also plotted by Pitt (1988, appendix figures 5.1–5.9).

Some noteworthy patterns emerge from examining the full set of price series. First, price-level-deflated effective exchange rates for the majority of goods were lower at the end of the liberalization period than in both September 1966 and January 1965. Of the 41 exchange rate indices, 35 were lower in November 1970 than in September 1966, and 39 were lower than in January 1965. Second, most series were at their minimum or close to it during 1967–8. This is most apparent for textiles and garments. This

Table 5.18 Real effective exchange rates, 1965–1970 (monthly)

	Commodity[a]																				
	1	2	3	4	5	6	7	8	9	10	11	12	13	14	15	16	17	18	19	20	21
1965																					
1	130	172	236	153	220	139	114	105	116	84	184	140	157	164	315	122	260	239	249	162	156
2	128	177	186	134	171	108	108	99	101	74	161	135	149	138	301	131	233	180	186	162	157
3	126	182	135	116	121	76	102	93	86	65	138	130	141	113	287	141	206	121	123	162	157
4	137	190	136	124	119	87	97	89	80	62	133	125	128	108	263	84	176	115	116	148	142
5	147	198	136	131	117	98	92	84	74	59	127	119	116	103	240	68	145	109	109	134	126
6	160	173	139	139	117	106	101	89	70	64	126	106	111	122	224	52	148	105	102	162	136
7	174	149	143	147	112	115	110	93	66	68	125	93	107	142	207	61	151	101	95	190	145
8	168	148	132	134	107	107	98	89	61	62	116	82	96	131	225	70	135	96	88	178	133
9	161	148	121	122	109	100	86	86	56	55	106	72	85	120	243	102	119	90	82	166	120
10	159	140	123	123	111	107	88	86	57	61	109	80	89	111	217	134	115	86	77	150	122
11	156	131	124	125	102	114	90	87	59	66	112	88	93	102	191	157	110	82	71	134	124
12	156	116	116	113	102	96	79	82	62	71	117	99	79	90	188		142	84	75	117	109
1966																					
1	155	101	108	102	93	78	69	78	65	76	123	110	65	77	185	179	174	86	80	100	94
2	136	86	102	95	91	77	69	71	56	72	117	98	59	80	146	133	149	70	65	79	83
3	116	71	96	89	89	76	69	64	48	68	112	85	54	82	107	87	123	54	50	59	72
4	102	72	100	97	90	85	76	79	55	65	111	85	61	87	139	100	108	47	45	60	62
5	88	73	103	105	91	93	84	94	62	63	110	85	69	92	172	114	94	41	41	60	51
6	98	83	111	113	102	99	84	104	65	59	105	103	69	101	139	106	116	59	62	70	60
7	108	93	119	121	113	105	84	115	68	55	101	120	69	110	106	98	138	76	82	80	69
8	104	96	110	111	107	103	92	107	84	77	101	110	84	105	103	99	119	88	91	90	85
9	100	100	100	100	100	100	100	100	100	100	100	100	100	100	100	100	100	100	100	100	100
10	100	97	82	83	77	80	75	96	81	90	87	90	90	98	124	96	107	118	113	109	117
11	100	93	63	66	55	59	50	93	62	81	73	81	80	96	149	93	114	137	127	118	134
12	104	92	66	65	60	66	58	106	69	77	83	85	96	93	141	87	108	135	126	121	136

(Continued)

Commodity[a]																				
1	2	3	4	5	6	7	8	9	10	11	12	13	14	15	16	17	18	19	20	21

1967

1	2	3	4	5	6	7	8	9	10	11	12	13	14	15	16	17	18	19	20	21
108	91	69	64	65	72	67	120	75	73	93	90	112	90	134	80	103	134	126	123	138
99	76	58	56	59	67	60	108	60	66	80	80	91	79	142	67	93	124	118	114	127
90	61	47	49	54	61	53	96	45	58	67	70	69	69	150	54	83	114	111	105	116
86	54	47	47	50	54	48	83	43	54	73	63	64	63	112	45	63	84	85	87	95
83	48	47	46	46	47	43	69	41	49	79	56	59	57	74	35	44	54	60	69	75
80	47	48	49	48	49	44	69	42	52	74	63	62	54	154	37	69	73	83	86	86
78	45	50	52	50	50	46	70	43	54	69	70	64	50	234	38	94	92	106	102	97
73	44	48	49	45	49	43	67	40	55	65	68	61	49	202	38	92	76	107	116	93
68	44	47	47	41	48	39	63	37	55	61	67	57	48	169	37	90	60	107	130	89
62	39	42	42	38	45	35	57	33	49	57	57	60	42	152	42	72	53	83	104	77
56	35	38	37	35	41	31	50	30	43	52	48	63	37	134	47	55	46	59	79	65
66	40	44	45	44	45	35	57	36	43	66	44	57	38	138	52	67	53	65	94	79

1968

1	2	3	4	5	6	7	8	9	10	11	12	13	14	15	16	17	18	19	20	21
76	46	51	54	53	49	38	63	42	42	80	40	50	40	143	58	80	60	70	109	92
73	52	54	54	54	53	36	60	38	40	78	37	50	39	132	55	71	57	67	100	90
71	58	56	54	54	57	34	56	33	38	76	34	49	38	121	52	63	55	64	92	88
67	54	55	57	52	54	31	54	36	39	78	38	54	46	151	47	61	53	62	112	88
63	51	55	60	51	51	28	53	38	41	81	43	59	55	180	42	58	51	60	132	86
65	50	56	60	58	56	36	56	42	40	80	42	57	54	197	42	58	50	58	125	86
66	49	58	61	65	60	43	60	46	40	79	40	54	54	214	42	57	49	56	119	84
69	53	69	58	70	59	48	60	45	39	79	51	60	56	214	40	58	49	55	115	89
72	58	79	55	75	58	54	60	45	38	78	63	65	57	214	37	58	49	54	112	93
75	66	75	58	74	58	56	66	46	41	86	69	69	57	233	39	62	52	58	114	95
78	75	71	60	72	58	58	71	48	44	95	75	72	57	252	41	65	55	61	115	97
84	91	75	66	76	64	64	80	57	50	106	83	82	70	262	46	81	60	67	121	102

1969

Month																					
1	89	107	79	71	81	69	69	89	66	56	117	91	92	82	271	50	98	65	73	126	108
2	85	104	80	69	76	65	66	86	63	54	112	88	89	83	230	56	97	63	70	110	91
3	82	100	81	67	72	62	64	82	61	52	108	84	85	84	188	63	97	60	68	110	75
4	75	95	76	64	68	60	59	78	58	50	102	77	87	74	168	61	93	57	65	103	70
5	68	90	70	62	64	58	54	74	55	48	97	69	89	63	147	58	90	54	61	97	64
6	68	88	67	61	62	56	54	73	54	47	96	67	93	63	145	55	92	55	62	95	71
7	69	85	64	59	61	54	54	72	54	47	95	65	97	63	142	51	95	56	63	93	79
8	64	77	64	58	60	53	53	70	52	46	92	62	95	60	121	49	86	57	66	97	80
9	58	68	63	57	59	52	52	68	51	45	90	59	93	60	101	47	76	58	68	101	82
10	58	61	61	55	57	51	51	69	49	46	93	59	91	60	121	48	77	60	77	100	93
11	59	54	58	54	55	50	49	71	46	47	95	59	90	60	142	49	78	63	86	99	104
12	66	58	60	54	61	53	54	77	50	51	95	59	98	64	161	53	85	68	92	105	110

1970

Month																					
1	73	62	62	54	67	57	59	82	55	54	95	60	107	69	180	57	91	73	99	112	116
2	69	61	64	53	63	54	58	83	56	55	98	57	100	68	163	55	91	72	100	200	140
3	65	60	66	51	60	52	57	83	56	56	101	55	94	66	146	53	90	70	101	288	163
4	63	56	62	47	56	48	51	78	55	52	95	50	92	62	138	52	88	64	81	280	155
5	60	52	58	43	52	45	45	74	53	48	88	46	89	58	129	51	86	57	61	272	147
6	58	77	55	42	51	44	46	73	52	47	86	45	86	56	122	65	79	64	65	280	146
7	56	103	53	41	51	43	47	71	52	46	85	45	83	55	115	78	73	70	68	287	145
8	57	103	50	39	51	42	45	71	53	45	84	46	86	51	114	72	74	70	69	289	148
9	58	103	46	37	51	41	44	71	53	45	84	47	88	47	116	65	75	71	69	291	151
10	56	102	49	37	51	41	44	74	56	44	88	44	88	47	119	59	76	71	70	277	146
11	55	102	51	38	50	41	45	76	59	44	91	42	88	46	121	54	77	71	70	263	142
12	53	102	54	38	50	41	45	78	62	43	94	39	87	46		48	78	72	70	249	138

(Continued)

	Commodity[a]																				
	22	23	24	25	26	27	28	29	30	31	32	33	34	35	36	37	38	39	40	41	42
1965																					
1	357	109	232	239	195	207	325	132	87	155	124	137	95	105	64	133	51	112	178	158	445
2	379	119	183	196	196	191	348	131	89	150	117	149	95	121	76	136	49	100	155	132	377
3	401	129	133	152	196	174	370	130	91	145	111	161	94	137	87	140	46	87	131	106	309
4	337	132	162	134	162	162	340	116	86	134	100	158	82	129	86	126	42	84	131	97	235
5	274	135	191	115	127	150	309	102	80	123	89	156	71	122	85	113	38	82	130	88	162
6	257	148	185	125	116	158	289	95	101	184	84	136	62	117	84	98	55	82	119	88	169
7	239	162	178	136	105	167	269	88	121	245	78	116	53	113	84	84	71	83	108	88	175
8	223	140	182	129	98	151	255	78	104	270	85	107	46	106	78	81	69	80	96	91	163
9	207	119	185	122	91	135	241	68	87	296	92	98	39	98	73	78	67	78	84	94	151
10	168	112	165	138	110	134	248	64	72	239	95	92	42	108	65	77	66	91	78	108	155
11	129	105	145	154	130	134	255	60	57	182	98	85	44	119	57	76	65	105	72	123	160
12	120	99	177	116	132	160	253	62	63	137	108	73	68	106	51	80	57	106	94	125	186
1966																					
1	111	93	209	77	134	185	251	64	68	92	117	61	92	92	45	84	50	107	115	126	212
2	104	75	182	83	122	162	221	77	75	70	127	97	91	85	47	85	46	94	94	89	161
3	96	57	156	88	111	138	192	89	82	48	136	134	90	78	50	86	42	82	72	51	109
4	85	47	125	93	109	115	173	89	81	49	168	122	106	76	69	94	37	78	63	52	90
5	74	37	94	98	106	92	154	90	81	50	200	110	123	74	89	102	33	74	55	54	71
6	81	46	99	98	102	108	149	84	86	59	168	105	117	79	113	100	37	87	60	61	85
7	87	54	103	98	98	123	145	77	91	69	135	99	110	84	138	98	41	101	65	68	99
8	94	77	102	99	99	112	122	89	95	84	117	99	105	92	119	99	71	100	83	84	99
9	100	100	100	100	100	100	100	100	100	100	100	100	100	100	100	100	100	100	100	100	100
10	121	95	100	95	95	101	102	97	96	132	93	112	96	107	110	90	87	88	121	111	96
11	141	90	100	91	91	103	105	95	91	164	87	124	92	113	119	80	73	76	143	122	92
12	161	97	111	99	97	110	106	103	128	148	103	137	102	130	127	92	60	74	141	91	91

1967

1	180	103	123	99	103	118	107	112	165	132	119	151	112	147	135	105	46	71	139	60	91
2	145	75	105	87	94	113	96	108	135	115	109	137	94	130	102	96	41	62	117	57	78
3	111	47	86	75	86	107	85	104	105	98	98	124	76	113	69	86	35	52	95	53	66
4	112	47	95	77	77	103	78	82	95	91	91	120	66	104	64	73	33	52	73	39	70
5	114	46	104	78	68	99	71	59	86	84	84	116	56	95	59	59	30	52	52	25	75
6	122	47	102	78	64	89	95	83	84	80	83	111	55	91	63	63	28	51	71	36	88
7	130	48	100	78	59	80	119	107	82	76	83	105	54	88	67	67	27	50	90	46	102
8	131	49	86	71	55	71	116	119	84	84	77	97	47	83	56	62	26	49	84	45	97
9	132	51	73	63	50	61	113	131	86	91	70	89	41	78	46	57	25	48	77	43	92
10	124	43	63	60	43	54	91	101	78	78	63	75	37	73	41	60	23	43	65	40	81
11	116	35	53	58	36	48	69	72	71	66	55	60	32	67	36	63	21	37	53	37	70
12	111	40	67	87	36	56	85	87	57	69	53	75	39	67	43	60	26	44	55	38	110

1968

1	107	45	81	116	37	63	100	103	42	72	51	89	47	66	50	58	31	50	57	39	150
2	104	41	73	97	34	58	93	99	45	77	63	88	46	67	46	53	30	48	52	36	135
3	100	38	64	78	31	54	85	95	48	81	74	88	45	67	42	49	29	46	47	33	121
4	88	39	61	88	30	49	99	97	43	82	72	86	49	67	45	49	31	45	50	35	124
5	75	41	58	99	29	44	113	100	39	83	69	83	54	66	48	48	32	44	54	37	128
6	71	41	58	94	28	42	95	96	39	78	67	87	66	70	40	54	38	46	52	49	136
7	67	40	57	88	28	39	77	92	39	74	64	90	78	74	32	59	43	49	50	40	144
8	70	45	58	86	31	41	84	96	38	71	66	89	84	80	31	57	48	55	53	39	141
9	73	51	58	83	34	43	90	101	37	69	67	87	90	86	30	56	54	61	56	38	139
10	73	57	62	82	36	45	99	107	41	80	74	87	96	87	31	58	57	61	56	52	146
11	73	64	66	82	38	48	108	112	45	90	81	87	101	88	31	61	61	61	56	65	154
12	77	65	66	88	36	52	115	113	57	94	92	99	109	100	34	72	64	62	58	63	156

(Continued)

	Commodity[a]																				
	22	23	24	25	26	27	28	29	30	31	32	33	34	35	36	37	38	39	40	41	42
1969																					
1	82	66	67	94	34	56	123	115	70	97	102	111	117	112	37	82	67	63	59	61	159
2	78	59	72	90	33	58	119	99	60	90	101	106	132	108	41	77	63	60	59	57	149
3	75	52	77	85	32	61	116	84	49	83	99	101	147	105	45	73	58	57	58	52	139
4	72	46	71	80	30	55	119	84	49	79	101	98	140	99	38	72	56	52	56	51	146
5	70	40	65	76	28	50	122	84	49	75	103	95	134	93	30	71	54	47	54	50	153
6	70	39	73	76	26	51	119	84	49	73	101	92	125	92	30	72	52	45	57	47	133
7	70	38	80	76	25	52	115	84	48	71	100	90	117	91	29	72	50	43	60	45	113
8	72	37	87	90	29	45	113	85	46	75	98	87	109	90	37	66	48	41	67	41	107
9	73	37	94	104	34	39	111	87	44	79	96	85	102	88	45	60	47	40	73	37	101
10	74	36	94	91	34	38	101	86	45	80	96	83	98	88	49	62	48	43	73	37	97
11	75	36	93	79	34	38	90	86	47	81	97	80	95	88	53	64	50	46	74	36	93
12	79	40	98	85	36	42	94	96	51	80	104	80	101	96	42	77	57	53	77	39	92
1970																					
1	83	43	104	91	39	47	99	106	56	80	112	80	106	103	31	90	63	59	80	41	91
2	81	45	102	88	36	46	97	107	54	76	110	77	108	100	35	84	61	53	78	47	91
3	79	47	100	86	34	45	95	109	52	72	107	75	110	98	40	78	59	47	75	53	92
4	73	49	105	81	30	42	89	109	49	73	100	75	93	95	33	77	55	47	73	55	82
5	67	51	109	77	26	39	83	108	45	73	94	76	76	92	26	76	51	46	72	57	71
6	68	49	114	74	25	35	77	106	46	69	91	77	73	88	25	74	50	44	69	60	67
7	68	47	119	70	23	31	71	104	47	66	88	78	71	84	24	72	49	41	66	63	62
8	69	48	141	68	20	31	74	120	48	67	86	72	68	83	32	71	43	40	65	64	63
9	70	48	163	65	17	31	76	135	49	68	84	66	65	82	40	69	36	38	64	64	64
10	71	44	146	69	17	30	75	150	49	68	84	69	66	83	44	68	33	37	64	59	64
11	71	40	130	73	17	29	74	166	49	69	84	73	67	85	48	67	31	37	65	54	65
12	71	36	113	77	17	29	73	181	50	69	84	76	69	86	51	66	29	36	65	49	65

a Commodities:
 1 sardines
 2 sewing thread
 3 printed shirting
 4 white shirting
 5 flowered poplin
 6 white jeans
 7 white drill
 8 trousers (short)
 9 blouse (women's, silk)
10 sarong (men's, cheap)
11 shirt (short sleeve)
12 handkerchief (men's)
13 socks (cotton)
14 singlet
15 concrete iron
16 galvanized sheet
17 iron hoop
18 water pipe ($\frac{3}{4}$ inch)
19 water pipe ($\frac{1}{2}$ inch)
20 brass plate
21 aluminum sheet
22 nails (iron, 2 + inch)
23 plastic-covered cable
24 electrical cable 1
25 electrical cable 2
26 transistor radio
27 television
28 refrigerator
29 plate glass
30 drinking glass
31 cement
32 bicycle inner tube
33 writing book
34 writing tablet
35 shoes (men's leather)
36 pins
37 buttons
38 canned milk
39 Kraft cheese
40 iron plate
41 galvanized wire
42 light bulb (incandescent)

increase coincides with the higher tariff rates introduced for many of these products in 1968. For example, the tariff on singlets rose from 70 to 175 percent in February 1968, the tariffs on trousers, shirts, and blouses had the same increase, the sock tariff rose from 50 to 150 percent, and the tariff on canned milk rose from 50 to 100 percent. Third, there were significant falls in many of the series in the year after January 1965, perhaps reflecting the "liberalizing" effects of the growing black-market economy in the chaotic months before and after the coup attempt. Some of these declines were very large and included some of the more important goods: all cotton fabrics, almost all garments, iron products, and cement.

In addition to exchange rates for commodities, the free-market (black-market) exchange rate (see table 5.13) gives some indication, albeit undependable, of the restrictiveness of the trade regime. Large-scale smuggling of commodities is often associated with an active black market for foreign exchange. The foreign exchange receipts of illegal export are a major source of supply to this market, while illegal importers are a major source of demand and restrictions on the movement of capital provide another source of demand.[10] As the allocation of foreign exchange for consumer goods – especially goods considered to be "inessential" – was reduced in the earlier 1960s, the ratio of the black-market exchange rate to the effective exchange rate for rubber exports rose (table 5.16), reflecting the scarcity value of consumer goods imports. At its peak in 1960, the black-market rate was almost 11 times the effective exchange rate for rubber exports, and over the five years 1960–4 it was, on average, more than five times as great. Since the black-market rate represents the exchange rate earned for foreign exchange acquired in smuggling exports, it is clear that the incentive to smuggle was enormous.

Real Rate of Foreign Exchange

Tables 5.19 and 5.20 provide calculations of real effective exchange rates using the four nominal exchange rates presented in table 5.11 deflated by a constructed implicit price index of the nontradeable components of GDP and inflated by foreign currency import and export price indices. These are necessarily presented on an annual basis because of the unavailability of quarterly price deflators. Annual values are just the average of the end-of-quarter values. The price deflators were based on 1965 = 100. Note that the real major export rate depreciated continuously from 1966 to 1971. The real other export rate appreciated over the same period, greatly reducing the difference between the two. Both the major and the other

---

[10] A theory linking black markets in foreign exchange and Indonesian-style smuggling is presented by Pitt (1984) and more briefly in the appendix.

Table 5.19 Real effective exchange rates: imports, 1965–1971 (annual averages, 1965 prices)

Year	Nominal major import rate	Real major import rate	Nominal other import rate	Real other import rate	Non-tradeables price index	Import price index
1965	0.25	0.25	8.57	8.57	100.00	100.00
1966	84.50	5.25	94.50	5.87	1,535.86	95.40
1967	154.50	4.05	172.00	4.51	3,850.41	100.99
1968	304.00	3.52	381.00	4.41	8,410.60	97.29
1969	326.00	2.81	379.75	3.28	10,457.86	90.26
1970	365.00	2.76	378.13	2.86	12,057.93	91.25
1971	396.50	2.71	396.50	2.71	13,175.93	90.17

Sources: nontradeables price index constructed from sectoral GDP deflators, Biro Pusat Statistik, *Pendapatan Nasional Indonesia*, various issues; import price index from Rosendale, 1975, p. 73

Table 5.20 Real effective exchange rates: exports, 1965–1971 (annual averages, 1965 prices)

Year	Nominal major export rate	Real major export rate	Nominal other export rate	Real other export rate	Nominal free rate	Real free rate	Export price index
1965	2.15	2.15	2.15	2.15	12.62	12.62	100.00
1966	29.70	1.84	58.36	3.62	107.88	6.69	95.22
1967	102.38	2.33	132.88	3.03	185.13	4.22	87.71
1968	236.00	2.38	273.50	2.76	390.00	3.94	84.99
1969	277.00	2.44	293.00	2.58	384.38	3.39	92.12
1970	324.25	2.50	356.75	2.76	382.25	2.95	93.15
1971	356.75	2.54	396.50	2.82	399.75	2.85	93.81

Sources: Nontradeables prices index constructed from sectoral GDP deflators, Biro Pusat Statistik, *Pendapatan Nasional Indonesia*, various issues; free rate, Biro Pusat Statistik, *Warta BPs* various issues, and *Indikator Ekonomi*, various issues; export price index from Rosendale, 1975, p. 73

import rate appreciated between 1966 and 1971. This trend occurred after the real major import rate depreciated 21-fold and the minor import rate appreciated by 31 percent in 1966 compared with 1965.

6

Stabilization, Liberalization, and Foreign Assistance

The chaotic state of the Indonesian economy when the trade liberalization was launched has been described in the previous chapter. Inflation was running at over 1,000 percent, while the service on Indonesia's external debt exceeded expected foreign exchange earnings for 1966 (Pitt, 1988, appendix table 6.1). Foreign exchange reserves were negative, and the central bank was unable to honor cash letters of credit for some time, which led Japan to cut off most of its exports to Indonesia by suspending export insurance arrangements. Over US$200 billion was owed to Japan – which had already financed some US$200 million in exports as war reparations during 1958–65 – and further credit was not forthcoming.

The greatest part of Indonesia's debt was owed to the Eastern bloc countries. The Soviet Union was Indonesia's largest single creditor (Pitt, 1988, appendix table 6.2), holding Indonesian debts of almost a billion US dollars. Of the US$1.4 billion of official capital inflow obtained from Eastern bloc nations during 1957–65 (none before 1957), US$0.9 billion was military aid; much of the rest was dedicated to monument building or to grandiose schemes such as the Tjilegon steel works, which in late 1965 consisted mostly of machinery rusting in a rice field.

The American-trained economists advising the government suggested that massive aid from abroad was necessary to solve the economic problems of the country, and that only the West had the requisite resources. A quick ending of confrontation with Malaysia and a declaration of Indonesia's intention to reapply for admission to the United Nations (announced April 4, 1966), to give private enterprise a role in the emerging economic order, and to return nationalized property and open the economy to foreign investment were important steps in reentering the graces of the West. However, after the pugnacious abandonment of the DEKON liberalization financed by the United States and the IMF, the Western aid community needed strong assurances both that a new political regime was being inaugurated and that it was committed to solving economic problems rationally.

Missions to Europe, Japan, and the United States in early 1966 failed to get debt rescheduling off the ground or to obtain appreciable aid. Some Indonesians felt that the United States was morally obliged to provide aid as a "reward" for extinguishing one of the largest Communist parties in the world. As the power of the New Order, its mass support, and its generally liberal economic tone became more apparent, particularly after the MPRS declarations of July 1966, prospects for aid improved.

One of the first measures of the New Order regime was to apply for readmission to the IMF, the World Bank, and the United Nations. Missions from the IMF and the World Bank visited Indonesia in mid-1966 to assist in formulating economic policy. They were instrumental in arranging a meeting of representatives of the non-Communist creditor nations at a conference in Tokyo in September 1966 to discuss proposals for a moratorium on Indonesia's debt commitments. With interest and amortization commitments in 1967 exceeding expected export receipts by nearly half, it was agreed in principle to defer some payments. A meeting in Paris in December concluded a moratorium arrangement that delayed all payments of interest and principal on all debt except short-term commercial credit until 1971. Payment schedules and interest charges were very favorable to Indonesia. The Soviet Union, Indonesia's largest single creditor, and other Eastern bloc nations also agreed, after some delay, to reschedule debt.

It was only after the Tokyo meeting, with the prospect of a debt moratorium at hand, and after having received assurances of new grants and credits of US$174 million from the United States, West Germany, Japan, and other nations, that Indonesia, in October 1966, initiated its first direct import liberalization measures, the end of import licensing, while at the same time enlarging the BE percentages for export. In February 1967, a meeting of Western creditor nations was convened in Amsterdam to consider Indonesia's need for aid. It was concluded that US$200 million was required in 1967 (Indonesia asked for US$212 million), and the United States declared its willingness to provide one third of any commitment. Japan later declared its willingness to match the US offer, and early in 1967 Indonesia began signing loan agreements with a number of the nations and agencies attending the Amsterdam meeting, a grouping which became known as the Inter-Governmental Group on Indonesia (IGGI). Indonesia proposed that foreign assistance be funneled into the Indonesian economy through the already existing BE system. Although it could not evade the donor countries' condition that their aid be "tied," it was able to prevent severe restrictions on the list of goods eligible for import. Table 6.1 provides some detail on official capital inflows. Aid utilization totaled US$128 million in 1966, jumped to US$219 million in 1967, and continued to expand through 1970. This aid contributed 29 percent of 1967 budget revenues and 19 percent of 1968 budget revenues, and would have been higher except that commodity aid was sold at subsidized prices. The operation of the Aid-BE system has already been described in the previous chapter.

Early in 1966 the government announced its intention of actively seeking foreign investment. Given the long history of professed aversion to foreign capital – a line still echoed by President Sukarno – and the relatively recent series of nationalizations without compensation, the foreign investment initiative was probably intended to impress the community of donors without much hope that it would result in significant private capital flows in the short run. In 1966, some industrial enterprises and agricultural estates that had been nationalized in previous years were returned to their previous owners. In 1967, a month before the crucial meeting of Indonesia's creditors in Paris, a new Foreign Investment Law was enacted. It provided a 30-year guarantee of nonnationalization and then compensation if nationalization took place. Tax holidays – exemptions from company tax with rates as high as 60 percent of net profits – were available for between two and six years depending on the priority of the investment. Losses could be carried forward for up to six years. Foreign managerial and technical personnel were permitted, as was the repatriation of profit.

The trade liberalization reinforced stabilization efforts because it was seen as a prerequisite for the rescheduling of debt and obtaining new foreign credits that Indonesia desperately needed to get its stabilization program going. There is no published evidence, however, that the sweeping liberalization measures of October 1966 were an overt *quid pro quo* for obtaining the blessing of the IMF (or any others) for rescheduling and new credits. Mas'oed (1983, p. 83) reviews the evidence and concludes that

> it would be oversimplified to conclude that the IMF or other external actors imposed such a program on Indonesia, as some believed they did. On the other hand, however, the facts tell us that the economists advising President Suharto designed the program in such a way as to get the favor of the Fund and other creditors.

The IMF, which had a team in Jakarta in June 1966, three months before the October liberalization, argued strongly in favor of rescheduling and granting Indonesia new credits at the September 1966 meeting of creditors in Tokyo. That meeting was inconclusive, since most creditors argued that a more specific program than the one submitted was needed (Posthumus, 1971, p. 13). The sweeping liberalization of October 3, 1966, followed, motivated at least partly by the need to gain credibility in the eyes of Western nations unconvinced of Indonesia's commitment to change. Clearly, promises of a balanced budget and monetary restraint require a measure of trust from creditors, since proving their effectiveness takes

Table 6.1 Official transfer and capital, 1966–1971 (million US dollars)

Item	1966 Carryover	1967 Commitment	1967 Utilized	1968 Commitment	1968 Utilized	1969 Commitment	1969 Utilized	1970 Commitment	1970 Utilized	1971 Commitment	1971 Utilized
Program aid	35	183	195	298	245	322	249	353	383	353	300
Aid-BE	16	132	137	119	93	129	93	119	134	141	123
BE grants	9	23	24	25	24	21	21	22	19	28	24
PL 480	8	22	28	143	125	147	119	170	177	140	112
Food aid	2	6	6	11	3	25	16	42	53	44	40
Project aid	182	—	69	71	29	227	66	249	84	293	90
Project aid (pre-1967)	182	—	69	—	29	—	17	—	12	—	2
Project aid (new)	—	—	—	71	—	227	49	249	72	293	88
Other (net)	—	—	9	—	32	—	7	—	−28	—	—
Debt repayment	—	—	−54	—	−75	—	−40	—	−66	—	−99
Total	217	183	219	369	231	549	282	602	373	646	291

—, negligible.
Source: Biro Pusat Statistik, *Statistik Keuangan*, various issues

time. Sweeping away all quantitative restrictions and effectively floating the exchange rate are measures that are immediately visible – and apparently convincing, since a rescheduling and aid package was worked out in Paris two months later. The importance of the new credits in achieving the balanced budget is highlighted in table 6.2. Official grants and credits contributed over 29 percent of total state revenues in 1967 and financed a significant proportion of imports (see table 5.4). All in all, receipts from trade taxes and official transfer resulting from the liberalization program made up 61.5 percent of budgetary receipts in 1967.

Liberalization and the Fight against Inflation

The primary demand of the student demonstrators in Jakarta in early 1966 was the control of inflation – and it was control of inflation that the Suharto regime publicly proclaimed to be its first priority. The fiscal deficit was widely seen as the source of Indonesia's triple-digit inflation, so it is not surprising that the only announced specific target of the government in any area of economic policy was the promise of a balanced budget by 1967. Trade liberalization helped to achieve that target by converting import premiums to revenue and by redirecting illegal trade into legal and taxed channels.

Anecdotal evidence suggests that import premiums were high by any standards before liberalization. For some important imported goods the black market was the major source of distribution. With triple-digit rates of inflation, a quantitative restrictions regime with fixed nominal exchange rates would result in ever-increasing losses in potential revenue. As table 6.2 demonstrates, the impact of liberalization on revenue was substantial.

Table 6.2 Trade taxes, aid flows, and the budget, 1965–1968

Revenue	1965	1966	1967	1968
Trade taxes				
Current Rp million	52	5,655	27,503	51,224
Constant prices (1965 = 100)	100	837	1,539	1,302
Percentage of total receipts	5.6	43.0	32.4	27.6
Aid receipts				
Current Rp million	0	0	24,689	35,537
Percentage of total receipts	0	0	29.1	19.2
Total trade and aid				
Current Rp million	52	5,655	52,192	86,761
Constant prices (1965 = 100)	100	837	2,920	2,206
Percentage of total receipts	5.6	43.0	61.5	46.8

Source: Biro Pusat Statistik, *Statistik Keuangan*, various issues

Revenues from trade taxes in 1966 (excluding payments related to petro-leum exploitation) were more than eight times the levels of the previous year in real terms. Real trade tax revenue in 1967 and 1968 was respec-tively 15 times and 13 times 1965 levels. It is not possible to dissect this revenue effect into the part that was due to the substitution of higher priced foreign exchange for quantitative restrictions and the part that was due to the redirection of illegal trade (mostly exports) into legal channels. Although the former was probably the most important source of new trade tax revenue, export tax receipts grew more quickly than those from imports, but from a much smaller base. Export tax receipts swelled to 38.5 percent of all trade tax receipts in 1967, and econometric evidence discussed in chapter 7 suggests that as much as 86 percent of the increased volume of smallholder rubber export – the largest single export item – may have been the result of diversion of illegal exports into legal channels rather than increased levels of total exports.

Real tariff collections per dollar of import also rose dramatically at the time of liberalization (figure 6.1). There was no large increase in tariff rates at the time that quotas were abandoned: rather, effective exchange rates were increased through the dual exchange rate system. Tariff receipts probably rose with the end of the quantitative restriction system as the mix of imports included more highly taxed "nonessential" goods and the collection effort intensified. Tariff collection rates fell by almost half from 1969 to 1972, perhaps because of changes in the tariff schedule and large imports of duty-free rice and wheat flour by the government food logistics agency.

In summary, controlling the budget deficit was crucial, and the direct revenue effects of liberalization were important in bringing inflation under control (see below). The success of the government in improving tax revenues is apparent from the top of figure 6.1, which shows a clear break in the trend at 1966 as the declining share of tax receipts in GNP was dramatically reversed.

Monetary Policy

The banking system, like everything else, had increasingly come under the control of the central government in the years before the liberalization. When the Bank Indonesia was given its post-colonial charter in 1953, it was accorded the sole right to issue notes and authority over foreign exchange transactions and reserves. By statute, note issue was subject to a 20 percent reserve requirement, while advances to the central government treasury were limited to 30 percent of government revenue in the preceding year. Later the Bank Indonesia was given the authority to set reserve require-ments for commercial banks, to control credit, and to fix maximum interest

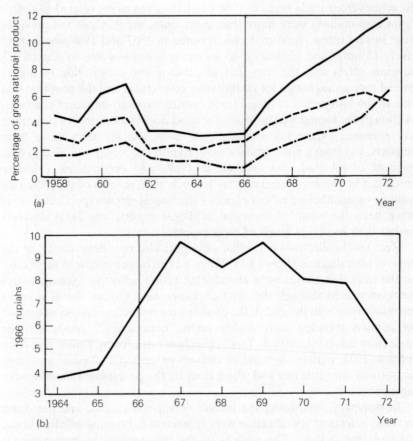

Figure 6.1 Government tax revenues before and after liberalization: (a) taxes as a percentage of gross national product (——, total; ---, indirect; -·-, direct); (b) real tariff collections per dollar of import

rates. Ever-widening budget deficits that could not be financed without resorting to money creation eventually brought an end to restrictions on the Bank Indonesia's financing of this deficit. As table 6.3 clearly shows, by the early 1960s, the financing of the budget deficit had become the principal source of money creation in Indonesia.

In 1965, Minister of Central Bank Affairs Jusuf Muda Dalam had reorganized the entire banking system under his sole control. The state banks were merged with the Bank Indonesia into the Bank Negara Indonesia (BNI) with units labeled I–V. The Bank Indonesia became BNI Unit I, and was delegated responsibility for budgetary finance and certain projects deemed "vital." The other units were similarly specialized. The state banks (Units II–V) depended on the central bank to finance their lending.

Table 6.3 Factors affecting money supply, 1952–1965 (billion rupiahs)

Year	Government	Enterprises		Foreign sector	Other	Total	Annual change in money supply (%)
		Public	Private				
1952	5.6	0.2	0.1	−3.2	−1.2	1.5	29.2
1953	2.5	−0.3	0.2	−1.6	−0.1	0.8	11.9
1954	3.3	0.2	0.3	−0.3	0.0	3.5	45.8
1955	1.6	0.2	−1.3	1.0	−0.4	1.1	10.0
1956	2.5	−0.2	1.0	−1.8	−0.3	1.2	9.4
1957	5.8	0.1	2.2	−1.0	−1.5	5.5	41.1
1958	9.5	1.3	−0.9	0.6	−0.1	10.5	55.5
1959	3.4	5.3	1.1	14.0	−18.2	5.5	18.7
1960	−0.8	3.3	−1.2	4.5	7.2	13.0	37.3
1961	23.4	3.1	7.1	−6.8	−7.0	19.8	35.1
1962	53.6	12.8	5.1	−9.4	6.1	68.3	100.6
1963	122.8	23.6	10.0	−11.0	−17.9	127.5	94.2
1964	369.7	81.7	32.5	−7.2	−37.0	439.8	65.8
1965	1,464.0	395.5	237.3	−6.8	−17.6	2,072.3	193.9

Source: Bank Indonesia, Annual Report, various issues

Much of this lending was "command credits" to state enterprises that did not need to demonstrate creditworthiness to qualify. In early 1965, 60 percent of new credit was mandatorily earmarked for state and cooperative enterprises. Political considerations dominated the specific allocation of credit, with President Sukarno's prestige projects receiving special priority. Ceiling interest rates for bank advances, which were far below the rate of inflation, were evaded through the use of administrative charges and profit-sharing arrangements. State enterprises may have been able to obtain credit at legal rates but, as Arndt (1971, p. 382) notes, this was immaterial, since neither they nor the state banks were under any effective accounting control and would not feel compelled to avoid losses. Indeed, state banks were implicated in massive illegal speculation in the market for SPP export–import link certificates in May 1965, an incident which may have precipitated their merger with the central bank. As bank credit for private firms became unavailable without political connections, the "unorganized" credit market centered on Chinese moneylenders became an import source of credit. Beginning in April 1965, in compliance with Sukarno's "New Course" (*Banting Stir*), credit was to be allocated only for the expansion of production on estates and farms and in key industries. None was officially set aside for imports, which were in any case to become a state monopoly by 1966.

With the liberalization came a dramatic change in monetary policy. After the "currency reform" of December 1965, which introduced the "new rupiah," the government implemented restrictive credit policies in

January and March 1966 without adequately adjusting interest rate ceilings. Arndt (1971, p. 382) reports that in the first months of 1966 moneylenders of the unorganized market publicly advertised interest rates of 15–20 percent per month. The most important measures aimed at restructuring the banking system and monetary policy were announced on October 3, 1966, the same day that import licensing ended and the BE system was extended. Interest charges were raised from their index levels of 26–53 percent a year (including commission charges) to between 6 and 9 percent per month. Lending interest rates by economic sector from 1966 through 1973 are presented by Pitt (1988, appendix tables 6.3 and 6.4). In practice, the cost of bank borrowing also included a 3 percent per month administrative charge and 2 percent per month in other charges. In comparison, interest rates in the unorganized money market ranged between 20 and 28 percent per month by the end of 1966. Short- and medium-term credits were severely restricted. Overdrafts were harshly penalized, and drawing uncovered checks was considered a criminal act punishable by death. Longer-term credits were strictly limited by the central bank. Credits to finance imports were entirely forbidden. Prefinancing of exports was prohibited and export credit was limited to 40 percent of the value of the confirmed exchange contract. Banks were instructed to stop discriminating between state enterprises and private firms, and "command credits" were terminated. Table 6.4 demonstrates the effect of this new policy in redirecting credit and reducing its volume.

The most significant effect of changes in monetary policy is seen in the dramatic slowdown of money growth between 1966 and 1967 (table 6.5). The dramatic increase in the rate of growth of narrow money (currency plus demand deposits) between 1960 and 1966, from a 12-month moving-average rate of 37.1 percent a year in December 1960 to a peak of 866 percent in August 1966, is matched by a fall almost as dramatic after 1966: by the end of 1967 it was down to 112 percent, and had fallen to 58 percent by the end of 1969. The primary cause of the reduction was the adoption of a balanced budget by the central government. Nonetheless the rate of growth remained large in absolute terms, as lending to public and private sector enterprises continued. Details of the factors affecting the growth of the money supply during the period 1965–72 are provided by Pitt (1988, appendix table 6.5).

The real supply of money, in contrast, fell sharply in the early 1980s, a decline that bottomed out during 1966 (table 6.5). In January 1966, the real stock of money was only a quarter of what it had been in 1960 and only half of what it had been just six months earlier. Such declines are characteristic of hyperinflation: economic agents expecting high rates of price inflation seek to reduce their real money balances and hence bid up prices faster than the money supply increases. Conversely, after 1966 the growth of the money supply outstripped that of the price level as agents sought to

Table 6.4 Total outstanding credit according to sector and purpose

Year (end of period)	Total credit outstanding (Rp million)	Increase in outstanding credits over sector previous period (%)	Distribution according to sector (%)		Distribution according to utilization (%)				
			Government	Private	Production	Export	Misc./special projects		
1965	997	—	57.3	42.7	13.5	10.2		76.3	
1966									
I	2,043	104.9	68.2	31.8	56.3	17.5	9.4		16.8
II	3,251	59.0	60.4	39.6	54.9	16.1	16.6		12.4
III	4,600	41.5	57.5	42.5	57.3	13.8	19.6		9.3
IV	6,342	37.8	59.8	40.2	59.8	14.8	18.0		7.4
1967									
I	7,639	20.4	54.5	45.5	54.9	21.4	16.5		7.2
II	12,430	62.7	53.0	47.0	57.1	20.6	16.5		5.7
Year	31,195	391.9[a]	55.6	44.4	44.9	15.6		39.5	
1968 Year	126,755	306.3	64.4	35.6	43.7	8.0		48.3	
1969 Year	245,434	93.6	53.4	46.6	39.4	8.6		52.0	
1970 Year	362,352	47.6	43.5	56.5	46.3	7.8		45.9	
1971 Year	495,363	36.7	39.8	60.2	50.1	6.4		43.5	
1972 Year	657,692	32.8	35.5	64.5	46.4	5.4		48.2	

—, not applicable.

[a] Over previous year.

Source: Biro Pusat Statistik, *Statistik Keuangan*, various issues

Table 6.5 Real and nominal money supply, 1960–1968

Year (month)	Currency (billion Rp)	Demand deposits (billion Rp)	Money supply (billion Rp)	Money supply change over 12 months	Prices change over 12 months	Real money supply (Dec 1960 = 100)
Dec 1960	34.079	13.757	47.836	37.1	29.5	100.0
Dec 1961	48.541	19.102	67.643	41.4	76.8	80.0
Dec 1962	102.280	33.618	135.898	100.9	156.8	62.6
Dec 1963	175.460	87.900	263.360	93.8	118.0	53.2
Dec 1964	453.100	222.000	675.100	156.3	135.2	57.9
1965						
Jan	509.4	214.8	724.2	172.3	183.4	46.7
Feb	564.3	187.8	752.1	171.5	177.7	42.2
Mar	629.3	193.7	823.0	180.9	127.6	49.7
Apr	665.9	207.8	873.7	173.9	189.9	51.7
May	707.2	305.0	1,012.2	196.0	199.6	57.3
Jun	812.9	304.0	1,116.9	204.3	212.6	59.1
Jul	911.5	338.6	1,250.1	214.1	260.9	55.4
Aug	1,016.0	369.5	1,385.5	229.9	286.0	52.6
Sep	1,188.9	438.8	1,627.7	247.8	290.0	50.9
Oct	1,364.0	516.0	1,880.0	262.9	374.3	44.9
Nov	1,549.7	641.1	2,190.8	283.3	433.4	43.5
Dec	1,966.6	615.4	2,582.0	282.5	594.4	31.9
1966						
Jan	2,478.0	834.1	3,312.1	357.3	704.0	26.6
Feb	3,436.4	1,057.5	4,493.9	497.5	740.1	30.0
Mar	4,261.2	1,427.6	5,688.8	591.2	1,078.2	29.1
Apr	5,305.9	1,609.2	6,915.1	691.5	1,164.7	32.4
May	7,184.8	2,010.4	9,195.2	808.4	1,191.4	40.3
Jun	8,363.0	1,905.0	10,268.0	819.3	1,526.7	33.5
Jul	9,287.8	2,028.1	11,315.9	805.2	1,369.4	34.1
Aug	10,887.1	2,502.4	13,387.5	866.3	1,385.3	34.3
Sep	12,027.5	2,445.6	14,473.1	789.2	1,296.0	32.4
Oct	13,139.3	3,143.2	16,283.0	766.1	1,169.0	30.7
Nov	14,091.7	3,731.6	17,823.3	714.6	1,045.9	30.9
Dec	15,720.1	5,304.3	21,024.4	714.3	635.4	35.3
1967						
Jan	15,924	7,108	23,032	595.4	420.8	35.5
Feb	16,961	6,685	23,646	426.2	417.8	30.5
Mar	17,647	6,970	24,617	332.7	312.3	30.6
Apr	18,923	8,139	27,062	291.3	279.1	33.4
May	21,475	9,309	30,784	234.8	254.3	38.1
Jun	22,660	10,330	32,990	221.3	171.8	39.5
Jul	24,719	11,580	36,298	220.8	156.6	40.6
Aug	26,209	12,336	38,545	187.9	129.5	43.0
Sep	27,766	11,411	39,177	170.7	121.8	39.6
Oct	28,758	14,133	42,891	163.4	99.8	40.4
Nov	29,902	15,589	45,491	155.2	122.0	35.5
Dec	34,585	17,134	51,719	146.0	112.2	41.0
1968						
Jan	37,145	20,089	57,234	148.5	171.8	32.4
Feb	39,729	21,443	61,172	158.7	148.5	31.7
Mar	42,304	20,297	62,601	154.3	147.0	31.5
Apr	46,297	23,835	70,131	159.1	130.9	37.5
May	51,058	28,172	79,229	157.4	145.0	40.0

Year (month)	Currency (billion Rp)	Demand deposits (billion Rp)	Money supply (billion Rp)	Money supply change over 12 months	Prices change over 12 months	Real money supply (Dec 1960 = 100)
Jun	58,415	31,544	89,960	172.7	143.6	44.3
Jul	60,603	36,309	96,912	167.0	148.9	45.7
Aug	61,826	32,755	94,580	145.4	145.0	43.0
Sep	64,881	33,414	98,295	150.9	122.5	44.6
Oct	66,699	35,398	102,097	138.0	104.8	47.0
Nov	67,897	36,029	103,927	128.5	75.8	46.1
Dec	78,163	35,522	113,685	119.8	85.1	48.7

Sources: money supply, Bulletin of Indonesian Economic Studies, various issues, and Biro Pusat Statistik, Warta BPS, various issues; price index, provided by Biro Pusat Statistik

increase real money balances in light of the new policy regime (see Appendix to this chapter).

The period 1966–7 is often depicted as a time of liquidity crisis. There was indeed a physical shortage of banknotes, which led to the use of promissory notes as a limited substitute for currency. The printing presses were incapable of producing sufficient currency to meet the government's needs in late 1965, particularly to pay the enormous New Year's salary bonuses that it had promised civil servants. Thus the "currency reform" of December 1965 was born. By introducing a "new rupiah" equal to 1,000 "old rupiahs" the government was able to make use of a warehoused stock of old but uncirculated bills of Rp 50 and Rp 100 denominations.

In early 1967, the government decided that the emphasis of policy should shift from halting inflation to "stimulating production." Interest rates were lowered and credit restrictions eased, although a priority credit ration system continued to exist. In 1968, the BNI conglomerate was broken up into its pre-1965 parts, with the Bank Indonesia returning to its role as a pure central bank. It was given limited autonomy by the government and a flexible ceiling on advances to the government was reestablished. The government kept to its balanced budget promise, although government agencies, such as the rice procurement agency BULOG, received large-scale advances in certain years. In October 1968, the Bank Indonesia authorized state banks to increase interest rates on time deposits significantly (Pitt, 1988, appendix table 6.6), offering a subsidy to the state banks to cover part of the cost. The deposits responded strongly, with new net additions in 1968 which were quadruple those of the previous year.

Fiscal Policy

The government budget was chronically in deficit in every post-Independence year before the liberalization. The deficit as a share of government revenues rose from 11.4 percent in 1960 to 163 percent in 1965; in the first quarter of 1966, it reached 618 percent of revenue. As table 6.6 demonstrates, the budget deficit rose not because the state's share of GDP grew rapidly and ahead of its tax receipts, but rather because the government sector could not shrink as fast as real tax revenues. The share of government expenditure in GDP peaked in 1961, and was only slightly more than half that peak in 1965. By 1965, government revenue was only 3.9 percent of GDP – unusually small by any standard.

In November 1965, less than two months after the attempted coup, the government sought to restrain budgetary deficits by ordering state enterprises to set prices that at least covered the costs of production. Subsidies on many other goods were reduced. For example, the official price of gasoline rose from Rp 4 to Rp 250 per liter in November, and then increased again a few weeks later to Rp 1,000 per liter, a 250-fold increase! Similar increases were enacted for railway, airline, and bus fares, postal and telegraph services, and other government services. The November 1965 budgetary package also called for tying civil service salaries to the cost of a basket of goods which met "minimum physical needs," the halt or slowdown of many development projects, and the sale of most of the government's fleet of motor vehicles, and mandated that interdepartmental transfers be in the form of recorded bank transactions. The

Table 6.6 The budget, 1951–1968 (percent)

Year	Ratio of trade taxes to revenue	Ratio of expenditure to GDP	Ratio of revenue to GDP	Ratio of deficit to GDP
1951	66.3	n.a.	n.a.	n.a.
1952	54.7	n.a.	n.a.	n.a.
1953	43.4	n.a.	n.a.	n.a.
1954	32.1	17.0	12.9	4.1
1955	35.9	13.3	11.6	1.7
1956	46.3	14.7	13.6	1.1
1957	47.3	15.6	12.4	3.2
1958	43.0	13.5	9.1	4.4
1959	35.3	15.6	8.2	7.4
1960	45.1	14.9	12.8	2.1
1961	34.2	18.7	13.2	5.5
1962	26.0	9.1	5.5	3.6
1963	31.1	10.3	5.0	5.3
1964	33.4	9.5	4.1	5.4
1965	29.3	10.6	3.9	6.7
1966	43.0	9.3	4.1	5.2
1967	32.4	10.3	10.0	0.3
1968	27.6	9.3	9.3	0.0

n.a., not available.
Sources: Rosendale, 1978, p. 158; Biro Pusat Statistik, Statistik Keuangan, 1972–3

subsidization of petroleum products alone had added Rp 150 billion to the deficit, almost equal to the government's revenue for the first quarter of 1965, and the government hoped to transform a large subsidy into a major revenue earner. November's revised budget estimates assumed that 40 percent would come from the tax on petroleum products – a target that could be achieved only if demand for petroleum products fell hardly at all in response to the 250-fold price rise. Demonstrations by the student organization KAMI in January 1966 led to a 50 percent rollback of gasoline and kerosene prices, and made the November budget worthless.

There was an effort to intensify tax collection efforts in late 1965 as well as the announced imposition of a new turnover tax. Indirect taxation was expected to contribute approximately 80 percent of budget revenues. Indirect tax rates were raised and resulted in a general sales tax of 20 percent – 50 percent on luxuries, a 5 percent retail surtax (revolution stamp), and excise taxes on beer, cigarettes, and sugar of 50 percent, 70 percent, and 10 percent respectively. Personal and corporate tax rates were revamped as well. Tax collectors were sent to the homes of the wealthy, and assessed income tax on the basis of their observed standard of living.

The budget deficit swelled enormously in the first half of 1966; deficits were 618 percent and 411 percent of revenue in the first two quarters respectively – the budget was certainly not the focus of government attention. The key budgetary act of the liberalization came in June and July 1966 when the MPRS called for a balanced budget and the government committed itself to its achievement. The government had already stopped work on President Sukarno's "special projects" and most other projects that did not promise a quick return. It restricted official travel and entertainment, cut the housing subsidies of civil servants, and left unwanted civil servants with falling real salaries. New tax schedules for corporate and personal income taxation were announced in April but, in the face of public opposition, the new turnover tax was never imposed. A further concerted drive to intensify tax collection efforts began in the third quarter of 1966. The deficit fell dramatically in the last two quarters of 1966 – to 69 percent and 55 percent of revenue respectively – and nominal government expenditure in the third quarter was actually less than that in the second quarter.

In December 1966, a budget for 1967 was approved which showed receipts and expenditures in balance. This was certainly not the first budget ever to make such a claim, but there were important differences: this government considered achieving a balanced budget crucial in demonstrating its credibility both to the domestic economy, which habitually discounted such claims, and to the community of aid donors, which insisted on such measures. Two new sources of revenue made important contributions. One was the profits on the sale of foreign exchange surrendered by exporters and then sold on the BE market. The second and more important source was the proceeds of the sale of foreign credits in the form of Aid-BEs. On the expenditure side, the government decreed that it would not permit supplementary budgets, a recurring feature of the past, and abolished all "special budgets." The latter had been created for the use of the President in carrying out special projects, including monument building and other prestige projects, for which no public accounting was ever made. There was to be just one budget and it was to be under the control of the Ministry of Finance, which strictly enforced budgetary ceilings. The government came very close to achieving their balanced-budget goal in 1967 and, according to budgetary definitions, achieved a balanced budget in 1968 (table 6.6).[1]

Table 6.7 demonstrates the declining share of tax receipts in the years preceding liberalization, as well as the large share of indirect taxes in total receipts. Tax receipts as a share of GDP rose over 70 percent in 1967, reflecting both new taxes and the increased intensity of collection efforts. This is most marked in the case of direct taxes. The share of total tax receipts in GDP continued its rise in the ensuing years, with direct tax revenue overtaking indirect tax revenue in 1972, largely as a result of higher oil company tax receipts.

Table 6.7 Central government tax receipts, 1960–1972

	Direct taxes		Indirect taxes		Total tax	
Year	Revenue (billion Rp)	Percentage of GDP	Revenue (billion Rp)	Percentage of GDP	Revenue (billion Rp)	Percentage of GDP
1960	8.7	2.2	40.9	10.5	49.6	12.7
1961	11.9	2.5	40.1	8.5	52.0	11.1
1962	17.8	1.3	54.6	4.1	72.4	5.4
1963	33.3	1.0	126.9	4.0	160.2	5.0
1964	70.3	1.0	209.4	2.9	279.8	3.9
1965	144.3	0.6	774.1	3.3	918.3	3.9
1966	1.8	0.6	10.7	3.4	12.5	4.0
1967	14.7	1.7	44.2	5.2	58.9	6.9
1968	51.0	2.5	94.0	4.7	145.0	7.2
1969	83.6	3.1	134.9	5.0	218.5	8.0
1970	113.4	3.4	188.3	5.6	301.7	9.0
1971	162.6	4.3	228.4	6.0	391.0	10.3
1972	272.8	6.0	241.3	5.3	514.3	11.3

Sources: 1960–7, Bank Indonesia, *Annual Report*, various issues; 1968–72, Biro Pusat Statistik, *Statistik Keuangan*, 1972–3, p. 26

[1] The trade liberalization of 1955 had an effect on the fiscal deficit similar to the liberalization of 1966. Redirection of import premiums into tariff revenue and illegal trade into legal trade helped reduce the deficit as a share of GDP from 4.1 percent in 1954 to 1.7 percent and 1.1 percent in 1955 and 1956 respectively.

Relaxation of Price Controls

Price control, characteristic of Indonesia since colonial times, reached an unprecedented level in 1965. The government had failed to include adjustment of nominally fixed prices in their campaign against triple-digit inflation. The result was massive corruption and diversion into black markets. State enterprises required massive subsidies because of their inefficiency but also as a result of the low prices for which they were forced to sell their products and services. Direct allocation of certain industrial inputs, such as weaving yarns and cloves, resulted in black-market sales of as much as half the allocated quantities.

As part of the ill-fated budget package for 1967 described above, the government declared its intention to end subsidies to state enterprises and insisted that they price their products so as to cover costs and to make a profit if possible. The ensuing massive price increases were partially reversed in the face of street demonstrations in January 1967, but later that year, when the new government felt secure, these prices were increased again.

In many cases, the increases were insufficient to eliminate black-market activity. Violent student opposition continued to delay the end of price control throughout 1966. By January 1967, the quarterly rate of subsidies to state enterprises was Rp 5.5 billion – three times the expenditure on civil servant salaries (Oei, 1968, p. 164). The new foreign exchange regulations introduced in 1966 explicitly recognized a list of "essential" commodities for which a special Rp 10 exchange rate applied. This was an apparent effort to conceal price subsidies in the government's budget.

Significant increases in prices occurred in November 1966 and again in February 1967. Price increases by eightfold or tenfold were common. Petrol prices were now Rp 4 per liter (new rupiah), 1,000 times their December 1965 level. The end of the newsprint subsidy led to an immediate 17.5-fold increase in its price and a fourfold increase in the price of newspapers. The direct allocation of yarns and other industrial inputs had ceased. The government distribution of "essential" commodities was greatly reduced in 1967 when the Kolognas (National Logistics Command) was reorganized; however, the government continued to intervene in the markets for these politically sensitive goods.

Private Capital Movements

Initial response to the 1967 Foreign Investment Law (briefly described above) was favorable. Over US$2.5 billion of foreign investment in 926 different projects was approved by the Foreign Investment Board between

1967 and 1971. In the 12 years following enactment of the Foreign Investment Law, over US$7.7 billion in foreign investment (known as PMA) had been approved (see table 6.8). Table 6.8 also reveals that 61 percent of foreign investment by value has been in the manufacturing sector, with mining and quarrying a distant second. (Investment in petroleum and banking are excluded from these data since they are not covered by the Foreign Investment Law.) In April 1967, new regulations authorized the reentry of foreign banks into Indonesia. Table 6.9 provides details of the implementation of the measures betweeen 1967 and 1974.

Complaints about the foreign investment process were numerous. Many investors were annoyed by the large bureaucracy that oversaw investment approvals and implementation. Often approvals were required from several ministries and a host of local government agencies. Domestic firms complained about the growth of foreign enterprises and the incentives they received. In 1968, a Domestic Investment Law was passed which provided similar incentives (known as PMDN) to local firms.

Table 6.8 Approvals of foreign investment projects by economic sector, 1967–1979[a] (million US dollars)

Sector	Number of projects 1967–79	Approvals 1967–74	1975–9	1967–79	Distribution of 1967–79 approvals
Agriculture	58	102	69	171	2.2
Forestry	78	475	132	607	7.8
Fishery	23	45	82	127	1.6
Mining and quarrying	11	547	906	1,453	18.3
Manufacturing	466	1,956	2,774	4,730	61.0
Food	53	123	187	310	4.1
Textiles and leather	70	891	314	1,205	15.5
Wood and wood products	12	16	35	51	0.6
Paper and paper products	14	16	101	117	1.5
Chemical and rubber	131	247	578	825	10.6
Nonmetallic minerals	29	233	319	552	7.1
Basic metals	23	234	916	1,150	14.8
Metal products	127	190	319	509	6.6
Other	7	6	7	13	0.1
Construction	63	58	19	77	1.0
Trade and hotels	14	134	49	183	2.3
Wholesale trade	3	11	1	12	0.2
Hotels	11	123	48	171	2.2
Transport and communication	20	32	65	97	1.2
Transportation	19	26	21	47	0.6
Communication	1	6	44	50	0.6
Social and personal services and others	51	195	112	307	3.9
Total	784	3,544	4,209	7,752	100.0

[a] Excludes investment in petroleum and banking.
Source: Bank Indonesia, Annual Reports, various issues

Table 6.9 Foreign investment implementation[a] by sector[b], 1967–1974 (million US dollars)

Sector	1967–9	1970	1971	1972	1973	1974	Total realized investment
Agriculture	9.3	1.8	2.1	3.4	7.9	4.5	29.0
Forestry	15.0	33.0	32.8	31.2	40.9	50.3	283.2
Fishery	3.1	4.7	8.4	3.4	6.5	21.9	48.0
Mining and quarrying	11.7	42.1	61.0	50.7	6.6	44.3	216.4
Manufacturing	34.6	48.4	103.7	171.1	306.7	368.5	1,033.0
Food	9.1	13.8	16.4	15.9	34.8	21.7	111.7
Textiles and leather	2.6	11.3	44.3	77.9	149.5	157.7	443.3
Wood and wood products	—	—	3.1	0.3	0.3	1.8	5.5
Paper and paper products	0.3	0.2	0.3	6.5	5.1	1.5	13.9
Chemical and rubber	8.0	11.4	17.9	21.2	37.1	50.8	146.4
Ferrous metals	1.0	0.7	2.5	4.9	29.3	44.2	82.6
Nonmetallic minerals	⎱ 13.6	⎱ 11.0	⎱ 19.2	⎱ 44.5	11.0	17.7	28.7
Metal products					37.7	72.2	198.2
Other					1.9	0.9	2.8
Construction	1.3	0.2	0.4	2.1	1.5	16.6	22.1
Trade and hotels	1.3	4.0	6.7	4.5	17.9	19.6	54.0
Wholesale trade	n.a.	n.a.	n.a.	n.a.	8.4	—	8.4
Hotels	n.a.	n.a.	n.a.	n.a.	9.5	19.6	29.1
Transport and communication	4.3	1.6	0.9	0.9	0.9	1.1	9.7
Transport	n.a.	n.a.	n.a.	n.a.	0.6	0.7	1.3
Communication	n.a.	n.a.	n.a.	n.a.	0.3	0.4	0.7
Real estate and business services	2.4	2.4	2.3	3.6	4.9	24.9	40.5
Other	—	—	—	—	—	82.2	82.2
Total	83.0	138.0	218.0	271.0	394.0	634.0	2,810.7

—, negligible; n.a., not available.
[a] Implementation is the recorded disbursement on projects approved based upon cash inflows, customs data on imported capital equipment, and the conversion of foreign claims under the DICS scheme.
[b] Excludes investment in petroleum and banking.
Source: Bank Indonesia, Annual Report, various issues

The private claims of foreigners pre-dating 1966 were taken care of by authorizing claimants to convert their claims into special rupiahs having essentially the same advantages as new foreign investment. This scheme, the Debt Investment Conversion Scheme (DICS), permitted these special rupiahs – DICS rupiahs – to be sold to third parties for working capital or used to import capital equipment or material inputs to run an enterprise. If they chose, previously expropriated enterprises were allowed to return with an incentive package at least as good as that provided under the Foreign Investment Law. The Dutch enterprises taken over in 1957 received compensation payments instead.

Private capital inflows were considerable in the immediate post-liberalization period. Table 6.10 provides Rosendale's (1978) estimates of private capital inflows by source for the period 1967–76 together with official estimates, which are widely held to be underestimates. Note than in 1967 and 1968, capital repatriation was a major source of private capital inflow. Most of this was capital flight kept abroad which reentered Indonesia through the DP market; only 10 percent was DICS rupiahs.

Table 6.10 Estimated net private capital inflow, 1967–1976 (million US dollars)

Source		1967	1968	1969	1970	1971	1972	1973	1974	1975	1976
PMA	(gross)	12	26	45	138	218	271	394	634	620	526
	(repayment)						−8	−17	−29	−90	−142
PMDN	(gross)	—	—	12	93	219	211	299	598	253	276
	(repayment)								−12	−93	−219
Foreign banks		—	4	6	2	—	—	—	—	—	—
Repatriation of capital		68	35	12	18	—	—	—	—	—	—
Bank deposits		—	—	26	72	2	226	287	12	−10	38
Merchants' L/C		—	—	—	76	172	19	33	124	128	150
Supplier credits[a]		28	−12	−1	−15	—	—	—	—	—	—
Oil exploration		n.a.	46	78	113	207	237	393	807	1,050	1,110
Total		108	99	178	497	818	956	1,389	2,134	1,858	1,739
Official estimate (net)		84	27	64	103	156	427	498	382	−1,439	237

—, negligible; n.a., not available.
[a] Excludes credit received through "red clause" exports.
Source: Rosendale, 1978, p. 99

Appendix

Many traditional hedges against inflation apparently fared very badly in the months before and after the liberalization. Favorite among the wealthy were luxury sedans, such as the Mercedes, and expensive wristwatches (on this subject see the reports of Roeder, 1965, and Cheng, 1964, in the *Far Eastern Economic Review*). Gold bullion and (illegal) dollars seemed likely inflation hedges as well. The data given below are index numbers of prices in the Jakarta free market deflated by the deseasonalized Jakarta 62-item cost of living index. The real value of the Mercedes sedan fell by nearly two thirds between January 1965 and January 1967. Gold and black dollars did not fare very well either – probably because the trade liberalization greatly reduced incentives to smuggle. Rice prices (not seasonally adjusted) just about kept pace with the overall price level while the price of an important nontraded good, firewood and wood charcoal, outperformed the cost of living index but with all its price increase coming in 1966. This reflected, in part, the huge increases in the government-controlled price of kerosene, the competing fuel.

	Mercedes 220S 1962	Gold (24 carat)	Black-market dollars	Rice (whole-sale)	Firewood and charcoal
Jan 1965	100	100	100	100	100
Jul 1965	77	79	76	72	94
Jan 1966	46	120	86	91	93
Jul 1966	33	65	52	67	121
Jan 1967	27	46	33	94	298

The absolute dollar prices of the Mercedes, gold, rice, and a 1950 Jeep are reported below, with rupiah prices converted at the black-market exchange rate. The Mercedes price had probably peaked in 1965; its price was US$5,333 in February 1964 and "free of foreign exchange" imports of such sedans continued until 1965. Note that between January 1965 and January 1967 the Mercedes price fell 19 percent while another motor vehicle, the 1952 Jeep (a model chosen so as to minimize the effect of economic depreciation), registered a price increase of 37 percent. Thus the luxury car market suffered a setback relative to more utilitarian vehicles. It is conjectured that many displaced rent earners were forced to dump their luxury sedans on the market in response to the drastically reduced possibilities of earning rents under the new trade regime. In January 1965, the Mercedes was worth 122 tons of rice but by January 1967 its value had fallen to only 42 tons.

	Mercedes 220S 1962	Gold (24 carat) (g)	Rice (whole-sale) (100 kg)	Jeep
Jan 1965	5,867	1.20	4.80	667
Jul 1965	5,978	1.25	5.22	614
Jan 1966	3,111	1.67	5.87	467
Jul 1966	3,707	1.51	6.44	585
Jan 1967	4,762	1.67	11.25	913

Economic Performance Following Liberalization

Figure 7.1 charts the time pattern of 18 economic indicators before and after the introduction of trade liberalization. It is quite clear from these charts that the performance of the Indonesian economy improved enormously in the years after 1966.

Legal exports, which were actually declining before 1966, grew rapidly after 1969, despite historically low levels of export prices. Legal exports benefited from the higher real effective exchange rate (table 5.11), the reduced black-market premium (table 5.16), and the diversion of illegal trade into legal channels.

Imports grew rapidly as well. The gap between the major import rate, applicable to goods considered "essential," and the other import rate ("less essential") fell considerably beginning in 1966 (table 5.11). The variance of these exchange rates also fell after liberalization. The GDP, which was almost flat in the years before liberalization, increased steeply after 1967. Manufacturing value added, which had actually been falling, increased at a faster rate than GDP, as did gross domestic capital formation.

The stabilization attempts of the government were seemingly effective. The rate of price inflation was reduced from 635 percent in 1966 to single-digit levels in just a few years. The rate of growth of the money supply and the budget deficit mirrored this pattern.

The data underlying figure 7.1 and, to the extent that the more limited data available permit, the output and employment response of individual manufacturing subsectors are examined in greater detail below.

Prices

The rate of inflation fell dramatically in the months following liberalization. In October 1966, the month in which the import license system was abolished, the Jakarta cost of living index was 1,169 percent higher than it had been 12 months earlier (table 7.1). Over the next 12 months, this price index rose only 100 percent, and over the calendar years 1969–71, price

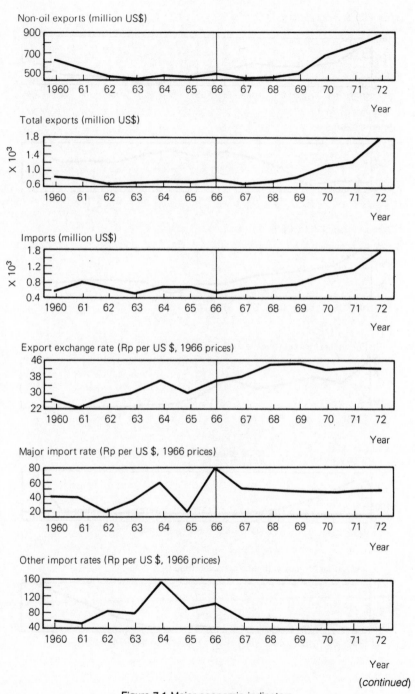

Figure 7.1 Major economic indicators

(*continued*)

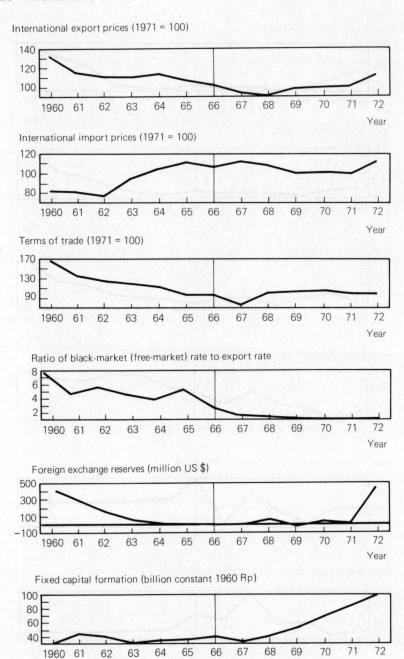

Figure 7.1 (*continued*)

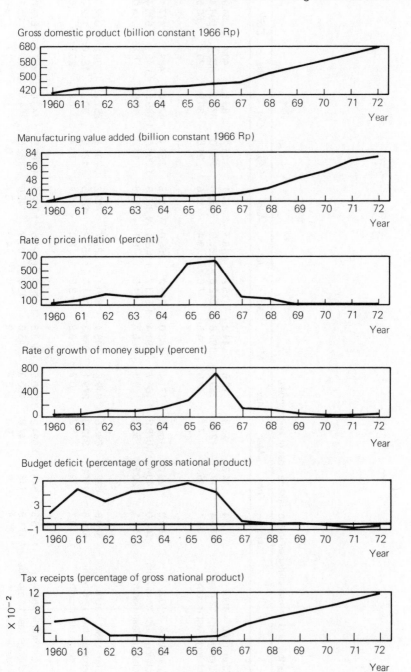

Figure 7.1 (*continued*)

Table 7.1 Monthly and annual changes in the Jakarta cost of living index

	Jan	Feb	Mar	Apr	May	Jun	Jul	Aug	Sep	Oct	Nov	Dec
1965												
Price index (Jan 1966 = 100)	12.4	14.3	13.3	13.6	14.2	15.2	18.1	21.1	25.7	33.6	40.4	64.9
Percentage change last 12 months	183.4	177.7	127.6	189.9	199.6	212.6	260.9	286.0	290.0	374.3	433.4	594.4
Percentage change last month	33.1	15.0	−7.1	2.0	4.5	7.0	19.4	16.6	21.6	30.9	20.5	60.5
1966												
Price index (Jan 1966 = 100)	100.0	120.2	156.6	171.4	183.0	246.2	266.0	313.5	358.1	426.0	463.3	477.1
Percentage change last 12 months	704.0	740.1	1,078.2	1,164.7	1,191.4	1,523.7	1,369.4	1,385.3	1,296.0	1,169.0	1,045.9	635.4
Percentage change last month	54.1	20.2	30.3	9.5	6.7	34.5	8.1	17.8	14.2	18.9	8.8	3.0
1967												
Price index (Jan 1966 = 100)	520.8	622.2	645.6	649.8	648.4	669.1	682.7	719.3	794.1	851.2	1,028.5	1,012.3
Percentage change last 12 months	420.8	417.8	312.3	279.1	254.3	171.8	156.7	129.5	121.8	99.8	122.0	112.2
Percentage change last month	9.2	19.5	3.8	0.7	−0.2	3.2	2.0	5.4	10.4	7.2	20.8	−1.6
1968												
Price index (Jan 1966 = 100)	1,415.3	1,546.0	1,594.2	1,500.5	1,588.3	1,629.7	1,699.5	1,762.5	1,766.9	1,743.6	1,807.9	1,873.8
Percentage change last 12 months	171.8	148.5	147.0	130.9	145.0	143.6	148.9	145.0	122.5	104.8	75.8	85.1
Percentage change last month	39.8	9.2	9.2	−5.9	5.9	2.6	4.3	3.7	0.3	−1.3	3.7	3.6

1969

Price index (Jan 1966 = 100)	Percentage change last 12 months	Percentage change last month
1,914.4	35.3	2.2
1,945.5	25.8	1.6
1,988.6	24.7	2.2
1,905.0	27.0	− 4.2
1,893.0	19.2	− 0.6
1,867.5	14.6	− 1.3
1,902.5	11.9	1.9
1,960.4	11.2	3.0
1,953.1	10.5	− 0.4
1,998.8	14.6	2.3
2,020.2	11.7	1.1
2,059.1	9.9	1.9

1970

Price index (Jan 1966 = 100)	Percentage change last 12 months	Percentage change last month
2,209.2	15.4	7.3
2,210.1	13.6	0.0
2,200.4	10.7	− 0.4
2,166.8	13.7	− 1.5
2,172.1	14.7	0.2
2,186.6	17.2	0.8
2,194.8	15.4	0.3
2,189.6	11.7	− 0.2
2,150.1	10.1	− 1.8
2,145.1	7.3	− 0.2
2,227.9	10.3	3.9
2,242.0	8.9	0.6

1971

Price index (Jan 1966 = 100)	Percentage change last 12 months	Percentage change last month
2,306.5	4.4	2.9
2,365.6	7.0	2.6
2,371.5	7.8	0.2
2,338.8	7.9	− 1.4
2,284.5	5.2	− 2.3
2,240.4	2.4	− 1.9
2,241.3	2.1	0.0
2,221.3	1.5	− 0.9
2,214.2	3.0	− 0.3
2,238.5	4.4	1.1
2,318.3	4.1	3.6
2,315.1	3.3	− 0.1

1972

Price index (Jan 1966 = 100)	Percentage change last 12 months	Percentage change last month
2,333.1	1.2	0.8
2,389.8	1.0	2.4
2,390.7	0.8	0.0
2,384.1	1.9	− 0.3
2,362.5	3.4	− 0.9
2,328.4	3.9	− 1.4
2,311.1	3.1	− 0.7
2,320.4	4.5	0.4
2,355.9	6.4	1.5
2,444.1	9.2	3.7
2,711.2	16.9	10.9
2,890.7	24.9	6.6

Source: data provided by Biro Pusat Statistik

increases were at single-digit levels. By any standard this record of price stabilization is remarkable.

Table 7.2 provides data on the annual movements of the four components of the Jakarta cost of living index, as well as the GDP deflator, and indices of the prices of domestically produced goods, imported goods, and agricultural exports. Examining the components of the cost of living index, it is interesting to note that all components grew at about the same rate from 1966 through 1972 except for apparel, a category which consists entirely of import-competing tradeables. Both "Other" and "Housing" include mostly services and other nontradeables, while the "Food" component is dominated by rice, in whose market the government has heavily intervened. The ready availability of food from the United States during the late 1960s and early 1970s certainly contributed to keeping its price below world-market levels (and the "Food" component of the index below the "General" index in 1969–71) except in years of drought such as 1972.

The GDP deflator moved essentially in accord with the Jakarta cost of living index – indeed, they share a common data base. Comparison of the imported-goods index with the other price indices is suggestive of the impact that the trade liberalization may have had on the price of the set of import-competing tradeables that make up this index. It seems likely that most of the difference between the increase in the import price level and other price indices is attributable to liberalization, and most of this to the elimination of the import premium rather than to a reduction in the effective exchange rate. Nevertheless, the trade liberalization *per se* most likely had only a small part to play in the reduction of the rate of inflation from over 1,000 percent per year to less than 10 percent. That feat is more the result of the financial discipline of the government.

Real Wages

One of the more remarkable developments of Indonesia's economic decline in the 1950s and early 1960s and its rapid recovery in the post-liberalization period is the dramatic swing in real wages. Every indication is that real wages fell by at least half from the early 1950s to the mid-1960s, and then rebounded just as dramatically by 1971. Table 7.3 provides time series data on wage rates in different types of employment. In column 1, note that the real annual wage in 1973 rupiahs in all large-scale manufacturing fell from the initial level of Rp 110,300 in 1954 to Rp 46,000 in 1962. This represents a fall of nearly 60 percent in real wages over eight years. Real wages remained near this level until 1967, and by 1973 had returned to 77 percent of their 1954 levels. The dramatic fall in wages before the liberalization is confirmed by other wage series. For example, the real

Table 7.2 Major price indices, 1963–1972 (1966 = 100)

| Year | Jakarta cost of living index[a] | | | | | GDP deflator | Retail price index of domestically produced goods | Retail price index of imported goods | Wholesale price index of agricultural exports |
	Food	Housing	Apparel	Other	General				
1963	1.6	1.1	1.6	1.1	1.5	1.1	0.91	1.1	n.a.
1964	3.6	2.7	1.1	2.6	3.4	2.3	1.8	2.4	n.a.
1965	28.3	18.0	17.3	15.9	23.7	7.7	8.6	12.14	n.a.
1966	169.9	174.0	165.6	194.4	174.5	100.0	100.0	100.0	100.0
1967	418.4	432.0	229.6	293.5	370.2	264.7	297.0	200.0	217.0
1968	689.2	734.3	591.8	717.8	685.2	582.5	652.7	454.7	608.0
1969	748.0	824.5	601.3	843.4	753.0	716.0	872.5	549.6	938.0
1970	757.5	1,226.3	713.0	943.2	820.0	818.2	854.4	562.0	856.0
1971	774.3	1,238.0	731.7	977.5	840.1	868.6	976.1	531.0	770.0
1972	1,120.0	1,255.9	729.6	1,012.3	1,057.2	972.8	1,060.0	548.2	816.0

n.a., not available.

[a] Values are for the month of December; the base is the average of 12 months of 1966.

Source: Biro Pusat Statistik, *Statistical Pocketbook of Indonesia*, various years.

Table 7.3 Real wages in Indonesia, 1951–1972

Year	1 Average yearly wage in large-scale manufacturing (1973 Rp)	2 Average yearly wage in medium-scale manufacturing (1973 Rp)	3 Average monthly wage on estates (1966 Rp)
1951	n.a.	n.a.	413
1952	n.a.	n.a.	524
1953	n.a.	n.a.	545
1954	110,300	n.a.	431
1955	102,600	n.a.	367
1956	100,400	n.a.	384
1957	97,600	n.a.	394
1958	80,500	27,500	344
1959	78,400	35,000	309
1960	71,600	33,300	314
1961	69,500	35,000	278
1962	46,000	20,700	n.a.
1963	50,400	20,800	202
1964	46,800	n.a.	n.a.
1965	51,400	23,500	n.a.
1966	55,200	18,700	268
1967	67,800	n.a.	275
1968	n.a.	n.a.	238
1969	n.a.	n.a.	291
1970	n.a.	n.a.	348
1971	74,100	37,600	348
1972	83,700	43,200	353

n.a., not available.
Source: Pitt, 1981a, p. 194

wage paid for handrolling 1,000 paper clove cigarettes (*kretek*) in Java fell 53 percent in real terms from 1951 to August 1964 (Castles, 1968).

Real wage data for some nonmanufacturing sectors demonstrate a pattern similar to that of manufacturing. Data on the average monthly wage (including payments in kind) paid on estates in constant 1966 rupiahs indicate a trend similar to that of the other time series. Real wages in large-scale manufacturing and on estates fell by almost equal percentages (54 percent) between 1954 and 1963, and then by 1973 regained a real wage of about 75 percent of that of 1954. Surprisingly, real wages paid to estate workers in 1938 were almost 80 percent higher than in 1972. Papanek (1980) reports that these real wages failed to increase further by 1978.

Certainly, the dramatic flexibility of wages in Indonesia is clear evidence that the labor market functioned fairly freely. Undoubtedly the liberalization played an important part in the rebound of real wages after the mid-1960s, both by increasing the level of overall economic activity and by altering the intersectoral distribution of economic activities in favor of relatively labor intensive ones. The latter issue has been addressed at length by Pitt (1981a).

Imports

Table 7.4 reports three measures of the real flow of imports during the period 1963–72. Column 6 of table 7.4 provides annual data on flows of merchandise import in current US dollars, column 7 provides a volume index of imports constructed by Rosendale (1978), and column 8 provides the national accounts estimate of merchandise plus nonfactor service imports in constant 1960 prices. All three measures concur that 1966, the year that the liberalization commenced, was the year with the lowest level of imports in the period 1963–72 – indeed, table 5.2 reveals that the volume of imports in 1966 was the lowest in the history of independent Indonesia. All three measures show significant growth in import flows thereafter. The volume measure in 1970 was more than double its 1966 value. Columns 9 and 10 of table 7.4 provide two measures of the share of merchandise plus nonfactor service imports (national accounts definition) in GDP. The series based on current price data (column 10) behaves oddly over time. In particular, the sharp movements between 1963 and 1967 seem unreasonably large. The same is true for similarly defined export series (column 5). It seems likely that in a hyperinflation the measurement of current prices falls prey to large errors – timing of surveys and methods of averaging to obtain annual averages become crucial in such circumstances. We therefore focus on the constant price share series (columns 9

Table 7.4 Measures of export and import flows, 1963–1972

	Export					Import					Openness	
Year	(1)	(2)	(3)	(4)	(5)	(6)	(7)	(8)	(9)	(10)	(11)	(12)
1963	697.9	50.6	48.7	11.9	9.1	521.4	54.8	47.5	11.6	9.3	23.4	18.4
1964	724.2	57.6	54.5	12.8	12.3	679.9	56.3	51.7	12.2	13.1	25.0	25.3
1965	707.7	59.3	56.2	13.1	5.3	694.7	45.4	47.5	11.0	5.7	24.1	11.0
1966	678.7	57.6	55.6	12.6	12.8	526.7	43.2	45.5	10.3	22.1	22.9	34.9
1967	665.4	65.1	55.5	12.4	8.8	649.2	50.7	58.3	13.0	16.9	25.4	25.6
1968	730.7	72.3	61.3	12.8	16.4	715.8	71.1	62.3	13.0	16.4	25.8	27.8
1969	853.7	82.9	70.0	13.2	9.0	780.7	77.2	75.0	14.1	14.8	27.3	23.8
1970	1,108.1	92.3	82.0	14.4	12.8	1,001.5	102.5	84.0	14.7	15.8	29.1	28.7
1971	1,233.6	100.0	92.0	15.1	13.4	1,102.8	100.0	92.0	15.1	16.0	30.1	29.4
1972	1,777.7	121.5	113.0	17.3	16.0	1,561.7	125.3	117.0	17.9	18.8	35.2	32.9

(1), (6), Merchandise (million US$).
(2), (7), Volume index (1971 = 100).
(3), (8), Merchandise plus nonfactor services (1960 prices, billion Rp).
(4), (9), Merchandise plus services as percentage of GDP (1960 prices).
(5), (10), Merchandise plus services as percentage of GDP (current prices).
(11) Total merchandise trade plus nonfactor services as percentage of GDP (1960 constant prices).
(12) Total merchandise trade plus nonfactor services as percentage of GDP (current prices).
Source: Biro Pusat Statistik, *Pendapatan Nasional Indonesia*, various issues, except columns 2 and 7 which are from Rosendale, 1975, p. 73; 1981, p. 167

and 4), which behave less erratically. These series demonstrate a rapid increase in the share of imports in GDP – 74 percent between 1966 and 1972.

Exports

Three measures of the real annual flow of exports are found in table 7.4. These measures tell basically the same story: real flows of exports grew fairly rapidly after the commencement of liberalization. Exports in 1972 were nearly triple the 1966 level in current US dollars, and nearly double in terms of volume. The volume index suggests that export response was much faster than the dollar value measure indicates. The share of exports in GDP at constant 1960 prices (column 4) rose from 12.6 percent to 17.3 percent over the same period.

A longer-term perspective on the growth and composition of exports is provided in tables 7.5 and 5.2. Note that the total annual export value in the four years before liberalization, 1962–5, averaged just over US$700 million compared with over US$900 million for the first eight years of the 1950s. As with imports, in the first four years following the introduction of liberalization (1966–9) average annual export value did not increase substantially. One reason for this is the historically low level of the commodity terms of trade during that period (see table 5.2). Export response would also be expected to be slow because most major exports were perennials – such as rubber, coffee, tea, pepper, palm oil, and copra – and investment in these has considerable gestation lags. Nevertheless, the volume indices presented in tables 5.2 and 7.4 reveal very rapid response. The growth of export volume in the first year of liberalization (1966–7) alone was as great as that attained over the previous 15 years. This same level of increase continued through 1976, the last year in table 5.2.

Table 7.5 Composition of exports, 1950–1981 (million US dollars (percent))

Year	Exports						
	Rubber		Petroleum		Other		Total
1950–3	421.3	(45)	174.1	(18)	351.7	(37)	947.1
1954–7	348.9	(38)	247.3	(27)	316.9	(35)	913.1
1958–61	341.2	(41)	262.4	(32)	225.2	(27)	828.8
1962–5	250.3	(36)	255.9	(36)	196.7	(28)	702.9
1966–9	198.5	(27)	280.8	(38)	252.8	(35)	732.1
1970–3	263.9	(14)	861.5	(47)	707.1	(39)	1,832.5
1974–7	464.0	(06)	5,956.0	(70)	2,062.0	(24)	8,482.0
1978–81	911.7	(05)	12,517.2	(65)	5,658.2	(30)	19,087.1

Figures are annual averages for the years indicated.
Source: Biro Pusat Statistik, *Ekspor*, various issues

The liberalization is probably responsible for most of this growth – both by increasing the returns to export production and by increasing legal trade at the expense of illegal trade. There is strong evidence that the latter response may be the most important, as the discussion of the phenomenon of price disparity in chapter 5 suggests. As table 5.3, column 7, indicates, the real effective exchange rate inclusive of price disparity was basically unaffected by liberalization. Elsewhere (Pitt, 1981b), a reduced-form legal export supply equation has been econometrically estimated that measures the effects of the smuggling incentive on the volume of legal smallholder rubber export. Simulation using that supply equation suggests that the diversion of illegal rubber export into legal channels would account for 86 percent of the increased volume of legal smallholder rubber export resulting from a complete liberalization – free trade – in the year 1965. As the price disparity for other major commodities, such as coffee and pepper, is known to have exceeded that of rubber, it should not be surprising to see a rapid increase in legal trade flows as a consequence of its increased attractiveness *vis-à-vis* smuggling. Finally, note from table 7.5 that, while the share of petroleum exports rose sharply after 1969, the rate of growth of non-oil exports was still very large. Annual average non-oil export value rose 2.2 times in 1970–3 compared with 1966–9, and 2.6 times in both 1974–7 and 1978–81 compared with the preceding four years.

Openness of the Economy

Table 7.4 provides two measures of the openness of the economy during the period 1963–72. As noted above, we have some reservations about the use of the trade-to-GDP ratios calculated from national accounts data at current prices. The calculated share of total merchandise trade plus nonfactor services in GDP (column 12) triples between 1965 and 1966 and then falls by nearly a third in the following year. The extremely high rate of inflation during this period makes the measurement of a "current" price difficult and is probably the cause of the problem. Instead, it is preferable to focus on column 11 of table 7.4, which is the same share but defined over constant 1960 prices. Here we see that the economy grew considerably more open in the years following the introduction of liberalization, with the trade share fully 54 percent higher in 1972 than in 1966.

Balance of Payments

Table 7.6 provides data on Indonesia's balance of payments for the years 1966–77. The trade balance was in surplus in 1966, but then fell into deficit for the years 1967–71. Thereafter, it has remained in surplus. The services

Table 7.6 The official balance-of-payments estimates, 1966–1977 (million US dollars)

Item	1966	1967	1968	1969	1970	1971	1972	1973	1974	1975	1976	1977
Exports	714	771	872	995	1,173	1,311	1,793	3,215	7,265	6,888	8,613	10,763
Imports c.i.f.	-671	-891	-926	-1,125	-1,263	-1,390	-1,633	-3,002	-5,290	-6,278	-7,723	-8,450[a]
Services excluding freight	-166	-162	-200	-253	-286	-339	-545	-743	-1,426	-1,746	-1,813	-2,387[a]
Official transfers	15	28	26	47	66	46	51	55	49	27	15	24
Current balance	-108	-254	-225	-336	-310	-372	-334	-475	598	-1,109	-908	-50
Nonmonetary capital												
Private	6	84	27	51	89	144	377	221	-136	-1,704	161	8
Official	100	191	190	215	227	238	293	505	541	755	1,389	1,291
Official monetary capital	13	6	-3	7	-23	55	-15	12	0	103	167	-198
Special drawing rights	0	0	0	0	35	28	30	0	0	0	0	0
Exceptional financing	0	0	0	0	0	0	0	0	0	1,201	278	0
Total of above items	119	281	214	273	328	465	685	738	405	355	1,995	1,101
Reserves and related items[b]	-2	3	15	13	-12	1	-407	-340	-688	857	-902	-997
Errors and omissions	-9	-30	-4	50	-6	-94	56	77	-315	-103	-185	-54

[a] Freight estimated at 13 percent of imports f.o.b.
[b] The minus sign indicates an increase.
Source: Rosendale, 1981, p. 165

balance has remained consistently in deficit (table 7.6), as has the current balance, except in 1974. Much of the recent growth in the services deficit is due to the increased profit remittances of foreign-owned firms. Official transfers and capital grew through 1976. Private capital inflows became substantial in the early 1970s and were almost US$400 million in 1972. Except for 1975, reserves increased substantially every year from 1972 to 1977. At the end of 1977 official reserve assets totaled US$8.45 billion, equivalent to 15 weeks of imports.

Since the liberalization, debt service has been a problem only once – in 1975. That episode, known as the Pertamina crisis, was due in large part to problems with managing liquidity within the state oil company Pertamina, which at the time had substantial independence in conducting its affairs. At the end of the liberalization period in 1971, the ratio of debt service to exports was 7.1 percent. It fell to 4.4 percent two years later but rose to 7.2 percent the next year as a result of Pertamina's difficulties. It continued to rise, peaking at 18.2 percent in 1978 before falling sharply again. Total debt outstanding as a share of GDP was 41 percent in 1973 and had fallen to 34 percent by 1980.

Aggregate Product and Employment

Table 7.7 provides index numbers on the growth of GDP by industrial origin and by expenditure at constant 1960 prices. In 1966, the year that liberalization began, total GDP was about 3 percent lower than it had been five years earlier and private consumption expenditure was 8.5 percent lower. Growth in 1967, the first full year after liberalization, was a mere 1.4 percent. This was partially due to the poor performance of farm agriculture resulting from abnormal weather. Thereafter, growth was rapid, rising an average of 7.9 percent a year between 1967 and 1972.

Tables 7.7 and 7.8 provide information on the sectoral growth of output and changes in output shares using standard national accounts definitions of industries of origin. Continuous measures of sectoral output are incomplete or difficult to obtain. Manufacturing output actually fell during the early 1960s and did not begin to grow significantly until after 1967. GDP originating in construction had actually declined, and manufacturing GDP was no higher than it had been five years earlier. Over the period 1967–72, the fastest growing sectors were bank and financial intermediaries, electricity and gas, mining and quarrying, and construction. The rapid increase in mining and quarrying output (at constant prices) is partly attributable to the opening to new foreign investment.

According to the 1971 population census, only 14.7 percent of the 1971 labor force was urban, and 6.2 percent were engaged in manufacturing compared with 60 percent in agriculture. The manufacturing labor force

Table 7.7 Trends of gross domestic product at constant 1960 market prices, 1960–1972

	1960	1961	1962	1963	1964	1965	1966	1967	1968	1969	1970	1971	1972
By industrial origin													
Agriculture, forestry, fisheries	100.0	101.6	105.0	101.1	106.3	107.1	112.3	110.3	121.3	123.6	128.7	133.3	136.6
Mining and quarrying	100.0	101.4	106.9	103.5	108.3	111.1	106.9	116.0	158.3	192.4	223.6	236.1	283.3
Manufacturing industries	100.0	112.3	113.8	111.7	110.1	109.2	111.4	115.0	125.2	142.9	156.7	176.1	185.9
Construction	100.0	129.1	108.9	82.3	82.3	93.7	106.3	92.4	116.5	153.2	192.4	230.4	282.3
Electricity and gas	100.0	109.1	118.2	136.4	154.5	154.5	154.5	200.0	209.1	236.4	272.7	300.0	318.2
Transport and communications	100.0	100.0	102.8	105.5	102.1	104.1	107.6	107.6	109.7	113.8	120.0	152.4	171.4
Wholesale and retail	100.0	115.9	115.4	118.6	122.0	120.8	115.6	126.9	141.2	159.1	179.6	194.4	221.9
Banking and intermediation	100.0	125.6	107.7	89.7	110.3	110.3	87.2	89.7	102.6	169.2	220.5	289.7	317.9
Ownership and dwellings	100.0	105.2	106.5	105.2	107.8	109.1	113.0	114.3	126.0	135.1	145.4	154.5	168.8
Public administration	100.0	109.1	111.4	112.5	113.1	115.3	138.1	140.3	163.6	166.5	172.7	180.7	186.4
Services	100.0	101.6	105.3	106.6	109.5	112.8	114.8	118.5	121.0	123.9	127.2	130.4	133.7
GDP 1960 prices	100.0	105.7	107.7	105.3	109.0	110.2	113.2	114.8	127.3	136.0	146.3	156.6	167.6
By kind of expenditure on GDP													
Private consumption	100.0	107.8	115.3	110.8	111.7	114.3	112.7	122.6	133.8	141.7	145.7	152.3	162.6
General government construction	100.0	93.1	74.9	75.4	88.7	64.3	89.3	79.4	90.0	93.3	109.1	116.8	115.3
Gross domestic capital formation	100.0	143.6	130.6	99.7	113.3	117.9	132.6	108.1	132.2	170.0	226.1	273.9	326.7
Export goods and services	100.0	109.1	99.5	93.8	104.8	108.0	103.3	106.7	117.9	134.4	158.3	176.3	216.5
Import goods and services	100.0	134.6	132.1	97.0	105.0	96.9	92.8	119.0	127.1	152.2	170.8	187.8	239.0
GDP 1960 prices	100.0	105.7	107.7	105.3	109.0	110.2	113.2	114.9	127.3	136.0	146.3	156.6	167.6

Source: Biro Pusat Statistik, *Pendapatan Nasional Indonesia*, various issues

Table 7.8 Gross domestic product by industrial origin, 1960–1971 (constant 1960 prices, percent)

Sector[a]	1960	1961	1962	1963	1964	1965	1966	1967	1968	1969	1970	1971
1	53.9	51.8	52.6	51.8	52.6	52.4	53.4	51.8	51.0	49.0	47.4	45.9
2	3.7	3.5	3.7	3.6	3.7	3.7	3.5	3.7	4.2	5.2	5.6	5.6
3	8.4	8.9	8.8	8.9	8.4	8.3	8.2	8.4	8.5	8.8	9.0	9.4
4	2.0	2.5	2.0	1.6	1.5	1.7	1.9	1.6	2.1	2.3	2.7	3.0
5	0.3	0.3	0.3	0.4	0.4	0.4	0.4	0.5	0.4	0.5	0.5	0.5
6	3.7	3.5	3.5	3.7	3.5	3.5	3.4	3.5	2.7	3.1	3.0	3.6
7	14.3	15.7	15.3	16.1	16.0	15.7	14.6	15.8	17.0	16.7	17.6	17.7
8	1.0	1.2	1.0	0.8	1.0	1.0	0.8	0.7	0.6	1.2	1.5	1.9
9	2.0	2.0	2.0	2.0	2.0	2.0	2.0	2.0	2.0	2.0	2.0	2.0
10	4.5	4.6	4.7	4.8	4.7	4.9	5.5	5.6	5.5	5.5	5.3	5.2
11	6.2	6.0	6.1	6.3	6.2	6.4	6.3	6.4	6.0	5.7	5.4	5.2
12	100.0	100.0	100.0	100.0	100.0	100.0	100.0	100.0	100.0	100.0	100.0	100.0

[a]Sectors: 1, agriculture, forestry, and fishery; 2, mining and quarrying; 3, manufacturing industries; 4, construction; 5, electricity and gas; 6, transport and communication; 7, wholesale and retail sale; 8, banking and intermediation; 9, ownership of dwellings; 10, public administration; 11, services; 12, GDP at market prices.
Source: Biro Pusat Statistik, Pendapatan Nasional Indonesia, various issues

in urban areas was only 23 percent of the total manufacturing labor force in 1971. The urban manufacturing labor force actually declined in absolute terms from 1961 to 1971 while the rural manufacturing labor force nearly doubled. Even when these data are adjusted for some changes in definitions (Sundrum, 1975), the urban share of the manufacturing labor force declined from 36.9 to 33.9 percent between 1961 and 1971. This may reflect the decline of import-competing sectors during the 1960s, since these sectors consisted of more urban firms than the agricultural processing sectors that composed the remainder of manufacturing.

Output and Employment by Manufacturing Subsectors

The data on aggregate output discussed above suggest that aggregate output and manufacturing output grew significantly faster after liberalization than it had before. Not all manufacturing subsectors would be expected to be affected uniformly since the distribution of protection across subsectors would probably be quite different after 1966. Unfortunately, not only are no sector-specific measures of effective protection available, data do not even exist on effective exchange rates by manufacturing sector. As a result we are unable to compare the liberalization's implementation across sectors with relative sectoral performance.

Measures of sectoral performance are also difficult to obtain or incomplete. For the period 1963–7 we have sectorally disaggregated data on value added and employment for large establishments only, constructed from some surveys carried out for national accounting purposes. Large establishments were defined as enterprises without mechanical power employing 100 or more persons, or establishments with mechanical power employing 50 or more persons. The relative performance of large and medium establishments (five or more employees with power, ten or more without) in manufacturing value added is illustrated in figure 7.2. Interestingly, the decline in manufacturing value added in the early 1960s was the result of a decline in value added of large and medium establishments only. While the value added of those firms declined 7 percent between 1961 and 1966, the value added originating in small firms grew by 12 percent. Large firms were disproportionately involved in activities that required imported raw materials and spare parts, while small firms tended to process locally produced agricultural products and thus were not as severely affected by the import stringency of those years. After 1967 and the end of import licensing, the value added of large and medium firms grew much faster than that of small firms.

Tables 7.9 and 7.10 present data on value added and employment by manufacturing subsector for large firms only. The measurement of real

Table 7.9 Indices of gross value added by manufacturing sector – large enterprises, 1963–1967

Sector	Code	1963	1964	1965	1966	1967
Food	20	100.00	85.86	87.97	34.62	45.94
Beverages	21	100.00	186.07	204.35	168.68	236.46
Tobacco	22	100.00	258.07	208.91	414.37	377.28
Textiles	23	100.00	44.32	66.44	26.65	33.47
Wearing apparel and other textiles	24	100.00	82.62	114.90	32.18	50.88
Wood, bamboo, etc.	25	100.00	133.80	145.87	68.88	57.34
Furniture and fixtures	26	100.00	114.14	74.32	11.02	3.24
Paper and paper products	27	100.00	52.53	227.95	121.01	81.95
Printing	28	100.00	82.02	345.71	254.31	416.29
Leather and leather products	29	100.00	54.78	33.66	19.31	29.65
Rubber and rubber products	30	100.00	21.66	22.34	22.01	29.91
Chemicals	31	100.00	60.68	36.36	7.96	32.93
Nonmetallic mineral products	33	100.00	50.03	30.82	18.93	23.30
Metal products	35	100.00	82.14	112.85	61.53	37.54
Manufacturing and repair of of machinery	36	100.00	95.70	94.13	25.36	57.81
Manufacturing and repair of electrical machinery	37	100.00	202.70	144.14	78.37	88.35
Transport equipment	38	100.00	302.66	417.47	85.21	165.28
Miscellaneous manufacturing	39	100.00	278.24	219.96	84.34	736.09
Total		100.00	104.03	103.79	108.30	117.45
Total excluding tobacco		100.00	68.53	79.39	38.39	57.84

Sector-specific deflators are unavailable. The value added of each sector is deflated to the 1963 value by a single price index: the implicit price deflator of the gross value added of large and medium establishments.

Source: Biro Pusat Statistik, Pendapatan Nasional Indonesia, 1960–8, p. 95

Table 7.10 Employment by manufacturing sector – large enterprises, 1963–1967

Sector	Code	1963	1964	1965	1966	1967
Food	20	107,983	83,017	70,647	65,504	64,148
Beverages	21	2,210	2,321	2,226	2,180	2,273
Tobacco	22	104,583	116,579	113,583	113,822	147,217
Textiles	23	79,408	67,084	71,297	71,539	69,994
Wearing apparel and other textiles	24	2,900	2,490	2,029	1,970	1,872
Wood, bamboo, etc.	25	3,912	4,241	4,180	4,356	3,808
Furniture and fixtures	26	493	446	428	388	326
Paper and paper products	27	3,596	3,442	4,146	4,093	2,757
Printing	28	12,525	10,927	15,204	13,500	12,874
Leather and leather products	29	1,592	1,624	1,542	1,577	1,503
Rubber and rubber products	30	47,481	49,822	46,520	47,395	39,589
Chemicals	31	14,531	14,493	15,658	15,622	15,092
Nonmetallic mineral products	33	10,421	10,286	9,255	8,260	7,285
Metal products	35	10,627	9,881	8,800	8,187	7,031
Manufacturing and repair of of machinery	36	3,520	4,005	3,586	3.379	2,791
Manufacturing and repair of electrical machinery	37	1,564	1,683	1,881	1,673	1,749
Transport equipment	38	7,089	6,079	1,497	1,389	842
Miscellaneous manufacturing	39	4,580	4,373	4,194	4,108	3,567
Total		419,015	392,793	376,673	368,942	384,718
Total excluding tobacco		314,432	276,214	263,080	255,120	237,501

Source: Biro Pusat Statistik, *Pendapatan Nasional Indonesia*, 1960–8, p. 92

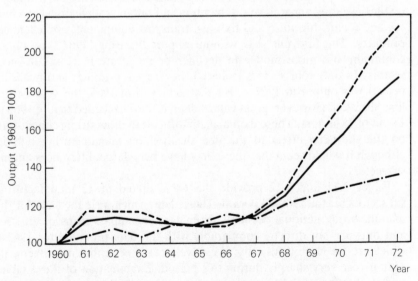

Figure 7.2 Manufacturing output: 1960–1972 (1960 = 100); ——, total; – – –, large enterprises; – · –, small and medium enterprises

output during this period may be more inaccurate than usual because of the rapid inflation and, as noted above, there are some problems with the national accounts at current prices from this period. The characterization in tables 7.9 and 7.10 of the performance of total large-enterprise manufacturing in years just before and just after the beginning of liberalization is thrown off by the inexplicably large growth in tobacco value added and its large share in total value added. There was no significant export of tobacco products or import of finished products to account for this surge. Cloves used in the production of the popular *kretek* cigarettes are imported in significant quantities, but clove import data do not correlate with these tobacco output data. Manufacturing value added which excludes the tobacco products sector in aggregation (table 7.9) demonstrates that the manufacturing output of nontobacco large firms had fallen sharply in 1964 before recovering somewhat in 1965. The year that liberalization began, 1966, brought a sharp drop of more than 50 percent in value added from these firms. It would be unfair to attribute this fall in output to the liberalization, since the end of the import-licensing system, the major act of liberalization, was only announced October 3, 1966. Output (excluding tobacco products) recovered somewhat in 1967 but still remained well below 1965 levels. Employment, as measured by number of workers, fell throughout the period 1963–7.

During the first (partial) year of liberalization output declined in every subsector except tobacco, whose output nearly doubled, and rubber, whose output was basically flat (table 7.9). Some of the output decreases were very sharp: declines in excess of 50 percent occurred in food products, textiles, wearing apparel, wood, bamboo and rattan, nonelectrical machinery and repair, furniture and fixtures, transport equipment, and chemical products. The first full year without import licensing, 1967, saw either continuing but more moderate declines or moderate increases in most sectors. In only four sectors (tobacco, beverages, printing, and miscellaneous) was output in 1967 above that achieved in 1965, the year before liberalization. However, gross value added in 1967 exceeded that of 1966 in 13 out of 18 sectors. These data make it difficult to draw strong conclusions on the short-run effect of the liberalization on manufacturing output, although it would seem that there may have been large differences among subsectors.

Tables 7.11 and 7.12 provide the value added of 12 manufacturing subsectors for the 1968–74 period. These data, which were the basis for the manufacturing national accounts estimates, encompass firms of all sizes and thus are not directly comparable with the data provided for 1963–7 which are for large firms only. We have already seen that manufacturing output rose very sharply during this period. Examination of these tables reveals that five of the 12 sectors grew more rapidly than average. Notable among them is textiles and apparel, which had a tripling of output between

Table 7.11 Manufacturing value added at constant 1971 prices, 1968–1974 (billion rupiahs)

Number	Manufacturing	1968	1969	1970	1971	1972	1973	1974
1	Food products	233.71	253.64	257.05	272.24	280.13	274.50	293.88
2	Beverages	6.00	6.42	6.54	6.90	7.14	7.14	7.64
3	Tobacco products	45.23	35.20	39.53	41.60	46.52	58.42	60.24
4	Textiles, wearing apparel, and leather	44.48	60.57	74.26	81.78	89.68	108.20	125.51
5	Wood and wood products	12.84	20.40	31.88	34.86	46.03	67.55	61.34
6	Paper, paper products, and printing and publishing	8.25	12.74	16.49	21.74	29.69	35.39	36.29
7	Rubber, plastic, and basic chemicals except petroleum products	43.98	42.87	45.06	46.41	50.06	56.12	60.09
8	Petroleum products	85.29	91.33	95.42	103.76	116.54	139.49	145.87
9	Ceramics, earthenware, lime, cement, glass, and other nonmetallic mineral products	17.41	23.02	24.50	23.30	31.43	35.53	36.12
10	Iron and basic metals	0.72	0.74	2.50	7.91	8.10	10.57	10.30
11	Metal products, machinery, and equipment	45.75	82.65	92.40	131.02	176.03	248.81	374.96
12	Others	5.21	5.32	5.44	5.56	5.70	5.84	5.98
	Total	548.88	634.90	691.05	777.09	887.05	1,047.55	1,218.20

Source: Biro Pusat Statistik, unpublished data

Table 7.12 Index numbers of manufacturing sector output, 1968–1974 (1971 = 100)

Number	Manufacturing	1968	1969	1970	1971	1972	1973	1974
1	Food products	85.85	93.17	94.42	100.00	102.90	100.83	107.95
2	Beverages	87.02	93.07	94.77	100.00	103.55	103.47	110.77
3	Tobacco products	108.71	84.60	95.01	100.00	111.81	140.42	144.79
4	Textiles, wearing apparel, and leather	54.39	74.06	90.80	100.00	109.66	132.30	153.47
5	Wood and wood products	36.84	58.51	91.43	100.00	132.02	193.74	175.93
6	Paper, paper products, and printing and publishing	37.93	58.62	75.86	100.00	136.55	162.76	166.90
7	Rubber, plastic, and basic chemicals except petroleum products	94.77	92.38	97.09	100.00	107.88	120.94	129.48
8	Petroleum products	82.20	88.02	91.96	100.00	112.32	134.44	140.59
9	Ceramics, earthenware, lime, cement, glass, and other nonmetallic mineral products	74.71	98.76	105.14	100.00	134.86	152.48	154.98
10	Iron and basic metals	9.12	9.42	31.57	100.00	102.48	133.63	130.26
11	Metal products, machinery, and equipment	34.92	63.08	70.52	100.00	134.35	189.90	286.18
12	Others	93.57	95.64	97.78	100.00	102.38	104.88	107.39
	All manufacturing	70.63	81.70	88.93	100.00	114.15	134.80	156.77

Source: Biro Pusat Statistik, unpublished data

1968 and 1974, suggesting the presence of significant excess capacity and perhaps the effect of new protective measures. Some of the other output increases were as steep. Metal and metal products output was up almost ninefold, but remained a very small sector comprising less than 0.5 percent of total manufacturing value added. Iron and basic metal output increased dramatically, but almost all of this increase can be attributed to a single new integrated steel works operated by a state enterprise.

8

Developments in the Post-liberalization Period

For the seven years after the August 1971 devaluation, the nominal value of the rupiah remained at Rp 415 per US dollar despite the real appreciation in the exchange rate caused by domestic prices, which continued to increase faster than foreign prices throughout the period. The government's ability to hold the nominal exchange rate at the 1971 level was supported by the rapid rise in receipts from petroleum exports. The strong rupiah led to increased pressure on the government to provide protection for the still small industrial sector. Thus Indonesia entered a period of increasing protection, relying on price measures, and to a lesser extent quantitative restrictions, to control imports.

A prohibited import list had reappeared in the late 1960s but did not include many significant items. Within months of the August 1971 devaluation the list began to expand. The imposition of new quantitative restrictions accelerated in 1974. Import bans were enacted on the import of a wide range of finished consumer durables in order to protect the mostly foreign-owned assembly industry. In October 1975, following pressure from manufacturers, the import of 23 varieties of textiles was prohibited. In time, a pattern developed by which industrial subsectors were able to have their products placed on the prohibited list. Two or more firms producing a certain good would petition for protection claiming that they could meet domestic demand at a "reasonable" price; often, the import prohibitions were granted. The strong incentives to invest provided by these trade barriers sometimes led to excess capacity in the protected sectors. The Foreign and Domestic Investment Board often removed subsectors protected by an import prohibition from its "priorities" list, thus further restricting competition. Nonetheless, the prohibited list still remained small compared with the pre-1966 era and with other developing countries.

The government, with the past experience of a quantitative restriction regime not yet forgotten, relied as much as possible on price interventions, such as tariffs, to increase protection for an increasingly troubled industrial sector. Pressure by manufacturers' associations and private firms brought haphazard tariff increases, mostly for finished goods, and tariff decreases, mostly for intermediate goods. Protection was also provided by an array of other price measures that were announced in scores of new regulations by a variety of government ministries. The very complex and uneven structure that resulted led to the growth of commercial advisory firms and newsletters which compiled and explained the rapidly evolving trade environment, and no doubt contributed to the fall in foreign investment.

One method of increasing nominal protection during this period was through the setting of checkprices on imports. The Ministry of Finance set checkprices for most import items to serve as the base upon which import levies are calculated. They were originally meant to reduce the time and effort necessary to expedite goods through customs by reducing the haggling and uncertainty over the value of goods and tax due. However, in the mid-1970s checkprices were used as a way of altering levels of protection without resetting listed tariff rates. For example, in April 1975 the checkprices for low quality textiles and weaving yarns were raised 20 percent, and those for higher quality textiles and weaving yarns were raised 50 percent. On May 1 both were raised an additional 25 percent.

Another protective device widely used during this period was restriction of the use of credit instruments for imports. Again, textiles were special targets of these restrictions. In February 1975 import of all textiles with DK (aid foreign exchange) was prohibited. Import with DK exchange qualified for a rebate of between RP 20 and RP 45 per US dollar of import depending on the origin of the aid and the origin of the import. Three months earlier, the use of merchants' letters of credit, a preferred means of financing imports, had been prohibited for the import of certain key textiles and apparel. At the same time the import of important types of cotton weaving yarns was monopolized by the state.

The prohibition of merchants' letters of credit for import spread to other commodities in 1976 and 1977; finally on May 17, 1977, their use was prohibited for all imports. Five months earlier, a wide-ranging set of protective measures had been announced. They included a 100 percent advance import deposit, an additional 100 percent "financial guarantee" deposit, and a 100 percent advance payment of import duties.

The pattern of protection in manufacturing over this period is suggested by the effective protection estimates for 11 subsectors in 1971, 1975, and 1978 provided by table 8.1. The 1971 estimates are from Pitt (1981a), and the 1975 and 1978 estimates are based on 1975 input–output coefficients at world prices. The 1978 estimates can be interpreted as the level of protection that would have existed in 1975 with 1978 levels of nominal protection.

Of the 11 sectors shown in table 8.1, protection was greater for seven of them (and for six of ten import-competing sectors) in 1978 than it was in 1975. All four sectors which experienced a fall in protection still had

Table 8.1 A comparison of effective protection over time for selected sectors, 1971–1978 (percent)

Sector	1971	1975	1978
Spinning	134	56	71
Weaving	Neg. IVA	192	117
Batik	− 38	− 35	− 23
Knitting	Neg. IVA	331	403
Wearing apparel	197	110	124
Pulp, paper, and cardboard	67	46	50
Tires and tubes	Neg. IVA	4,315	1,415
Other rubber products	195	406	226
Cutlery, hand tools, and general hardware	77	36	85
Other fabricated metal products	50	66	76
Accumulators and dry batteries	193	116	112

Neg. IVA, negative international value added.
Source: 1971, Pitt, 1981a, pp. 226–9

effective rates in excess of 100 percent. Of some interest is the fall in effective protection received by the weaving sector. This may be indicative of increased efficiency in this sector since 1971 when it had negative international value added.

One pattern that emerges from the admittedly small sample of sectors in table 8.1 is a reduction in the variance of effective protection rates. All six of the sectors having the lowest protection in 1975 had increased protection in 1978, and four of the five sectors with highest protection showed declines. Although the coverage of table 8.1 is too limited to support on its own conclusions on the overall level of protection afforded to manufacturing in 1978 relative to 1975 or 1971, these 1978 estimates along with other evidence support the conclusion that manufacturing protection increased between 1971 and 1978.

The Devaluation of November 1978

On November 15, 1978, the rupiah was devalued from Rp 415 to Rp 625 per US dollar. An accompanying policy package reduced tariffs, liberalized import prepayment requirements, and introduced an export certificate scheme which appears to have reduced the import substitution bias.

Before the devaluation, a duty drawback scheme existed to provide exporters of manufactures with rebates of customs duty, import sales tax, and other indirect taxes paid on imports. The exporters were required to submit detailed information and receipts to the Ministry of Finance to obtain a drawback. The procedure was costly and time consuming and very few firms were able to take advantage of it. An alternative to the drawback scheme was the export certificate scheme, inaugurated at the time of the devaluation, which listed commodities for which exporters could obtain a "rebate," determined as the product of an item's checkprice and the export certificate percentage. The checkprice was intended to represent the ex-factory cost of the item while the certificate percentage was intended to represent the average duty paid on imported inputs. There is some evidence that the rebate obtained under the export certificate scheme exceeded that obtainable under the drawback scheme, implying that there was an element of subsidy in the former.

With the nominal devaluation, the export certificate scheme appears to have been crucial in instigating the boom in manufactured exports that followed soon after their introduction. Most of the manufactured exports that demonstrated rapid growth between 1978 and 1979 received export certificates. Of 39 trade classifications (six-digit UN Standard International Trade Classification (SITC) codes) having exports in excess of US$1 million in 1979, 23 had export certificates representing 69 percent of the export of these 39 classifications. Exports of manufactures receiving export certificates grew by 446 percent in 1979, while all others grew by only 105 percent. This manufactured export promotion initiative proved unquest-ionably successful and has altered the focus of trade incentives in succeed-ing years. Government policy since 1978 has demonstrated a strong awareness of the importance of providing adequate incentives to export and has halted – but not reversed – the slide toward an inward-looking trade policy.

9
Examining the Indonesia Trade Liberalization with a Vector Autoregression

In this chapter the behavior of some important time series in the period after the introduction of the liberalization of 1966 is analyzed using a method known as innovation accounting. An innovation is the difference between the realized outcome of a time series and the best (linear) forecast made at an earlier point in time. Policy actions which, from the point of view of private economic agents, are generated by a more or less stable stochastic process are anticipated and are not innovations. Innovations are unforecast changes in economic variables, such as an unanticipated change in an exchange rate or other trade control instrument. A rational public will condition their economic choices on their expectations about future values of policy and not just on current values. Obviously, in order to distinguish anticipated changes in policy variables from unanticipated changes, a statistical model that provides a probability distribution of future paths of the policy variables is needed.

Christopher Sims (1980) has persuasively argued that economic theory is unlikely to provide complete and uniquely specified macroeconometric models, claiming that "what 'economic theory' tells us about them is mainly that any variable which appears on the right-hand-side of one of these equations belongs in principle on the right-hand-side of all of them" (Sims, 1980, p. 3). Identifying restrictions of existing models are often not based on theory and are false. Sims argues that it should be feasible to estimate these models as reduced forms, treating all variables as endogenous. Following this approach, a six-variable (192-parameter) vector autoregression (VAR) containing Indonesian international-trade-related time series is estimated. In the VAR "policy variables" such as effective exchange rates are treated as random variables symmetrically with all other variables. The residuals of the VAR are the estimated innovations.

Under fairly general conditions, a time series can be expressed as a linear combination of current and past innovations – called the moving-average representation of the series. Innovation accounting is a method by which innovations and moving-average representations are used to summarize the behavior of a set of time series over some period of time. In contrast, the common procedure for tracing the effects of a policy begins with an equation or set of equations in which nonpolicy variables at a given date are expressed as a function of predetermined policy variables at that date. The effect of policy variables on the economy are then directly solved from the equations of the model. Sims (1986) illustrates why such a procedure to evaluate policy can be seriously mistaken.

Innovation accounting based upon the estimated VAR is used to study the effects of trade policy innovations on the behavior of important Indonesian time series. In addition, the movement of these time series in the years following the liberalization of 1966 is historically decomposed in order to estimate what part of their movement can be attributed to innovations in trade policies. In particular, the nearly total end to quantitative restrictions without pre-announcement, the major component of the liberalization begun in 1966, is explicitly treated as an innovation – a policy action that, from the point of view of economic agents, deviated from the stochastic process that is presumed to have generated policy in the past.

Innovation Accounting

If deterministic variables are ignored, an autoregressive representation of the $m \times 1$ vector time series $y(t)$ is of the form

$$y(t) = \sum_{s=1}^{q} A(s)y(t-s) + e(t) \qquad (9.1)$$

where A is a matrix of coefficients to be estimated and $e(t)$ is a vector of innovations. These innovations are a white noise process, serially uncorrelated with covariance matrix Σ. Once the As have been estimated, it is possible to compute the coefficients of the moving average representation

$$y(t) = \sum_{s=1}^{\infty} B(s)e(t-s) + X(t)C \qquad (9.2)$$

In equation (9.2) we have allowed $y(t)$ to have a deterministic (exogenous) component $X(t)C$. A change in a component of e will affect all values of y from that point onwards. The coefficient in $B(s)$ trace out these responses and can be thought of as obtained from simulations of the model. These coefficients are thus the "dynamic multipliers" of the system.

The components of e can be contemporaneously correlated, so that it is not possible to partition the variance of y into the innovations of each series. Thus it is useful to orthogonalize the innovation $e(t)$. The vector $e(t)$ can be obtained from a vector $v(t)$ of orthonormal random variables by premultiplication of v by a matrix S, where S is chosen so that $SS' = \Sigma$. If S is lower triangular, this factorization is known as the Choleski decomposition. There is only one factorization of Σ into SS' such that S is lower triangular with positive elements on the diagonal. The Choleski decomposition attributes to series 1 all the contemporaneous correlation between series 1 and all others, 2, . . . m; to the new series 2, the contemporaneous correlation between it and series 3, . . . m; and so on. The impulse responses and the decomposition of variance with these innovations will depend on the particular ordering chosen. Placing a variable later in the order will usually result in its having reduced importance in explaining its own movements and those of other variables. This issue is considered again in the explanation of results presented below. The moving average representation of $y(t)$ with orthogonalized residuals can be written as

$$
y(t) = \sum_{s=0}^{\infty} B(s)SS^{-1}u(t - s) + X(t)C
$$

$$
= \sum_{s=0}^{\infty} D(s)v(t) + X(t)C \tag{9.3}
$$

Where the coefficients in $D(s)$ trace out the response to orthogonalized shocks $v(t)$.

Our particular interest here is to analyze one particularly large innovation, the trade liberalization commencing in 1966. We can use the moving average representation to estimate what part of the evolution of the time series in the system after 1966 can be accounted for by the trade liberalization innovation. The historical decomposition is based upon the following partitioning of the moving average representation:

$$
y(T + j) = \sum_{s=0}^{j-1} D(s)v(T + j - s) + \left[\sum_{s=j}^{\infty} D(s)v(T + j - s) + X(T + j)C \right] \tag{9.4}
$$

The first sum represents that part of $y(T + j)$ due to (orthogonalized) innovations in periods $T + 1$ to $T + j$; the second term in brackets is the forecast of $y(T + j)$ based upon the information available at time T about $y(t)$ and from the deterministic variables up to $T + j$. The historical decomposition above decomposes the differences between forecast values and actual values of $y(t)$ among the m components of $v(t)$.

The Data and Specification of the Vector Autoregression

Six endogenous variables were chosen for inclusion in the system. They are import flows in US dollars (IMPORT), non-oil export flows in US dollars (EXPORT), the effective exchange rate for non-oil exports (EERX), the effective exchange rate for imports (EERM), the import premium associated with import licensing (PREMIUM), and the free- or black-market exchange rate (FREE RATE). The data are quarterly series for the period 1950, quarter I, through 1973, quarter I. The PREMIUM variable is defined as 1 plus the rate of premium, as given by the relationship.

$$1 + s = \frac{P_{\mathrm{d}}}{P_{\mathrm{w}} \times \mathrm{EERM}}$$

where s is the rate of premium, P_{d} is the domestic price of imports and P_{w} is the world price. The variable PREMIUM is a weighted average of some of the goods described in table 5.18. The series EERX, EERM, and FREE RATE have been deflated by the Jakarta 62-item cost of living index. Logarithms are taken of all these series. Indices of export prices and import prices in world markets are included as deterministic variables, in addition to seasonal dummies, a trend, and a constant term. Lack of data prevented the inclusion of GDP or some other output measure as an endogenous variable. Even annual output series for the entire period 1950–73 are unavailable.

A few words need to be said about the interpretation of these series in the Indonesian context. Illegal transactions were a significant factor for most of the period under review. The importance of price disparity in Indonesia has been noted in previous chapters. In a theoretical model of smuggling with price disparity (Pitt, 1981b) the domestic price of a traded good is the weighted average of the returns to legal and illegal trade with the profit-maximizing mix of these types of trade as weights. Thus the variable PREMIUM in fact measures the product of two phenomena: (1 plus the rate of premium in the absence of illegal transactions) multiplied by (1 plus the rate of import price disparity). This product may be greater than or less than unity since the rate of import price disparity is typically negative. Furthermore, it is important to remember that our measures of import and exports are for *legal* trade only. Obviously, direct observations on the flows of illegal trade are unavailable. A model of Indonesian-style illegal trade with black markets for foreign exchange (Pitt, 1984) finds that the share of trade flows diverted to illegal channels is determined only by the effective exchange rate and the black-market price of foreign exchange.

In order to capture the effect of import licensing above and beyond that captured by the variable PREMIUM, which also captures price disparity, a dummy variable for import restriction is included in the system as a deterministic variable. This variable has a value of zero whenever binding quantitative restrictions were pervasive and a value of unity otherwise. While in some contexts such a dichotomization may be problematical, that is fortunately not the case in Indonesia. Quantitative restrictions were either pervasive in that an overwhelming share of imports was affected, or almost nonexistent, as during the Burhanuddin Harahap cabinet of 1955–6 and the period beginning with 1966, quarter IV. There was no sequencing that led to intermediate phases. Treating the quantitative restrictions dummy as a deterministic variable in the VAR implies that the end of all quantitative restrictions announced and enacted on October 3, 1966, was an innovation in that it was not predicted by past values of the variables of the system. No evidence has been found that would tend to undermine such a claim.

The inclusion of this dummy variable permits an examination of the role that abandoning quantitative restrictions played in determining the evolution of important time series, conditioning on any other innovations associated with the liberalization *including* import premium innovations. The inclusion of both a quantitative restriction dummy variable and a measure of import premium is consistent with the findings of the ten country studies of the National Bureau for Economic Research's Foreign Trade Regimes and Economic Development project. In their synthesis volumes, both Anne Krueger (1978) and Jagdish Bhagwati (1978) make the case that the conventional Marshallian equivalence proposition, that tariffs and quotas are basically equivalent in their real effects, has almost negligible scope in light of the special theoretical restrictions under which it holds and the nature of the quantitative restrictions regimes observed. They argue that the distribution of the premium among economic agents affects resource allocation and efficiency. Furthermore, Krueger (1978, p. 112) provides evidence supporting the assertion that "the significant difference between tariffs and QRs lies in the greater variation [in implicit protection] that occurs under QR regimes." To construct a measure of the variation in implicit protection directly would require considerable effort, and even if we could do it, the other arguments for nonequivalency would still hold. Thus, in the absence of measurement errors, we can think of a test of the hypothesis that the coefficients of these dummy variables are jointly zero as a test of the nonequivalency proposition. The null hypothesis is clearly rejected with our data ($\chi^2(6) = 17.91$, significant at the 0.01 level).

The final problem of specification is to choose a lag length. Models with different numbers of lags were compared using the transformed likelihood ratio test statistic suggested by Sims (1980). It was found that little benefit was to be gained by working with lag lengths greater than 4, so a lag length of 4 was chosen.

Description of the Estimated System

A vector autoregressive system such as this is best described by computing the system's response to "typical" random shocks (innovations). Typical shocks are positive residuals of one standard deviation unit in each equation of the system. An economic interpretation of how an innovation affects the evolution of a set of time series is obtained by connecting innovations with policy actions in particular sectors. For example, we might wish to know whether a large rise in exports at date t can be attributed to real export exchange rate devaluation. If we found no large innovation in the real export exchange rate in periods prior to t we might not want to conclude that devaluation was the cause. If there was a large export exchange rate innovation, we could use the moving-average representation to determine whether it was substantially responsible for the change in exports. If the export innovation accounting does not assign much influence to the devaluation innovation, then we might conclude that, although an export exchange rate devaluation occurred before the export increase, it was not substantially responsible for it.

Table 9.1 provides the response of each variable to one standard deviation unit innovations of each of the six variables in turn. Response patterns are traced for 16 quarters, with the innovation occurring in quarter 0. As noted above, it is useful to examine orthogonalized innovations; however, impulse responses may be sensitive to the variable ordering. A "primary" ordering of EERX, EERM, PREMIUM, FREE RATE, IMPORT, and EXPORT has been chosen to reflect our interest in the effects of exchange rate innovations. However, in calculating each innovation response, these variables have been reordered so that the source of the innovation is always ordered first, followed by the remaining variables according to their "primary" order.

Some of the results of this innovation accounting exercise are summarized below; the reader is urged to examine the table and remember that the response is log scaled.

1 Effective exchange rate innovations are not very persistent on almost all variables. Exports seem to be increased fairly persistently by an EERX innovation and imports are reduced fairly persistently by an EERM innovation.
2 Each effective exchange rate innovation generates similar response patterns in both the effective exchange rates.
3 The import premium responds persistently negatively to innovation in the EERM and IMPORT, a result consistent with commonly held wisdom. The opposite result would not invalidate our model. Although increases in EERM and IMPORT are likely to be negatively related to

Table 9.1 Responses to innovation ($\times 10^{-2}$)

Quarter	Export exchange rate	Import exchange rate	Import premium	Free rate	Imports	Exports
Responses to export exchange rate innovation						
0	8.932	9.077	−8.193	3.862	−2.031	1.466
1	6.476	5.686	−3.980	3.478	−2.417	−0.759
2	1.016	−0.602	1.616	−1.675	−0.272	−0.303
3	−0.073	−3.895	2.269	−1.781	0.372	0.084
4	−0.726	−2.082	−0.536	−1.377	−1.100	0.629
5	−0.973	0.230	−2.723	−0.996	−0.923	0.955
6	−0.760	0.499	−1.392	−0.169	−0.672	0.022
7	0.710	1.750	−1.566	0.689	0.359	0.378
8	1.613	2.081	−1.188	1.311	0.346	0.208
9	1.256	0.727	0.592	0.840	−0.145	−0.006
10	0.595	−0.703	1.579	0.194	−0.179	−0.132
11	−0.163	−1.438	1.534	−0.299	−0.081	−0.087
12	−0.715	−1.286	0.846	−0.563	−0.137	0.138
13	−0.821	−0.734	0.228	−0.481	−0.082	0.237
14	−0.500	0.029	−0.282	−0.210	0.090	0.248
15	−0.011	0.637	−0.550	0.109	0.239	0.220
Responses to import exchange rate innovation						
0	5.622	14.421	−12.854	0.983	−2.437	1.885
1	4.272	8.531	−6.757	3.472	−0.174	0.081
2	1.325	3.599	−1.450	0.572	0.251	−0.058
3	1.215	1.698	−3.414	1.124	1.831	1.870
4	−1.653	−0.576	−1.283	0.972	−2.117	−0.190
5	−2.246	−0.510	−1.725	0.549	−1.082	0.273
6	−1.695	0.258	−1.818	1.589	−0.753	−1.183
7	−0.487	1.845	−2.268	1.770	−0.044	−0.579
8	0.791	2.418	−1.758	1.983	−0.344	−0.953
9	1.188	1.450	−0.242	1.281	−0.371	−1.136
10	1.129	0.594	0.100	0.427	−0.437	−1.086
11	0.526	−0.432	0.311	−0.270	−0.516	−0.914
12	−0.111	−0.811	0.002	−0.767	−0.705	0.602
13	−0.403	−0.532	−0.658	−0.802	−0.631	0.251
14	−0.292	0.130	−1.159	−0.474	−0.596	−0.067
15	0.129	0.786	−1.339	0.014	−0.464	0.070
Responses to premium innovation						
0	−4.794	−12.144	15.264	0.173	1.972	−1.705
1	−5.164	−9.164	10.977	−2.063	1.167	0.961
2	−3.079	−4.686	5.787	−0.246	0.655	1.662
3	−2.020	−2.295	5.904	0.338	−1.237	0.279
4	−0.569	−0.219	3.778	0.164	1.957	1.292
5	−0.297	−0.447	3.791	0.150	2.389	0.819
6	−0.494	−1.054	3.604	−0.488	1.948	1.461
7	−1.025	−1.651	2.967	−0.766	1.454	0.977
8	−1.801	−2.001	2.198	−1.140	1.458	0.693

9	−1.941	−1.328	0.787	−0.958	1.367	0.550
10	−1.530	−0.443	−0.157	−0.460	1.339	0.349
11	−0.838	0.487	−0.805	−0.090	1.149	0.110
12	−0.163	0.919	−0.955	0.134	0.986	−0.157
13	0.287	0.807	−0.714	0.145	0.720	−0.453
14	0.423	0.444	−0.541	−0.053	0.488	−0.564
15	0.276	0.029	−0.468	−0.328	0.204	−0.594

Responses to free-rate innovation

0	2.868	1.179	0.219	12.025	2.227	0.376
1	1.692	1.781	2.848	11.737	0.096	1.695
2	−1.319	0.103	4.908	6.450	−0.588	2.919
3	−3.233	−3.022	8.079	3.144	−1.238	0.274
4	−2.051	−1.168	4.033	1.242	1.292	−0.103
5	−1.338	1.063	−0.265	0.381	2.240	−0.574
6	−1.616	0.763	−0.728	−0.885	2.026	−0.717
7	−1.148	0.559	−1.556	−1.499	1.910	−0.920
8	−0.520	1.064	−3.116	−1.516	1.519	−1.065
9	−0.018	1.585	−4.052	−1.237	0.604	−1.208
10	0.444	1.548	−3.912	−0.808	0.032	−1.393
11	0.868	1.521	−3.659	−0.472	−0.288	−1.368
12	1.155	1.469	−3.311	−0.205	−0.672	−1.171
13	1.270	1.180	−2.585	−0.027	−1.104	−1.032
14	1.272	0.863	−1.907	−0.047	−1.270	−0.832
15	1.147	0.596	−1.365	0.086	−1.286	−0.591

Responses to import innovation

0	−1.352	−2.620	2.244	1.996	13.416	−2.356
1	−2.196	−1.063	−0.548	0.625	4.971	0.348
2	−0.624	1.859	−2.688	0.389	0.689	1.495
3	1.006	1.629	−2.010	−0.107	0.763	−2.232
4	0.641	2.876	−5.077	−2.140	1.804	−1.798
5	1.320	2.712	−5.686	−1.654	1.573	−1.725
6	1.751	1.553	−4.472	−1.448	0.280	−1.928
7	1.556	2.008	−5.638	−1.888	−0.346	−1.226
8	1.273	1.417	−4.914	−1.482	−1.116	−1.431
9	1.528	1.289	−4.114	−0.851	−1.604	−1.286
10	1.931	1.811	−4.080	−0.155	−1.453	−0.814
11	1.852	1.514	−2.849	0.242	−1.681	−0.623
12	1.714	0.936	−1.462	0.402	−1.757	−0.329
13	1.506	0.436	−0.507	0.522	−1.554	−0.114
14	1.053	−0.023	0.235	0.467	−1.374	0.131
15	0.551	−0.414	0.825	0.385	−1.160	0.355

Responses to export innovation

0	1.186	2.462	−2.357	0.409	−2.862	11.041
1	−1.697	0.228	2.275	−0.859	−3.049	3.975
2	−2.800	−3.052	4.816	−1.922	0.545	2.329
3	−0.821	−0.613	2.384	1.962	0.481	1.125
4	0.013	−1.092	3.949	3.506	2.596	1.299
5	−1.727	−2.462	5.762	1.610	1.217	0.886

(continued)

Table 9.1 (continued)

Quarter	Export exchange rate	Import exchange rate	Import premium	Free rate	Imports	Exports
6	−2.598	−3.645	6.288	0.138	1.477	1.106
7	−2.029	−2.947	4.867	−0.071	1.154	0.139
8	−1.594	−1.150	2.044	−0.524	1.717	0.422
9	−1.441	−0.392	0.885	−0.757	1.644	0.099
10	−1.027	−0.256	0.471	−0.897	1.692	0.016
11	−0.443	0.382	−0.681	−0.813	1.475	−0.064
12	−0.174	0.559	−1.198	−0.706	1.066	−0.233
13	−0.050	0.416	−1.209	−0.628	0.594	−0.458
14	0.093	0.349	−1.322	−0.513	0.420	−0.509
15	0.192	0.397	−1.423	−0.391	0.136	−0.518

PREMIUM in a structural relationship, this may not hold in a reduced-form relationship. Innovations to EERM and IMPORT may affect other series and through complicated cross-equation feedbacks ultimately result in an unchanged or higher level of PREMIUM. Indeed, by 15 quarters after the innovations, their effects on PREMIUM have all but disappeared.

4 Innovations to the free- or black-market exchange rate lead to a sustained increase in the EERM (after quarter 4), a sustained decrease in the PREMIUM (after quarter 5), and a sustained decrease in exports (after quarter 4). (A static model of smuggling and the black market for foreign exchange (Pitt, 1984), with exogenous policy rules, predicts that the share of export smuggled will increase in response to an "exogenous" shock in the black-market rate while the share of import smuggled will decrease, but because of its characteristic homogeneity it offers no predictions on absolute flows.)

5 Export innovations are followed by higher imports (beginning with quarter 2), while import innovations are followed by mostly lower levels of export.

In addition to these impulse responses, the response of the system to a change in the quantitative restrictions dummy variable is traced. This shock takes the form of a permanent end to a quantitative restrictions system. Computationally it is the same as a vector of unchanging perpetual innovations equal to the coefficient vector of the dummy variable in the system's autoregressive representation (9.1). Figure 9.1 provides the response of imports and exports to this quantitative restrictions innovation over a period of 24 quarters. The figure reveals that the initial response is a fairly sharp and positive import response, peaking at about quarter 4, and a somewhat less sharp but negative export response, bottoming out at about the same time. The two response curves meet at around quarter 10, where the net response is positive, and then both responses continue positive

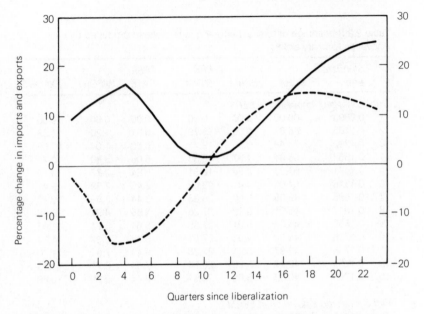

Figure 9.1 Trade responses to the end of quantitative restrictions: ——, imports; ———, exports

throughout the remaining quarters. Thus these data reveal that in Indonesia the elimination of a quantitative restrictions system (in the absence of any other innovations, including import premium) would initially tend to worsen a balance-of-trade deficit through import increase and export reduction but would eventually (after $2\frac{1}{2}$ years) result in higher levels of both imports and exports.

Table 9.2 provides the results of a decomposition of the variance of each series into each of the orthogonalized innovations. If there were no sampling errors in the estimated system, a variable would be strictly exogenous if its own innovations explained 100 percent of its forecast error. The share of forecast error explained by the innovations of other variables indicates interactions among variables. In table 9.2, which uses the "primary" ordering, the free-market exchange rate, imports, and exports have more than half their variance accounted for by own-innovations after 16 quarters. For PREMIUM, own-innovations account for less than one third of forecast variance. Substantial feedback into PREMIUM comes from EERM, IMPORT, and FREE RATE. The major source of feedback into the export exchange rate is PREMIUM, and the greatest feedback for the import exchange rate is from export rate innovations. The largest source of feedback into imports and exports is PREMIUM, with FREE RATE second in both cases. Table 9.3 provides variance decompositions with a different ordering: trade flows are put first rather than last. There is very little qualitative difference between the

Table 9.2 Percentage of forecast error *k* quarters ahead produced by each innovation (primary order)

k	Standard error	EERX	EERM	PRE-MIUM	FREE RATE	IMPORT	EXPORT
Orthogonalized innovation in EERX							
1	0.0893	100.00	0.00	0.00	0.00	0.00	0.00
2	0.1185	86.67	0.05	5.70	0.01	1.20	6.38
3	0.1292	73.48	0.50	12.71	0.62	1.04	11.66
4	0.1362	66.21	1.87	13.33	5.06	2.80	10.74
5	0.1431	60.23	2.86	18.51	5.84	2.77	9.79
6	0.1516	54.05	4.47	23.62	5.45	2.99	9.41
7	0.1595	49.08	5.00	26.33	5.44	3.89	10.27
8	0.1647	46.21	5.22	27.26	5.66	4.91	10.73
9	0.1686	45.02	5.01	27.55	5.64	5.71	11.07
10	0.1716	44.00	4.93	27.61	5.44	6.67	11.34
11	0.1738	42.97	5.11	27.28	5.43	7.91	11.30
12	0.1755	42.17	5.23	26.94	5.85	8.71	11.10
16	0.1799	40.58	5.05	25.91	8.44	9.39	10.63
Orthogonalized innovation in EERM							
1	0.1442	39.62	60.38	0.00	0.00	0.00	0.00
2	0.1729	38.37	55.59	4.49	0.92	0.00	0.62
3	0.1880	32.54	54.41	6.57	1.62	1.15	3.71
4	0.2011	32.22	54.64	6.47	1.55	1.85	3.28
5	0.2048	32.09	52.89	6.66	1.50	3.65	3.21
6	0.2084	30.99	51.21	7.03	1.79	4.93	4.05
7	0.2128	29.78	49.12	7.27	1.90	5.21	6.73
8	0.2172	29.26	47.38	6.99	1.83	6.26	8.28
9	0.2198	29.44	46.65	6.82	1.88	6.80	8.42
10	0.2214	29.13	46.33	6.73	2.45	7.01	8.34
11	0.2234	28.71	45.85	6.61	3.32	7.31	8.19
12	0.2254	28.62	45.14	6.51	4.24	7.35	8.14
16	0.2285	28.35	43.98	6.97	5.38	7.20	8.13
Orthogonalized innovation in import PREMIUM							
1	0.1526	28.81	42.11	29.08	0.00	0.00	0.00
2	0.1984	21.07	32.52	41.64	0.88	1.16	2.74
3	0.2279	16.47	26.59	45.53	2.12	3.15	6.12
4	0.2550	13.96	27.23	41.40	7.13	4.66	5.62
5	0.2716	12.33	24.19	39.87	7.94	9.41	6.27
6	0.2881	11.85	21.49	37.66	7.06	13.13	8.80
7	0.3013	11.05	19.82	36.06	6.60	14.46	12.01
8	0.3121	10.56	18.76	34.02	6.48	17.06	13.13
9	0.3185	10.27	18.17	32.82	7.37	18.53	12.84
10	0.3243	9.95	17.59	31.79	9.43	18.84	12.41
11	0.3300	9.83	17.11	30.69	11.37	19.02	11.98
12	0.3343	9.79	16.73	29.99	12.88	18.83	11.79
16	0.3436	9.36	16.24	30.52	14.28	17.93	11.66

Orthogonalized innovation in FREE RATE

1	0.1202	10.31	2.40	2.56	84.73	0.00	0.00
2	0.1733	9.00	2.06	2.11	85.13	0.47	1.23
3	0.1942	7.91	2.81	1.72	84.20	0.89	2.47
4	0.2037	7.95	4.56	2.87	80.61	1.03	2.98
5	0.2110	7.83	5.51	3.39	75.95	2.47	4.85
6	0.2135	7.87	5.89	3.58	74.38	3.19	5.09
7	0.2156	7.73	6.79	4.03	73.06	3.38	5.01
8	0.2180	7.66	7.27	4.32	72.16	3.63	4.97
9	0.2203	7.85	7.57	4.42	71.45	3.65	5.06
10	0.2215	7.91	7.68	4.39	71.17	3.63	5.23
11	0.2219	7.88	7.68	4.38	71.04	3.62	5.40
12	0.2222	7.88	7.67	4.44	70.89	3.62	5.50
16	0.2235	7.91	7.76	4.97	70.09	3.67	5.60

Orthogonalized innovation in IMPORT

1	0.1342	2.29	1.24	0.01	4.69	91.77	0.00
2	0.1485	4.52	2.37	1.55	4.21	85.45	1.89
3	0.1501	4.46	2.45	2.65	4.35	83.97	2.11
4	0.1529	4.36	4.17	2.69	4.84	81.80	2.15
5	0.1589	4.51	5.19	2.53	5.28	76.25	6.23
6	0.1642	4.54	5.01	5.14	6.69	71.73	6.88
7	0.1682	4.49	4.85	7.00	7.71	68.44	7.51
8	0.1714	4.37	4.71	9.11	8.13	66.05	7.64
9	0.1745	4.25	4.71	10.34	8.19	64.34	8.18
10	0.1772	4.13	4.61	11.25	7.97	63.44	8.60
11	0.1795	4.03	4.55	11.97	7.79	62.51	9.14
12	0.1814	3.95	4.56	12.25	7.74	62.03	9.46
16	0.1867	3.76	5.03	11.80	9.48	60.67	9.26

Orthogonalized innovation in EXPORT

1	0.1104	1.76	1.26	0.04	0.02	3.68	93.24
2	0.1214	1.85	1.39	2.46	2.46	3.05	88.79
3	0.1311	1.64	1.21	7.29	6.63	3.13	80.11
4	0.1391	1.46	3.90	12.51	5.89	4.88	71.35
5	0.1426	1.58	3.99	14.10	5.94	5.99	68.41
6	0.1458	1.94	3.90	15.31	6.57	6.61	65.68
7	0.1489	1.86	4.81	15.02	6.94	7.97	63.39
8	0.1507	1.88	5.19	15.05	7.73	8.23	61.92
9	0.1526	1.85	5.89	14.68	8.42	8.75	60.41
10	0.1546	1.81	6.63	14.53	9.05	9.13	58.85
11	0.1564	1.77	7.16	14.64	9.78	9.12	57.53
12	0.1579	1.74	7.51	14.94	10.40	9.03	56.38
16	0.1615	1.74	7.61	16.31	11.39	8.78	54.17

Table 9.3 Percentage of forecast error *k* quarters ahead produced by each innovation (alternative order)

k	Standard error	EX-PORT	IM-PORT	EERX	EERM	PRE-MIUM	FREE RATE
Orthogonalized innovation in EXPORT							
1	0.1104	100.00	0.00	0.00	0.00	0.00	0.00
2	0.1214	93.50	1.02	0.90	0.09	2.69	1.81
3	0.1311	83.24	3.29	0.85	0.08	7.77	4.78
4	0.1391	74.64	5.07	0.81	2.23	12.89	4.37
5	0.1426	71.80	6.01	0.80	2.65	14.46	4.28
6	0.1458	69.11	6.92	0.97	2.74	15.64	4.63
7	0.1489	66.80	7.99	0.98	4.16	15.33	4.73
8	0.1507	65.26	8.46	0.98	4.68	15.34	5.27
9	0.1526	63.69	9.06	0.95	5.64	14.97	5.68
10	0.1546	62.06	9.53	0.94	6.58	14.83	6.07
11	0.1564	60.66	9.59	0.95	7.22	14.94	6.64
12	0.1579	59.45	9.57	0.94	7.62	15.24	7.17
16	0.1615	57.15	9.25	1.01	7.71	16.63	8.24
Orthogonalized innovation in IMPORT							
1	0.1342	4.55	95.45	0.00	0.00	0.00	0.00
2	0.1485	7.93	86.77	0.99	2.74	1.56	0.00
3	0.1501	7.89	85.19	1.00	2.82	2.70	0.41
4	0.1529	7.71	82.49	1.04	4.63	2.74	1.39
5	0.1589	9.80	78.65	1.50	5.81	2.61	1.63
6	0.1642	9.72	74.94	1.68	5.59	5.33	2.74
7	0.1682	10.05	71.60	1.83	5.44	7.25	3.83
8	0.1714	10.13	68.96	1.77	5.32	9.38	4.43
9	0.1745	10.74	66.70	1.71	5.46	10.64	4.76
10	0.1772	11.28	65.23	1.75	5.44	11.56	4.74
11	0.1795	11.88	63.95	1.80	5.47	12.29	4.62
12	0.1814	12.28	63.17	1.83	5.60	12.57	4.55
16	0.1867	12.09	61.88	1.83	6.43	12.10	5.66
Orthogonalized innovation in EERX							
1	0.0893	1.76	1.59	96.65	0.00	0.00	0.00
2	0.1185	3.05	5.78	84.81	0.11	6.02	0.23
3	0.1292	7.26	5.80	72.24	0.85	13.32	0.53
4	0.1362	6.90	5.62	65.10	2.54	13.89	5.95
5	0.1431	6.25	5.30	59.18	3.43	18.98	6.86
6	0.1516	6.87	5.13	52.87	4.55	24.10	6.48
7	0.1595	8.86	5.23	47.81	4.67	26.84	6.59
8	0.1647	9.83	5.39	45.32	4.64	27.79	7.02
9	0.1686	10.27	5.47	44.64	4.43	28.07	7.12
10	0.1716	10.62	5.81	44.00	4.52	28.13	6.92
11	0.1738	10.70	6.67	43.16	4.94	27.78	6.76
12	0.1755	10.56	7.60	42.35	5.20	27.42	6.87
16	0.1799	10.07	9.35	40.55	5.10	26.37	8.55

Orthogonalized innovation in EERM

1	0.1442	2.91	2.21	35.77	59.10	0.00	0.00
2	0.1729	2.04	1.90	35.45	55.13	4.55	0.93
3	0.1880	4.36	2.04	29.97	55.57	6.69	1.37
4	0.2011	3.91	2.36	29.57	56.10	6.56	1.49
5	0.2048	4.05	4.02	29.13	54.48	6.74	1.57
6	0.2084	5.31	5.04	28.29	52.61	7.12	1.65
7	0.2128	8.02	4.97	27.40	50.50	7.39	1.71
8	0.2172	9.55	5.20	27.50	48.99	7.11	1.65
9	0.2198	9.59	5.37	28.05	48.42	6.94	1.63
10	0.2214	9.49	5.60	27.84	48.19	6.85	2.02
11	0.2234	9.33	6.15	27.38	47.79	6.73	2.61
12	0.2254	9.20	6.57	27.25	47.07	6.62	3.29
16	0.2285	9.10	6.69	26.97	45.84	7.09	4.30

Orthogonalized innovation in PREMIUM

1	0.1526	2.39	1.36	26.03	41.17	29.06	0.00
2	0.1984	2.72	0.81	20.23	33.23	41.89	1.11
3	0.2279	6.53	1.17	15.45	28.10	45.96	2.79
4	0.2550	6.09	1.30	12.84	29.28	41.78	8.70
5	0.2716	7.48	3.69	11.67	26.40	40.22	10.54
6	0.2881	10.65	5.78	12.43	23.63	38.02	9.49
7	0.3013	14.09	6.42	12.16	22.19	36.45	8.70
8	0.3121	15.57	8.26	12.17	21.45	34.39	8.15
9	0.3185	15.35	10.00	12.10	20.99	33.16	8.39
10	0.3243	14.89	11.19	11.68	20.41	32.11	9.72
11	0.3300	14.40	12.32	11.37	19.92	31.00	10.98
12	0.3343	14.07	12.85	11.22	19.50	30.30	12.06
16	0.3436	13.89	12.50	10.69	18.80	30.87	13.25

Orthogonalized innovation in FREE RATE

1	0.1202	0.12	3.15	11.89	1.83	2.67	80.35
2	0.1733	0.30	1.58	10.32	2.09	2.15	83.56
3	0.1942	1.22	1.26	8.77	3.06	1.75	83.95
4	0.2037	2.04	1.17	8.96	4.50	2.95	80.38
5	0.2110	4.66	1.55	9.30	4.93	3.49	76.07
6	0.2135	5.12	1.91	9.53	5.13	3.69	74.63
7	0.2156	5.03	2.32	9.37	5.93	4.12	73.23
8	0.2180	4.92	3.07	9.21	6.33	4.39	72.09
9	0.2203	4.87	3.55	9.31	6.63	4.48	71.17
10	0.2215	4.93	3.73	9.35	6.76	4.44	70.79
11	0.2219	5.08	3.74	9.33	6.78	4.43	70.65
12	0.2222	5.20	3.74	9.31	6.76	4.49	70.50
16	0.2235	5.40	3.78	9.28	6.81	5.03	69.70

orderings in this case, even though some of the off-diagonal elements of the correlation matrix of innovations (not shown) are not small. This lack of sensitivity to ordering is reassuring although other orderings may produce more significant changes.

Historical Decomposition of the Indonesian Trade Liberalization

A historical decomposition of the performance of the six endogenous variables of the model was performed using the partitioning of the moving-average representation of equation (9.4). The decomposition begins with 1966, quarter I, the period in which the *Bonus Ekspor* import entitlement certificate system began. The quantitative restrictions system was abolished on October 3, 1966. Figure 9.2 plots the paths of three time series: (a) the actual level of quarterly import flows (labeled ACTUAL); (b) the forecast level of import flows based on information on endogenous variables available at time 1966, quarter I, and the actual contemporaneous values of all deterministic variables (labeled WITHOUT QRS); (c) the forecast level of import flows based on information on endogenous variables available at time 1966, quarter I, and the contemporaneous value of all deterministic variables *except* the quantitative restrictions dummy variable, which instead has the value zero indicating the existence of a quantitative restrictions regime (labeled WITH QRS). The difference

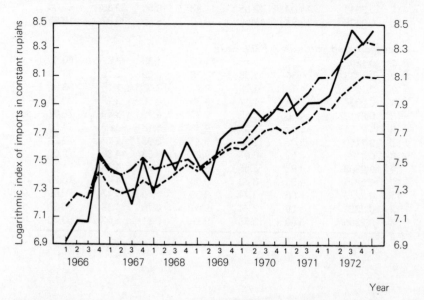

Figure 9.2 Historical import decomposition (BE begins in 1966, quarter I; quantitative restrictions end in 1966, quarter IV): ——, actual; – – –, with QRS; – · – without QRS

between ACTUAL and WITH QRS is the accumulated historical effect on imports of the sum of all the innovations of the six endogenous variables of the system. The difference between WITH QRS and WITHOUT QRS is the effect of ending the quantitative restrictions regime (as indicated by the dummy variable) on historical flows of import.

Figure 9.3 plots the difference ACTUAL minus WITH QRS as the series OTHER INNOVATIONS and the difference WITHOUT QRS minus WITH QRS as the series QR INNOVATION. The series OTHER INNOVATIONS demonstrates a rather erratic pattern for the sum of the six innovations. There is a rather sharp negative "other" innovation in 1966, quarter I, which remains mostly negative until early 1968. The negative response in 1966 is mostly due to a large import innovation plus lesser innovations in PREMIUM, FREE RATE, and both effective exchange rates. Table 9.4 provides the details on innovations. There is very little pattern to the innovations after 1966. The FREE RATE is perhaps the most consistent source of innovations negatively affecting import throughout the period (it contributes negatively to OTHER INNOVA-TIONS in 20 out of 29 quarters). Nevertheless, it is remarkable that, with the possible exception of 1966, innovations from the other endogenous variables had very little persistent effect on imports. It is quite clear from figure 9.3 that only the end of quantitative restrictions liberalization persistently affected imports.

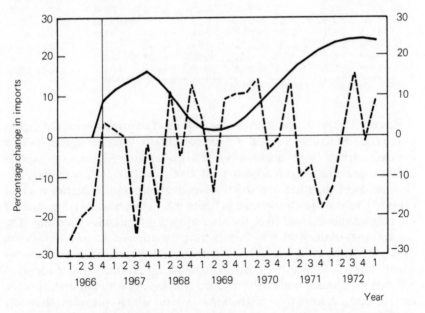

Figure 9.3 Sources of innovation for imports (BE begins in 1966, quarter I; quantitative restrictions end in 1966, quarter IV): ——, QR innovation; ‒‒‒, other innovations

Table 9.4 Historical decomposition of import series, 1966, quarter I, to 1973, quarter I

Date	Actual	Forecast[a]	Innovations contributing to the difference between actual and forecast imports						
			QRs	EERX	EERM	PREMIUM	FREE	IMPORT	EXPORT
66 I	6.918	7.174	0.000	− 0.031	− 0.037	0.001	− 0.023	− 0.167	0.000
66 II	7.070	7.268	0.000	− 0.024	0.050	− 0.015	− 0.021	− 0.171	− 0.017
66 III	7.061	7.234	0.000	0.028	− 0.004	− 0.020	− 0.067	− 0.084	− 0.026
66 IV	7.558	7.430	0.092	0.032	0.066	0.051	− 0.014	− 0.112	0.013
67 I	7.440	7.304	0.116	0.004	− 0.058	0.041	− 0.021	− 0.013	0.041
67 II	7.400	7.266	0.134	0.010	0.005	− 0.038	− 0.010	− 0.035	0.067
67 III	7.194	7.291	0.147	− 0.018	− 0.028	− 0.052	− 0.039	− 0.172	0.064
67 IV	7.508	7.360	0.163	− 0.043	− 0.006	0.048	−. 0.062	0.028	0.021
68 I	7.269	7.304	0.141	0.001	− 0.043	0.002	− 0.089	− 0.058	0.012
68 II	7.575	7.351	0.108	0.031	0.006	− 0.045	− 0.051	0.172	0.003
68 III	7.434	7.413	0.070	− 0.002	− 0.010	− 0.045	− 0.016	0.011	0.012
68 IV	7.640	7.472	0.039	− 0.040	0.015	− 0.027	0.014	0.105	0.063
69 I	7.489	7.428	0.020	0.003	− 0.058	− 0.049	− 0.034	0.092	0.089
69 II	7.366	7.489	0.016	0.023	0.007	− 0.067	0.004	− 0.102	− 0.003
69 III	7.668	7.556	0.018	0.029	− 0.019	− 0.105	0.078	0.104	0.006
69 IV	7.740	7.603	0.029	0.025	0.041	− 0.110	0.107	0.145	− 0.101
70 I	7.747	7.587	0.051	0.020	− 0.028	− 0.044	0.064	0.100	− 0.002
70 II	7.877	7.654	0.078	0.002	0.006	0.001	0.048	0.167	− 0.078
70 III	7.795	7.723	0.105	− 0.003	− 0.011	− 0.017	0.097	− 0.008	− 0.091
70 IV	.7.876	7.748	0.133	− 0.017	− 0.008	− 0.013	0.072	0.068	− 0.109
71 I	7.995	7.699	0.160	− 0.005	0.009	0.041	− 0.008	0.224	− 0.124
71 II	7.831	7.747	0.184	− 0.015	0.020	0.103	− 0.033	− 0.090	− 0.085
71 III	7.927	7.794	0.205	− 0.034	0.020	0.102	0.005	− 0.110	− 0.054
71 IV	7.927	7.887	0.222	− 0.004	0.011	0.080	− 0.015	− 0.248	− 0.005
72 I	7.981	7.875	0.235	− 0.014	0.036	0.121	− 0.057	− 0.227	0.013
72 II	8.231	7.977	0.242	− 0.028	0.041	0.157	− 0.061	− 0.112	0.014
72 III	8.454	8.044	0.246	− 0.021	0.055	0.148	− 0.015	0.002	− 0.006
72 IV.	8.353	8.120	0.245	0.005	0.012	0.094	− 0.025	− 0.072	− 0.026
73 I	8.448	8.110	0.242	0.027	0.015	0.074	− 0.011	− 0.040	0.032

[a] Forecast imports with QRs remaining in existence.

Figures 9.4 and 9.5 provide the same types of information for the export time series as figures 9.2 and 9.3 did for import. Note in figure 9.4 that forecast exports with quantitative restrictions exceed forecast exports without quantitative restrictions until 1969, quarter II. Thereafter, the elimination of quantitative restrictions innovation results in higher levels of export. This is more clearly seen in figure 9.5. As with imports, the sum of the innovations derived from the six endogenous variables is erratic. The greatest part of this variation derives from variation in the own-innovation of exports (see table 9.5). This is perhaps not surprising in an economy where non-oil exports are primarily agricultural products whose supply is affected by climatic and environmental shocks. As with imports, it is the end of the quantitative restrictions system which provides the only persistent source of the deviation of exports from forecast values.

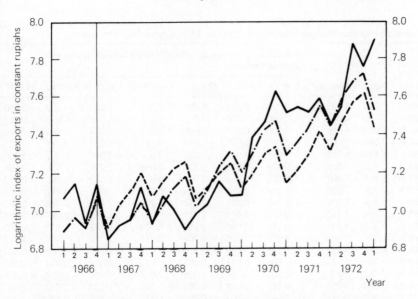

Figure 9.4 Historical export decomposition (BE begins in 1966, quarter I; quantitative restrictions end in 1966, quarter IV): —, actual; – – –, with QRS; – · –, without QRS

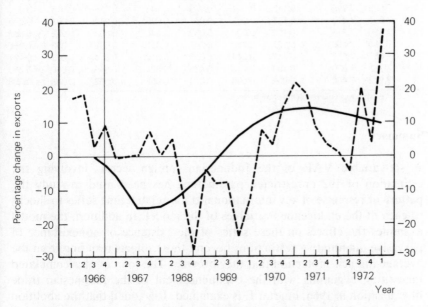

Figure 9.5 Sources of innovation for exports (BE begins in 1966, quarter I; quantitative restrictions end in 1966, quarter IV): —, QR innovation; – – –, other innovations

Table 9.5 Historical decomposition of export series, 1966, quarter I, to 1973, quarter I

			Innovations contributing to the difference between actual and forecast imports						
Date	Actual	Forecast[a]	QRs	EERX	EERM	PREMIUM	FREE	IMPORT	EXPORT
66 I	7.070	6.899	0.000	0.022	0.031	0.002	− 0.001	0.028	0.090
66 II	7.150	6.968	0.000	− 0.020	0.012	− 0.015	− 0.016	0.019	0.203
66 III	6.939	6.910	0.000	− 0.012	0.008	− 0.033	− 0.034	− 0.006	0.106
66 IV	7.148	7.080	− 0.025	0.007	0.055	0.027	− 0.059	0.031	0.031
67 I	6.851	6.913	− 0.058	0.001	− 0.035	0.066	− 0.064	0.025	0.004
67 II	6.926	7.030	− 0.105	0.016	0.001	0.049	− 0.013	0.036	− 0.088
67 III	6.957	7.103	− 0.153	0.010	− 0.061	− 0.015	0.002	0.082	− 0.010
67 IV	7.126	7.202	− 0.154	0.008	− 0.035	− 0.017	0.052	0.017	0.053
68 I	6.934	7.076	− 0.148	− 0.036	− 0.042	− 0.063	0.064	0.038	0.045
68 II	7.084	7.161	− 0.128	− 0.011	− 0.041	− 0.089	0.062	0.037	0.094
68 III	7.012	7.231	− 0.105	0.009	− 0.046	− 0.129	0.078	0.033	− 0.060
68 IV	6.910	7.266	− 0.077	0.020	− 0.006	− 0.117	0.106	0.041	− 0.323
69 I	6.989	7.068	− 0.045	− 0.009	− 0.009	− 0.073	0.107	0.002	− 0.052
69 II	7.041	7.125	− 0.006	0.014	0.003	− 0.016	0.070	0.034	− 0.184
69 III	7.161	7.204	0.031	− 0.004	0.005	− 0.004	0.016	− 0.017	− 0.070
69 IV	7.084	7.255	0.063	− 0.001	0.052	− 0.005	0.033	− 0.050	− 0.262
70 I	7.084	7.114	0.090	− 0.007	0.002	0.031	0.025	0.010	− 0.180
70 II	7.390	7.200	0.111	− 0.016	0.033	0.088	− 0.015	− 0.042	− 0.031
70 III	7.466	7.301	0.127	0.009	− 0.010	0.120	− 0.045	− 0.021	− 0.014
70 IV	7.630	7.339	0.137	− 0.016	0.008	0.123	− 0.027	− 0.030	0.096
71 I	7.517	7.152	0.143	0.004	0.008	0.122	− 0.007	− 0.100	0.194
71 II	7.546	7.214	0.145	0.009	0.005	0.146	− 0.044	− 0.003	0.073
71 III	7.520	7.296	0.143	0.004	0.029	0.142	− 0.055	− 0.015	− 0.023
71 IV	7.591	7.419	0.138	− 0.008	0.041	0.090	− 0.017	− 0.052	− 0.020
72 I	7.458	7.316	0.130	0.020	0.033	0.046	0.005	− 0.006	− 0.087
72 II	7.550	7.466	0.122	− 0.002	0.047	0.017	0.000	− 0.033	− 0.066
72 III	7.887	7.567	0.113	0.014	0.058	0.012	0.014	− 0.012	0.121
72 IV	7.762	7.620	0.104	− 0.013	0.025	− 0.024	0.045	0.056	− 0.050
73 I	7.912	7.430	0.096	− 0.006	0.024	− 0.058	0.062	0.036	0.328

[a] Forecast exports with QRs remaining in existence.

Summary

A six-variable VAR of the Indonesian foreign sector, involving the estimation of 192 unrestricted parameters, has been used to study the pattern of response of key international-trade-related time series to shocks to each of the endogenous variables of the model. In addition, the model examines the effects on these series of the existence or nonexistence of pervasive quantitative restrictions beyond those effects resulting from the average implicit protection that they provide. The sources of accumulated innovation beginning with the commencement of the Indonesian trade liberalization in 1966, quarter I, is examined. It is found that the abolition of the quantitative restrictions regime was the only persistent innovation affecting import and export in the post-liberalization period studied (1966, quarter I, to 1973, quarter II) and resulted in a higher level of both, but with some lag. Exchange rate innovations were not important determinants of imports and exports during this period. In summary, the level of trade flows in the post-liberalization period was not persistently affected by innovations in exchange rate or the implicit protection resulting from quantitative restrictions. It was only the alteration in the method of exchange control from quantitative restriction to the price mechanism which persistently affected trade.

10

Lessons of the Indonesian Experience for the Timing and Sequencing of a Trade Liberalization

In this chapter we examine the Indonesian experience for insights as to the appropriate path for a liberalization policy. Economic theory and our reading of the literature on the experience of other countries with liberalization strongly support the conviction that liberalization is important in fostering development and also suggest how we might determine optimal liberalization paths. Below, the intention is not to draw conclusions or make general statements on these liberalization issues on the basis of this wide body of existing evidence, but merely to determine what additional evidence is provided by the Indonesian experience.

Even though four liberalization episodes are described above, one in detail, our ability to draw inferences based solely on the resulting observations is somewhat limited. The number of factors that may affect the timing and success of a liberalization far exceed the number of observations that the Indonesian experience offers. Moreover, the liberalizations of 1955 and 1957–8 are not very informative about the issues of timing and sequencing because they were carried out for specific non-economic reasons. The 1955 liberalization was an attempt by a caretaker cabinet to leave a strong impression on the electorate just weeks before a national election. The coalition partners did poorly in the election, in which economic issues were not central. The succeeding cabinet reversed the liberalization that their opponents had fashioned and tried to use against them in the election. The 1957–8 liberalization was an attempt to forestall civil war between the central government and the export-oriented regions of Sumatra and Sulawesi: had these regions not declared a "State of War and Siege" there would not have been a liberalization. When the revolt was crushed, the liberalization was swiftly ended. The peculiarity of the 1950–1 liberalization is that it was the first economic policy package of a newly independent nation; again, economic issues were overwhelmed by other concerns, paramount among them being ethnic identity and patriotic rhetoric. Because of the special circumstances of these early liberalizations and their short duration, the discussion below of inferences for timing and sequencing of trade liberalization (see the preface to this volume) will focus on factors which may have been important determinants of the success of the 1966 liberalization.

Was this really a liberalization? In the months before the liberalization the instruments of economic control were widely evaded by black markets. As a result, a substantial part of the response to liberalization (as typically measured) represented the redirection of illegal market activities into legal market activities. It was found for example that the real return to rubber export *inclusive* of illegal receipts was no greater after the liberalization than before. Furthermore, econometric evidence suggests that most of the increase in smallholder rubber export reflected the redirection of smuggling into legal channels. Thus, while the pre-liberalization trade regime was in principle extraordinarily restrictive, the pervasiveness of illegal transactions meant that in practice resource misallocation, though still large, was probably less than it might have been. Nonetheless, this was unquestionably a liberalization. In 1965 Indonesia, economic agents were unwilling to save and invest in an uncertain climate in which the state could seize assets without compensation, where market signals (prices) were obscured by the manipulation of monopolies and the whims of the state, and where private information – who you knew rather than what you knew – were key determinants of economic success. Private information, quantitative controls, and corruption are still elements of the Indonesian economy, as they always have been. However, these problems were an order of magnitude greater in the pre-liberalization period.

The Staging and Length of the Liberalization Process

The successful Indonesian liberalization of 1966 did not consist of pre-announced stages. It occurred quite suddenly, and the most important liberalizing initiatives were introduced in rapid succession between May 1966 and July 1967. Most notably, the highly restrictive import-licensing system was swept away in a single day in October 1966. Might the speed and suddenness with which it took place account for the success of the liberalization? Such a conclusion is not supported by the whole of the Indonesian experience. The Sumitro reforms of 1955 and the BE system of 1957 were also sudden dramatic one-stage liberalizations. The liberalization of 1950–1 was a staged affair. Why did the sudden and sweeping liberalizations of 1955 and 1957–8 fail while the 1966 liberalization succeeded?

The economic situation in Indonesia before the 1966 liberalization differed markedly from the situation before the earlier attempts. The virtual breakdown of the economy discredited the Guided Economy notions that the state must regulate and control prices, trade, and production in order to achieve desirable social objectives. Most economic groups were willing to see the instruments of control dismantled. Before the two earlier liberalizations, in 1955 and 1957, the state of the economy was not nearly so desperate. The rates of growth of gross national product were generally positive in those years and inflation was only in single or double digits. Moreover, the control of the state was not nearly as comprehensive as it was in 1966, and thus it was both popular and patriotic to blame economic woes on the Dutch, who still dominated trade, and on an unfair international economic system.

The political situation in 1966 also differed radically from that of earlier liberalization attempts. In the immediate aftermath of the coup attempt of September 30, 1965, the Communist Party, a leading proponent of economic control, was eliminated – its members were murdered or driven underground. President Sukarno's power and that of his political establishment, rooted in the Guided Economy, began to disintegrate. Recall that this was no ordinary political struggle: the opposing parties had more to lose than their power and livelihoods. The level of violence was extraordinary – perhaps half a million dead, including many notable political leaders – and the annihilation of opposition meant liquidating their source of power, the state apparatus, and a revolutionary change in ideology. Political opposition to liberalization may have been identified with support of the Old Order (and hence Communism) and therefore considered dangerous. In contrast, the 1955 and 1957 liberalizations were strategic moves aimed toward short-term political objectives, rather than a response to a desperate economic situation. There was no sweeping political change or revolutionary change in ideology.

What about the private sector? Why did they not oppose the 1966 liberalization at the time of its introduction? First, the private sector had been almost completely eliminated from direct international trade, and the state trading corporations, their agents in trade, were probably able to capture most premiums. Second, it was official policy for state enterprises and "cooperatives" to have higher priority in the foreign exchange allocation process. A free-market system must have seemed preferable to private sector enterprises, even if it might mean an increase in competitive imports. Overall capacity utilization in manufacturing was 25 percent, and it was lower still among privately owned enterprises. There could be few worries among private firms about economic dislocation resulting from liberalization with utilization rates already at historically low levels. Third, indigenous private sector entrepreneurs in Indonesia tended to come from reformist Moslem groups. During parliamentary days, they were the backbone of the Masjumi political party, the primary opposition to Sukarno's PNI and to the PKI. On ideological and religious grounds alone, private sector entrepreneurs were keenly interested in the success of the New Order forces over President Sukarno.

It is true that there was equally little opposition to liberalization by private sector entrepreneurs at the time of the 1950–1 liberalization. This simply reflected the fact that there were very few Indonesian entrepreneurs in 1950, and those few were not closely associated with trade or reliant on the state. However, by the time of the 1955 liberalization, there was an important class of private entrepreneurs – the *Benteng* and monopoly importers – whose livelihoods were threatened by liberalization. This class was closely attached to, or were one and the same as, important political figures. They represented the vanguard of the new "national economy" which was eventually to displace the "colonial economy" still controlled by the Dutch. Between the 1950s and 1966 this entrepreneurial class had simply become part of the state itself – the "bureaucratic capitalists" – and was thus discredited with it as the economy disintegrated in the 1960s.

The Length of the Liberalization Process and the Appropriate Speed of Liberalization

The political situation explains not only the radical economic changes of 1966 but also why they took place over such a short period of time. The regulatory and trade apparatus – bureaucrats and the managers of state enterprises – were made up of Sukarno's cronies who could not be trusted to faithfully carry out a staged liberalization and were actively opposing the emerging New Order government. Ending their control over international trade was an effective method of reducing their power and that of the rentier class who were strongly aligned with President Sukarno.

The speed of the liberalization may also have been impelled by the need to impress upon foreign creditors, particularly Western nations, and the IMF and World Bank that the change in course of the Indonesian economy was genuine. In early 1966 imports had almost come to a complete halt, foreign reserves were negative, Japan had cut off most of its exports to Indonesia, and borrowing from the Soviet Union and China was no longer possible. Indonesia desperately needed foreign credits from those nations and institutions it had spurned as "neocolonialist and imperialist" just months earlier, and many of whom had had their assets nationalized without compensation. Thus its desperate economic straits, the end of aid from the Communist bloc, and its reputation as mercurial and untrustworthy in international affairs may have required Indonesia to put its liberalization program in effect *before* qualifying for aid and rapprochement with the West.

Not only did the Indonesian government suffer from a lack of credibility with other nations, it had very little with its own people. The proclamations of the Indonesian government in early 1966 were not believed by the public. The revolutionary rhetoric of the past years did not match up to the economic reality. This was a nation familiar with the announcement of grandiose schemes – such as the man-in-space scheme – and the use of Orwellian "Newspeak." More to the point, earlier liberalization attempts had been scuttled very soon after their initiation, and announced changes in policy, such as President Sukarno's DEKON of 1963, were never carried out in their entirety. In such an environment, announcements of future liberalization stages or policy changes would probably be totally discounted by economic agents. Thus, in order to establish credibility, the government could not hope to alter behavior through announcement of the future course of policy but only through an immediate and profound change in policy.

The Desirability of a Separate Stage Concerned with the Promotion of Exports and/or Foreign Capital Flows and its Place in the Policy Sequencing

Importing could not be liberalized until after the "export drive" initiative, of which the BE and checkprice–overprice systems were the central elements, began to yield results and until Indonesia could reschedule its enormous debt and obtain fresh credits abroad. One of the first measures of the New Order regime was to apply for readmission to the IMF, the World Bank, and the United Nations from which Indonesia had withdrawn in 1965. Missions from the IMF and World Bank visited Indonesia in mid-1966 to assist in the formulation of economic policy. They were instrumental in arranging a meeting of representatives of the non-Communist creditor nations at the Tokyo conference in September 1966 to discuss proposals for a moratorium on Indonesia's debt commitments. With interest and amortization commitments in 1967 exceeding expected export receipts by nearly half, it was agreed in principle to defer some payments. A December meeting in Paris concluded a moratorium arrangement that delayed until 1971 all payments of interest and principal on all debt except short-term commercial credit. Payment schedules and interest charges were very favorable to Indonesia. The Soviet Union, Indonesia's largest single creditor, and other Eastern bloc nations also agreed to reschedule debt.

With the prospect of a debt moratorium and having received assurances of new grants and credits of US$174 million from the United States, the Federal Republic of Germany, Japan, and other nations, Indonesia initiated its first direct import liberalization measures in October 1966 at the same time as the BE percentages for export were enlarged. Import license restrictions were almost entirely swept away. Direct foreign exchange allocations to manufacturing firms were ended. Importers were free to buy almost any good they wished. Reinvigorated legal export flows, a large infusion of foreign grants and loans, and the guarantees of support (and perhaps the insistence) of the donor countries allowed the dramatic end of quantitative restrictions to occur in the virtual absence of foreign exchange reserves.

The Appropriate Circumstances for the Introduction of a Liberalization Policy and its Sustainability under and Relationship to other Policy Measures

It is claimed above that the extraordinary economic and political circumstances at the time of the 1966 Indonesian liberalization were important factors in its success. However, total economic breakdown and political and social upheaval are hardly useful policy prescriptions as prerequisites for successful liberalization. In the Indonesian context it is more useful to consider the manner in which other policy measures reinforced and helped sustain the trade liberalization.

The control of inflation insistently demanded by the student demonstrators in Jakarta in early 1966 was proclaimed as the first priority of the Suharto regime. The only specific target announced by the government in any area of economic policy was the promise (in December 1966) of a balanced budget by 1967. In pursuit of this goal, the government turned its attention to the fiscal deficit, widely regarded as the source of Indonesia's triple-digit inflation, and went after subsidies and public expenditure with an ax. In the Indonesian case it may be more appropriate to ask how liberalization reinforced this stabilization effort rather than the other way around. As early as November 1965, the government declared its intention of ending subsidies. The government clearly recognized that its budgetary problems would be vastly improved by redirecting quota and black-market premiums into the treasury, and the trade liberalization effectively achieved this. The BE (and Aid-BE) system, key elements of the trade liberalization, became important new sources of revenue for the government in their balanced budget drive. The popular response to the dramatic reductions in subsidies was surprisingly mild. One reason is that black markets were so important that the end of quotas and subsidies did not significantly change relative prices so much as capture premiums.

Undoubtedly the capital market liberalization begun in 1966 also played an important part in sustaining the liberalization. The BE system became the mechanism of choice for aid from the newly organized IGGI. In addition, private capital inflows became considerable, reflecting both a substantial return of flight capital and new foreign investment under the liberal Foreign Investment Law. Most of this flight capital returned in the form of DP exchange and significantly contributed to supporting the new foreign exchange market.

The General Applicability of the Indonesian Case

While every liberalization episode and every country has unique aspects, the Indonesian experience of 1966 differs considerably from many of the liberalization episodes considered in this project. Issues of the speed and staging of liberalization and the uniform or discriminatory treatment of sectors are important when there are major economic and political groups whose fortunes are closely tied to the liberalization process, and who have the ability to reverse such a process by virtue of the magnitude of the harm inflicted upon them by liberalization or by virtue of their political power. Manufacturing in Indonesia was probably less important, economic straits were probably more desperate, and standard avenues of political expression were probably less open than for any other liberalization episode of this research project. The Indonesian liberalization, although dramatic by most standards, was part of a revolution of such historical magnitude that it was not the major innovation of the state at the time of its introduction. While the Indonesian experience strongly suggests that its improved economic performance was a result of its liberalized trade regime, the liberalization itself occurred during a period of such chaos that generalizable inferences on sequencing and desirable discrimination are nearly impossible to make.

Appendix 1

Smuggling, Price Disparity, and the Black Market for Foreign Exchange

A model of smuggling relevant to the Indonesian experience must be able to explain the coexistence of three phenomena: smuggling, legal trade, and price disparity in a commodity. Price disparity is defined as the positive (negative) difference between the domestic market price and the tax-inclusive world price of an exported (imported) commodity. Price disparity means that the domestic price of an exportable is greater than its return from legal export, that is, any legal export seemingly occurs at a loss.

A natural justification for legal trade at a loss is its ability to reduce the costs of smuggling. To hide their smuggling, it is necessary for trading firms to trade legally. Obviously, in order to underinvoice an import, it is necessary to declare some positive value. Furthermore, it is logical to assume that success in avoiding detection is inversely related to the degree of underinvoicing. For example, an item worth US$100 declared to be worth US$99 has a greater chance of fooling the customs officer than the same item declared at US$10. This reasoning extends to other types of faked declarations as well. A trader seeking to undervalue a good whose unit price is well known may do so by declaring it to be something else, or may declare an incorrect number of units. For example, 10,000 tons of rubber may be declared to weight 9,000 tons. Alternatively, grade I rubber may be declared as grade II or, with greater risk of detection, as grade V. In all the above cases the declared value of a shipment is legal trade, while smuggling is the difference between the actual and the declared values. The type of invoice faking is not of consequence here, although it can be important in the detection of smuggling. The point is that the less the ratio of the declared value to the actual value, the greater is the risk of detection and thus the cost of smuggling.

Consider a small economy, that is, one for which the terms of trade are fixed, that produces two traded goods X and M, an exportable and importable respectively, with primary factors in perfect competition. Production and trade are carried out by identical firms. Each firm can trade illegally according to the "smuggling function"

$$\bar{s} = g(l,s) \tag{A1.1}$$

where $\bar{s}$ is the quantity of good X smuggled, l is the quantity of good X legally trade, s is the quantity of good X input into the smuggling activity, and $g(\cdot)$ is a strictly concave and twice continuously differentiable linear homogenous function. It is further assumed that it has the properties

$$g_l \geq 0 \tag{A1.1a}$$
$$1 \geq g_s \geq 0 \tag{A1.1b}$$
$$s \geq \bar{s} \tag{A1.1c}$$

Assumption (A1.1a) states that the marginal product of legal trade in the smuggling activity is nonnegative. Assumption (A1.1b) states that a unit increase in the smuggling input results in a positive but less than unit increase in actual (*ex post*) smuggling. The difference between *ex ante* smuggling s and *ex post* smuggling $\bar{s}$ is the cost of smuggling. Assumption (A1.1c) prohibits this cost from being negative.

Profit maximization in production implies producing on the production possibility curve where the marginal rate of transformation equals the domestic relative price q^s. The traders'/smugglers' decision is then to maximize profits given by

$$\pi = q^f g(l,s) - q^f(1-t)l - q^s(l+s) \tag{A1.2}$$

with first-order conditions

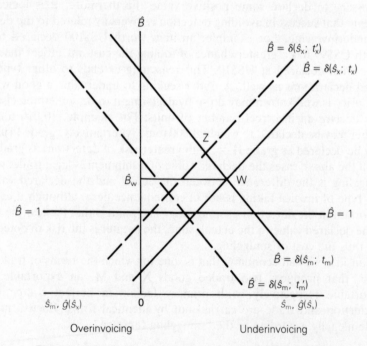

Figure A1.1 Equilibrium in the black market for foreign exchange

$$q^f g_l + q^f(1 - t) = q^s \qquad \text{(A1.2a)}$$
$$q^f g_s = q^s \qquad \text{(A1.2b)}$$

where q^f represents the fixed international terms of trade and t is the tax rate.[1] Conditions (A1.2a) and (A1.2b) state the marginal cost of an additional unit of tradeable will just equal its revenue in trade, be it legal or illegal trade. Note that an additional unit of legal trade results in both additional legal revenue of $q^f(1 - t)$ and additional smuggling revenue of $q^f g_l$. Furthermore, firms will earn zero economic profits because the revenue from all foreign trade is just equal to the domestic cost of tradeables. Setting (A1.2) equal to zero and solving for q^s yields an expression for the equilibrium domestic price as the weighted average of all trade:

$$q^s = q^f \frac{\bar{s}}{l + s} + q^f(1 - t) \frac{l}{l + s} \qquad \text{(A1.3)}$$

Note that the optimization problem of firms could have been equivalently stated as maximizing q^s, the domestic price ratio given by equation (A1.3). That is, firms choose the mix of legal trade and smuggling that provides the highest rate of transformation in trade. The price equation (A1.3) demonstrates that the domestic price of a commodity which is both legally traded and smuggled is not its legal trade price. Furthermore, because the domestic price will exceed the legal trade price, the international value of output in the presence of smuggling will exceed that value in its absence.

An equivalent representation of this model would have firms maximizing expected profit given a function describing the probability of being caught. Note that the linear homogeneous smuggling function (A1.1) can be written as

$$\bar{s} = s\hat{g}\left(\frac{l}{s}\right) \qquad \text{(A1.4)}$$

where $\hat{g}(\cdot)$ is the original function $\hat{g}(\cdot)$ transformed through division by s. The function $\hat{g}(l/s)$ is bounded by zero and unity, and can be thought of as the probability of smuggling success, an increasing function of the legal component of trade.

If legal trade requires the sale or purchase of legal foreign exchange, the coexistence of legal trade and smuggling implies the coexistence of legal and black markets for foreign exchange. Importers who underinvoice in order to avoid tariffs will need to obtain illegally an amount of foreign exchange equal to the difference between the actual and the declared value of their shipments. Exporters who underinvoice to avoid export taxes will

---

[1] While the algebra here applies to export smuggling, the theory applies equally to import and export smuggling in a manner analogous to the symmetry of import and export taxes demonstrated by Lerner.

be willing to sell. The market formed by these illegal traders is referred to as the "black market for foreign exchange."

Equilibrium in this market can be characterized by denormalizing the two-by-two barter model of smuggling above so as to admit money prices in two currencies. Since legal foreign exchange purchases (sales) are assumed to be identically equal to the declared (legal) value of imports (exports), in the absence of quantitative restrictions the market for legal foreign exchange can be characterized as perfectly competitive, with domestic exchange freely convertible into legal foreign exchange at some market clearing price E for foreign exchange in terms of domestic exchange. Similarly, if there are no quantitative restrictions on sales or purchases in the black market, it is cleared as a price B of foreign exchange in terms of domestic exchange.

Exporters maximize profits (in domestic currency units in this case) given by

$$\pi_x = p_x^w B g(l_x, s_x) + p_x^w E(1 - t_x) l_x - p_x^d(s_x + l_x) \tag{A1.5}$$

where l_x and s_x represents legal and *ex ante* smuggled exports respectively, $g(l_x, s_x)$ is the export smuggling function discussed above, and p_x^w and p_x^d are the world and domestic prices respectively of the exportable.

Similarly, importers maximize profit by

$$\pi_m = p_m^d h(l_m, s_m) + p_m^d l_m - p_m^w E(1 + t_m) l_m - p_m^w B s_m \tag{A1.6}$$

where $h(\cdot)$ is the import smuggling function having the same properties as $g(\cdot)$ above.

First-order conditions for the exporter with respect to l_x and s_x are

$$p_x^w B g_l + p_x^w E(1 - t_x) = p_x^d \tag{A1.7}$$

$$p_x^w B g_s = p_x^d \tag{A1.8}$$

and first-order conditions for the importer with respect to l_m and s_m are

$$p_m^d h_l + p_m^d = p_m^w E(1 + t_m) \tag{A1.9}$$

$$p_m^d h_s = p_m^w B \tag{A1.10}$$

Conditions (A1.7)–(A1.10) state that the cost of an additional unit of tradeable to the firm will just equal the revenue to be earned by trading it, be it legally or illegally. These conditions have been expressed in domestic currency units. Also note from (A1.7) and (A1.9) that price disparity will exist for both commodities.

As profits will be zero, (A1.5) and (A1.6) can be set equal to zero and solved for the domestic prices of the exportable and importable as the weighted average of all trade. If world prices are set equal to unity, (A1.5) is divided by l_x, and (A1.6) is divided by l_m, these domestic price equations are

$$p_x^d = \frac{B\hat{g}(s_x) + E(1 - t_x)}{\hat{s}_x + 1} \tag{A1.11}$$

$$p_m^d = \frac{B\hat{s}_m + E(1 + t_m)}{\hbar(\hat{s}_m + 1)} \tag{A1.12}$$

where $\hat{g}(\cdot)$ and $\hbar(\cdot)$ are the smuggling functions in terms of $\hat{s}_x = s_x/l_x$ and $\hat{s}_m = s_m/l_m$ respectively. Maximizing (A1.11) and minimizing (A1.12) is equivalent to maximizing the profits and results in the first-order conditions

$$\hat{B} - \frac{(1 + t_x)}{(\hat{s}_x + 1)\hat{g}' - \hat{g}} = 0 \tag{A1.13}$$

$$\hat{B} - \frac{(1 + t_m)\hbar'}{\hbar - \hat{s}_m\hbar' + 1} = 0 \tag{A1.14}$$

where $\hat{B} = B/E$, $\hat{g}' = \partial\hat{g}(\hat{s}_x)/\partial\hat{s}_x$, and $\hbar = \partial\hbar(\hat{s}_m)/\partial\hat{s}_m$.[2]

For notational convenience, equation (A1.13), the supply curve for black-market foreign exchange given a tax rate, is written as

$$\hat{B} = \sigma(\hat{s}_x) \tag{A1.15}$$

and equation (A1.14), the demand curve for black-market foreign exchange given a tariff rate, is written as

$$\hat{B} = \delta(\hat{s}_m) \tag{A1.16}$$

We can readily sign the derivatives $\sigma' = \partial\sigma(\hat{s}_x)/\partial\hat{s}_x > 0$ and $\delta' = \partial\delta(\hat{s}_m)/\partial\hat{s}_m > 0$, allowing us to draw supply and demand curves for black-market foreign exchange as in figure A1.1.[3]

Note that in this model the supply of black-market foreign exchange is simply the value (quantity) of *ex post* export smuggling $g(l_x, s_x)$ and the demand is the value (quantity) of *ex ante* import smuggling s_m. The equilibrium conditions in the markets for foreign exchange are

$$l_x = l_m \qquad \text{equilibrium in the legal foreign exchange market} \tag{A1.17}$$

[2] From this point on, references to the black-market exchange rate, import smuggling, and export smuggling refer to the normalized terms $\hat{B}$, $\hat{s}_m$, and $\hat{s}_x$.

[3] Figure A1.1 has been drawn over the space of two quadrants because t_x or t_m may have negative values representing subsidies. As smuggling is defined here as declared value less than actual value, overinvoicing represents "negative" smuggling.

$$g(s_x, l_x) = s_m \qquad \text{equilibrium in the black market for foreign}$$
$$\text{exchange} \qquad \text{(A1.18)}$$

which together imply a single normalized equilibrium condition

$$\hat{g} = \hat{s}_m \qquad\qquad\qquad\qquad\qquad\qquad\qquad \text{(A1.19)}$$

Equations (A1.15), (A1.16), and (A1.19) constitute a system of three equations in three unknowns. In figure A1.1, equilibrium is at W with exchange rate $\hat{B}_w$ where condition (A1.19) is satisfied. Equilibrium at W illustrates the case of a positive black-market premium ($\hat{B} > 1$). An increase in the tariff from t_m to t'_m results in equilibrium at Z with an increased black-market rate of exchange and reduced level of smuggling. The black-market price of foreign exchange can be *less* than the legal price with a lower rate of import tariff $t'_m < t_m$, with a new equilibrium at Y. In general, reductions in the import tariff reduce import and export smuggling but *increase* the relative black-market rate of exchange. Note that only one of the goods needs to be taxed for both to be smuggled and exhibit price disparity.

Pitt (1984) demonstrates that quotas are equivalent to tariffs in this model. Thus the effects of a fall in the quota on the normalized levels of smuggling and black-market exchange rate are the same as a rise in the tariff, the effects of which are illustrated in figure A1.1.

Bibliography

Adiratma, Roekasah E. (1969) *Pola Penghasilan dan Pengeluaran dari Produsen Padi dalam Hubungan dengan Produksi dan Djumlah Pendjualan Padi*. Bogor, Indonesia: Institut Pertanian Bogor.

Aidit, Dipa N. (1964) "Mismanagement, corruption and the bureaucratic capitalists." In Herbert Feith and Lance Castles, eds (1974) *Indonesian Political Thinking 1945–1965*. Ithaca, NY: Cornell University Press.

Arndt, Heinz (1971) "Banking in hyperinflation and stabilization." In Bruce Glassburner, ed., *The Economy of Indonesia: Selected Readings*. Ithaca, NY: Cornell University Press.

Arndt, Heinz (1966) "Survey of recent developments." *Bulletin of Indonesian Economic Studies*, 5, October, 1–21.

Bank Indonesia, *Annual Report*, various issues (see Java Bank for pre-1953).

Bank of Japan, Statistics Department, *Price Indexes Annual*, various issues.

Bhagwati, Jagdish (1978) *Anatomy and Consequences of Exchange Control Regimes*. Cambridge, MA: Ballinger.

Biro Pusat Statistik, *Ekspor: Menurut Jenis Barang, Negeri Asal dan Pelabuhan Ekspor*, annual, Jakarta.

Biro Pusat Statistik, *Impor: Menurut Jenis Barang dan Negeri Asal*, annual, Jakarta.

Biro Pusat Statistik, *Pendapatan Nasional Indonesia*, irregular series, Jakarta.

Biro Pusat Statistik, *Statistical Pocketbook of Indonesia*, annual, Jakarta.

Biro Pusat Statistik, *Statistik Industri*, annual, Jakarta.

Biro Pusat Statistik, *Statistik Keuangan*, annual Jakarta.

Biro Pusat Statistik, *Statistik Konjunktur*, monthly.

Biro Pusat Statistik, *Warta BPS*, monthly.

Boeke, Julius H. (1946) *The Evolution of the Netherlands Indies Economy*. New York: Institute of Pacific Relations.

Boeke, Julius H. (1953) *Economics and Economic Policy of Dual Societies*. New York: Institute of Pacific Relations.

British Chamber of Commerce in Indonesia. *Annual Review*, various issues, Jakarta.

Broek, Jan O. M. (1942) *The Economic Development of the Netherlands Indies*. New York: Institute of Pacific Relations.

Bulletin of Indonesian Economic Studies (1968), October, p. 117.

Business News, newspaper, Jakarta.

Castles, Lance (1965) "Socialism and private business: the latest phase." *Bulletin of Indonesian Economic Studies*, 1, June, 13–39.

Castles, Lance (1968) *Religion, Politics, and Economic Behavior in Java: the Kudus Cigarette Industry*. New Haven, CT: Yale University Press, Southeast Asia Studies, Yale University, Cultural Report no. 15.

Cheng, K. O. (1964) "Indonesia: better than currency." *Far Eastern Economic Review*, 44, April 2, 46–7.

Commercial Advisory Foundation in Indonesia (1960) *The New Import Regulations and Lists of Commodities, 1960*. Jakarta: Commercial Advisory Foundation in Indonesia.

Commodity Yearbook. New York: Commodity Research Bureau Inc., various issues.

Cooper, Richard N. (1974) "Tariffs and smuggling in Indonesia." In Jagdish Bhagwati, ed., *Illegal Transactions in International Trade*. Amsterdam: North-Holland.

de Klerck, E. S. (1978) *History of the Netherlands East Indies*, 2 vols, reprint of the Rotterdam 1938 edn. Amsterdam: B. M. Israel.

de Wilde, A. Neytzell and J. Th. Moll (1936) *The Netherlands Indies during the Depression: a Brief Economic Survey*. Amsterdam: Meulenhoff.

Feith, Herbert (1958) *The Wilopo Cabinet, 1952–1953: a Turning Point in Post-Revolutionary Indonesia*, Ithaca, NY: Cornell University Press, Monograph Series, Modern Indonesia Project, Cornell University.

Feith, Herbert (1962) *The Decline of Constitutional Democracy in Indonesia*. Ithaca, NY: Cornell University Press.

Furnivall, John S. (1939) *Netherlands India*. Cambridge: Cambridge University Press.

Geertz, Hildred (1971) "Indonesian cultures and communities." In Ruth T. McVey, ed., *Indonesia*. New Haven, CT: HRAF.

Glassburner, Bruce (1960) "Problems of economic policy in Indonesia, 1950–1957." *Ekonomi dan Keuangan Indonesian*, 13 July–August, 302–21.

Glassburner, Bruce (1971) "Economic policy making in Indonesia." In Bruce Glassburner, ed., *The Economy of Indonesia: Selected Readings*. Ithaca, NY: Cornell University Press.

Glassburner, Bruce (1978) "Political economy and the Suharto regime." *Bulletin of Indonesian Economic Studies*. 14 (3), November, 24–51.

Higgins, Benjamin (1957) *Indonesia's Economic Stabilization and Development*. New York: Institute of Pacific Relations.

International Monetary Fund (1979) *International Financial Statistics*. Washington, DC: IMF.

International Monetary Fund, *Balance of Payments Yearbook*, various issues. Washington, DC: IMF.

International Rubber Study Group, *Rubber Statistical Bulletin*. London: Secretariat of the International Rubber Study Group, monthly.

Java Bank, *Report for the Financial Year*, annual, Jakarta (until 1953)

Kahin, George McT. (1963) "Indonesia." In Harold C. Hinton, N. Ike, N. Palmer, K. Callard, R. Wheeler, and G. Kahin, eds., *Major Governments of Asia*, 2nd edn. Ithaca, NY: Cornell University Press.

Kraal, A. (1956) "De Nieuwe Regelingen voor Import en Export." *Ekonomi dan Keuangan Indonesia*, 9 (12), December, 799–818.

Kraal, A. (1957) "Enige Aspecten van de Ontwikkeling der Industrie in Indonesia." *Ekonomi dan Keuangan Indonesia*, 10, April–May, 252–313.

Krueger, Anne O. (1978) *Liberalization Attempts and Consequences*. Cambridge, MA: Ballinger.

Mackie, J. A. C. (1967) *Problems of the Indonesian Inflation*. Ithaca, NY: Cornell University Press, Monograph Series, Modern Indonesia Project, Southeast Asia Program, Cornell University.

Mas'oed, Mochtar (1983) "The Indonesian economy and political structure during the early New Order 1966–1971." PhD thesis, Ohio State University.

Mintz, Jeanne S. (1965) *Mohammed, Marx and Marhaen*. New York: Praeger.

Mortimer, Rex (1974) *Indonesian Communism under Sukarno: Ideology and Politics, 1959–1965*. Ithaca, NY: Cornell University Press.

Mulia, Wanda (1964) "Masalah administrasi dan kebidjaksanaan perdagangan luar negeri." Lembaga Penjelidikan Ekonomi dan Masjarakat, Fakultas Ekonomi, Universitas Indonesia, No. 004B.

Oei, Hong Lan (1968) "Indonesia's economic stabilization and rehabilitation program: an evaluation." *Indonesia*, April, 135–74.

Palmer, Ingrid (1972) *Textiles in Indonesia: Problems of Import Substitution*. New York: Praeger.

Palmier, Leslie (1973) *Communists in Indonesia: Power Pursued in Vain*. New York: Anchor.

Panglaykim, Jusuf (1963) "Some notes from the history of marketing (trading regulationsets [sic]) Indonesia from 1933 to the B.E.L. [sic] system of 1957." *Ekonomi dan Keuangan Indonesia*, 16 (2), 5–33.

Panglaykim, Jusuf and Heinz Arndt (1966) "Survey of recent developments." *Bulletin of Indonesian Economic Studies*, 4, June, 1–35.

Panglaykim, Jusuf and Ingrid Palmer (1969) *State Trading Corporations in Developing Countries with Special Reference to Indonesia and Selected Asian Countries*. Rotterdam: Rotterdam University Press.

Panglaykim, Jusuf and Kenneth Thomas (1967) "The New Order and the economy." *Indonesia*, April, 73–120.

Papanek, Gustav (1980) "The effects of economic growth and inflation on workers' income." In Gustav Papanek, ed., *The Indonesian Economy*. New York: Praeger.

Pick's Currency Yearbook. New York: Pick Publishing Corporation, various issues.

Pitt, Mark M. (1981a) "Alternative trade strategies and employment in Indonesia." In Anne O. Krueger, Hal B. Lary, Terry Monson, and Narongchai Akrasanee, eds, *Trade and Employment in Development Countries I: Individual Studies*. Chicago. IL: University of Chicago Press.

Pitt, Mark M. (1981b) "Smuggling and price disparity." *Journal of International Economics*, 11, 447–58.

Pitt, Mark M. (1984) "Smuggling and the black market for foreign exchange." *Journal of International Economics*, 16, 243–57.

Pitt, Mark (1988) "Timing and sequencing of trade liberalization policies: the case of Indonesia, statistical appendix." Available from the Brazil Department, World Bank, Washington, DC.

Posthumus, G. A. (1971) *Inter-Governmental Group on Indonesia*. Rotterdam: Rotterdam University Press.

Roeder, O. G. (1965) "Six tons of rice." *Far Eastern Economic Review*, 49, September 2, 452, 455.

Roeder, O. G. (1966) "Taking stock." *Far Eastern Economic Review*, 54, December 29, 679–81.

Rosendale, Phyllis (1975) "The Indonesian terms of trade, 1950–1973." *Bulletin of Indonesian Economic Studies*, 11 (3), November, 50–80.

Rosendale, Phyllis (1978) "The Indonesian balance of payments 1950–1976: some new estimates." PhD thesis, Australian National University (unpublished).

Rosendale, Phyllis (1981) "The balance of payments." In Ann Booth and Peter McCawley, eds, *The Indonesian Economy during the Soeharto Era*. Kuala Lumpur: Oxford University Press.

Schmitt, Hans Otto (1959) "Some monetary and fiscal consequences of social conflict in Indonesia, 1950–1958." PhD thesis, Department of Economics, University of California, Berkeley, CA.

Shepard, Jack (1941) *Industry in Southeast Asia*. New York: Institute of Pacific Relations.

Sims, Christopher A. (1980) "Macroeconomics and reality." *Econometrica*, 48, January, 1–48.

Sims, Christopher A. (1986) "Are 'forecasting models' usuable for policy analysis?" *Federal Reserve Bank of Minneapolis, Quarterly Review*, Winter, 2–16.

Sumitro, Djojohadikusumo (1953) "Macro-economics and public policy in economically underdeveloped areas." *Ekonomi dan Keuangan Indonesia*, April.

Sumitro, Djojohadikusumo (1955) *Ekonomi Pembangunan*. Jakarta: P. T. Pembangunan

Djakarta.

Sumitro, Djojohadikusumo (1956) "Stabilization policies in 1955." *Ekonomi dan Keuangan Indonesia*, January.

Sumitro, Djojohadikusumo (1959) "Searchlight on Indonesia." unpublished paper.

Sundhaussen, Ulf (1982) *The Road to Power: Indonesian Military Politics 1945–1967*. Kuala Lumpur: Oxford University Press.

Sundrum, R. M. (1975) "Manufacturing employment 1969–71." *Bulletin of Indonesian Economic Studies*, 12 (1), 58–65.

Sutter, John O. (1959) *Indonesianisasi, Politics in a Changing Ecomony, 1940–1955*. Ithaca, NY: Southeast Asia Program, Cornell University, Data Paper no. 36.

Takens, G. F. (1954) "Letter to the Editor." *Ekonomi dan Keuangan Indonesia*. 7, 510–11.

Thomas, Kenneth D. (1966) "Price disparity in export trade." *Bulletin of Indonesian Economic Studies*, 2 (4), June 101–2.

van der Waals, Leendert Jan (1926) "De Indische Invoerrechten een Fiscaal-Economische Studie." Proefschrift (thesis), Nederlandsche Handelshoogschool, Rotterdam (unpublished).

Warta Perdagangan (also known as *Warta Ekonomi untuk Indonesia*), monthly, Jakarta.

Wirodihardjo, Saroso (1957) *Masalah Perdagangan dan Politik Ekonomi*. Jakarta: Djakarta Press.

World Bank (1968) *Current Economic Position and Prospects for Indonesia*. Washington, DC: World Bank.

Part II

Pakistan

Stephen Guisinger and Gerald Scully

Contents

List of Figures

List of Tables

Acknowledgments

This study forms part of the research project entitled the "Timing and Sequencing of Trade Liberalization" (see the preface to the volume). The authors have benefited greatly from the direction provided by the organizers of the study, Armeane M. Choksi, Michael Michaely, and Demetris Papageorgiou, as well as from comments and suggestions from other consultants at various stages of this study's preparation. The excellent administrative assistance provided by the World Bank staff deserves our special thanks.

In addition, the authors have a lengthy list of people to thank for their help in this study. In Pakistan, research assistance was provided by staff of The Pakistan Institute of Development Economics. We are especially grateful to the Institute's Director, S. N. H. Naqvi, and Research Director, Sarfraz Qureshi, for their cooperation and suggestions. In the United States, Grace Gao, Hilary Brooks, and John Gaspar provided valuable help in compiling data and reviewing research material. The project could not have been completed without the expert administrative skills of Sharon Fickes.

Douglas Nelson was involved in the early phases of the study before he left to join the World Bank staff. He is responsible for much of the analysis of Pakistan's trade and exchange control policies, and especially the construction of the import liberalization index in chapter 2.

Introduction

Compared with most developing countries that have undergone trade liberalization, Pakistan is a tortoise rather than a hare. Hares start and stop suddenly, often with great flamboyance; tortoises plod. In Pakistan, trade liberalization has made slow but fairly steady progress since 1960. This is not to claim that the race is yet approaching a successful conclusion: at the end of our study (1983) there was still a long way to go in terms of loosening quotas and reducing tariffs. Nevertheless, the theme of our study is that the race is not always won by the swift and flamboyant; substantial trade liberalization may be possible in a series of small moves extended over a period of time. For some countries this may be the only politically feasible route.

In this tortoise-like progression toward liberalization, two episodes stand out in Pakistan's history – 1960–5 and 1972–8 – when the pace of liberalization accelerated and concerted government campaigns were made on its behalf. These two episodes differ in two important respects from the episodes identified in other countries studied in terms of sequencing and timing of liberalization. First, the degree to which trade was liberalized during these episodes appears to be smaller than in other cases. Since there is no precise measure of magnitudes of liberalization, this is strictly a subjective judgment based on our reading of the companion pieces in the study. If our assertion is correct, many consequences of liberalization for Pakistan's economy would then be hard to discern from macroeconomic data. This is especially so because trade represented only a small fraction of Pakistan's gross national product (GNP) during this period. Liberalization had no readily apparent adverse effects on Pakistan's economy and yielded many benefits that simply do not show up in the macroeconomic indicators. In the absence of clear statistical "footprints" that can be convincingly assigned to liberalization, we have chosen to concentrate more on liberalization itself than on its consequences.

The second difference is that, because of the piecemeal nature of Pakistan's liberalization, the episodes tell an important part of the story but not all of it. Of two approaches to making trade policy – one characterized by detailed planning of large discrete policy shifts and the other by small policy changes with each sequential step based on the success or failure of its predecessor – Pakistan's policymaking definitely falls into the latter category. This process – whether appropriate or not as a general prescription for trade policy liberalization in developing countries – is a central focus of our attention because it was a guiding principle for Pakistan's policymakers throughout the entire period of our study.

How to tell the tortoise's story? To understand the significance of the two liberalization episodes, the reader must have some appreciation of the economic and political setting in which these episodes took place. Our study begins with two chapters that provide a selective review of Pakistan's economy – selective in the sense that only trends and data germane to understanding the nature of the economy and the problems of liberalization peculiar to Pakistan were included. We have perhaps erred on the side of providing too little rather than too much statistical background. For a fuller treatment, the reader seeking more detail can turn to any of several good treatises on Pakistan's economic development cited in the references.

The third and fourth chapters examine, respectively, the 1960–5 and 1972–8 episodes in terms of antecedent conditions, liberalization policies adopted and consequences for the economy. The final chapter presents lessons from these two episodes that might apply to later liberalizations in Pakistan or to other countries facing similar conditions.

A cursory summary of our main findings about Pakistan's liberalizations is perhaps useful at the outset. The two liberalizations made positive long-lasting contributions to Pakistan's economic development with no *apparent* adverse effects on employment, industrial output, or inflation. For the first episode, this was due primarily to the limited scope of the liberalizations and to the fact that the initial liberalizing step was, perhaps somewhat paradoxically, to *increase* distortions in export trade in an effort to raise the incentives for exports relative to the highly protected market for import substitutes. In the 1972–8 episode, economic distress in the form of unemployment, inflation, and underutilization of capacity was rampant. However, this distress could not be traced logically to the effects of liberalization, for in the space of two years (1971–3) Pakistan experienced more chaotic events than most nations see in a decade: a political schism that spun off half the population into the new nation of Bangladesh; a war with India; a new political regime that taxed, expropriated, and regulated ruthlessly in an effort to alter the distribution of income and wealth; and, finally, a worldwide inflation triggered by the increase in the price of oil. Neither economic science nor the statistical data are refined enough to extract the independent effects of liberalization from these other factors.

A special word is in order on the units of time for which data are collected in Pakistan and the naming of these units. Like many countries, Pakistan operates on a fiscal year basis, in Pakistan's case a year that runs from July 1 of one year to June 30 of the next. Thus the government statistical services record data as, for example, "1959–60" or sometimes "1959/60," but never "FY60." Data are not recorded on a calendar year basis, nor can the researcher easily transform fiscal year into calendar year series.

The following convention has been adopted in this study. All data are presented on a fiscal year basis and the "name" for the data unit is the calendar year in which the fiscal year ends. So, "1959–60" becomes "1960." Historical events remain identified by the calendar year in which they fall. In our view, this convention provides fluidity in the sometimes tedious recounting of statistical data, with no loss of accuracy for the reader aware of the convention.

1

The Domestic Economy of Pakistan

Pakistan began its economic and political life rather inauspiciously in a political reconfiguration of the Indian subcontinent, conceived in an earnest desire for peace and realized under conditions of extreme violence. In 1947 new boundaries were drawn across the subcontinent to provide Muslims with their own political state. The desire to end communal strife between Hindus and Muslims led to the creation of Pakistan at an enormous price in terms of human suffering. Millions of people were uprooted from farms and villages occupied by their ancestors for generations and were forced to relocate to a strange land many hundreds of miles away. Almost half a million people lost their lives, and many more were stripped of all their possessions. Turmoil surrounding Partition, as it was called, haunted Pakistan's economic progress for years after. Among problems created by Partition, none was more intractable than the existence of two noncontiguous divisions of the country, separated by more than 1,000 miles of unfriendly Indian territory. The two wings, East and West Pakistan, differed in almost every respect but religion, causing one observer to note that three men were responsible for maintaining Pakistan's integrity – the Prophet Mohammed and the Wright brothers.

Differences between the two wings, glaringly apparent at the beginning, only widened with time. West Pakistan's agriculture was based on wheat, cotton, and sugar, while East Pakistan's farmers, for the most part, planted rice and jute. Productivity growth in West Pakistan's agricultural sector required large public investments in tube wells and dams, while changes in productivity in the East were more dependent on monsoons than government programs. In 1950 East Pakistan had a per capita income equal to 85 percent of that of West Pakistan, a differential that increased steadily through the 1950s because of an absolute decline in per capita income in the East. During the 1960s the gap widened still further as income in the West rose by 2 percentage points more than in the East. By 1969–70, per capita income in the West was more than 60 percent above that in the East. The wide disparity in quality of life, alleged by those living in East Pakistan to be the result of systematic discrimination by a government dominated by

West Pakistanis, became the rallying point for the political crisis that subsequently produced Bangladesh.

Population Structure, Growth, and Migrations

In 1981 Pakistan had a population of more than 83 million, making it the seventh largest developing country in the world (table 1.1). Already a large country at the time of its creation, Pakistan's population numbered more than 75 million in 1947, with approximately 35 million people located in the West, now Pakistan. The nation has maintained, at almost 4 percent, one of the fastest rates of population growth of any developing country. Over the past two decades (1960–80) the crude birth rate has declined by only 5 per 1,000 (from 51 to 46 per 1,000), while the crude death rate has dropped from 24 to 16 per 1,000, causing a rise in the rate of population growth (Asian Research Team on Employment Promotion (ARTEP), 1983).

In family planning, Pakistan's performance compares unfavorably with that of India, where the crude birth rate has fallen by 20 percent. As recently as 1980, fewer than one in 16 eligible couples in Pakistan practiced contraception (Burki and Laporte, 1984, p. 409).

One consequence of the rapid rate of growth is that 45 percent of the population is less than 15 years old. Furthermore, partly for religious reasons, women have historically had a low rate of participation in the labor force. In 1973, female workers were 9.1 percent of the total population (Government of Pakistan, *Pakistan Economic Survey*, 1981, statistical annex, p. 6). These factors lead to a rather high dependency ratio of approximately 3.3 dependents for each worker (ARTEP, 1983; World Bank, 1982).

Table 1.1 Population estimates totaled by province, urban, and rural, 1965 and 1981 (thousands)

Area	1965	1981	Average annual percentage change
Total in Pakistan	51,836	83,782	3.85
Baluchistan	1,928	4,305	7.71
Northwest Frontier Province	8,636	13,060	3.20
Punjab	30,039	47,451	3.62
Sind	11,233	18,966	4.30
Urban	12,173	23,694	5.92
Rural	39,663	60,088	3.21

Source: World Bank, 1982

More than 70 percent of Pakistan's population lives in the countryside. The country is divided into four major provinces, which roughly correspond to the four major language and ethnic groupings of the people. Slightly more than half the population lives in the Punjab, whose capital is Lahore. About a quarter of the population is found in the Sind, whose capital Karachi is the principal port for Pakistan. The balance of the population is divided among the northwest frontier province, Baluchistan, and various territories administered by the central government.

Pakistan, like India, has had a tradition of overseas migration. The trend in overseas employment was dramatically accelerated by increased demand for employment in the Middle East during the 1970s. Between 1971 and 1980, approximately 600,000 workers emigrated, mainly to the Middle East for temporary employment. It was estimated that in 1980 there were some 1.4 million Pakistanis working abroad who remitted home about US$1.5 billion (Government of Pakistan, *Pakistan Economic Survey*, 1981, p. 8). The average remittance of US$1,070 per capita was thee times the GNP per capita of Pakistan in 1980.

Gross National Product: Expenditure and Sectoral Composition

In 1960 GNP per capita in Pakistan was less than US$100. By 1983 per capita GNP stood at approximately US$350. Pakistan ranks as one of the poorest countries in the world – not as poor as Bangladesh and India but less well off than a number of countries in Africa.

Pakistan's economic structure has responded to the natural forces of income growth and productivity change. Agriculture's share of both employment and GNP have diminished. From 46 percent of GNP in 1960 (table 1.2), the share of agriculture dropped to 25 percent in 1984 (measured in 1960 constant market prices). The growth rate of agricultural crops has been 3.7 percent per year. Noncrop agricultural output has shown the weakest performance (2.7 percent annual growth). Manufacturing output grew by 7.8 percent per year over this same period and as a consequence its share of GNP rose from 12 to almost 18 percent. Manufacturing's increased share of GNP has been driven by an 8.9 percent growth in the large-scale sector, while the relatively slow growth of small-scale manufacturing caused its share of GNP to fall slightly during the period.

Fiscal and Monetary Policy

Pakistan's governments have maintained relatively stable fiscal and monetary policies over the three and a half decades since Partition. Pakistan has

Table 1.2 Gross domestic product at factor cost by industrial origin, 1960 and 1983 (million 1960 rupees)

Sector	1960	Percentage of GNP	1983	Percentage of GNP
Total	16,803	100.00	59,985	100.00
Agriculture	7,711	45.89	17,826	29.70
Crop	4,775	28.42	12,536	20.90
Noncrop	2,936	17.47	5,290	11.33
Manufacturing	2,018	12.01	10,507	17.51
Large-scale	1,159	6.90	7,647	12.75
Small-scale	859	5.11	2,860	4.77
Construction	427	2.54	2,952	4.92
Wholesale and retail trade	2,105	12.53	8,770	14.62
Public administration and defense	1,048	6.24	5,866	9.78
Mining and quarrying	70	0.42	322	0.54
Ownership (dwellings)	837	4.98	1,754	2.92
Other services	1,411	8.40	4,639	7.73

Source: World Bank, data files

not experienced the runaway inflation or staggering fiscal deficits of some Latin American countries. Credit expansion has been tightly controlled through limits on bank lending.

Tax and Expenditure Policy

Pakistan's tax policy is characterized by a relatively low income inelasticity, primarily because the government has relied on indirect taxes for revenue. Tables 1.3 and 1.4 present data on the sources of government revenue that show the importance of customs duties, sales, and excise taxes. In the consolidated Federal and Provincial Government's Budgets for 1974 and 1984, indirect taxes represent more than 80 percent of tax collections. The tax burden has risen over time: in 1961, tax revenues amounted to 7.8 percent of GNP but were 14 percent in 1984.

Deficits grew during the decade of the 1970s but not to the heights experienced in other countries. For example, during 1976–80, when the government was expanding rapidly, the overall deficit (current plus capital accounts) averaged 8 percent of GNP.

Savings and Investment

Time and savings deposits as a fraction of GNP were quite low in Pakistan in the late 1950s. Partly because of the low rate of inflation during the 1970s, real rates of interest were positive (table 1.5). Savings rose to 16.7 percent of GNP in 1968 but fell during the 1970s, partly as a result of

Table 1.3 Federal government tax revenues and expenditures for selected years (1961, 1974, 1984) (million rupees)

Revenues and expenditures	1961[a,b]			1974			1984		
	Revenues or expenditures	Percentage of total taxes or expenditures	Percentage of GNP	Revenues or expenditures	Percentage of total taxes or expenditure	Percentage of GNP	Revenues or expenditures	Percentage of total taxes or expenditures	Percentage of GNP
Current tax revenues	1,426	100.0	7.8	9,445	100.0	11.7	58,388	100.0	14.0
Customs duties	552	38.7	3.0	4,169	44.1	5.1	22,041	37.7	5.3
Excise taxes	316	22.2	1.7	2,742	29.0	3.4	16,430	28.1	3.9
Sales taxes	192	13.5	1.0	692	7.3	0.9	4,063	7.0	1.0
Income and corporation taxes	294	20.6	1.6	1,191	12.6	1.5	9,797	16.8	2.4
Other taxes	72	5.0	0.4	651	6.9	0.8	6,057	10.4	1.5
Current expenditures	1,423	100.0	7.8	10,605	100.0	13.1	58,208	100.0	14.0
Nondevelopment	n.a.	—	—	10,216	96.3	12.6	52,115	89.5	12.5
Defense	n.a.	78.1	—	4,949	46.7	6.1	25,219	43.3	6.1
Internal security	n.a.	—	—	333	3.1	0.4	1,397	2.4	0.3
Interest payments	n.a.	13.1	—	1,509	14.2	1.9	12,144	20.9	2.9
General administration	n.a.	25.6	—	762	7.2	0.9	3,517	6.0	0.8
Community services	n.a.	—	—	—	—	—	1,254	2.2	0.3
Social services	n.a.	—	—	—	—	—	2,168	3.7	0.5
Economic services	n.a.	—	—	—	—	—	2,023	3.5	0.5
Subsidies	n.a.	—	—	2,243	21.2	2.8	1,916	3.3	0.5
Others	n.a.	—	—	420	4.0	0.5	2,477	4.3	0.6
Development	n.a.	—	—	389	3.7	0.5	6,093	10.5	1.5

n.a., not applicable; —, not applicable.
a Federal tax revenues were obtained by subtracting the central revenue receipts of East Pakistan from those of the Central Pakistan government.
b Federal expenditures were obtained by subtracting the central expenditures of Pakistan from those of the central Pakistan government.
Sources: 1961 revenues, Government of Pakistan, 1975, and World Bank 1976, table 7.1; 1961 expenditures, Government of Pakistan. Pakistan Economic Survey, 1969–70, appendix, p. 45, and World Bank, 1976, table 7.2; 1974, 1984, Government of Pakistan, 1983, pp. 153 and 156

Table 1.4 Consolidated federal and provincial governments' tax revenues and expenditures, 1974 and 1984 (million rupees)

Item	1974			1984		
	Revenues or expenditures	Percentage of total taxes or expenditures	Percentage of GDP	Revenues or expenditures	Percentage of total taxes or expenditures	Percentage of GNP
Current tax revenues	10,487	100.0	12.9	60,374	100.0	14.5
Direct taxes	1,665	15.9	2.1	10,002	16.6	2.4
Indirect taxes	8,822	84.1	10.9	50,372	83.4	12.1
Domestic transactions	4,160	39.7	5.1	25,174	41.7	6.0
International transactions	4,622	44.5	5.8	25,238	41.8	6.1
Current nondevelopment expenditures	13,022	100.0	16.1	66,342	100.0	15.9
General administration	1,110	8.5	1.4	5,171	7.8	1.2
Defense	4,949	38.0	6.1	25,219	38.0	6.1
Law and order	605	0.5	0.7	3,099	4.7	0.7
Community services	n.a.	n.a.	n.a.	2,641	4.0	0.6
Social services	n.a.	n.a.	n.a.	9,337	14.1	2.2
Economic services	n.a.	n.a.	n.a.	3,700	5.6	0.9
Subsidies	2,465	18.9	3.0	3,167	4.8	0.8
Debt servicing	n.a.	n.a.	n.a.	12,572	19.0	3.0
Economy cut	n.a.	n.a.	n.a.	1,737	2.6	0.4
Relief to government servants	n.a.	n.a.	n.a.	2,650	4.0	0.6
Grants to local authorities	n.a.	n.a.	n.a.	513	0.8	0.1
Other	2,307	17.7	2.8	10	n.a.	n.a.

n.a., not available.
Source: Government of Pakistan, *Pakistan Economic Survey*, 1983–4, pp. 223–5

the relatively high rate of inflation which reached a decade low of 10.6 percent of GNP in 1975. During the 1980s savings recovered somewhat but have not yet reached the 1968 peak. In 1984 time and savings deposits were 15.5 percent of GNP.

Unlike Japan, Korea, or even its neighbor, India, Pakistan has never demonstrated the capacity for investing large fractions of GNP. In 1965, gross capital formation was 23.2 percent of GNP (table 1.5). The investment share declined until 1975, reaching a historical low of 12.5 percent

Table 1.5 Savings and gross fixed capital formation, 1960–1983

	1	2	3	4	5	6	7
Year	Time and savings deposits[a]	Gross fixed capital formation	Savings bank deposits interest rate	Real interest rate	Savings as a percentage of GNP	Investment as a percentage of GNP	Public investment as a percentage of total investment
1960	946	n.a.	2.67	n.a.	5.6	n.a.	n.a.
1961	1,228	n.a.	3.01	−0.96	6.7	n.a.	n.a.
1962	1,507	n.a.	3.21	4.83	7.9	n.a.	n.a.
1963	1,935	n.a.	3.20	3.33	9.5	n.a.	n.a.
1964	2,432	5,055	3.20	−1.97	10.6	22.1	43.2
1965	3,228	6,064	3.52	−0.88	12.3	23.2	46.7
1966	4,039	5,507	3.96	1.18	14.0	19.0	45.2
1967	5,140	5,890	4.15	−5.10	15.8	18.1	46.4
1968	5,933	5,819	4.59	2.56	16.7	16.4	45.6
1969	6,201	5,669	5.09	4.73	16.3	14.9	47.5
1970	6,876	6,835	5.26	1.31	15.9	15.8	48.9
1971	6,668	7,045	5.32	0.20	14.6	15.4	49.9
1972	7,758	6,813	5.50	−0.77	15.7	13.8	48.0
1973	9,553	7,647	5.50	−9.83	15.6	12.6	51.3
1974	9,557	10,614	6.75	−17.31	11.8	13.1	63.8
1975	11,249	16,218	7.50	−18.41	10.6	15.3	67.9
1976	14,980	22,770	8.00	−4.81	12.0	18.3	71.5
1977	17,852	26,421	8.50	−1.05	12.5	18.4	70.6
1978	22,873	28,961	8.50	0.62	13.2	16.7	69.9
1979	27,094	31,605	8.50	1.34	13.9	16.2	69.2
1980	31,618	39,376	8.50	−5.27	13.6	17.0	67.1
1981	33,314	41,003	8.50	−5.46	12.2	15.0	63.7
1982	38,895	47,466	8.50	6.10	12.3	15.0	65.9
1983	53,184	54,544	8.50	n.a.	14.4	14.8	63.9

n.a., not available.

[a] All figures are for June of the fiscal year.

[b] The real interest rate is the nominal interest rate less the change in the consumer price index.

Sources: column 1, 1960–9, Government of Pakistan, Pakistan Economic Survey, 1970; 1970–84, Government of Pakistan, Pakistan Economic Survey, 1983–4, appendix, p. 83; column 2, Government of Pakistan, Pakistan Economic Survey, 1983–4, appendix, pp. 24–2; column 3, 1960–71, Pakistan Institute of Development Economics, 1983, p. 107; 1972–83, Government of Pakistan, Pakistan Economic Survey, 1983, p. 164

in 1973, then increased steadily throughout the Bhutto period, reaching a peak of 18.4 percent in the last year of the Bhutto regime (1977). However, the increased investment activity during the Bhutto period was due almost entirely to public sector investment. During the 1960s public investment averaged about 46 percent of total investment. At the height of the Bhutto regime it reached 71.5 percent. Under the Zia government this policy was somewhat reversed, as is evidenced by the declining trend in the share of public investment beginning in 1978.

Monetary Policy and Inflation

Pakistan is typical of many developing countries in being "under-intermediated:" the public holds money but few other financial instruments. The State Bank rations credit to the private sector in accordance with an annual credit plan. The traditional instruments of monetary control used in industrialized countries – reserve requirements, open-market operations, and the discount rate – play almost no role in regulating the money supply in Pakistan.

During 1960–83 the money supply grew at a 12 percent compound rate, while prices rose at 8 percent (table 1.6). The 1960s witnessed a period of conservative monetary policy and relative price stability. The money supply grew at an 8 percent annual rate, prices at slightly more than 3 percent. In the 1970s prices rose more than 12 percent a year, while money supply grew at 16 percent. The period 1980–3 brought no diminution in monetary expansion, but prices rose somewhat more slowly.

Factors of Production

Composition and Sectoral Distribution of the Labor Force

Rates of participation in the labor force have traditionally been low in Pakistan because of (a) the rapid population growth that increases the number of young people who are by definition excluded from the labor force, and (b) a low participation of women. Table 1.7 shows the trend in labor force participation adjusted for changing age and sex distributions of the population. The table also includes the reported unemployment rates, which have historically shown low levels of open unemployment. Almost everyone in Pakistan reports themselves to be employed in some degree, if only as unpaid family helpers.

Over the 1970s Pakistan's labor force grew even faster than the population as large numbers of young workers and more female workers entered the labor market. Table 1.8 shows that between 1972 and 1983 the

Table 1.6 Money supply, velocity, and inflation, 1959–1983 (million rupees)

Year	Money supply[a]	Percentage change in money supply	Percentage change in consumer price index	Velocity[b]
1960	6,159	—	—	2.7
1961	5,878	4.6	1.8	3.1
1962	6,105	3.9	2.7	3.1
1963	6,987	14.4	− 1.3	2.9
1964	7,989	14.3	3.2	2.9
1965	8,757	10.0	6.1	3.0
1966	9,976	13.9	5.1	2.9
1967	10,504	5.3	8.8	3.1
1968	10,861	3.4	2.3	3.3
1969	12,258	12.9	1.5	3.1
1970	13,327	8.7	4.5	3.3
1971	15,125	13.5	5.1	3.0
1972	15,130	0.0	5.2	3.2
1973	18,046	19.3	9.2	3.4
1974	21,545	19.4	30.4	3.8
1975	22,655	5.2	26.9	4.7
1976	27,681	22.2	11.3	4.5
1977	35,254	27.4	11.9	4.1
1978	42,192	19.7	7.9	4.1
1979	51,871	11.9	6.7	3.8
1980	60,373	16.4	10.6	3.8
1981	72,781	20.6	12.4	3.8
1982	80,010	9.9	10.5	4.0
1983	96,542	20.7	4.2	3.8

—, not applicable.
[a] Money supply is the currency in circulation plus scheduled banks' demand deposits plus other deposits at the State Bank of Pakistan. All figures are for June of the fiscal year.
[b] Velocity is GNP divided by money supply.
Source: Government of Pakistan, *Pakistan Economic Survey*, various issues

Table 1.7 Trends in labor force participation rates (percent)

Year	Total	Male	Female	Unemployment rate
1951	30.70	55.10	2.10	n.a.
1961	32.40	55.00	6.10	0.56
1972	29.43	51.79	5.34	0.61
1975	29.05	52.01	4.21	0.50
1978	29.38	52.28	6.47	0.50
1980	31.00	51.94	8.09	n.a.
1983[a]	29.99	52.67	5.55	0.50

n.a., not available.
[a] Projections.
Source: ARTEP, 1983

Table 1.8 Estimates of the labor force (thousands)

Year	Total	Male	Female
1961 Census[a]	12,763	11,641	1,122
Planning Commission[a]	13,720	12,514	1,206
Planning Commission[b]	14,921	13,603	1,318
1972	18,650	17,020	1,630
1978	22,220	20,510	1,710
1983	26,060	23,740	2,320

The Planning Commission data are based on increasing census
estimates by 7.5 percent.
[a] Excluding frontier region.
[b] Including frontier region.
Source: ARTEP, 1983

labor force rose by 40 percent compared with a population increase of 35 percent (table 1.1).

Table 1.9 shows the sectoral distribution of employment. Most workers are still employed in agriculture; the manufacturing employment share has remained unchanged for the past two decades. Services, especially transportation and commerce, have absorbed workers mainly from the rural sector. Table 1.10 shows the sectoral growth rates of employment that explain the changing labor force shares. Manufacturing employment slowed sharply in the 1960s to about a third of the rate experienced in the 1950s. The service sectors grew, until very recently, at rates several times the national average.

Three important features of the labor force over the recent past have been the relatively low levels of education of workers, the rapid rise in temporary migration of workers to the Middle East, and the weak role played by unions.

Table 1.9 Sectoral distribution of the employed labor force (percent)

Sector	1951	1961	1972	1978	1983[a]
Agriculture	66.40	60.80	57.30	56.60	55.40
Manufacturing	9.90	13.60	12.92	13.37	13.78
Mining	0.10	0.20	n.a.	n.a.	n.a.
Transport and communications	1.70	2.90	4.84	4.70	4.80
Electricity, gas, water	1.80	0.20	0.37	0.50	0.52
Construction	n.a.	2.10	3.41	4.10	4.20
Commerce	7.00	71.00	9.89	10.50	11.00
Services	11.30	12.40	8.13	10.50	10.30
Others	1.80	0.70	n.a.	n.a.	n.a.
Total	100.00	100.00	100.00	100.00	100.00

n.a., not available.
[a] Projected.
Source: ARTEP, 1983

Table 1.10 Sectoral growth rate of employment (percent)

Sector	1951–61	1961–72	1972–8	1978–83
Agriculture	2.1	2.2	2.8	2.5
Manufacturing and mining	6.4	2.1	3.9	3.5
Transport and communication	8.4	7.7	2.5	3.5
Electricity, gas, water	2.7	8.4	8.4	3.0
Construction	5.9	7.8	6.4	3.3
Commerce	3.2	5.9	4.1	3.9
Other services	3.8	a	5.9	3.0
All	3.0	2.6	3.0	2.9

a Negative value.
Source: ARTEP, 1983

Education and Skills

In 1980, only 21 percent of adults (and 30 percent of males) were literate (Burki, 1981, p. 306). In 1981, 78 percent of school-aged males and only 30 percent of school-aged females were enrolled in primary schools, compared with 93 percent and 64 percent, respectively, for India. One study suggests that low levels of educational attainment are at least partly due to unattractive rates of return on investments in education (Guisinger et al., 1984). Primary schooling yields returns of less than 5 percent.

Emigration

Temporary migration has been an important feature of Pakistan's labor force since the 1973 oil price increase. In 1971 fewer than 4,000 workers left Pakistan to work abroad, mainly in the Middle East; in 1981, the peak year of emigration, 168,000 workers departed. The growth rate of emigration over this period was an extraordinary 47.2 percent per year. It was estimated that about 2 million Pakistanis (10 percent of the labor force) were employed in the Middle East in 1981 (Government of Pakistan, *Pakistan Economic Survey*, 1984, p. 109). By 1978 remittances amounted to more than US$1.2 billion.

While the export of skilled labor resulted in periodic shortages in key skill categories at home and contributed to the rise in real wages for both skilled and unskilled workers, studies have shown that, on balance, social gains from migration have outweighed social costs, especially for unskilled workers (Guisinger, 1984).

Unionization

The third notable feature of Pakistan's labor force is the absence of a strong labor movement. Throughout Pakistan's history, unions have had no effective power over wages and working conditions except during a brief spell in the last half of the Bhutto period, and even then their powers were severely circumscribed by the government's desire to maintain control over wages and prices.

Economic Growth and Factor Productivity

Pakistan's growth during the period 1950–80 has been consistently above the average for developing countries and superior to that of low-income developing countries as a group and that of its neighbors in Asia. For example, between 1950 and 1975, annual increases in real GNP averaged 4.6 percent for Pakistan but only 3.4 percent for developing countries as a group. During the 1960s, when Pakistan had its greatest spurt of growth, the 6.7 percent average annual rate of increase in GNP exceeded that for all developing countries by 1.8 percentage points and that for the Asian region as a whole by 3.5 percentage points. During 1970–80, Pakistan's relative performance slid because the country's absolute growth rate fell (to an annual rate of 5.5 percent), while developing countries raised their rates of growth to 5.4 percent.

Differences in the rate of growth during the 1960s and the 1970s for the economy as a whole and for the economic sectors can be seen in table 1.11. During 1964–70 the real rate of growth for the economy was 7.1 percent. During 1971–83, the growth rate slipped to 5.5 percent.

The most precipitous declines in economic performance were in the critical sectors of large-scale manufacturing and agriculture. Small-scale manufacturing, in contrast, improved its performance during the 1970s. Unlike large-scale manufacturing, the small-scale manufacturing sector is more or less left alone by the government. This fact, coupled with the inflow of capital and entrepreneurs from large-scale manufacturing firms faced with the threat of nationalization during the Bhutto regime, may account for the increase in the growth rate of the small-scale manufacturing sector from 2.8 to 7.3 percent. Factor productivity and the economy began to slow during the 1970s. Except in small-scale manufacturing, labor productivity grew at 3 percent or better during 1964–70, with the highest growth rate of labor productivity in large-scale manufacturing. Partly because of the introduction of new disease-resistant seeds, insecticides, and fertilizers, and to increased water availability, labor productivity in agriculture grew at a very respectable 3 percent annual rate. For the economy as a whole, labor productivity grew at 4.1 percent during this period.

During 1971–83, labor productivity growth fell throughout the economy except in small-scale manufacturing, where it grew at almost four times the rate achieved in the previous period. In large-scale manufacturing, the rate of labor productivity growth was less than half that experienced during the earlier period. In agriculture, labor productivity growth virtually stagnated from 1971 to 1983.

Table 1.11 Growth rates by sector (percent)

Time period and sector	Real rate of growth of output	Rate of growth of labor employed	Rate of growth of labor produc- tivity	Employment elasticity	Incremental capital-to- output ratio
1964–83					
Aggregate economy	5.7	3.0	2.7	0.53	2.96
Manufacturing					
Large-scale	7.2	3.3	3.9	0.46	3.65
Small-scale	5.9	2.7	3.2	0.55	1.58
Agriculture	3.8	3.1	0.7	0.83	0.80
1964–70					
Aggregate economy	7.1	3.0	4.1	0.42	2.59
Manufacturing					
Large-scale	10.5	3.1	7.4	0.30	3.18
Small-scale	2.8	1.8	1.0	0.64	4.35
Agriculture	6.1	3.1	3.0	0.51	0.45
1971–83					
Aggregate economy	5.5	3.0	2.5	0.55	2.92
Manufacturing					
Large-scale	6.1	3.3	2.8	0.54	3.89
Small-scale	7.3	3.5	3.8	0.48	1.36
Agriculture	3.2	3.1	0.1	0.97	1.06

Source: Government of Pakistan, *Pakistan Economic Survey*, various issues

Factor Prices and Income Distribution

Factor Prices

Manufacturing Wages

Real wages fluctuated during 1960–81 (table 1.12), but on the whole a rising trend can be observed. Real wages in large-scale manufacturing grew at an annual rate of 3.4 percent. Guisinger and Irfan (1975) found little evidence that significant wage disparities existed across industry groups. This uniform spread of real wage increases suggests that labor markets were fairly efficient with no barriers to inter-industry mobility of factors.

Agricultural Wages

Data on agricultural wages are not readily available but scattered surveys shed some light on the movements of rural wages during the period covered by the manufacturing data. Guisinger and Hicks (1978) found evidence to suggest substantial increases in real agricultural wages over the

Table 1.12 Wages in manufacturing and agriculture (rupees per worker per year)

	Nominal wages			Real wages[c]		
Year	Large-scale manufacturing wages[a]	Agricultural wages	General wages[b]	Large-scale manufacturing wages	Agricultural wages	General wages
1960	1,091	498	607	1,091	498	607
1961	1,135	510	625	1,115	501	614
1962	1,156	587	692	1,105	561	662
1963	1,189	610	716	1,152	591	739
1964	1,195	666	763	1,122	625	716
1965	1,340	731	843	1,187	647	747
1966	1,464	801	923	1,234	675	778
1968	1,536	949	1,057	1,164	719	801
1969	1,735	1,028	1,158	1,295	767	864
1970	1,931	1,114	1,264	1,379	796	903
1971	2,094	1,207	1,370	1,424	821	931
1972	2,389	1,308	1,507	1,544	846	974
1973	2,914	1,417	6,692	1,724	838	1,001
1974	4,012	2,469	2,769	1,820	1,120	1,256
1975	4,953	2,851	3,238	1,771	1,019	1,158
1976	5,665	3,233	3,680	1,820	1,039	1,182
1977	6,035	3,302	3,805	1,732	947	1,092
1978	6,376	3,899	4,355	1,695	1,036	1,158
1979	6,974	4,208	4,717	1,738	1,049	1,176
1980	8,597	4,913[d]	5,591	1,937	1,107	1,260
1981	11,215	5,618[d]	6,648	2,247	1,126	1,332

[a] 1976–81 wages were obtained by multiplication of the Industrial Worker Index of Money Wage Rates (1974–5 = 100) and the 1974–5 money wage rate from Guisinger (1978).
[b] In 1972, 57.3 percent of the labor force was in agriculture and 12.9 percent in manufacturing (ARTEP, 1983, p. 16), and these percentages were used to weigh sectoral wage rates in evaluating the general wage rate.
[c] Nominal wages divided by the consumer price index.
[d] Estimated.
Sources: large-scale manufacturing wages, 1960–75, Guisinger, 1978; agricultural wages, 1960–79, Pakistan Institute of Development Economics, 1983, p. 198, and 1982, ARTEP, 1983, p. 27

period 1960–75. Data from national income accounts and labor force surveys lead to estimates of real income per worker in the agricultural sector that displays significant increases between 1961 and 1970 but a slight tapering off between 1970 and 1975. From one source of data (Guisinger, 1978, p. 11) it was concluded that the real wages of both daily and permanent workers rose, on average, by 2.6 percent a year. Another study (ARTEP, 1983, p. 84) found evidence for a similar increase in agricultural real wages. On combining the available data sources into the wage series in table 1.12, the annual growth of real wages in the agricultural sector is found to be nearly 4 percent.

Urban Informal Sector Wages

In many developing countries, urban informal sector wages have drifted down in spite of improvements in real incomes in both the rural and the urban informal sector. In Pakistan, however, urban informal sector wages appear not to have suffered the same fate. Although the evidence is mixed and fragmentary, Guisinger and Irfan (1980) found that some urban informal sector occupations improved their real income positions between 1959 and 1975.

Public Sector Wages

At its inception, Pakistan inherited a civil service system based on the British model, which included artificially high wages with a wide disparity between the entry level and top ranks. Between 1960 and 1975, the disparity had been narrowed (Guisinger, 1978, p. 6) and the real public sector wage actually declined, in contrast with the upward trend in the real wage in manufacturing.

These wage trends for the major sectors of the economy suggest a pattern that differs from that in many other developing countries: the wage structure appears to be far more uniform, both across skill levels and across industry groups. The large gap found in other developing countries between the formal and informal sectors does not occur.

Income Distribution

This evenness in wage levels allowed Pakistan to avoid sharp deteriorations in income distribution that many other developing countries have experienced. While Pakistan has consistently had substantial numbers of urban and rural families living in poverty, there is no evidence that the distribution of income worsened during the period of most rapid growth, the 1960s. Data on income shares and Gini coefficients (Guisinger and Hicks, 1978) suggest no deterioration in income distribution.

Capital

Unlike wages, the price of capital varies substantially among sectors in Pakistan. Because no single source exists and capital is far from a homogeneous commodity, data to substantiate the preceding assertion is difficult to find. Some evidence is provided by Guisinger (1978) who examined the ratio between equilibrium and market prices of capital created by subsidies and taxes. Guisinger found a range of variation in the ratio over time due to variations in the incidence of policies such as tax holidays and accelerated depreciation. These policies are also applied unequally among sectors of the economy. One effect of the capital subsidization policies during 1960–75 was a skewing of the wage-to-rental ratio in favor of capital-intensive projects.

Summary and Conclusions

Pakistan is a low-income developing country with a high rate of population growth and a population that largely resides in rural areas and earns its income from agriculture and related activities. Nevertheless, the economy has made generally good progress during the 1960s and 1970s despite two wars, the dismemberment of the original Pakistan and the oil shock of 1973. In the 1960s the government pursued a generally conservative monetary and fiscal policy that produced low rates of inflation. Perhaps as a legacy of the British civil service or because of the discipline of the military governments that ruled Pakistan between 1958 and 1971, the government displayed a preference for small corrective actions rather than sweeping reforms and a relatively modest role for the state. After Bhutto assumed power in 1971, the role of the state – and especially public sector investment – increased. Inflation levels rose, growth rates gyrated, and private investors abandoned large-scale industry for safer investments in small-scale manufacturing and housing. Not all disruptions during the Bhutto period were self-inflicted: the oil price shock delivered a double blow by increasing the import bill and paralyzing foreign markets for Pakistan's exports.

The oil price shock was not without its silver lining for Pakistan. The demand for labor in the Middle East drew thousands of Pakistani workers abroad; at one point more than 2 million Pakistanis were at work in foreign countries and remittances became the country's single most important source of foreign exchange. That workers were able to move out of their traditional occupations into new jobs in the Middle East and then regain employment in Pakistan at the end of their overseas assignments is a reflection of the fluidity of Pakistan's labor markets. Unlike many developing countries suffering from distorted labor markets as a result of public sector wage policies and minimum wage laws, Pakistan has few legal or institutional barriers to the movement of labor and the uniformity of wage levels for workers of similar skills in different sectors of the economy reflects this.

2

Pakistan in the International Economy

As in many developing countries, governments in Pakistan intervened extensively in international trade. Imports were subject to either quantitative restrictions or high and discriminatory tariffs. Exports were controlled through subsidies, taxes, and quota restrictions. Foreign exchange rates were fixed until 1982 and private access to foreign currency is strictly regulated. Foreign investment in either direction has not been encouraged. However, over the 1960–78 period, Pakistan moved toward liberalization of its trade and investment policy and this liberalization is reflected in the trends in exports and imports.

Background to Liberalization

Export and Import Trends

Data on Pakistan's nominal external trade and balance of payments for 1960–83 are presented in table 2.1. The same data are reported as a percentage of nominal GNP in table 2.2. Examination of the pattern of relative imports, exports, and openness of the economy reveals three important features of the evolution of external trade and commercial policy in Pakistan. First, exports and imports, as a share of GNP, are secularly increasing. Exports as a share of GNP increased 0.33 percent a year over the period, while imports rose 0.41 percent. Second, the share of both exports and imports rose significantly beginning in 1973, after a major devaluation of the rupee. From 1960 to 1972, exports averaged approximately 4 percent of GNP, while from 1973 to 1983 they averaged approximately 9 percent. Imports were an average 10 percent of GNP in the former period, but rose to 18 percent in the latter. Export shares are quite stable within each period while import shares show a downward trend between 1960 and 1972, and then a rising trend between 1973 and 1983. However, the shift in the openness of the economy between 1960 and 1983

Table 2.1 External trade and balance of payments, 1960–1983
(billion current rupees)

Year	GNP	Exports	Imports	Trade balance	Net factor income from abroad
1960	16.8	0.76	1.81	−1.04	−0.02
1961	18.3	0.54	2.17	−1.63	−0.03
1962	19.1	0.54	2.24	−1.70	−0.03
1963	20.4	1.00	2.80	−1.80	−0.05
1964	22.9	1.08	2.98	−1.91	−0.04
1965	26.1	1.14	3.67	−2.53	−0.06
1966	28.9	1.20	2.88	−1.68	−0.05
1967	32.6	1.30	3.63	−2.33	−0.05
1968	35.5	1.65	3.33	−1.68	−0.02
1969	38.0	1.70	3.05	−1.35	−0.03
1970	43.3	1.61	3.29	−1.68	0.00
1971	45.6	2.00	3.60	−1.60	−0.08
1972	49.3	3.37	3.50	−0.12	0.10
1973	61.3	8.55	8.40	0.15	0.46
1974	81.1	10.16	13.48	−3.32	0.62
1975	105.8	10.29	20.93	−10.64	1.15
1976	124.4	11.25	20.47	−9.21	2.99
1977	143.3	11.29	23.01	−11.72	5.48
1978	173.9	12.98	27.82	−14.84	12.14
1981	273.7	29.28	53.54	−24.26	22.69
1982	317.5	26.27	59.48	−33.21	25.35
1983	368.2	34.44	68.15	−33.17	39.46

Source: Government of Pakistan, Pakistan Economic Survey, 1983–4

was due as much to the revaluation of imports following the 1972 devaluation as it was to import liberalization.

Trade Balance

Except for the year of devaluation, 1972, Pakistan experienced a negative trade balance throughout the 1960–83 period. When the trade balance is expressed as a share of GNP, a difference between the two subperiods is evident: on the whole, the trade balance share, in absolute value terms, declined before and rose after the devaluation. From the previous discussion of export and import shares, the rising trade imbalance seems due in part to import revaluation following the devaluation. Imports also increased because import controls were liberalized in the post-devaluation period, the price of imported oil and related products rose dramatically in late 1973, and workers' remittances from abroad provided a new source of unilateral transfers.

Table 2.2 External trade relative to gross national product, 1960–1983 (percent)

Year	Ratio of exports to GNP	Ratio of imports to GNP	Ratio of exports plus imports to GNP (openness)	Ratio of trade balance to GNP
1960	4.5	10.8	15.3	−6.2
1961	3.0	11.9	14.9	−8.9
1962	2.8	11.7	14.5	−8.9
1963	4.9	13.7	18.6	−8.8
1964	4.7	13.0	17.7	−8.3
1965	4.4	14.1	18.5	−9.7
1966	4.2	10.0	14.2	−5.8
1967	4.0	11.1	15.1	−7.1
1968	4.6	9.4	14.0	−4.7
1969	4.5	8.0	12.5	−3.5
1970	3.7	7.6	11.3	−3.9
1971	4.4	7.9	12.3	−3.5
1972	6.8	7.1	13.9	−0.3
1973	13.9	13.7	27.6	0.2
1974	12.5	16.6	29.1	−4.1
1975	9.7	19.8	29.5	−9.8
1976	9.0	16.5	25.5	−7.4
1977	7.9	16.1	24.0	−8.2
1978	7.5	16.0	23.5	−8.5
1979	8.7	18.7	27.4	−10.0
1980	10.1	20.3	20.4	−10.2
1981	10.7	19.6	30.3	−8.9
1982	8.3	18.7	27.0	−10.6
1983	9.4	18.5	27.9	−7.9

Source: based on data from Government of Pakistan, *Pakistan Economic Survey*, 1983–4

Pakistan's Pattern of Trade Liberalization

Between 1960 and 1978, Pakistan adopted a number of policy changes that moved the country generally in the direction of a more liberal trade regime. There were several reversals along the way, and at times the progress was very slow, but on the whole it became easier to import and export goods during this time.

Import Restraint

From 1960 to 1978 the dominant influence on the level and composition of imports was import licensing. Adopted in 1952 in response to the sharp decline in Pakistan's foreign exchange earnings when raw material prices sagged, import licensing was a far more important determinant of domestic prices of importable goods than tariffs were. Permission to import was granted to specific importers and ceilings were placed on goods that could be imported during a shipping period, generally six months. Tariffs played only a minor role in limiting imports because the premium that an importer could earn by selling scarce imports on the domestic market was usually higher than the tariff on the product. Tariffs served only to siphon off a part of the scarcity premium into government revenues.

The restrictiveness of licensing varied with the availability of foreign exchange. For roughly the first half of the period, attempts at liberalization of the import control system focused on expanding the value of licenses issued and making the licensing process automatic while maintaining a constant official exchange rate. (The particulars of adjustments to import licensing are discussed in chapters 3 and 4.)

Export Promotion

The tight restrictions on imports produced a highly overvalued rupee that discouraged exports. Until 1972, liberalization on the export side focused on subsidization by granting exporters rights to part of the scarcity premiums on imports.

Devaluation

Devaluation was attempted in 1955 but the government did not consider the results satisfactory. A constant official rate was maintained until 1972 when a massive (130 percent) devaluation was put into effect. A slight revaluation of the official rate was made in February 1973.

Index of Trade Liberalization for Pakistan

Trade liberalization can be perceived as a continuum of export and import policies that are bounded between two extremes. A completely illiberal regime is characterized by autarky; a completely liberal trade regime is the theorist's idealized free-trade condition. Pakistan's trade policies have been rated on a scale that ranges from 0 to 20, with 0 representing absolute illiberality and 20 complete liberality. The index represents the composite of two indices, one for imports and one for exports.

Index of Import Liberalization

Rather than relying on subjective ratings, the index of import liberalization has been constructed by transforming objective measures of the stringency of import quota restrictions. The source of information on quota restrictions is the Import Trade Control Orders in various issues of the *Gazette of Pakistan*. Table 2.3 presents data on quota restrictions for 39 commodities from 1960 to 1984. The cell entries in the table represent the modal policy treatment for the commodity as determined from the annual *Import Policy Statement*. The entries range from 1, the most liberal treatment of imports in Pakistan, to 5, the most illiberal. The value of 1 is given to commodities on the free list, on Open General Licensing (OGL), or subject to automatic licensing. The value of 5 is assigned to commodities on the tied list, the negative list, the restricted list, the banned list, or imported through the Trading Corporation of Pakistan. The values of these measures were grouped into three identified categories of imports: consumer goods, intermediate goods, and capital goods. The average score in each category as well as an average score for all commodities are presented in table 2.4 and shown graphically in figure 2.1.

The import quota restriction index was converted to an index of import liberalization first by reversing the value of the score – a 1 becomes a 5, a 2 becomes a 4, and so forth – and then by rescaling the values from a range bounded between 1 and 5 to a range bounded between 0 and 20. The terminal value of the index of import liberalization for Pakistan in 1984 is based on the authors' judgment of where Pakistan belongs on the continuum of import trade policies that ranges between complete autarky and free trade. The basis for coding the import liberalization index is presented in table 2.5 (for exports, table 2.6), the liberalization index for both imports and exports appears in table 2.7, and a graphic presentation of the indices is given in figures 2.2 and 2.3.

Index of Export Liberalization

Among the key ingredients of export policy are export restrictions, tax (subsidy) policies, exchange rate flexibility and exchange rate convertibility. Complete liberality of exports (an index value of 20) would be a policy of freely floating exchange rates, an absence of quota restrictions, and free convertibility of currency. Complete illiberality would be characterized by complete ban of exports. Until 1982 Pakistan's export policy was based on fixed exchange rates, restricted currency convertibility, and export taxes and subsidies. In our judgment, the most liberal export policy occurred during the period 1960–83 with Pakistan moving to a regime of freely floating exchange rates in 1982. A value of 10 was assigned to Pakistan's 1982 export regime (see tables 2.6 and 2.7 and figure 2.2).

Guisinger (1978) found that in 1960 the official exchange rate (OER) of Rs 4.76 fell below the equilibrium exchange rate, estimated at Rs 7.56 to the US dollar. We assume arbitrarily that the exchange rate of Rs 9.90 in 1974 was an equilibrium one, we calculate the equilibrium OER as a simple

Table 2.3 Quantitative restrictions of imports by sector. 1960–1983

Sector	60		62		64		66		68		70		72		74		76		78		80		82	
Sugar	3	3	2	3	3	3	3	5	3	3	5	5	5	1	1	5	1	5	1	5	5	1	1	5
Edible oils	3	5	5	5	5	3	3	1	3	3	5	5	3	3	3	1	1	1	5	5	5	1	1	1
Tea	3	5	5	5	5	5	5	5	3	3	5	3	3	1	1	1	1	1	1	1	1	1	1	1
Cotton textiles	5	3	5	5	5	3	3	2	3	3	5	5	1	1	1	1	1	1	1	1	1	1	1	1
Silk textiles 1	5	3	5	5	5	3	5	1	3	5	5	5	5	1	1	1	1	1	1	1	1	1	1	1
Silk textiles 2	5	3	5	5	5	3	5	1	3	5	5	5	5	1	5	5	5	5	5	5	5	5	5	5
Footwear	5	5	5	5	5	3	3	3	5	5	5	5	5	5	5	5	5	5	5	5	5	5	5	5
Apparel	3	5	5	5	5	3	3	5	5	5	5	5	5	5	5	5	5	5	5	5	5	5	5	5
Printing and publishing 1	3	1	1	1	1	2	2	2	3	3	3	3	5	1	1	1	1	1	1	1	1	1	1	1
Printing and publishing 2	3	3	5	5	3	3	3	2	3	3	5	5	5	5	5	5	5	5	5	5	5	5	5	5
Soaps	5	5	3	5	5	3	3	5	3	5	5	5	1	1	5	5	5	5	5	5	5	5	1	5
Matches	5	5	5	5	5	5	5	5	3	5	5	5	5	1	5	5	5	5	5	5	5	5	1	5
Plastic goods	3	5	5	5	5	3	2	1	3	3	5	5	3	1	1	1	1	1	5	1	1	5	1	1
Sports goods	3	3	5	5	5	5	3	1	5	5	5	5	5	5	5	5	5	5	5	5	5	5	1	5
Electrical appliances	3	3	5	5	3	2	2	2	3	3	1	1	5	1	1	1	5	5	1	1	5	5	5	5
Motor vehicles	3	3	1	1	1	2	3	5	3	3	3	3	3	5	1	5	1	5	1	1	1	1	1	5
Jute textiles	5	5	5	5	5	5	5	5	5	5	5	5	1	5	1	1	1	1	1	1	1	1	1	5
Wood and lumber 1	3	3	5	5	5	4	2	4	3	3	5	5	5	1	1	1	1	1	1	1	1	1	1	5
Wood and lumber 2	5	5	5	5	5	3	5	3	3	3	5	5	1	1	5	5	5	5	5	5	5	5	5	5
Leather tanning	5	5	5	5	5	3	3	3	3	5	5	5	1	1	1	1	1	1	1	1	1	1	1	5
Rubber products	3	3	5	5	1	3	3	2	3	3	5	5	3	1	1	5	1	1	1	1	1	1	1	1
Fertilizer	5	5	5	5	5	1	1	1	1	1	1	1	1	5	1	1	1	1	1	1	1	1	1	5
Paints and varnishes	3	3	5	5	3	2	2	1	3	3	3	3	1	1	1	1	1	1	1	5	1	1	1	1
Chemicals 1	3	3	1	1	1	2	2	2	3	1	1	1	1	1	1	1	1	1	1	1	1	1	1	1
Chemicals 2	3	3	1	1	1	2	2	2	3	1	5	5	5	1	1	1	1	1	1	1	1	1	1	1
Petroleum products	3	5	1	1	1	3	3	2	3	3	5	3	3	1	1	1	1	1	1	1	1	1	1	1
Paper products	3	3	5	5	5	3	3	3	3	3	5	5	5	1	1	1	1	1	1	1	1	1	1	1
Nonmetallic minerals 1	3	3	3	3	3	1	3	1	3	3	3	3	3	1	1	1	1	1	1	1	1	1	1	1
Nonmetallic minerals 2	5	5	5	5	5	1	3	1	3	2	5	5	3	1	1	1	1	1	1	1	1	1	1	1
Cement 1	3	3	5	5	3	1	3	5	3	3	5	5	3	1	4	1	1	3	1	1	1	1	1	1
Cement 2	3	3	5	5	3	1	3	5	3	3	5	5	3	1	5	1	5	5	5	5	5	5	1	1
Iron and steel	3	3	1	1	1	1	3	1	3	1	1	1	1	1	1	1	1	1	1	1	1	1	1	1
Aluminum and copper	5	5	1	1	1	5	3	1	3	3	5	1	1	1	1	1	1	1	1	1	1	1	1	1
Metal products 1	3	3	5	5	3	3	3	2	3	3	3	3	1	1	1	1	1	1	1	1	1	1	1	1
Metal products 2	5	5	1	1	1	1	3	1	3	3	5	5	2	1	1	1	1	1	1	1	1	1	5	1
Nonelectrical machinery	3	3	5	5	3	2	2	1	3	2	3	3	3	5	1	1	1	1	5	5	5	5	5	1
Machining tools	3	5	5	5	5	5	5	1	3	3	5	1	1	5	5	5	5	5	5	5	5	5	5	5
Sewing machines	3	3	5	5	3	2	2	1	3	2	2	2	3	1	1	1	1	1	5	5	5	5	5	5
Electrical machinery	3	3	5	5	3	2	2	2	3	3	3	3	3	1	1	1	5	1	1	1	1	1	1	1

The cell entries represent the modal policy treatment of the given sector as determined from the annual *Import Policy Statement* of the Government of Pakistan: 1, free list, OGL, automatic licensing: 2, score moved from 1 to 3 during year: 3, licensed list, bonus list, cash-cum-bonus list, export performance list: 4, score moves from 1 to 5 or 3 to 5 during year: 5, tied list, trading corporation of Pakistan, negative list, restricted list, banned list.

trend from 7.60 to 9.90 over the interval 1960–74, and extrapolate this trend through 1984. Since subsidies to exports are liberalizing in this context, we divide the nominal effective exchange rate (NEER) by the estimated equilibrium exchange rate and obtain a fraction of the observed liberality on the export side. For example, in 1978 with the NEER equal to Rs 10.19 and the estimated equilibrium rate equal to Rs 10.55, the ratio is 97 percent. This yielded a scale number of 9.7 on the 0–20 scale.

Table 2.4 Mean values of import quota restrictions indices by category of imports, 1960–1983

Year	Imports	Consumer goods imports	Intermediate goods imports	Capital goods imports
1960	3.7	3.8	3.7	3.5
1961	3.7	3.8	3.5	3.7
1962	4.1	4.1	3.9	3.8
1963	4.1	4.4	3.9	3.8
1964	3.5	4.1	3.4	2.8
1965	2.9	3.2	3.2	2.1
1966	2.9	3.2	2.6	2.9
1967	2.5	3.0	2.7	1.8
1968	3.2	3.5	3.0	3.0
1969	3.2	3.9	2.8	2.6
1970	4.2	4.5	4.1	3.8
1971	3.9	4.4	3.9	3.1
1972	3.4	4.4	3.2	2.4
1973	1.9	2.3	1.4	1.7
1974	2.0	2.6	1.4	1.9
1975	2.1	3.3	1.4	1.3
1976	2.3	3.0	1.7	2.3
1977	2.3	3.3	1.4	1.8
1978	2.4	3.3	1.4	2.0
1979	2.5	3.5	1.4	2.3
1980	2.6	3.5	1.7	2.3
1981	2.5	3.3	1.4	2.3
1982	2.1	2.5	1.4	2.3
1983	2.7	3.3	2.8	1.7

Source: Government of Pakistan, *Pakistan Economic Survey*, various issues

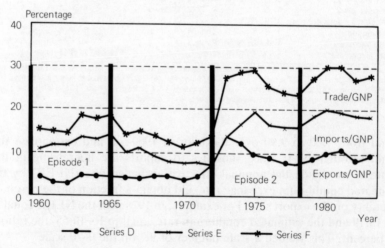

Figure 2.1 Openness of the economy, Pakistan, 1960–1983

Table 2.5 Coding of import liberalization index

Index value	Description of basis for assignment of index value
20	Free trade
19	Very low tariffs, < 5%
18	Moderate tariffs, 5 to < 15%
17	Moderate tariffs, < 15%; some restrictions
16	
15	
14	Tariffs 50–100%; moderate restrictions
13	
12	Pakistan regime = 1
11	
10	Pakistan regime = 2
9	
8	Pakistan regime = 3
7	
6	Pakistan regime = 4
5	
4	Pakistan regime = 5
3	
2	
1	State trading, nonmarket
0	Autarky

The index values are rescaled average quota restraint codes from table 2.3.

Table 2.6 Coding of export liberalization index

Index value	Description of basis for assignment of index value
20	Freely floating exchange rate, no currency restriction
19	
18	
17	
16	
15	Periodic adjustments, moderate exchange restriction
14	
13	
12	
11	
10	Fixed exchange (tax or subsidy to exports to keep alignment)
9	
8	
7	
6	
5	
4	
3	
2	
1	
0	No convertibility

Table 2.7 Import, export, and trade liberalization indices, 1960–1983

Year	Quota restraint index	Import liberalization index (M)	Export liberalization index (X)	$\frac{M + X}{2}$	Integer scale
1960	3.5	7.0	5.6	6.3	6
1961	3.7	6.6	6.4	6.5	7
1962	3.9	6.2	6.4	6.3	6
1963	4.1	5.8	6.1	6.0	6
1964	3.4	7.2	6.1	6.7	7
1965	2.7	8.6	6.8	7.7	8
1966	2.9	8.2	6.9	7.6	8
1967	2.3	9.4	6.4	7.9	8
1968	3.2	7.6	7.0	7.3	7
1969	3.1	7.8	7.2	7.5	8
1970	4.0	8.0	7.0	7.5	8
1971	3.6	6.8	8.0	7.4	7
1972	3.3	7.4	7.9	7.7	8
1973	2.0	10.0	8.8	9.4	9
1974	2.0	10.0	8.2	9.1	9
1975	2.0	10.0	7.7	8.9	9
1976	2.3	9.4	7.5	8.5	9
1977	2.2	9.6	8.4	9.0	9
1978	2.3	9.4	9.7	9.6	10
1979	2.7	8.6	9.0	8.8	9
1980	2.6	8.8	7.9	8.4	8
1981	2.4	9.2	8.5	8.9	9
1982	2.1	9.8	10.0	9.9	10
1983	2.6	8.8	10.0	9.4	9

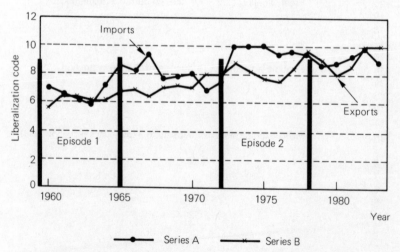

Figure 2.2 Liberalization indices, Pakistan's imports and exports

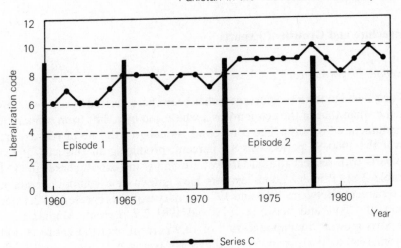

Series C

Figure 2.3 Trade liberalization index, Pakistan, 1960–1983

The Index of Trade Liberalization

Our index of trade liberalization is an unweighted average of the index of import liberalization and the index of export liberalization. The values for the trade liberalization index are presented in table 2.7 and the trade liberalization index derived from these two component indices is shown graphically in figure 2.3, above.

The Path of Trade Liberalization and the Pattern of Discrimination toward Imports

The import, export, and trade liberalization indices over the whole 1960–83 period exhibit a moderate, discernible trend toward liberalization. However, this trend is not continuous but fluctuates over a policy cycle. The period 1960–5 can be described as a moderate liberalization with respect to both export and import policy. The period 1967–71 witnessed a retrenchment from liberality on imports but some further liberalization in export policy. The period 1972–8 witnessed a liberalization of import policy but, except for the devaluation, a more restrictive export policy through the application of taxes on exports. The post-1978 period represents a slight retrenchment from liberal import policy and a rather variable export policy. Throughout the 1960–83 period consumer goods have been the most restricted and, at least since 1974, intermediate goods the least restricted (table 2.4).

Structure and Growth of Exports

Export Performance

Since 1960 Pakistan's export sector has been characterized by a growth rate higher than that of the economy as a whole and by a shift from primary to manufactured exports. The compound annual growth rate of real exports over the 1960–83 period was 8.0 percent, producing an elasticity of real exports with respect to real GNP of 1.6 and rising export shares in GNP (table 2.8). Primary goods exports have grown at a compound rate of 5.6 percent. Between 1960 and 1971 primary exports represented 2.1 percent of GNP, and between 1972 and 1983 2.7 percent. Manufactured exports grew at a compound rate of 10.9 percent over the entire period. From 1960 to 1971, manufactured exports averaged 1.7 percent of GNP, while over the later period they averaged 4.1 percent.

Table 2.8 Share of real exports in gross national product, 1960–1983 (percent, constant 1960 prices)

Year	Total exports as percentage of GNP	Primary exports as percentage of GNP	Manufactured exports as percentage of GNP
1960	4.54	2.59	1.95
1961	3.13	1.70	1.46
1962	2.80	1.78	1.05
1963	4.83	3.18	1.84
1964	4.98	2.62	2.42
1965	5.00	2.72	2.43
1966	3.87	1.91	1.96
1967	4.71	1.91	2.87
1968	5.57	2.45	3.34
1969	5.81	1.70	4.34
1970	4.96	1.30	3.82
1971	5.79	1.53	4.32
1972	7.97	2.94	4.52
1973	8.90	3.51	5.33
1974	6.10	2.45	3.80
1975	6.36	2.88	3.50
1976	6.64	2.25	3.62
1977	5.39	2.38	2.98
1978	5.40	2.03	3.19
1979	5.92	1.87	4.14
1980	6.45	3.12	4.10
1981	7.37	3.67	4.62
1982	6.12	2.35	4.48
1983	6.86	2.33	5.39

Source: based on data from Government of Pakistan, Pakistan Economic Survey, 1983–4

Composition of Exports

The composition of Pakistan's exports has changed significantly over the period. The principal changes have been, in relative terms, the decline in exports of primary goods (mainly raw cotton and Basmati rice), the ascendancy of manufactured exports, and the decline of cotton-based exports (cotton thread, yarn, and cloth). During the Ayub liberalization, primary exports constituted almost two thirds of all exports; by 1971, they were less than one third. While primary exports recovered periodically over the remaining years, their decline continued (table 2.9): in 1983, primary exports were 30 percent of exports. Up to 1973, raw cotton and cotton-manufactured products constituted almost half of all Pakistan's exports; beginning in 1974 their share dropped precipitously to slightly less than a third until 1983.

Table 2.9 Composition of exports, 1960–1983

Year	Exports (million Rs)	Primary exports (million Rs)	Manufac- tured exports (million Rs)	Share of primary exports (%)	Share of manufactured exports (%)
1960	763	436[a]	327[a]	57.1	42.9
1961	540	322	218	59.6	40.4
1962	543	368	175	67.0	33.0
1963	998	729	269	73.0	27.0
1964	1,075	618	457	57.5	42.5
1965	1,140	683	457	59.9	40.1
1966	1,204	556	648	48.6	51.4
1967	1,297	589	708	47.3	52.7
1968	1,645	855	790	52.0	48.0
1969	1,700	632	1,068	37.2	62.8
1970	1,609	532	1,077	33.1	66.9
1971	1,998	650	1,348	32.5	67.5
1972	3,371	1,510	1,861	44.8	55.2
1973	8,551	3,366	5,185	39.4	60.6
1974	10,161	4,007	6,154	39.4	60.6
1975	10,286	4,932	5,354	47.9	52.1
1976	11,253	4,902	6,351	43.6	56.4
1977	11,294	4,622	6,672	10.9	59.1
1978	12,980	4,634	8,346	35.7	64.3
1979	16,925	5,474	11,451	32.3	67.7
1980	23,410	9,838	13,572	42.0	58.0
1981	29,280	12,824	16,456	43.8	56.2
1982	26,270	9,112	17,158	34.7	65.3
1983	34,442	10,326	24,116	30.0	70.0

[a] Estimated.
Source: Government of Pakistan, Pakistan Economic Survey, 1983–4

Export Exchange Rates

From 1955 until May 11, 1972, the rupee was pegged at Rs 4.76 to the US dollar. The 1972 devaluation pushed the rupee to Rs 11 to the dollar, but less than a year later, in February 1973, it was revalued to Rs 9.9 to the dollar, where it remained until January 1982 when it was allowed to float. Export taxes and subsidies have created a divergence between the official and effective exchange rates faced by exporters.

Data on the OER, the NEER, and the real effective exchange rate (REER) for the period 1960–80 are presented in tables 2.10 and 2.11. The NEER equals the OER multiplied by $1 \pm t$ where t is equal to the subsidy (tax) rate. The REER is the NEER multiplied by p_f/p_d, where p_f is the export unit value index and p_d is the domestic price index. Two different REERs can be calculated: the REER when the domestic price index is the consumer price index, and the REER2 when the domestic price index is the wholesale price index.

The statistical relationships between REERs, GNP, and real exports are shown in table 2.12. Log transformations have been used, and thus the

Table 2.10 Exchange rates: official and effective, 1959–1979 (rupees per US dollar)

Year	OER	NEER	Nominal percentage subsidy (tax)
1960	4.76	5.30	11.3
1961	4.76	5.39	13.2
1962	4.76	5.40	13.4
1963	4.76	5.78	21.4
1964	4.76	5.72	20.2
1965	4.76	5.73	20.4
1966	4.76	5.74	20.6
1967	4.76	5.10	7.1
1968	4.76	5.32	11.8
1969	4.76	5.40	13.4
1970	4.76	5.58	17.2
1971	4.76	6.10	28.2
1972	5.80	6.45	11.2
1973	10.63	7.31	− 31.2
1974	9.90	8.14	− 17.8
1975	9.90	6.94	− 29.9
1976	9.90	7.04	− 28.9
1977	9.90	7.84	− 20.8
1978	9.90	9.84	− 0.6
1979	9.90	8.80	− 11.1
1980	9.90	7.93	− 20.9

Source: Pakistan Institute of Development Economics, 1983

Table 2.11 Real effective exchange rates for exports, 1960–1980 (rupees per US dollar)

| | 1 | 2 | 3 | |
| | | Primary | Manufactured | Column 3 divided by |
Year	Exports	exports	exports	column 2
1960	4.23	3.91	9.25	2.37
1961	7.14	5.90	7.38	1.25
1962	5.87	5.48	6.75	1.23
1963	5.41	4.88	9.74	1.38
1964	5.38	4.22	7.30	1.73
1965	6.37	5.20	7.71	1.48
1966	6.27	4.99	8.82	1.77
1967	5.52	4.25	8.16	1.92
1968	6.12	4.92	8.68	1.76
1969	6.25	4.29	8.52	1.99
1970	5.99	4.75	7.27	1.53
1971	7.02	5.50	7.79	1.42
1972	7.49	5.38	9.75	1.81
1973	14.19	10.40	23.98	2.31
1974	14.01	12.13	24.79	2.04
1975	13.86	12.37	21.92	1.77
1976	12.70	9.35	19.77	2.11
1977	15.19	13.40	22.46	1.68
1978	17.56	19.21	23.47	1.22
1979	17.56	14.07	24.54	1.74
1980	16.88	12.35	24.40	1.98

Source: Government of Pakistan, *Pakistan Economic Survey*, various issues

Table 2.12 Export regression equations

Dependent variable	Constant (t value)	Coefficient (t value)	Independent variable	Coefficient (t value)	Independent variable	$\bar{R}^2$ (F value)
Log real exports	−6.5711 (2.08)	1.2198 (3.45)	LRGNP	0.6820 (2.62)	LREER	0.8842 (77.35)
Log real primary exports	−2.3413 (0.67)	0.7517 (1.99)	LRGNP	0.6582 (2.48)	LPREER	0.7217 (26.94)
Log real manufactured exports	−12.8855 (5.20)	1.7563 (6.38)	LRGNP	0.6376 (3.55)	LMREER2	0.9382 (155.87)

LRGNP, log of real GNP; LREER, log of REER; LPREER, log of REER for primary goods; LMREER2, log of REER2 for manufactured exports.

coefficients reflect elasticities. The elasticity of total exports with respect to GNP is 1.22, while the elasticity of the REER is 0.68, both coefficients being significant at the 1 percent level. Some 88 percent of the variance in real exports is associated with the variance in real GNP and the variance in REER2. Among subcategories of exports, real primary exports appear to respond inelastically to real GNP ($\beta = 0.75$), while real manufacturing exports appear to respond elastically ($\beta = 1.75$). The responses of primary and manufactured goods exports to their REERs appear to be nearly identical.

In table 2.13, the various components of the REER – the OER, the tax-to-subsidy rate, and relative prices – are regressed against real exports to ascertain their relative importance. The elasticity of real exports with respect to the OER is 1.13, indicating a mildly elastic response of exports with respect to devaluation, contrary to normal devaluation pessimism. Interestingly, devaluation, *ceteris paribus*, had a much greater impact on primary exports than on manufacturing exports. The elasticity of real primary exports with respect to the OER was 1.49, while the corresponding elasticity of real manufacturing exports was 0.81. Over the period, as a matter of trade policy, Pakistan favored a relative increase in its manufactured exports. The somewhat inelastic response of real manufacturing exports with respect to the OER may help explain Pakistan's reluctance to devalue.

The elasticity of real exports with respect to the ratio of the foreign price to the domestic price is 0.76, indicating an elasticity of foreign demand for Pakistan's output lower than the elasticity of domestic demand. The elasticity of real primary exports with respect to relative prices is 0.99. This implies that the foreign elasticity of demand is equivalent to the domestic elasticity of demand. The elasticity of real manufacturing exports with respect to relative prices is 0.61, suggesting that the foreign elasticity of demand for Pakistan's manufactured output is well below the domestic elasticity of demand.

Under normal circumstances, an increase in export subsidies (or a decrease in export taxes) will increase real exports. Examination of the elasticities in table 2.13 for real exports, real primary exports, and real manufactured exports with respect to the corresponding ratio of the NEER divided by the OER indicates a negative relationship. Such a result is paradoxical if the argument is that the subsidization of exports is for the purpose of promoting exports. The results suggest that Pakistan's export subsidy (tax) policy responded to exogenous relative prices. Over the period when Pakistan's export prices were falling relative to domestic prices, exports were subsidized. Over the period when export prices rose relative to domestic prices, exports were taxed. The tax–subsidy policy over the period may have served as a partially correcting mechanism for the disequilibrium induced by the overvalued rupee.

The tradeoff between relative prices and export subsidies can be discerned more precisely by regressing the relative prices of exports, primary exports, and manufacturing exports against the respective ratios of the NEER to the OER. These results are shown in table 2.14. For real exports the tradeoff is just above unity ($\beta = 1.07$), for real primary exports

Table 2.13 Real exports and the components of the real effective exchange rate

Dependent variable	Constant (t value)	Coefficient (t value)	Independent variable	Coefficient (t value)	Independent variable	$\bar{R}^2$ (F value)
Log real exports	−5.6389 (2.89)	1.0686 (4.87)	LRGNP	1.1295 (5.32)	LOER	0.9378 (151.79)
Log real exports	−11.4009 (8.02)	1.8355 (13.36)	LRGNP	−1.1130 (4.77)	LXSUB	0.9293 (132.42)
Log real exports	−9.6513 (4.2469)	1.6425 (7.31)	LRGNP	0.7563 (2.62)	LXTOT	0.8842 (77.35)
Log real primary exports	1.45519 (0.60)	0.2408 (0.88)	LRGNP	1.4878 (5.63)	LOER	0.8648 (64.95)
Log real primary exports	−4.8487 (2.48)	1.1001 (5.76)	LRGNP	−1.3504 (5.7589)	LPSUB	0.8332 (50.94)
Log real primary exports	−2.9311 (1.05)	0.9102 (3.29)	LRGNP	0.9916 (3.21)	LPTOT	0.7627 (33.15)
Log real manufactured exports	−14.1028 (5.47)	1.8825 (6.50)	LRGNP	0.8085 (2.88)	LOER	0.9281 (130.16)
Log real manufactured exports	−17.3787 (6.76)	2.3576 (9.69)	LRGNP	−0.5003 (1.38)	LMSUB	0.9051 (96.39)
Log real manufactured exports	−14.5735 (5.53)	2.0514 (7.83)	LRGNP	0.6078 (2.59)	LMTOT	0.9236 (121.85)

LRGNP, log of real GNP; LOER, log of OER; LXSUB, log of export subsidies; LXTOT, log of export terms of trade; LPSUB, log of export subsidies to primary exports; LPTOT, log of primary export terms of trade; LMSUB, log of manufacturing subsidies; LMTOT, log of manufacturing terms of trade.

Table 2.14 Tradeoffs between relative export prices and export subsidies

Dependent variable	Constant (t value)	Coefficient (t value)	Independent variable	$\bar{R}^2$ (F value)
LXTOT	0.2982 (8.01)	− 1.0711 (6.01)	LXSUB	0.6371 (36.12)
LPTOT	0.0881 (1.67)	− 1.0392 (5.35)	LPSUB	0.5802 (28.64)
LMTOT	0.7702 (16.52)	− 1.5525 (11.52)	LMSUB	0.8681 (132.64)

For a definition of the variables, see table 2.13.

it is even close to unity ($\beta = -1.04$) and for real manufactured exports the response is elastic ($\beta = -1.55$).

Whether Pakistan's export tax–subsidy program served to promote exports depends upon how subsidies were geared to relative prices. If subsidies (taxes) were set so as to compensate exactly for changes in relative prices, the elasticity of (NEER/OER) $\times p_f / p_d$ with respect to real exports would be zero. If subsidies (taxes) were set to promote exports, the elasticity of (NEER/OER) $\times p_f / p_d$ with respect to real exports would be positive. The logarithm of the product of NEER/OER and relative prices for primary exports and for manufactured exports was calculated and, along with the logarithms of real GNP, was regressed against the respective real exports. For real primary exports the coefficient was -0.21 ($t = 0.41$), which is not statistically different from zero. For real manufactured exports the elasticity was 1.57 ($t = 3.47$). These results suggest that Pakistan attempted to maintain relatively constant prices for its primary goods exporters and increasing prices for its manufactured goods exports.

Structure and Growth of Imports

Import Performance

The compound growth rate of real imports over the period 1960–83 was 3.8 percent. Since this growth rate is less than the growth rate of real GNP, the share of real imports in real GNP declined, even though the share of nominal inputs in nominal GNP increased. During the Ayub liberalization, real import shares rose from 10.8 percent of real GNP in 1960 to 13.4 percent in 1965 (table 2.15). However, after 1965 import shares dropped sharply, reaching a low of 5.7 percent in 1972. Over the period 1973–80 real import shares recovered, attaining a level of 9.2 percent in 1978, but dwindling somewhat thereafter.

Table 2.15 Share of real imports in real gross national product, 1960–1983 (constant 1960 prices)

Year	Imports as a percentage of GNP	Consumer goods imports as a percentage of GNP	Capital goods imports as a percentage of GNP	Intermediate goods imports as a percentage of GNP
1960	10.75	3.72	4.09	2.94
1961	10.22	2.92	4.17	3.13
1962	10.61	2.45	5.05	3.00
1963	11.58	2.13	6.25	3.20
1964	11.45	2.23	5.73	3.49
1965	13.44	3.49	6.38	3.57
1966	9.77	1.66	5.38	2.73
1967	11.76	2.66	5.34	3.76
1968	9.82	2.14	4.75	2.93
1969	8.71	0.97	4.56	3.18
1970	8.47	0.86	4.28	3.33
1971	7.75	0.84	4.06	2.85
1972	5.68	1.28	2.41	1.99
1973	6.94	2.05	2.07	2.82
1974	7.15	1.68	2.11	3.36
1975	7.16	1.53	2.13	3.50
1976	7.07	1.50	2.49	3.08
1977	7.61	1.21	2.90	3.50
1978	7.77	1.57	2.60	3.60
1979	9.23	2.00	2.79	4.44
1980	9.00	1.44	3.20	4.36
1981	7.00	1.02	1.95	4.03
1982	6.61	0.93	1.94	3.74
1983	6.48	0.91	2.01	3.56

Source: Government of Pakistan, *Pakistan Economic Survey*, various issues

The Composition of Imports

The composition of Pakistan's imports had undergone considerable structural change over the period, reflecting effects of import substitution (table 2.16). In 1960, 35 percent of Pakistan's imports were finished consumer products, 38 percent capital goods, and 27 percent intermediate goods. By 1971 the share of consumer goods had fallen to 11 percent of imports, with shares of capital and intermediate goods rising to 52 percent and 37 percent respectively. In 1983, consumer goods were 14 percent of imports, capital goods 31 percent and intermediate goods 55 percent.

Determinants of Imports: 1960–1979

In the import functions, GNP represents demand, facilitating comparison with the export regressions discussed previously. A second determinant of

Table 2.16 Import share by category of import, 1960–1983 (percent)

Year	Share of consumer goods	Share of intermediate consumer goods	Share of capital goods	Share of intermediate capital goods
1960	34.6	13.8	38.0	13.3
1961	28.6	13.8	40.8	16.8
1962	24.1	16.1	47.6	12.1
1963	18.4	15.8	54.0	11.7
1964	19.5	16.4	50.0	14.1
1965	26.0	14.8	47.5	11.8
1966	17.0	17.8	55.1	10.1
1967	22.6	20.7	45.4	11.3
1968	21.8	20.4	48.4	9.4
1969	11.1	23.8	52.3	12.9
1970	10.2	28.9	50.5	10.4
1971	10.9	25.0	52.4	11.7
1972	22.5	23.4	42.4	11.7
1973	29.5	29.5	29.8	11.3
1974	23.5	38.4	29.5	8.7
1975	21.4	36.7	29.8	12.1
1976	21.2	33.8	35.2	9.8
1977	15.9	36.6	38.1	9.4
1978	20.2	36.8	33.5	9.6
1979	21.7	39.0	30.2	9.1
1980	16.0	42.3	35.5	6.2
1981	14.5	50.1	27.8	7.6
1982	14.1	48.3	29.4	8.2
1983	14.1	49.0	31.0	5.9

Source: based on Government of Pakistan, Pakistan Economic Survey, 1983–4

imports is the REER for imports. In a regime in which quota restraints are employed, the effective exchange rate should be calculated by taking into account the implicit protection (percentage price differential) of imports. Unfortunately, such measures are not available for the entire period under study. In the absence of REERs for imports, the quota restriction indices for total imports as well as for the three subsectors are employed as explanatory variables.

Results of the import regressions are presented in table 2.17. The elasticity of total real imports is approximately 0.9 with respect to real GNP and − 0.9 with respect to the quota restriction index. Thus, a one-point reduction in the index as its mean value of 2.5 represents a 40 percent decline in the index, producing a roughly 35 percent increase in real imports. The two independent variables are significant and explain about three quarters of the variance in real imports. The regressions for the import subsector show broadly the same pattern, with consumer goods showing more, and capital goods less, "price" elasticity than the average for all imports.

Table 2.17 Import regression equations

Dependent variable	Constant (t value)	Coefficient (t value)	Independent variable	Coefficient (t value)	Independent variable	$\bar{R}^2$ (F value)
Log real imports	− 0.4007 (0.15)	0.9241 (3.94)	LRGNP	− 0.8752 (2.76)	QR	0.7764 (33.99)
Log real consumer imports	2.3394 (0.66)	0.6824 (2.18)	LRGNP	− 2.2296 (3.73)	QRCONS	0.5740 (13.80)
Log real capital imports	− 2.3770 (1.13)	0.9444 (4.91)	LRGNP	− 0.0376 (0.19)	QRCAP	0.6433 (18.13)
Log real intermediate imports	− 3.0538 (1.06)	1.0708 (4.038)	LRGNP	− 0.9135 (4.26)	QRINMD	0.8916 (79.13)

LRGNP, log of real GNP; QR, average quota restraint code for all industries; QRCONS, average quota restraint code for consumer imports; QRCAP, average quota restraint code for capital goods imports; QRINMD, average quota restraint code for intermediate goods imports.

Summary and Conclusions

From 1960 to 1983 Pakistan moved toward more liberalized trade, on both the import and the export side. Movement was gradual rather than accelerated and the liberalization was moderate. On a scale running from free trade (20) to autarky (0), Pakistan moved from 6 to a high of 10, ending the period at 9. Thus, while much room for improvement exists, progress was definitely made.

Our analysis found trade policy effective in altering the magnitude of both imports and exports. Consumer goods imports were especially sensitive to changes in the index of quota restraint, which was the operative price variable for imports as quotas, not tariffs, governed domestic prices of consumer goods in Pakistan during most of this period. Consumer goods imports were subject to more restrictive trade policies than either capital or intermediate goods, and consequently import substitution proceeded faster in that sector. Even after a period of substantial import substitution before 1960, consumer goods' share in total imports still fell from 35 to 14 percent over the period 1960–83.

Exports responded to changes in the REERs. Manufactured exports, in particular, displayed a relatively high elasticity compared with that for primary goods exports. Primarily because of a tax–subsidy policy for exports that generally favored development of manufactured goods, the share of manufactures in total exports rose from 43 to 70 percent over the period.

3

The Ayub Liberalization

Between Partition and the end of the Bhutto era (1977), two episodes can be identified as deliberate moves toward liberalization: 1960–5 and 1972–8. The first of these (which we term the Ayub liberalization since it began shortly after Field Marshall Ayub Khan seized the reins of government in a military coup in 1958) marked the first time in Pakistan's short history that the government moved decisively and comprehensively to relax the direct control system that permeated both the internal and external economy. As such, the motives for liberalization, the instruments, and especially the strategy adopted to put it into effect, deserve careful consideration.

Antecedents to Liberalization

It is important to understand that much of the confusion in economic policies before Ayub, as well as the government's predilection for direct controls, stems from the newness of Pakistan as a nation. With no political history and no indigenous political institutions, Pakistan was engrossed, immediately following Partition, in intense efforts at nation building. In the absence of well-established parties or political coalitions, no strong leader emerged who could force a consensus behind a coherent economic policy. This political chaos, combined with a deteriorating international environment following the Korean War, led the government to adopt a risk-averse reliance on direct controls. Imports and even exports of certain products were banned; interregional shipments of grain were limited and in some instances banned; price controls were imposed on key products; quantitative limitations were imposed on all imported goods; all major industrial investments had to be sanctioned by the government; and all foreign exchange receipts earned by exporters had to be surrendered to the State Bank. The proximate cause of Pakistan's trade problems, which made quantitative restrictions appear necessary, was the overvalued exchange rate. Foreign demand for raw materials to feed the Korean War effort produced a surge in demand for Pakistan's exports that fueled domestic inflation. The collapse of the export boom in 1952 left Pakistan with a large potential trade deficit and an overvalued currency. India had devalued in 1949, but Pakistan failed to follow suit both for political reasons and because of misguided economic judgment.

The rupee overvaluation predictably reduced the availability of foreign exchange. The government, instead of devaluing, began an allocation system, controlled by a high-level Foreign Exchange Committee, which distributed foreign exchange receipts across three categories: government imports, capital imports for industry, and consumer goods, raw materials, and spare parts. The Ayub liberalizations were focused on the last of these.

In the period just preceding Ayub, imports of consumer goods, raw materials, and spare parts accounted for roughly 50 percent of Pakistan's total imports. The Chief Controller of Imports and Exports (CCIE) administered the import-licensing system. Because the system was assembled hurriedly in 1952, the principal criterion for allocating licenses to individuals and companies was the level of imports during the OGL period which prevailed during the Korean boom (1950–2). For each commodity a firm had imported during the OGL period, the firm was given a monetary "category" equal to its average imports per six-month shipping period during a base period. The amount of a commodity imported was controlled by changing the percentage of the category that the permit holders could import in any shipping period. This type of licensing system is commonly referred to in Pakistan as the category system.

In allocating exchange among importers, the CCIE attempted to rank commodities on the basis of "essentiality" to the economy. In practice, this meant a higher priority to raw materials than to consumer goods, which were themselves ranked from "essential" to "luxury." The CCIE also allocated exchange between two categories of importers: commercial importers who imported for resale, and industrial importers. In the beginning, the majority of imports were handled by commercial importers, but by 1958 industrial licenses accounted for the greater proportion of imports.

The category system was most effective at coping with short-term balance-of-payments crises, but as time passed it became clear that the system was more a cause of the problem than a solution. First, licenses issued for capital goods did not sufficiently take into account the raw material requirements they would entail. Many of the industrial plants established during the early 1950s were operating at less than a third of rated capacity. Second, the system spawned inequalities, both between income groups and between geographic areas, especially East and West Pakistan. These inequalities, coupled with the pervasive view that the scarcity premiums on import licenses were ill-gotten and tainted by corruption, fueled the fires of public agitation against the government and, as we will see, ultimately became the impetus for Pakistan's second liberalization movement.

The directions for policy reform under Ayub were fairly clearly spelled out. The value of import licenses had to be expanded and this required an expansion of exports. To expand exports, the government had little choice but to increase incentives to exporters either through subsidies or devaluation.

Devaluation was ruled out in 1959 by Ayub largely because of the widely held view that the devaluation four years earlier, Pakistan's first, was a failure. In 1955 Pakistan had devalued the rupee by a third – from Rs 3.57 to Rs 4.76 to the US dollar. The expected increase in exports never materialized, however; world demand in general was expanding only slowly at the time, while Pakistan's own demand for exportables reduced the surplus available for sales abroad. Moreover, the devaluation was not large in relation to Pakistan's trade deficit, and in a few industries the government imposed export taxes that reduced incentives (for example, an export tax on tea to stabilize the domestic price of this politically sensitive commodity).

1960–1965 Reforms

In view of the perceived futility of official devaluations, on January 14, 1959, the government chose to announce several export promotion measures that resulted in a substantial implicit devaluation of the rupee for exporters. The first of these represented an important shift in attitude about foreign trade. Before 1959 only goods on an approved list could be exported; export of all other goods was banned. This discouraged development of many new export items because of the arduous efforts needed to change the list. The positive list was replaced by a negative list that included the names of 16 banned goods; all other goods could be exported.

Export Bonus Scheme

By far the most important change, basically the takeoff point for the Ayub liberalization, was the introduction of the Export Bonus Scheme (EBS). Throughout the 1950s the government had experimented with a variety of export promotion schemes, most of which provided to exporters of certain products import licenses equal to a fixed percentage of the value of their exports. With these licenses, exporters could import scarce raw materials and spares or other valuable items from a restricted list of imports.

The EBS adopted in 1959 differed in several important ways from earlier schemes. The list of importable commodities was considerably expanded. The list of export industries with access to the scheme was extended to include minor primary and service exports as well as manufactured exports. Finally, and perhaps most importantly, the bonus vouchers were freely transferable; they could be sold for cash, and in fact were quoted on the Karachi stock exchange.

With the introduction of the EBS the government established new procedures to control the spending of foreign exchange.

Sequence of Policy Changes

Major changes in policies that followed the introduction of the EBS are described in the following sections. The chronological sequence is listed in semiannual steps because, until 1966, policy announcements covered one six-month period at a time rather than the whole fiscal year.

January–June 1959

The government put a freeze on all unutilized import licenses in order to build up foreign exchange reserves, which were extremely low.

July–December 1959

Pakistan's foreign exchange reserve position improved as the fruits of the EBS began to be realized. Meanwhile, aid from the United States increased. The number of licensable items was increased from 174 to 201.

Another important development during this period was that the government publicly acknowledged a bias toward allocating licenses directly to industrial users, bypassing commercial importers who resold imports to consumers or industries. The government maintained that the industrial bias was necessary to promote the rapid growth of industry.

January–June 1960

The number of importable items remained constant but the total value of licensable imports increased slightly. The major liberalizing policy adopted in this period was the automatic approval system for drugs and pharmaceuticals, which permitted pharmacists to apply for additional licenses once existing licenses had been used up. This system was the precursor to a renewal of OGL and automatic licensing. The industrial bias of licensing continued, though a slight movement toward liberalization of consumer goods could be discerned.

July–December 1960

The experiment in automatic approval was continued and expanded by the addition of another 28 goods, mostly essential industrial raw materials and consumer goods. The reason offered for this change was the desire to stabilize domestic prices and to allow domestic industry to produce efficiently through better capacity utilization. For the first time in Pakistan's history, raw materials were available in sufficient quantity to ensure operation to full capacity on a one-shift basis for the majority of firms, and newcomers were invited to enter import trade. On the negative side, the licensable list for this period contained only 188 items, 13 items fewer than before.

January–June 1961

Automatic renewal of licenses was continued and extended and more newcomers were allowed to enter. A total of 118 industries enjoyed automatic licensing compared with 14 industries in the previous period. The share of firms receiving imports equal to 100 percent of their one-shift capacity rose to 80 percent.

A definite export bias began to emerge during this period. In selecting both newcomers and firms for automatic renewal privileges, previous export performance was taken into consideration. The government also withheld automatic privileges from firms that did not achieve operating efficiency through better use of raw materials and did not lower prices.

On March 8, 1961, the cabinet agreed to place 11 items on OGL. OGL consolidated the automatic renewal system and expanded the newcomer provisions of the previous liberalization efforts. The two essential features of OGL were that (a) separate classes of importers were not established and (b) anyone could apply for an import license (up to a maximum specified amount) for one of the 11 items and be assured of repeat licensing. The list of acceptable imports under OGL included industrial items (iron, steel, and cement) and agricultural items (tractors) but was primarily aimed at consumers (tires and tubes, milk products, typewriters, books, and tools). The intention was to remove the scarcity margins on these items caused by restrictive licensing.

July–December 1961

The path of liberalization becomes murky during this period because of the proliferation of different import schemes. Automatic licensing was de-emphasized while something called "request basis" licensing was introduced. The total number of importable items fell slightly, from 186 to 184. The OGL list expanded from 11 to 49, while the automatic licensing list shrank from 51 to 14. Request-basis licensing was available for 173 industries. Industrial consumers made requests for a value of licensing that would allow them to operate at full (one-shift) capacity for 12 months. These requests were granted within the limits of foreign exchange availability and the reasonableness of the requests. In general, more case-by-case allocations were made in this period than previously. As before, industries with export potential were singled out for special treatment.

January–June 1962

The CCIE announced the policy for this period in a speech in which he assessed performance of the liberalization measures introduced in previous periods. He stated that industrial output had benefited from the increased availability of raw materials but that the increase in nonbonus imports had not been matched by an increase in nonbonus exports, even though special privileges, such as licenses to import balancing and modernization equipment, had been afforded firms with export potential.

The export-oriented revisions established categories of industries on the basis of their export performance. Those with the best performance received the most liberal treatment insofar as licenses were concerned; the less favored categories had to show proof of export orders before import licenses necessary for export production could be released.

In March, the government announced an expanded program of advanced licensing for raw materials for firms with export potential. Advanced licenses permitted firms to plan their production over a longer period of time, eliminating unwanted downtime and increasing efficiency overall. The primary condition of the advanced licensing scheme was that all imports brought in under this provision had to be used for export. Products eligible for EBS could also take advantage of advanced licensing.

July–December 1962

For the first time in three years, no substantial changes in import policy were introduced. The method of linking import licensing to export performance proved successful and was expanded. By the end of 1962, about half of CCIE imports (about 20 percent of all imports) were subject to liberalized import procedures.

January–June 1963

The only change introduced during this period was imposition of a penalty on request-basis firms that did not meet their export quotas.

July–December 1963

This period saw only minor changes in eligible products under the various import categories.

January–June 1964

The objectives of the import policy for January–June 1984 were announced by the CCIE on December 31, 1963: fuller utilization of installed capacity, encouragement to exports, and reduced imports of goods competing with local products.

The major innovation during this period was the free list. Four items from the iron and steel category were placed on a free import system which required no licensing, and any resident national of Pakistan was free to import them.

July–December 1964

On the basis of the successful implementation of the free list in the previous period, the list's scope was expanded to 50 items. Almost all the requirements of industries for imported raw materials and spares were placed on the free list. The free list was not quite as liberal as its name implies, however; many of the raw materials were made available under tied aid agreements so that the national origin, price, and value of imports were constrained. Import duties on free-list imports were increased from 5 to 20 percent.

January–June 1965

The import policy during January–June 1965 was as liberal as in the preceding period. As in the previous period, tariffs were raised on a number of items to restrain their import under the liberalized licensing system. Duties on capital equipment doubled, from 12.5 to 25 percent in West Pakistan and from 7.5 to 20 percent in East Pakistan.

July 1965–June 1966

For the first time in Pakistan's history, the import policy was announced for the entire fiscal year, not just for a six-month period. The free list was expanded to 51 items, but in all other respects the import policy remained unchanged. In November 1965, war was declared on India. Foreign aid ceased abruptly. An emergency 25 percent surcharge sales tax was imposed.

Assessment of the Ayub Liberalization

The war with India prematurely ended the most ambitious trade reforms of any Pakistani government up to that time. The share of CCIE imports that entered under liberalized procedures rose from almost zero to more than 70 percent. Under the new system, import licenses were issued only upon accrual of foreign exchange earnings. Three accounts were created and replenished by foreign exchange earnings: one account contained 20–40 percent of foreign exchange earnings from items eligible for the bonus scheme; another account was used for government imports; a third account was used for private nonbonus imports.

Since exporters of different products received different rates of bonus (that is, the percentage of the value of their exports to be received in vouchers), the effect of this scheme was a partial devaluation and the creation of some flexibility in the existing system of multiple exchange rates. In spite of its expanded coverage, the size of the EBS was rather small, accounting for about 10 percent of total CCIE-licensed imports (or about 5 percent of total imports); thus the degree of liberalization must be considered to be fairly marginal. In addition to its limited coverage, the system was also criticized for extensive experimentation with various bonus-list items, bonus rates, and bonus recipients, which created considerable uncertainty and induced a wide variety of speculative behavior, including stockpiling. The major reason for these experiments was to maintain a stable premium on bonus vouchers and to regulate the domestic selling price of commodities on the bonus list.

To facilitate comparison with the other country studies in our project, and hence the drawing of general inferences, the assessment that follows (and its counterpart, for the second liberalization episode in chapter 4) focuses on the issues selected by the original research plan as critical in analyzing an attempted liberalization (see the preface to the volume).

Timing and Sequencing: 1959–1965

As demonstrated earlier, both imports and exports are price sensitive: changes in effective exchange rates are positively correlated with exports and negatively with imports. However, because of the simultaneous occurrence of often unrelated events – floods, droughts, the creation of Bangladesh – it is impossible to show the *independent* effect of liberalization on macroeconomic data. Moreover, data for the sectors most likely to be affected by liberalization – industry, for example – are simply too unreliable to submit to statistical analysis.

Nevertheless, within constraints imposed on inferences by these conditions in Pakistan, it is possible to give broad generalizations about the timing and sequencing of liberalization measures in Pakistan undertaken during the 1959–65 period. Certain patterns recur in the process, not with absolute regularity but enough to intimate a strategy or an attitude that policymakers adopted in making their choices.

One such pattern is the preference of the Ayub regime for liberalizations that were *directly self-funding*. All liberalizations are ultimately self-funding, but officials in the Ayub regime needed more assurance of this than the educated guesses of economists about price elasticities seemed to provide. Ayub's liberalizations were on a "cash," rather than a "credit," basis. Increased imports were permitted only when firm commitments for increased foreign exchange availability were possible. The best example of the self-funding concept is the special bank account established for the Export Bonus Scheme (EBS). The central bank collected all export proceeds and deposited the amounts that would be redeemed for imports (20–40 percent of exports, depending on the bonus rate) in a special account. All bonus imports had to be paid out of this account, virtually guaranteeing that any increase in foreign exchange expenditures under EBS had been "prepaid" through deposits in the special account.

The emphasis on self-funding was a result not only of the control mentality of its bureaucrats but also of Pakistan's economic conditions. Pakistan could not borrow commercially on international markets to cover shortfalls in foreign exchange earnings. (Thus, in another example, the free-list liberalizations were only undertaken after aid donors pledged to cover the additional import costs of items on the free list, and even with these pledges planners hedged and circumscribed the uses of the free list to prevent rapid increases in imports.) The need for self-funding may also explain why liberalizations were limited to quantitative restrictions and not tariffs. No self-funding scheme was obvious for tariff reductions.

The implications of self-funding for the timing and sequencing of liberalizations are fairly obvious. With regard to timing, import liberalizations dependent on increased aid obviously need both a willing donor and a government committed to liberalization. The two coincided in 1964 in connection with the free list. By the same token, import liberalization dependent on earmarked funds from export promotion schemes was undertaken more frequently.

One-stage versus Gradual Liberalization

The self-funding requirement dictated the sequence of liberalization measures. "Naked" liberalizations were unheard of during the Ayub regime; import liberalization depended upon export promotion measures or additional aid commitments. The self-funding requirement also led to *multistage* liberalization. Rather than one large liberalization, several small liberalizations were introduced sequentially, each stage being limited to a small list of imports. Testing the waters in this way, planners developed confidence in the possibility of successful liberalization.

Length of the Process

No time limits were attached by the Ayub government to the liberalization process. In part, this can be explained by the absence of any specific goals. While the second five-year plan spoke in general terms of the need for liberalization throughout the economy, including the trade sector, few specific goals were set. The lack of quantitative objectives was consistent with the cautious step-by-step approach of the bureaucrats. By not committing themselves to a specific goal, they could experiment without the pressure of having to meet targets within a given period.

Desirability of a Separate Stage for Quota Removal

In one sense the list was an attempt at a separate stage for quota removal. In principle, items on the list were freely importable. Tariffs on free-list items were generally low and remained unchanged. However, no goal of tariff elimination or reduction for free-list items was ever announced. Liberalization was seen only as a means of eliminating direct controls, not as the first step in tariff reform.

The other liberalization schemes – EBS, Pay As You Earn (PAYE), OGL – did not contain measures designed to replace import quotas by tariffs as a first step. These liberalization measures were designed to relax the stringency of the quotas themselves.

Export Promotion as a Separate Stage

Export promotion was seen as the initiating step in liberalization, not as a separate stage. The exception to this was the free-list liberalization that was financed by foreign aid rather than export earnings. The principal export promotion measure adopted under Ayub, the EBS, funded itself by granting exporters access to scarce imports. Thus export promotion was directly linked to import liberalization.

Discriminatory Treatment

The liberalizations under Ayub were all discriminatory in nature, partly because of the piecemeal implementation of the reforms. Rather than attempt small uniform liberalization on all commodities, the government preferred to liberalize commodities sequentially in the order of their "essentiality." Items needed by industry to attain full-capacity operation were the first to be put on the bonus and free lists. Items competing with domestic industry were the last to be liberalized.

Appropriate Circumstances for Liberalization

Liberalization of imports began within a year of the accession of Ayub to power. General Ayub Khan seized power in order to establish political order and revive the economy. The timing of the liberalization was determined by Ayub's need to show decisive and effective measures that would achieve both these goals. From an economic standpoint the timing was not crucial, largely because of the tentative nature of the measures adopted, but from a political standpoint Ayub had no alternative but to launch his liberalization campaign in the first few years.

While in many countries liberalizations were initiated as part of some type of stabilization program, the Ayub liberalization was preceded by a period of relative economic stability. Admittedly, the slow growth of foreign exchange earnings was a motive, but the period immediately preceding the reforms could not be characterized as a crisis in the normally understood meaning of the term.

Sustainability of Liberalization Policy

Pakistan's liberalizations, being self-funding, multistaged, and spread out over a period of years, were easily sustainable. Adjustment costs were low because exports expanded while noncompeting imports were liberalized. Most importantly, the trade sector accounted for only a small portion of national income. Small changes in a small sector had few repercussions in the economy.

The Ayub liberalizations proceeded as long as the requisites for the self-funding system were in place, but when the 1965 war erupted and aid was cut off they were halted. After the war, liberalization was resumed. During the Ayub period, no liberalization measure was ever withdrawn because of any adverse consequence that could be attributed to liberalization itself.

Relationship of Liberalization to Other Policy Measures

For the reasons just stated, the government made no significant effort to adjust fiscal and monetary policies to accommodate changes in the trade sector. Nor does evidence exist to suggest that liberalization initiatives were delayed or accelerated to coincide with changes in economic policies elsewhere in the economy.

4

The Bhutto Liberalization

Antecedents to Liberalization

The political movement that swept first Ayub Khan and then his successor Yahya Khan from power and ushered in the Bhutto era was rooted in classical populism. A variety of social and political groups that had little in common except their desire to see Ayub, Yahya, and their major supporters (industrialists and the elite corps of civil servants) removed from power formed a coalition. Among important issues that emerged on the agenda of Bhutto's party – the Pakistan People's Party (PPP) – were income redistribution and political restructuring. The former was interpreted primarily to mean an attack on the major industrialists while the latter meant an assault on the civil service of Pakistan. To the extent that these were two of the three legs upon which the stability of the pre-Bhutto government rested – the third being the military – Bhutto began his regime by tearing at the foundations of the government itself. Remember that in 1971 Pakistan had received a stunning blow from the secession of Bangladesh. Bhutto devoted much of his own effort to reestablishing the legitimacy of government and to building political institutions. Responsibility for economic policymaking fell almost by default to the left wing of the PPP. Thus, from the very beginning of PPP authority, the attack on economic concentration became a central part of Pakistani economic policy, with the expected negative effect on capital accumulation and overall economic growth.

Bhutto attacked the industrialists and bureaucratic elite by liberalizing the system of import licensing. The trade and exchange control system was widely perceived as the major contributor to economic concentration under Ayub, with corrupt bureaucrats and influential businessmen sharing the rents created by restrictive licensing. Although the bonus scheme had moved effective exchange rates closer to equilibrium exchange rates, rural populations, who had to bear the higher prices of bonus imports and were forced to sell their exportable output at the OER without bonus vouchers, saw the scheme as discriminatory. Thus liberalization could be sold to

Bhutto's constituency as an attack on economic privilege. No evidence exists to suggest that efficiency gains from liberalization were a prime motive for initiating the reforms.

1972–1978 Reforms

The three most significant components of the 1972–8 liberalization were devaluation, the end of restrictive licensing, and the elimination of the bonus scheme. The rupee was devalued by 131 percent on May 12, 1972. No one had doubted that the rupee was overvalued. However, the Ayub and Yahya governments had believed that devaluation would be self-defeating by generating inflation, which in turn would undermine political stability. This was no longer a crucial issue for Bhutto, since political stability had already been undermined by the breakup of Pakistan and war with India. Moreover, because of the simultaneous reduction in import licensing, the average effective devaluation on the import side was only about 40 percent rather than 131 percent.

The second major change was simplification and liberalization of the category system regulating imports. Specifically, where the previous system had six separate import lists, the new system had only two: a free list of items which, in principle, could enter the country without restriction, and a tied list of items importable only from tied aid or barter sources. In addition, the Trading Corporation of Pakistan, a state-owned agency, held the monopoly to import certain goods, including steel billets and strips, most nonferrous metals in ingot form, newsprint, and sugar. As in the previous system, all goods not on a so-called "positive" list were banned.

Although significant liberalizations were achieved by this simplification, several problems remained. Many consumer products were omitted from the positive lists, producing infinite protection in theory although in practice smuggling set an effective upper limit on the prices of domestically produced substitutes. Banning makes it especially difficult to judge the degree of protection afforded by the government since, officially, there are no imports on which to make price comparisons. Further, the free list permitted unlimited imports only to those buyers who held foreign exchange. Whenever foreign exchange supplies were scarce, importers without foreign funds found that, even though they possessed a license to import, they had to queue up for foreign exchange. The effects of foreign exchange licensing on prices of importable goods were identical with those of import licensing.

The final reform was elimination of the EBS. It seems paradoxical that introduction of the scheme in 1959 and its elimination in 1972 could both be considered as liberalizing actions, but the paradox is resolved by recognizing that the scheme's benefit in the earlier period was to introduce market forces into a rigid license control system. When the licensing system was sharply curtailed in 1972, the scheme became a cumbersome way to maintain what was effectively a multiple exchange rate system. The decision to eliminate the scheme was a movement toward more uniform effective exchange rates for exports.

For goods qualifying for the EBS, the effective devaluation fell short of the nominal devaluation because the scheme ensured that exporters received more rupees per US dollar of exports than they would earn at the official rate. For these goods, the gain from the official devaluation was partially offset by the loss of market value of bonus vouchers. Moreover, for many goods that did not qualify for the bonus scheme, the effective devaluations were also less than the nominal devaluation because the government levied export taxes on these goods. On average, effective devaluation on exports amounted to only 25 percent.

Assessment of the Bhutto Liberalization

Timing and Sequencing: 1972–1978

The timing and sequencing of the 1972–8 liberalization seem, at first sight, to stand in sharp contrast with the 1960–5 effort. Currency devaluation, totally absent from the first liberalization, was the centerpiece of the second episode. The gradual step-by-step measures of the 1960–5 episode were swept away in favor of bold quantum leaps. While Ayub's march toward liberalization required six years, all Bhutto's significant liberalizations were implemented in just one month (May 1972).

Beneath these superficial dissimilarities, however, strong congruities can be discerned. Currency devaluation was implemented but, because of the adoption of export taxes, the effective devaluation on the export side was not too different from the increase achieved by the EBS in the first liberalization. On the import side, the government tried to keep domestic prices stable for many items. Domestic prices of services and some capital items rose sharply, but for most products the government adjusted tariffs to ensure equality between pre- and post-devaluation prices. Finally, in spite of the appearance of a one-time liberalization, the government continued to adjust export taxes and import duties throughout the 1972–6 period in response to both internal and external developments.

Preference for a One-stage Liberalization

There is no question that the Bhutto government preferred the one-stage over the gradual approach of trade liberalization, for reasons that were more political than economic. Throughout his campaign, Bhutto promised a "new broom" government, one that would sweep away the cobwebs of profiteering from trade regulations. One cannot avoid a sense of irony in Bhutto's dismantling the EBS in 1972. In 1959 it was Bhutto, as Minister of Commerce, who had proudly announced the creation of the EBS as a means of improving efficiency in the economy; in 1972 he ordered its termination as a way to improve equity by eliminating scarcity rents from import licenses.

The one-stage liberalization of trade was just one of several major economic policy reforms introduced by Bhutto. Within a month of assuming office, he announced the nationalization of a major part of basic industry: iron and steel, heavy engineering, automobiles, basic metals, cement, and petrochemicals. In a single government act, more than one fifth of Pakistan's large-scale manufacturing sector came under state management, although ownership remained in the hands of the private sector. Banks and insurance companies were nationalized in January 1974.

In the first year of his regime, Bhutto announced other reforms that, at least on paper, appeared to be quite comprehensive and sweeping. For example, he announced a major land reform in March 1972. Ceilings on individual holdings were dropped by about two thirds – from 500 hectares for irrigated land and 1,000 hectares for unirrigated land to 150 hectares and 300 hectares, respectively. Timing of these reforms in the first few months of the Bhutto regime was designed to convey determination of the government to eradicate inequalities at one fell swoop.

In summary, 1972 was a year filled with sharp departures from previous policies. The timing and means of announcement were carefully staged for maximum dramatic effect. The Bhutto government hammered home the notion that power had shifted from the elite to the masses by a succession of policies that sought to reverse what the government saw as a widening income distribution gap by removing elements of oligopolistic control from the economy. In the event, however, all the policies announced in this period were either subsequently modified, as in the case of trade liberalization, or only partially implemented, as in the case of labor and land reforms, making the reforms much less radical than they at first seemed. One could plausibly argue that the 1972 liberalization episode only lasted a few short months before the first backward step was taken.

Length and Speed of Liberalization

Bhutto's desire for dramatic and decisive action dictated a short period of implementation. Given that the reforms in trade and exchange rate policy reforms were announced within six months of Bhutto's accession to power, very little preparatory work had been done to ensure smooth implementation. Nevertheless, the new trade and exchange rate policies were announced simultaneously and put into immediate effect.

Separate Stage for Quota Elimination

Since elimination of quotas was one of the objectives of the reforms and was accomplished in one act, it could be concluded that a separate stage for quota elimination was attempted. The effective devaluation of imports of 40 percent compensated for the loss of scarcity markups on licenses and checked the expansion of demand.

Separate Export Promotion State

Promotion of exports was stimulated by the 24 percent increase in the effective exchange rate, but a separate stage was not attempted.

Uniform versus Discriminatory Treatment

The government attempted to maintain stable rupee prices of both imports and exports of traded commodities. Imports of services bore the full brunt of devaluation, and relative prices therefore shifted against importers of services. However, for traded goods, tariffs were changed in a nonuniform fashion in order to treat imports uniformly, that is, to leave their domestic prices unchanged. The exchange and trade control reforms did reduce the variability of tariff levels.

Desirable Discrimination

The overhaul of the trade licensing system was designed to leave the relative prices of manufactured goods as unchanged as possible. No deliberate discrimination among traded goods was built into the tariff, export tax, and exchange rate changes. Of course, by leaving relative prices unchanged, the pre-1972 pattern of discrimination reflected different levels of effective protection and was allowed to continue.

One way in which discrimination among products was pursued was through product-by-product changes in effective export exchange rates. The government made changes based on their own forecasts of market demand and supply. After 1972, when world demand for a product sagged, for example, export taxes were dropped or subsidies added to stabilize domestic prices or maintain international market shares. These decisions were *ad hoc*, prompted by changes in world or domestic conditions, and not part of a plan.

Appropriate Circumstances

In the second liberalization, the appropriate time to initiate trade exchange reforms clearly was immediately following Bhutto's accession to the position of prime minister, when his power was at a peak. In the aftermath of the East Pakistan debacle and the humiliating military encounter with India, Bhutto emerged from the elections without any close rivals or an effective opposition. Pakistan's economy was in a state of turmoil, half of its former market having been lopped off. It was a serendipitous coincidence of interests: trade liberalization served the political aims of the PPP as well as economic efficiency.

The timing of reforms aroused little criticism. Only the amount of devaluation was questioned by the press. *The Pakistan and Gulf Economist* (May 27, 1972) noted that, because exports had almost doubled between the fiscal years of 1971 and 1972, the 131 percent devaluation seemed excessive, though the writer clearly failed to appreciate how small the effective devaluation was.

Like the Ayub reforms, the Bhutto liberalization was not an offshoot of a stabilization program initiated in response to abnormal economic conditions. Reforms were certainly launched in a period of economic turmoil, but here it is important to draw the lines of causality very carefully. Both the economic turmoil and the emergence of the Bhutto regime can be traced to the same basic causes: international political instability that resulted in the collapse of united Pakistan, and domestic political instability that brought to power a reform-minded government. Thus it would be incorrect to assert that the economic chaos of early 1972 prompted the Bhutto reforms. In fact, it is reasonable to speculate that Bhutto would have initiated the same reforms regardless of the state of the economy. For Bhutto, any economic gain from liberalization was an incidental bonus: the principal objective was to dethrone the small number of industrialists and traders who had cornered the rents produced by direct controls on imports.

Sustainability

The Bhutto liberalizations began to run into trouble almost immediately. Imports rose sharply; export growth tapered off after an initial burst; inflation began to accelerate. How much of the increase in imports was due to Bhutto's policy changes in other areas, especially nationalization and labor relations, how much to exogenous factors such as floods and droughts, and how much to external factors, especially the oil price shock and subsequent worldwide recession, is hard to determine. It is obvious that the exogenous and external factors were significant and their absence would have improved the prospects for survival of Bhutto's liberalization policies, and indeed of the regime itself.

Other Policy Measures

The most important policy change accompanying the trade reforms was devaluation. Because of the disparity between the official rate of exchange

(Rs 4.76 per US dollar) and the effective import rate on many commodities (Rs 10–14 per US dollar), devaluation was inevitable if the various import-licensing and export subsidy schemes were to be eliminated. Many different combinations of exchange rate and tariff or tax changes were possible and no explanation for the Rs 11 per US dollar official rate was ever provided.

The only other major policy change made at the time of trade reforms was an increase in the discount rate from 5.6 percent. Although the change was announced as part of the devaluation package, this restraint on credit expansion may have had other motives. Domestic prices had been rising well before May 1972. The change in the discount rate was probably only cosmetic; the main source of credit was expansion in the immediate pre-devaluation period due to the government's deficit financing. The actual increase in credit to the public sector was three times the planned level in 1972 (Guisinger, 1981, p. 395).

5

An Interpretation of Pakistan's Liberalizations

The review of the two liberalization episodes leaves a number of key questions unanswered. First, to what extent were they a deliberate strategy planned with a specifically economic end in view? Second, what can explain the government's predilection, both during and outside the episodes, for tinkering with the trade control system? Third, what were the consequences of liberalization for the economy? And finally, why did the government not go further than it did in the liberalizations that were undertaken?

These questions do not lend themselves well to statistical testing, and our interpretations necessarily contain a strong element of subjective judgment. Our conclusions should be regarded more as reasoned conjectures than analytical results; yet, the importance of these issues demands some attempt. Some insights may be sought in an examination of the motives, and resultant policy design, of the two liberalizations, in the context of the objectives that have preoccupied Pakistan's economic policymakers over the whole period.

Pattern of Reform

On the face of it, the two episodes differ significantly, both in motivation and in the mechanisms adopted for implementation. With respect to objectives, the Ayub liberalization was essentially aimed at improving the *efficiency* of the economic system. That efficiency gains were accompanied by an improvement in income distribution was a welcomed by-product but not the primary object of the liberalization. In contrast, the Bhutto liberalization was motivated by concerns for *equity*. That liberalization might also improve the efficiency of the economy was welcomed, but it is quite tenable that the Bhutto reforms would have been launched even if no efficiency gains were predicted.

With respect to implementation, the two episodes differed in terms not only of strategy but also of tactics. The Ayub regime began with export promotion measures and then moved to liberalize imports. Bhutto tackled export and import liberalization simultaneously. The Ayub reforms were parceled out over six years, whereas the bulk of the Bhutto reforms were completed in just one month. The Ayub reforms focused on the relaxation of quotas while the Bhutto liberalization involved not only quota relaxation but also changes in import tariffs and export taxes.

Nonetheless, the two episodes shared many common features, many of them characteristic of persisting trends in the pattern of Pakistani policy-making. Prominent among them were an absence of long-range planning and a related predilection for incessant policy adjustment.

Absence of Long-range Planning

Policy reforms seldom go forward through the Pakistan bureaucracy without some degree of forethought and review of options. Moreover, Pakistan's second five-year plan, whose drafting and implementation largely coincided with Ayub's first seven years in power, took the theme of liberalization of economic controls in all sectors as one of its centerpieces, and in that sense it could be said that the Ayub reforms in trade conformed to a comprehensive plan. Nevertheless, both the Ayub and the Bhutto reforms were unplanned in the important sense that no period of careful study preceded implementation of policy changes, and for both (though in different respects) components of the liberalization process were essentially uncoordinated.

The Ayub liberalization began on a small scale with the EBS, followed by other reforms introduced serially but not in a predetermined sequence. Instead, each reform measure had its own genesis, only indirectly related to other measures. The Bhutto reforms, by contrast, may have initially been more carefully coordinated, but the period from plan to implementation was extremely short – six months – and modifications to the initial package began soon after implementation. Thus, in neither episode can one claim that the reforms were part of a planned program of liberalization.

Continuous Intervention

Characteristic of both episodes, and indeed of trade policy in Pakistan in general, was the constant tinkering with the system of trade controls. The government made numerous small modifications in trade policies, both during and between episodes, that ultimately had a significant bearing on liberalization. Episodes merely represent periods of heightened activity.

For example, both imports and import traders were assigned to a bewildering array of categories, and frequent changes were made in these classifications. At one time or another during the first eight years of the

EBS, changes were made in expiration dates of vouchers, qualifying export products, rate of bonus, and list of goods importable under bonus. Significant changes were made every six months and the bonus scheme itself was not made permanent until 1968, almost ten years after it had been introduced as a temporary expedient.

The resultant uncertainty introduced a number of inefficiencies into the trade system. For example, importers hoarded raw materials to guard against import scarcities. Whenever the government announced any type of liberalization, importers placed massive orders for fear that the "window" would soon close again; and their fears were often self-fulfilling. Another example of policy-induced inefficiency was the proof required of industrial importers that imported raw materials were used before new licenses were issued. This created needless paperwork and invited corruption.

Similar uncertainty was found among exporters, who did not know from one period to the next what profit they would earn. The normal commercial risk encountered in foreign sales was compounded by uncertainty about the effective exchange rates. The value of bonus vouchers fluctuated not only with the rate and coverage of the bonus scheme, but also with the premium that vouchers sold for in the open market.

What were the benefits perceived by the government as compelling enough to justify the costs incurred by these frequent changes in trade policies? Paradoxically, the main objective seems to have been stability – in prices and exchange rates, in distribution of profits, and in maintaining a hierarchy of essentiality.

Stable Domestic Prices
One objective of policymakers in Pakistan has always been maintenance of stable domestic prices for basic consumer goods such as tea, rice, and wheat. In the event of shocks to the internal supply or external demand of these products, policymakers in Pakistan have never hesitated to stabilize prices through taxes and subsidies. For example, a ban on the export of raw cotton was instituted in 1973 when flooding reduced the size of the crop, endangering the supply of raw cotton to domestic mills.

Stable Effective Exchange Rates
To reduce the uncertainty facing importers and exporters, the government attempted to maintain the bonus voucher premium within a range. The desirable range varied, but in general a bonus voucher premium below 100 or above 200 was considered inappropriate. To maintain the rate within this range, the government added items to the list of exports eligible for bonus vouchers and to the list of goods eligible for import under bonus vouchers as well as changing the rate of bonus vouchers.

Avoidance of Windfalls
On occasion, the government altered the composition of eligibility lists (both exports and imports) and bonus rates to prevent windfalls. For example, for products imported under either regular license or bonus, importers holding regular licenses received windfalls to the extent of the bonus premium. The government tried to limit windfalls by making such products importable by one of the two means but not both.

Maintaining an Order of Priority for Imports
From time to time, the government decided that prices of certain luxury imports were too low. Adjustments were then made on ineligibility lists to raise prices for these goods.

Consequences of Liberalization

Statistical evidence on the impact of Pakistan's liberalizations on major economic indicators is particularly hard to come by for three reasons. First, the scale of both liberalizations has been small, both in relation to those attempted by other countries and in proportion to the initial level of trade distortions. Compounding the problem of size is the fact that, in the Ayub episode, liberalization was spread out over a number of years, making the impact that was felt in any one year smaller than the total amount of liberalization achieved during the episode. All other things being equal, single-stage liberalizations should leave a more readily identifiable imprint on economic variables such as GNP, trade flows, and price levels than multistage liberalizations achieved over a period of years.

Second, trade has been a relatively small sector in Pakistan, largely because of Pakistan's large population. During the period 1960–83, imports never represented more than 20 percent of GNP, in contrast with smaller economies such as Singapore, Israel, or Uruguay in which the trade sector occupies a much more important place. For this reason, it is hard to link changes in imports and exports to changes in macroeconomic variables.

Third, other economic events that occurred at the same time as liberalization have to some degree obscured the impact of trade reforms on economic indicators. In the Ayub period, trade reforms were accompanied by major shifts in agricultural price policy, while large inflows of foreign capital appeared for the first time in Pakistan's history. The Bhutto reforms were preceded by war and the bisection of the country, and were soon followed by the oil price crisis of 1973 that triggered a slump in foreign demand for Pakistan's exports. In econometric terms, the identification of the impact of liberalization at the macroeconomic level calls for multivariate analysis that, in the case of Pakistan, cannot be undertaken with the data at hand.

In spite of the impracticality of accurate measurement, it is still useful to sift through the time series data on Pakistan's primary economic indicators to look for the influence of liberalization, at least for the first longer episode. Table 5.1 shows data on several important variables for the 1960–70 period. The balance of trade, in real terms, widened sharply in the first year owing as much to a fall-off in exports as to an increase in imports. While the value of exports, expressed in constant 1959 prices, rose in 1963, there is no further tendency to expand until 1968. The performance of imports was erratic, rising substantially in four of the years but either growing modestly (1–5 percent) or even declining in the remaining seven. Liberalization was obviously not reflected in steady increases in total imports and exports. Manufacturing exports showed greater responsiveness. After declines in fiscal years 1961 and 1962, the volume of manufactured exports increased in all but two of the following years.

Industrial output shows a fairly steady increase during the episode. Liberalization contributed to the higher level of capacity utilization by making raw materials available, but much of industrial growth can be attributed to the working off of disequilibrium created by Partition and shifts in the internal terms of trade. The early 1960s was a period of price stability compared with the 1970s. Industry grew fast, but demand grew even faster, and the wholesale price of manufactured goods increased by roughly 3 percent a year.

In drawing a balance sheet on the 1960–5 liberalization, trade and exchange reforms may have had a favorable effect and few, if any, significant negative effects on the economy, but statistical evidence for these conclusions is difficult to find.

Another way to examine the impact of liberalization on the economy is to look beyond the episodes themselves and ask whether changes in exports and imports have any impact on macroeconomic indicators, such as prices. Regressions of two variables (export and import shares in domestic supply, that is, exports or imports divided by domestic supply (= production + imports − exports)) and three price indices (all commodities, primary goods, and manufactured goods) for two time periods – a pre-devaluation (1960–72) period and a post-devaluation (1973–83) period – yielded 12 correlation coefficients. The normal expectation would be for export shares to be positively, and import shares negatively, correlated with prices. Data show that only four of the 12 possible correlations are significant and one of the four has the wrong sign. These results do not support the notion that changes in import and export shares in Pakistan have had significant impact on domestic prices.

Table 5.1 Economic trends for the fiscal years 1959–1960 to 1969–1970

Item	Fiscal year										
	1960	1961	1962	1963	1964	1965	1966	1967	1968	1969	1970
Exports (1960 prices)	763	519	531	972	1,001	1,016	1,044	1,030	1,200	1,318	1,200
Imports (1960 prices)	1,806	2,090	2,186	2,741	2,776	3,274	2,498	2,879	2,589	2,363	2,451
Trade deficit (1960 prices)	−1,043	−1,571	−1,635	−1,769	−1,775	−2,258	−1,454	−1,849	−1,309	−1,045	−1,251
Growth rates											
Exports (%)	n.a.	−32	2	83	3	1	3	−1	24	3	−9
Imports (%)	n.a.	16	3	25	1	18	−24	15	−10	−9	4
Industrial output, CSO index[a]	100	119	138	159	100	201	213	235	253	278	301
Wholesale price index manufacturing	100	99	101	106	107	107	113	117	122	130	134
Capacity utilization (% of one shift)	n.a.	n.a.	n.a.	n.a.	5	79	n.a.	n.a.	n.a.	n.a.	n.a.
Manufactured exports	100	79	68	113	157	174	150	227	203	391	378

n.a., not available.

[a] Index prepared by the Central Statistical Office.

Source: Government of Pakistan, *Pakistan Economic Survey*, various issues.

Limits of Liberalization

The final question is why Pakistan did not pursue liberalization more vigorously. If the Ayub and Bhutto liberalizations had little apparent adverse effect on the economy, why did the government not continue to liberalize, and liberalize in greater amounts? Did the government pursue liberalization to the point where the marginal benefit just equaled the marginal cost or did it stop short? The limited scope and infrequent appearances of liberalization efforts suggest that strong forces operated to preserve trade restrictions and that liberalizations only occurred in unusual circumstances.

We conjecture, and it can be little more than that given the absence of reliable data, that government policymakers relied on *estimated foreign exchange availability* to determine the extent of the liberalizations attempted and, importantly, that their method for estimating foreign exchange availability ignored the efficiency gains that liberalization was meant to bring about. In sum, the government used a narrow definition of expected foreign exchange receipts that limited Pakistan's liberalizations to fairly modest efforts compared with measures adopted in other developing countries.

It must be recalled that in the Ayub period the government did not regard Pakistani exports as being very elastic in terms of foreign demand or domestic supply. Liberalization on the import side had then to be "purchased" out of foreign exchange reserves or foreign aid inflows. This attitude produced the EBS, which virtually ensured that import liberalization was paid for by export earnings, but this scheme was thought applicable only to certain manufactured goods where supply and demand elasticities seemed more congenial. It should also be recalled that export earnings provided only 20 percent of Pakistan's foreign exchange receipts, the remainder coming from capital inflows, principally foreign aid.

In addition, foreign exchange reserves were very limited. During the 1960s, reserves generally provided coverage for five to six months of imports. Thus any substantial liberalization had to come principally from new capital inflows. For example, the free list was introduced only after funds were made available through the Pakistan Consortium and was curtailed when the funds dried up. The promise of efficiency gains alone seemed insufficient to drive the liberalization process.

The situation had changed somewhat at the time of the Bhutto liberalization. Exports provided much higher shares of foreign exchange receipts – approximately 80, 60, and 40 percent in fiscal years 1972, 1973, and 1974. However, the reserve coverage of imports fell to two to three months.

Thus in neither the Ayub nor the Bhutto episodes did the government perceive a satisfactory "cushion" of foreign exchange availability that could underwrite a substantial liberalization – a cushion provided either by ample reserves, adequate lines of commercial credit, or additional foreign aid. The corollary to this is that liberalizations were undertaken strictly in proportion to anticipated additions to foreign exchange receipts.

Statistical evidence for the relationship between liberalization efforts and foreign exchange receipts is provided in the appendix. Evidence suggests certain patterns in the behavior of Pakistan's policymakers. First, there is a significant inverse relationship between changes in Pakistan's balance-of-trade and foreign exchange reserve positions. A 10 percent increase in the balance-of-trade deficit was associated with a 10 percent *increase* in foreign exchange reserves. This paradoxical finding can be explained by reference to the preceding discussion of capital-inflow-constrained liberalization. Any increase in capital inflows was apportioned in a very consistent fashion between liberalization (reflected in the worsening trade deficit) and additions to foreign exchange reserves.

Second, data also suggest that export and import policies were set conditional on anticipated foreign exchange receipts, principally capital inflows. Since the relationship of the import quota restraint index to the level of imports has already been established (chapter 2), the import quota restraint index needed to maintain equilibrium for the balance of payments was estimated for every year between 1959 and 1979, assuming that the REER observed in each year prevailed. This estimated import quota restraint was then compared with the actual value for each year from 1959 to 1979 and the two series were found to be highly correlated. The same procedure was followed for the REER (again assuming the prevailing levels of the import quota restraint index) and the same results were obtained, that is, the "required" levels of the REER were not too different from observed levels.

If policymakers made decisions about liberalization based on a narrowly determined estimate of future foreign exchange availability – essentially foreign exchange reserves in hand plus capital inflows (principally foreign aid commitments) plus a conservatively estimated growth in export earnings (ignoring efficiency gains from liberalization itself) – then the question can be asked: what incremental capital inflows were necessary to induce Pakistani officials to undertake substantial liberalization? For example, at what "price" in terms of new aid commitments would liberalizations begin to look attractive to the government?

Table 5.2 reports the results of a simulation presented in the appendix that shows present value of capital inflows necessary to sustain different import and export regimes over the period 1959–79. The row and column marked "actual" refer to the import and export policies actually experienced by Pakistan over the period 1960–83. The net present value of Pakistan's foreign capital inflows during this period was approximately US$6 billion. The actual value of the import restraint index varied between

Table 5.2 Present value of capital inflows necessary to sustain alternative trade and exchange rate policies (billion constant 1960 US dollars)

Exchange rate regime	Import liberalization index			
	Actual	2.0	1.0	Special
Actual	6	8	18	—
Improved[a]	—	6	16	—
Special[a]	—	—	—	3

—, not calculated.

[a] Assumes that the 1972 REER prevailed during the period 1959–71.

[b] Assumes a tightening of the import liberalization index to 4.0 from 1959 to 1971 but then a liberalization to 2.0 thereafter.

4.1 and 2.2 with an average around 3.0. Thus, if Pakistan had lowered its import restraint index from the observed level of 3.5 to 2.0 in 1959 and maintained that level for the entire period without altering its export exchange rate policy, a capital inflow of US$8 billion rather than US$6 billion would have been required to maintain balance-of-payments equilibrium. Had the index been lowered to 1.0, then US$18 billion would have been required. The second row of the table reports similar results, except that the REERs for exports prevailing during the period 1960–71 are assumed to be equal to the 1972 REER for exports. In other words, had Pakistan undertaken an effective devaluation of the rupee much earlier, then the required capital inflows would have been approximately US$2 billion less for each of the liberalization assumptions.

The row and column marked "special" indicate a regime in which an initial tightening of import quotas had taken place (a uniform index of 4.0 from 1960 to 1971) followed by a liberalization to 2.0 in each year from 1972 until 1979. In this case, reserves accumulate until 1972, at which time they are drawn down as liberalization takes place.

These simulations of alternative trade and exchange rate regimes are made on the conservative assumption that liberalization has no efficiency effects on the economy that would reduce import demand or expand export supply. They also ignore the possibility that a substantial adjustment in Pakistan's OER could have been undertaken at an early point in the period. In that sense, they represent the outer limits of the "cost" of liberalizations represented in the simulations. However, to the extent that policymakers ignored these possibilities and focused on the additional foreign exchange costs of liberalization, it is not difficult to understand why liberalization has occurred in such small amounts and why it has typically been on a directly "self-funding" basis.

Appendix 1

Trade Liberalization in the Context of Pakistan's Economic Development Strategy

It is fair to ask why Pakistan did not attempt more far-reaching or more frequent liberalizations. Neither episode studied was brought to a halt because of a failure of the liberalization policies *per se*, and liberalization operated successfully at some point during each episode. This appendix offers the following fairly simple explanation of the timing of liberalization efforts: at any point in time, the ratio of projected foreign exchange earnings to a "safety" threshold determined the government's willingness to liberalize. When this ratio triggered liberalizations, the scope was limited by the estimated availability of foreign exchange.

Most developing countries maintain negative trade balances, which are offset by net inflows of capital. Since 1959 Pakistan has fitted this pattern (except for 1973, the year of the major devaluation of the rupee). Pakistan has not attracted much private foreign direct investment. Over the six-year period 1972–8, annual foreign private capital investment averaged US$97 million or less than 2.5 percent of total capital inflows (Government of Pakistan, *Pakistan Economic Survey*, 1983–4, p. 80). Bhutto's nationalization of much of large-scale manufacturing and the heavy influence of the state in the allocation of resources in the economy soured the climate for foreign capital during 1971–7. The Bhutto nationalization program resulted in capital flight. The value of foreign investment in Pakistan in 1973 has been estimated to be in the rate of US$200–300 million (Kocyhanek, 1983, p. 274). Repatriable foreign direct investment from 1977 to 1983 in Pakistan totaled US$581 million. Thus a stock of foreign direct investment in the neighborhood of US$1 billion seems reasonable for 1983. This amount pales to insignificance compared with the US$22.4 billion of foreign loans and grants that Pakistan received from 1951 to 1983 (Government of Pakistan, *Pakistan Economic Survey*, 1983–4, p. 81).

Estimates of Pakistan's foreign exchange availability are presented in table A1.1. During the first liberalization episode roughly 30 percent of Pakistan's foreign exchange rate was obtained through grants, 50 percent

Table A1.1 Estimated foreign exchange availability in Pakistan by source, 1960–1983 (million US dollars)

	1	2	3	4	5	6	7	8	9	10
Year	Foreign aid	Loans	Net factor income from abroad	Exports	Subtotal of foreign exchange	Foreign exchange reserves	Total foreign exchange	Real foreign exchange	Exports as percentage of total foreign exchange	Foreign exchange reserves as percentage of imports
1960	116	99	−5	160	370	258	628	628	43.2	67.9
1961	221	361	−6	113	689	272	961	844	16.4	59.5
1962	221	361	−6	114	690	238	928	854	16.5	50.7
1963	221	361	−10	210	782	249	1,031	876	28.9	42.3
1964	221	361	−7	226	801	280	1,081	1,058	28.2	44.5
1965	221	361	−12	239	809	219	1,028	985	29.5	28.4
1966	141	447	−11	253	830	208	1,038	943	30.5	34.4
1967	141	447	−10	272	850	197	1,047	1,092	37.5	26.0
1968	141	447	−5	346	929	160	1,089	1,129	37.2	22.8
1969	141	447	−6	357	939	239	1,178	1,260	38.0	37.3
1970	141	447	1	338	927	311	1,238	1,177	36.5	45.1
1971	95	778	−17	420	1,276	184	1,460	1,300	32.9	24.3
1972	62	82	17	581	742	140	882	603	78.3	23.3
1973	49	494	44	804	1,391	296	1,687	630	57.8	37.4
1974	69	1,199	62	1,026	2,356	489	2,845	735	43.5	35.9
1975	100	1,015	116	1,039	2,270	472	2,742	475	45.8	22.3
1976	102	856	302	1,137	2,397	418	2,815	515	47.4	20.2
1977	187	927	554	1,141	2,809	539	3,348	609	40.6	23.2
1978	222	1,187	1,226	1,311	3,516	535	4,051	687	37.3	19.0
1979	222	1,187	1,468	1,710	4,587	832	5,419	880	37.3	22.6
1980	310	1,403	1,847	2,668	6,228	1,210	7,438	n.a.	42.8	n.a.
1981	233	755	2,292	2,958	6,238	1,816	8,054	n.a.	47.4	n.a.
1982	486	1,191	2,403	2,490	6,570	1,491	8,062	n.a.	37.9	n.a.
1983	464	1,226	3,095	2,701	7,486	1,541	9,027	n.a.	36.1	n.a.

n.a. not available.

The values for exports in column 4 are those given in table 2.9, converted at the OER. Column 5 is the sum of columns 1–4. Column 7 is the sum of columns 5 and 6. Column 8 is column 5 divided by the consumer price index. Column 9 is column 4 divided by column 7. Column 10 is column 6 divided by the values for imports, which are those given in table 2.1, converted at the OER.

Source: columns 1, 2, World Bank (unpublished data); column 3, Government of Pakistan, *Pakistan Economic Survey,* 1983–4; column 4, Government of Pakistan, *Pakistan Economic Survey,* 1983–4, p. 204.

6. Government of Pakistan, *Pakistan Economic Survey,* 1983–4, p. 204.

through foreign loans, and 20 percent through exports. Of the US$1,105 million of foreign aid to Pakistan during the second plan (1960–5), 46 percent was provided by the United States. Of the US$1,805 million in loans and credits granted, one half by the United States and 20 percent by the World Bank and the International Development Association. Thus Pakistan's first liberalization episode occurred in the context of a relatively large commitment of external resources to Pakistan. In 1961 and 1962 export earnings represented only 17 percent of total foreign exchange availability. Technically, Pakistan could have imported six times the value of its exports and still have maintained an overall balance of international accounts. In the third plan period (1965–70), foreign aid fell by 36 percent to US$704 million, with the United States supplying about 28 percent of the aid.

The Bhutto trade liberalization episode differed from the Ayub episode in its greater reliance on Pakistan's own resources. Foreign aid was only 3–8 percent of exchange earnings during the early 1970s and has remained in the 4–6 percent range thereafter. In 1972 and 1973 exports represented 78 percent and 58 percent, respectively, of Pakistans's foreign exchange earnings. Thereafter, exports accounted for 42 percent of Pakistan's foreign exchange. Foreign loans in 1974 of US$1.2 billion were more than twice the total average for the previous year. This was followed in 1975 by loans totaling US$1 billion. The fraction of foreign exchange earnings arising from borrowings declined after 1973 as temporarily emigrating Pakistani workers repatriated increasing amounts of earnings from the Middle East. By the late 1970s, a third or more of Pakistan's foreign exchange earnings arose from repatriations.

The liberalization of 1972–8 also differs from the 1960–5 liberalization in the government's willingness to accept a narrower safety margin in international transactions. In 1972, foreign exchange reserves equaled 23 percent of the annual value of imports, a foreign exchange reserve equivalent to 2.8 months of imports or half that of the previous episode. While the foreign exchange constraint loosened somewhat in 1972–4 with increased loans and relatively good export performance, Pakistan operated in the latter half of the 1970s with half the foreign exchange reserves of the early 1960s.

By the end of 1983, Pakistan owed US$13.7 billion of loans repayable in foreign exchange. Table A1.2 indicates Pakistan's debt servicing during the period 1975–84. Debt servicing is about 25 percent of export earnings.

Trade Liberalization and Foreign Exchange Constraint

Evidence that Pakistan's propensity to liberalize at any given point is related to its available foreign exchange appears in table A1.3, which

Table A1.2 Debt servicing of Pakistan, 1975–1984 (million US dollars)

Year	Principal	Interest	Total	Percentage of foreign exchange earnings	Percentage of exports
1975	144	104	248	16.3	25.4
1978	165	167	332	11.4	25.9
1981	360	242	602	10.4	21.5
1982	288	203	491	8.8	21.2
1983	390	244	634	9.6	24.1
1984	496	289	785	11.6	28.7

Source: Government of Pakistan, Pakistan Economic Survey, 1983–4, p. 84

Table A1.3 Nominal balance of trade and foreign exchange reserves, 1960–1983

Year	Balance of trade (RS million)	Foreign exchange reserves (Rs million)	Foreign exchange reserves (Rs million)
1960	−1,043	1,227	257.8
1961	−1,633	1,294	271.8
1962	−1,693	1,133	238.0
1963	−1,802	1,184	248.7
1964	−1,907	1,328	280.0
1965	−2,532	1,043	219.1
1966	−1,676	990	208.0
1967	−2,329	939	197.3
1968	−1,682	759	159.5
1969	−1,347	1,138	239.1
1970	−1,676	1,482	311.3
1971	−1,604	877	184.2
1972	−124	814	140.3
1973	−153	3,145	295.9
1974	−3,318	4,840	488.9
1975	−10,639	4,669	471.6
1976	−9,212	4,133	417.5
1977	−11,718	5,336	539.0
1978	−14,835	5,294	534.7
1979	−19,463	8,241	832.4
1980	−23,519	11,978	1,209.9
1981	−24,264	17,974	1,815.6
1982	−33,212	15,737	1,491.7
1983	−33,709	19,648	1,541.0

Source: Government of Pakistan, Pakistan Economic Survey, 1983–4, pp. 174, 204

presents data on Pakistan's balance of trade and foreign exchange reserves over the period 1960–83. A regression of the balance of trade on foreign exchange reserves yielded a regression coefficient that, converted to an elasticity about the mean, was equal to − 0.99. The simple correlation between the variables was − 0.95. Thus 91 percent of the variance in Pakistan's balance of trade is associated with the variance in foreign exchange reserves.

The unitary response of the balance of trade with respect to foreign exchange reserves suggests that the government followed a fairly clear policy guideline on trade: the balance of trade was kept proportional to the level of foreign exchange reserves. A 1 percent increase in the balance-of-trade deficit was associated with a 1 percent increase in foreign exchange reserves. Thus, for more than two decades any increase in foreign exchange availability in a given year was allocated in fixed percentages between trade liberalization (reflected in a widening trade deficit) and additions to reserves.

The unitary elasticity suggests that export policy via the REER and import policy via the import quota restraint index were set conditional on foreign exchange reserves. If this is so, then given the REER and the foreign exchange at hand, the value of the import quota restraint index causes the overall trade balance to equal zero, which should correspond to the actual import quota restraint index. Further, given the actual import quota restraint index and the foreign exchange at hand, the value of the REER that causes the overall balance to equal zero, which should correspond to the actual REER. The predicted and theoretical values of the REER and the import quota restraint index are given in table A1.4. The theoretical value of the import quota restraint index is calculated in the following manner. Using the real export and real import regression equations in tables 3.12 and 3.17, the real foreign exchange acquired from nontrade sources (dominated by foreign aid and repatriated earnings) was added to the constant term in the export equation, and the import equation was then solved for the value of the import quota restraint index that yielded equilibrium in the overall balance. These theoretical values of the quota restraint index appear in table A1.4. Comparison of the actual index reveals a close correspondence. A similar procedure, *mutatis mutandis*, was employed to obtain the predicted values of the REER that yielded equilibrium in the overall balance. Comparison of actual and predicted values of the REER also reveals a close correspondence.

The exact degree of correspondence between the actual values of the import quota restraint index and the REER and their equilibrium values is obtained by regression analysis, the results of which are as follows:

$$\log(QR^*) = 0.027 + 1.2 \log(QR) \qquad R = 0.1154 \quad (A1.1)$$
$$\qquad\qquad (1.07) \quad (4.80)$$

Table A1.4 Actual values of REER2 and the quota restraint index and values of REER2 and the quota restraint index that result in zero overall balance

Year	Actual REER2	Actual QR	QR assumption 1	REER2 assumption 2
1960	4.23	3.5	4.7	6.1
1961	7.14	3.7 +	3.1	5.6
1962	5.87	3.9	4.2	6.5
1963	5.41	4.1 +	3.1	3.8
1964	5.36	3.4	3.6	5.8
1965	6.37	2.7 +	2.0	4.4
1966	6.27	2.9 +	2.8	6.1
1967	5.52	2.3	2.5	6.3
1968	6.19	3.2 +	2.6	4.8
1969	6.25	3.1 +	3.0	5.9
1970	5.99	4.0 +	3.3	4.7
1971	7.02	3.6 +	2.7	4.8
1972	7.49	3.3	3.4	7.7
1973	14.19	2.0	2.6	19.6
1974	14.01	2.0 +	1.9	13.0
1975	13.86	2.0 +	1.5	9.2
1976	12.70	2.3 +	1.7	8.7
1977	15.19	2.2 +	1.5	9.6
1978	17.56	2.3 +	1.5	9.8
1979	17.56	2.7 +	1.3	6.6

Assumption 1, given the actual REER2 and the foreign exchange the value of the quota restraint index (QR) which results in zero overall balance; assumption 2, given the QR and the foreign exchange at hand, the value of REER2 which results in zero overall balance.

$$\log(REER2^*) = 0.608 + 0.623 \log(REER2) \quad R = 0.51 \quad (A1.2)$$
$$(2.04) \quad (4.53)$$

The elasticity of the equilibrium quota restraint index with respect to the actual index is slightly greater than unity and statistically significant at the 1 percent level. An increase in the quota restraint index is import restricting and, since the regression coefficient indicates that the actual index is less than the equilibrium value of the index, an interpretation of this result is that Pakistan pursued a marginally more liberal import policy than was required to maintain equilibrium in the trade account.

Trade liberalization on imports was also linked to export policy in a fairly predictable way. The equation

$$\log(QR) = 1.91 - 0.403 \log(REER2) \quad R = 0.55 \quad (A1.3)$$
$$(10.68) \quad (4.88)$$

reveals a significant negative relationship between the quota restraint index and the REER. The implied elasticity suggests that a 10 percent depreciation of the REER was accompanied by a 4 percent reduction in the quota restraint index. In other words, for the government to feel comfortable in lowering the quota restraint index from 3 to 2, it would seek an 80 percent depreciation of the REER.

Foreign Exchange Requirements for a Sustained Trade Liberalization

We have presented evidence that Pakistan's import liberalization policy is constrained by its available foreign exchange reserves. An interesting speculation is by what amount Pakistan's foreign exchange reserves would have had to increase in order for it to sustain import liberalization of a certain level throughout the period of analysis. To answer this question we use the regression results for real exports and real imports calculated in table A1.4 and hypothesize various values of the import quota restraint index, the export REERs, and the required foreign exchange reserves necessary to sustain those hypothetical values. Two critical assumptions underlie this analysis. First, it is assumed that the parameters of the export and import equations are invariant to the fairly dramatic shifts in trade policy hypothesized here. Second, the effects of such shifts in trade policy for economic growth efficiency and income distribution are necessarily completely ignored, since it is beyond the scope of this study to specify and estimate a complete macroeconomic model of Pakistan. Nevertheless, it should be recognized that dramatic shifts in trade policy are likely to induce changes in other macroeconomic variables and that these changes will feed back into the trade sector.

It is reasonable to assume that, if trade liberalization improves industrial efficiency, the foreign exchange outlays associated with liberalization will be lessened. Since we have no evidence on the response to liberalization in efficiency terms, we cannot make allowances for this relationship in our calculations. Thus, if liberalization is regarded as having favorable effects on income distribution, efficiency, and growth, then our approach will overestimate the foreign exchange requirements for liberalization. Table A1.5 presents five scenarios of trade liberalization and the additional foreign exchange requirements required to achieve these scenarios.

In case 1, Pakistan adopts a relatively liberal quota restraint index equal to 2.0 and imposes no additional subsidies on exports. The foreign exchange requirement, converted to real values and discounted to present value at a real interest rate of 3 percent, amounts to US$8.2 billion. In case 2, Pakistan adopts a liberal regime of quota restraints, an index of 1.0, and imposes no additional subsidies on exports. The present value of the foreign exchange requirements is US$18.4 billion. In case 3, Pakistan opts for an import quota restraint index of 2.0 and applies export subsidies during the period 1960–72 so as to maintain a REER of approximately

Table A1.5 Additional foreign exchange requirements necessary to sustain trade liberalization compared with actual flows (million constant 1960 US dollars)

Plan	Year	Case 1	Case 2	Case 3	Case 4	Case 5	Actual real value of foreign aid (annual averages)
First	1959	503.9	1,017.8	359.9	873.8	223.7	215
Second	1960	492.7	1,051.1	387.1	945.5	188.2	534
	1961	530.7	1,109.2	396.2	974.7	215.3	534
	1962	571.8	1,188.7	415.8	1,032.7	235.4	534
	1963	635.4	1,323.5	456.9	1,145.0	260.3	534
	1964	688.0	1,469.3	507.4	1,288.7	262.1	534
Third	1965	752.6	1,610.4	547.1	1,404.9	284.9	539
	1966	868.8	1,832.6	609.8	1,573.6	343.3	539
	1967	910.8	1,956.7	649.9	1,695.8	340.6	539
	1968	959.2	2,071.4	679.1	1,791.3	352.9	539
	1969	1,088.5	2,350.1	749.3	2,010.8	400.7	539
None	1970	1,094.0	2,421.0	788.0	2,115.0	370.5	280
	1971	946.9	2,122.3	694.6	1,870.0	306.1	280
	1972	457.0	1,247.9	457.0	1,247.9	—	280
	1973	636.1	1,753.2	636.1	1,753.2	—	280
	1974	822.2	2,273.3	822.2	2,273.3	—	280
	1975	1,010.2	2,706.8	1,011.2	2,706.8	—	280
	1976	987.8	2,906.1	987.8	2,906.1	—	280
	1977	962.7	3,280.9	962.7	3,280.9	—	280
Fifth	1978	1,034.0	3,600.6	1,034.0	3,600.6	—	265
Net present value of all flows at 3% (1960)		8,200	18,400	6,200	16,400	2,600	6,200

—, not applicable.

Case 1: given an import quota restraint index of 2.0 and the actual REER, the required foreign exchange rate for zero balance of trade.

Case 2: Given an import quota restraint of 1.0 and the actual REER, the required foreign exchange for zero balance of trade.

Case 3: Given an import quota restraint index of 2.0, a REER from 1959–60 to 1971–2 equal to REER2 in 1972–3, the required foreign exchange for zero balance of trade.

Case 4: Given an import quota restraint index of 1.0, and a REER from 1959–69 to 1971–2 equal to the REER2 in 1972–3, the required exchange rate for 1959–69 zero balance of trade.

Case 5: Actual aid flows for table A1.1; net present value only approximate owing to use of average data for annual aid flows.

Rs 14 per US dollar, the REER2 in 1973. The present discounted value of the loan or transfer is US$6.2 billion. In case 4, Pakistan selects a quota restraint index of 1.0 and imposes export subsidies during the period 1960–72 as before. The present value of the foreign exchange requirement is US$16.5 billion. In case 5, a two-tier trade policy is adopted. Over the period 1960–72, a more restrictive import regime is imposed than in fact existed, and exports are subsidized by external aid sufficient to produce equilibrium. Foreign exchange reserves, principally foreign aid and remittances, are allowed to accumulate to finance import liberalization in 1973 and thereafter. The value of the import quota restraint index is 4.0 from 1959 to 1971 and 1.0 thereafter. The present value of the foreign exchange requirements over the period 1960–72 is US$2.6 billion. The path of the real dollar foreign exchange reserves over the whole period of analysis is presented in table A1.6. Under this scenario of trade policy and export subsidies, real dollar reserves accumulated to US$4.1 billion in 1972. Reduced quota restrictions in 1973 and removal of the export subsidy reduced the foreign exchange reserves, but the large increase in repatriated earnings allows maintenance of a respectable level of foreign exchange reserves.

Table A1.6 Accumulated real dollar foreign exchange reserves under case 5, 1959–1979

Year	Foreign exchange reserves, case 5 (million real US$)
1960	181.6
1961	455.2
1962	646.8
1963	972.8
1964	1,251.4
1965	1,857.6
1966	2,274.8
1967	2,792.2
1968	3,298.9
1969	3,740.4
1970	4,158.7
1971	4,677.8
1972	4,124.6
1973	2,142.7
1974	2,332.7
1975	2,543.6
1976	2,643.6
1977	2,824.8
1978	3,071.8
1979	3,482.2

The last column of table A1.5 shows the approximate flow of real aid to Pakistan over the 20-year period. The present value of the real aid flows, using the same 3 percent discount rate, is US$6.2 billion. This suggests, for example, that to achieve an import quota restraint index of 1.0 while maintaining balance-of-trade equilibrium would have required a quadrupling of the net present value of aid inflows over the period from the value actually observed – from US$6.2 billion to US$24.6 billion ($18.4 + $6.2).

These scenarios suggest that a unit drop in the index of import quota restraint from 2.0 to 1.0 requires an additional US$10 billion in capital inflows (compare the net present values of foreign exchange between cases 1 and 2 and also between cases 3 and 4). They also suggest that the stream of additional foreign exchange earnings to Pakistan from a devaluation in 1959 that would have achieved the 1972 REER level would have generated a net present value of US$2 billion. Remembering that the real devaluation achieved in 1972 was approximately 25 percent, it is probable that had Pakistan liberalized imports in 1959 to the level of a quota restraint index of 1.0, maintenance of balance-of-trade equilibrium would have required a very substantial real devaluation, which would have to have been maintained throughout the 1960s.

References

ARTEP (Asian Research Team on Employment Promotion) (1983) *Pakistan's Labor Force*. Mimeo.

Burki, Shahid (1981) *Pakistan under Bhutto, 1971–77*, London: Macmillan.

Burki, Shahid and Robert Laporte Jr (1984) *Pakistan's Development Priorities*, Karachi: Oxford University Press.

Government of Pakistan (1975) *Twenty-five Years of Pakistan in Statistics*. Islamabad: Printing Corporation of Pakistan Press.

Government of Pakistan (1983) *Review of the Sixth Five Year Plan*. Islamabad: Printing Corporation of Pakistan Press.

Government of Pakistan *Import Policy Statement*, annual. Islamabad and Karachi: Printing Corporation of Pakistan Press.

Government of Pakistan *Pakistan Economic Survey*, various issues. Islamabad and Karachi: Printing Corporation of Pakistan Press.

Guisinger, Stephen (1978) *Wages, Capital Rental Values and Relative Factor Prices in Pakistan*. Washington, DC: World Bank, Staff Working Paper no. 287, June 1979.

Guisinger, Stephen (1981) "Stabilization policies in Pakistan: the 1970–77 experience." In William Cline and Sidney Weintraub, eds, *Economic Stabilization in Developing Countries*, chapter 11. Washington DC: The Brookings Institution.

Guisinger, Stephen (1984) "The impact of temporary worker migration on Pakistan." In Shahid J. Burki and Robert Laporte Jr, eds, *Pakistan's Development Priorities: Choices for the Future*, chapter 7. Karachi: Oxford University Press.

Guisinger, Stephen, James W. Henderson, and Gerald W. Scully (1984) "Earnings, rates of return to education, and the earnings distribution in Pakistan." *Economics of Education Review*, 3 (4), 25–67.

Guisinger, Stephen and M. Hicks (1978) "Long-term trends in income distribution in Pakistan." *World Development*, 6, 1271–80.

Guisinger, Stephen and Mohammed Irfan (1975) "Inter-industry differentials in wages and earnings in Pakistan's manufacturing sector." *Pakistan Development Review*, 14(3), Autumn, 274–95.

Guisinger, Stephen and Mohammed Irfan (1980) "Pakistan's informal sector." *Journal of Development Studies*, 16 (4), July, 412–26.

Kochanek, Stanley A. (1983) *Interest Groups and Development*, Oxford: Oxford University Press.

The Pakistan and Gulf Economist (1972), May 27.

Pakistan Institute of Development Economics (1983) *The PIDE Macroeconometric Model of Pakistan's Economy*. Islamabad: The Pakistan Institute of Development Economics.

World Bank (1976) *Bangladesh: Development in a Rural Economy*. Washington DC: World Bank, Report no. 455a–BD.

World Bank (1982) *Pakistan: Economic Development and Prospects*. Washington, DC: World Bank, Report no. 3802–PAK, April 14.

Part III

Sri Lanka

*Andrew G. Cuthbertson and
Premachandra Athukorala*

Contents

List of Figures and Tables

Figures

Tables

288 Sri Lanka/Cuthbertson and Athukorala

1

Introduction

In its nearly 40 years of modern independent rule Sri Lanka has had two policy programs of trade liberalization. What follows is the story of what made those programs happen, how well they worked, and what if anything brought them to a close – in short, this case study is about Sri Lanka's experience with the timing and sequencing of a trade liberalization policy.

The story begins with a political, geographic, and economic scene-setting description. The features of Sri Lanka's land, people, and heritage that ought to be considered in drawing lessons about the timing and sequencing of a trade liberalization are as follows: 200 years of British rule, a well-educated predominantly rural population, relatively ambitious social welfare programs, a significant minority group with simmering political tensions, a well-established basically two-party system, an important strategic location, and, from time to time, large flows of aid.

Chapter 2 goes on to tell how evenly balanced center-left and center-right governments have managed an economy driven by commodity exports – tea, rubber, and coconut. Economic policy is partly explained in terms of the way successive governments responded to fluctuations in these commodity prices – sometimes with attempts to diversify the productive structure of the economy and sometimes with selective import controls so that politically vulnerable imports might continue. The steady increase of government ownership of manufacturing industry, and in the 1970s of the plantation sector, is an important part of Sri Lanka's economic policy story. The experience illustrates the difficulty of undoing policy experiments as successive center-right governments have repeatedly failed to carry out promised policies for privatization.

In chapter 3 the ebbs and flows of policy are documented in terms of the almost regular changes of government that have been a feature of Sri Lanka's political economy. Out of this discussion two liberalization episodes are identified: one a tentative and short-lived attempt in 1968, and the other a bold dismantling of import-licensing barriers in 1977. An index of liberalization is derived that traces these openings and closings of trade policy. Focusing on the two identified episodes, in the remainder of the case study we suggest inferences – disentangling what actually led to a particular combination of opening-up measures and the outcomes that may persuasively be attributed to them.

Chapters 4 and 5 detail the circumstances, events, and outcomes of each episode to set up a basis for testing the hypotheses. The testing, in turn, is the task of chapter 6, which brings together the two episodes, their origins, and their outcome to draw conclusions on the lessons and inferences about the timing and sequencing of trade liberalization that can be derived from the Sri Lankan experience.

A first look at the Sri Lankan experience suggests some preliminary plausible propositions about the timing and sequencing of a trade liberalization:

1 one or a few stages are preferable to a gradual approach;
2 the quicker the better;
3 the early days of a government provide the best change of effective sustainable liberalization;
4 an unhappy experience with a closed regime fosters political receptiveness to liberalization, and a lucky coincidence of external prices helps to sustain it;
5 replacing quantitative restrictions with tariffs is desirable, but subsequent reductions in those tariffs are hard won;
6 an export promotion stage makes at best only a small contribution to neutrality;
7 uniform treatment of sectors is desirable;
8 accompanying macroeconomic policies are crucial for successful liberalization;
9 economy-wide growth can be identified as a liberalization outcome;
10 unemployment is not an inevitable outcome of a liberalization episode.

These are working hypotheses. Much of the case study is concerned with testing in detail how safe it is to attribute outcomes to liberalization actions and not to something else. In Sri Lanka the largest set of forces, apart from liberalization, combines the aid flows, which began in 1978, with the related public sector policies and macromanagement.

The detailed analysis suggests that there are large gains to be made from initiating significant reforms early in the life of the government. These gains arise because at that time the vested interests pressing for protection are likely to be in disarray. The hindsight interpretation of Sri Lanka's experience suggests that these interests regenerate quite quickly, hence the desirability of early decisive action. Benefits of switching from quotas to tariffs possibly arise in the form of easier entry to industry and thus greater domestic competition. However, if the switch is to high tariffs, these seem as hard to shift as the quotas were before them.

Particularly in the 1977 episode, subsequent steps for reducing tariffs turned on detailed fine tuning of estimates of effective protection with the idea of forcing these estimates within some narrower band. A positive outcome of this process could have been a holding-off of demands for protection increases. However, a negative effect was that the program of reform became bogged down in detail.

For widespread reform to happen, the main ingredient has to be bold across-the-board changes. While this may be difficult politically, the important lesson is that, with widespread change, employment and invest-ment opportunities are created, not lost. One of the clearest lessons of the study concerns the fears of unemployment and disruption which so frequently stifle liberalization attempts. Sri Lanka's policymakers, when contemplating what manner of liberalization to introduce in 1977, had a choice between one big shot and a first-stage less sweeping change with follow-up. Their eventual choice of the latter reflected perceptions that the unemployment effects of the former would be large. However, the experience following the changes that were introduced suggests that employment opportunities actually grew. Thus it is presumed that they would have grown even more had the liberalization been more sweeping. As it was, even detailed investigation of the individual sectors likely to have been most affected shows no identifiable unemployment effects. A number of qualifications to this conclusion – mainly relative to data – are examined, and it appears to be a robust finding!

Another finding after detailed review is that to embark on a compre-hensive and ambitious program of export promotion is to set an uncertain course towards a neutral incentive regime. The lesson is that problems are created with each intervention and that the revenue-raising impacts on the macroeconomy are also significant. In Sri Lanka's case, the funding of export development by way of import taxes almost certainly meant that, on balance, the scheme worsened disparities.

The 1977 episode occurred in tandem with a program of public invest-ment on a grand scale. At times through the late 1970s and early 1980s this program nearly ran out of control. Fiscal deficits and accompanying trade deficits fueled protectionist pressures. From time to time revenue collec-tion imperatives saw the application of import duties which had quite selective protective effects. In this climate the bidding-up of domestic resources for the government-run projects slowed down the growth of the traded sector and made further steps in a reform process less likely.

While the years following the 1977 episode have been difficult, the liberalization which began in 1977 has not been abruptly reversed. In many ways it now seems that liberalization of trade is a bipartisan policy. Sri Lanka has not retreated to a closed economy, and hence the cyclical pattern of regularly closing and opening the economy appears to have been broken.

2

Economic Background

Sri Lanka (known until 1972 as Ceylon) is a small island nation situated a few degrees north of the equator at the extreme southern tip of India. It is separated from India by the Palk Strait, which is about 22 miles across at its narrowest. Adam's Bridge, a series of small islands stretching from Marnar in the northwest of Sri Lanka to Ramesvaram in India, runs between the two countries. Sri Lanka's land area is a little more than 25,000 square miles. Its central position in the Indian Ocean has for centuries made it an attractive resting and trading place.

Because of its closeness to India, Sri Lanka shares some of the cultural and institutional features of the subcontinent. However, it has a recorded history of more than 2,500 years as a separate economic entity with a distinct civilization. From the early 1500s to 1948 there was some form of European rule. Portuguese and Dutch rule of the coastal areas (1517–1638 and 1638–1776 respectively) had no lasting effect on the country's production structure. It was not until the arrival of the British (1815) that the island was welded into an effective political entity by the conquest of the central highland kingdom of Kandy.

It was during the British period, particularly after the 1840s with the introduction of coffee as a plantation crop, that the transformation of a feudal agrarian economy into an export-oriented plantation economy began. By the 1860s coconut had emerged as another plantation crop. The coffee plantations were almost totally destroyed by a leaf disease during the 1880s, and the plantation industry successfully shifted to tea and rubber. By the dawn of the twentieth century, the pattern of overwhelming dominance of the three major plantation crops – tea, rubber, and coconut – in the modern sector of the economy was firmly established (Snodgrass, 1966). The colonial experience also shaped the political and social fabric of the island and provided the framework for the present political, governmental, and educational system. With this colonial background, Sri Lanka became independent on February 4, 1948, as the culmination of a process of orderly and peaceful transfer of power from the colonial government to Western-educated local political leaders.

Land and Resources

About 60 percent of the island is cultivable and about 30 percent is under cultivation. Tea, rubber, and coconut occupy about 11 percent of the land, while paddy (rice) cultivation accounts for about 8 percent, other crops 15 percent, and gardens and orchards 9 percent (Department of Census and Statistics, 1983). Being about 500 miles north of the equator, Sri Lanka is warm all the year round with little seasonal change of temperature. The island can be divided into wet and dry zones, reflecting differences in the seasonal distribution and amount of rainfall. In the dry zones, because of the nature of the soil, much of the rainfall is lost to rapid run-off. In ancient times huge reservoirs were built for irrigation. Since Independence several extensive projects to renovate these ancient irrigation schemes have been prominent in the development programs of different governments.

Large reserves of economically exploitable mineral deposits include gems, graphite, mica, mineral sands, and several types of clay. Gems, graphite, and mineral sands are mined chiefly for export, while the other minerals are used mainly in local industry. No coal, copper, iron, lead, or zinc deposits have been discovered. There are no proven oil deposits either, but there is vast potential for generating hydroelectricity which, in 1982, accounted for about 22 percent of total commercial energy usage. The coastal lagoons and the coral reef surrounding the southern half of the island abound with fish – another potentially important resource endowment of the economy.

Population, Labor Force, and Employment

Population growth

The population of Sri Lanka more than doubled between the 1946 census and the 1981 census, when it reached 14.8 million (table 2.1). This upsurge was mainly the outcome of natural increase reflecting the combination of a "primitive birth rate with a modernized death rate" (Robinson, 1959, p. 39). The crude death rate declined from 23 per thousand in 1946 to 17 per thousand in 1953, and then to 6 per thousand in 1981. In contrast, the birth rate remained very high at about 37 per thousand until the late 1960s. The much reduced death rate can be attributed to the overwhelming success in combating malaria in the mid-1940s. The birth rate has declined since the late 1960s, reflecting the impact of a family planning program (which has bipartisan support) and a continuing rise in the average age of marriage. As an outcome of this decline, the rate of overall population

Table 2.1 Population of Sri Lanka

Census year	1 Total population[a] (thousands)	2 Intercensal increase[a] (thousands)	3 Annual average growth (%)	4 Natural increase[a] (thousands)	5 Migration increase[a] (thousands)	Column 4 as % of column 2	Column 5 as % of column 2	Birth rate (per 1000)	Death rate (per 1000)
1871	2,400.4	359.4	—	119.8	239.6	33.3	66.7	—	—
1881	2,759.7	248.1	0.89	144.3	103.3	58.1	41.9	27.4	22.7
1891	3,007.8	558.2	0.85	225.4	332.8	40.4	59.6	29.4	24.3
1901	3,566.0	540.4	1.51	356.1	184.2	65.9	34.1	34.4	27.6
1911	4,106.4	392.3	0.95	319.4	72.8	81.4	18.6	38.1	28.8
1921	4,498.6	808.3	1.79	657.0	151.3	81.3	18.7	37.6	30.4
1931	5,306.9	1,350.5	2.54	1,281.0	69.6	94.8	5.2	39.8	26.5
1946	6,657.3	1,440.6	1.80	1,328.2	112.4	92.2	7.8	36.8	23.0
1953	8,099.0	2,484.2	3.60	2,513.2	-29.1	101.2	-1.2	37.7	17.1
1963	10,582.1	2,129.1	2.51	2,208.1	-79.0	103.7	-3.7	37.3	10.4
1971	12,711.1	2,137.0	1.68	3,105.0	-252.8	145.9	-11.8	32.7	8.2
1981	14,848.0	751.0	1.69	1,023.8	-272.8	136.3	-36.3	28.0	6.0
1984[b]	15,599.0	—	—	—	—	—	—	n.a.	n.a.

n.a., not available; —, not applicable.

[a] Rounded.

[b] Estimated by the Central Bank on the basis of the 1981 census.

Sources: Department of Census and Statistics, *Statistical Abstract*, various issues; Central Bank of Ceylon (CBC), *Review of the Economy – 1984*, 1984 data

growth, which had been more than 2.5 percent up to the late 1960s, declined to about 1.7 percent by 1984.

Net population increases from migration were significant until about the 1930s, a reflection of the dependence of the plantation sector on indentured laborers from south India (Dutta, 1973). Since then migration has not significantly affected population growth. From about the early 1950s, the net flow of migration has been outward, mainly because of the ban on emigration of Indians in 1957 and the repatriation of laborers since the early 1970s in a phased program between Sri Lanka and India agreed in 1964. Since about 1977 the emigration of Sri Lankans in search of temporary employment in oil-exporting Middle East countries has further augmented out-migration. Gross annual out-migration to the Middle East increased from about 7,900 in 1977 to about 70,000 in 1982 when the total stock of Sri Lankan workers in these countries was about 125,000 (Athukorala, 1986, p. 7).

The population remains overwhelmingly rural; the urban proportion increased from 15 percent in 1946 to about 20 percent by 1981. One of the striking features of population growth in Sri Lanka is the relative absence of huge cities on the scale of most other Asian nations. While internal migration has been an important facet of Sri Lanka's population dynamics, rural-to-urban migration is low compared with urban-to-rural migration and migration within the rural sector (International Labor Organization) (ILO), 1971).

The largest city by far is Colombo; its population (261,000 in 1983) and that in the immediate area have grown rapidly over the past few years. None of the other five principal cities has more than 60,000 residents. Population density overall increased from 196 people per square mile in 1971 to 230 per square mile in 1981.

Ethnic Composition

About 75 percent of the population of Sri Lanka is Sinhalese. The largest minority group, the Tamils, makes up about 18 percent of the population. The remainder are Ceylon Moor (7 percent) with less than 1 percent of the total consisting of Burghers, Eurasians, and Malays. Over the past 40 years, the Sinhalese proportion has increased slightly (table 2.2). Religious affiliations closely follow ethnic composition: most Sinhalese are Buddhist and most Tamils are Hindus. There is some regional concentration of ethnic population. The Sinhalese predominate everywhere except in the northern and eastern provinces, where the Tamils are the largest ethnic group, but, like the population as a whole, they are most densely concentrated along the western coastal belt.

The relationship between the ethnic communities has always been a significant factor in the social, political, and economic life of Sri Lanka

Table 2.2 Ethnic composition of the population

	Percentage of total population				
Ethnicity	1946	1953	1963	1971	1981
Sinhalese	69.4	69.4	71.6	72.0	74.0
Low Country Sinhalese	43.6	42.8	42.8	42.8	44.2
Kandyan Sinhalese	25.8	26.5	28.8	29.2	29.8
Tamils	22.7	23.0	21.6	20.5	18.2
Ceylon Tamils	11.0	11.0	11.0	11.2	12.6
Indian Tamils	11.7	12.0	10.6	9.3	5.6
Muslims	7.1	6.3	6.4	6.7	7.1
Others[a]	5.8	1.3	0.4	0.8	0.7

[a] Burghers and Eurasians, Malays, Europeans, and Veddhas.
Source: Department of Census and Statistics, Statistical Abstract, various issues

(Mathews, 1981; Manor, 1984). In particular, since Independence relations between the Sinhalese and the Sri Lankan Tamils have been characterized by rivalry, with outbursts of anti-Tamil violence in 1958, 1977, and 1983. Since the late 1970s, the main Tamil party, the Tamil United Liberalization Front (TULF), has sought an autonomous Tamil state in the northern and eastern portions of the island where the Tamils form the largest ethnic group. The long-standing rivalry between these two communities escalated into sustained and widespread violence starting in July 1983. These conflicts have dominated the policy agenda since, and have considerably damaged economic performance and quality of life.

Education

For many years the Sri Lankan population has been regarded as very well educated. Literacy rates exceed 85 percent and primary school enrollment is over 80 percent. The pupil-to-teacher ratio was 28 in 1970 and 24 in 1980. There are nine universities, and the number of students attending them doubled from 10,000 in 1960 to 20,000 in 1980. Since 1931 education has been free at all levels. Until the early 1960s, secondary and university education was in English. In the 1960s, a Swabhasha (native language) policy came into effect. While literacy remained relatively high, those educated in the 1960s typically spoke mainly Sinhala or Tamil. The communication gap thus created is often blamed for aggravating communal tensions.

Labor Force and Employment

At the census of 1981 Sri Lanka had an estimated labor force of 5.0 million. The rate of growth of the labor force between the censuses of 1971 and

1981 is estimated at between 2.5 and 3 percent per year, and the labor force is forecast to reach 6.2–6.8 million by 1990. The 1981 census recorded that the labor force was 75 percent male and 25 percent female.

Chronic unemployment has prevailed since the early 1960s. Various surveys conducted in the late 1960s reported unemployment rates of between 10 and 14 percent (Gunasekara, 1974). The Central Bank's *Consumer Finances Survey* of 1973 reported an unemployment rate as high as 24 percent (table 2.3). During the post-1977 period of policy reform, unemployment declined significantly, though it still remains well above 10 percent. Young people, often those with higher levels of education, figure disproportionately among the unemployed.

The distribution of labor deployment by major production sectors together with data relating to the relative importance of each sector is presented in table 2.4. The employment share of the primary sector (agriculture, forestry, fishing, and hunting) has marginally declined over time in line with the decline in the output share of that sector. However, its employment share remains above 45 percent – much higher than its 28 percent output share. It is particularly interesting that within the primary sector the employment share of the domestic agricultural sector has continuously expanded while that of the plantation sector has significantly declined. Employment shares of the industrial and services sectors remain around 10 percent and 30 percent respectively.

From about the 1930s the trade union movement was very powerful in industry, commerce, and plantation agriculture, but its influence has declined since the election in 1977 of the center-right party led by Jayawardene. This decline is commonly ascribed to what was almost a rout

Table 2.3 Unemployment as a percentage of workforce

Population	1973	1978–9	1981–2
By sector			
Urban	32.1	20.7	14.2
Rural	24.5	14.6	12.0
Estate	12.0	5.6	5.0
All island	24.0	14.7	11.7
By age group			
14–18 years	65.8	30.7	30.8
19–25 years	47.5	31.1	28.8
26–35 years	15.2	13.1	8.8
36–45 years	3.9	2.7	1.7
46–55 years	1.2	0.8	0.5
Over 55 years	0.8	0.2	0.4
All ages	24.0	14.7	11.7

Source: CBC, *Consumer Finance and Socio-economic Survey*, 1973, 1978–9, 1981–2

Table 2.4 Sectoral distribution of gross domestic product and labor deployment (percent)

Sector	Distribution of GDP				Distribution of employment				Allocation of increase in employment		
	1953	1963	1971	1981	1953	1963	1971	1981	1953–63	1963–71	1971–81
Agriculture, forestry, fishing, and hunting	43.6	47.1	38.5	28.4	52.9	52.6	50.4	45.9	48.5	32.2	31.5
Export agriculture	29.5	26.3	19.1	9.5	28.6	24.6	20.1	18.5	− 33.8	− 14.2	− 8.2
Domestic agriculture	13.3	15.7	16.8	17.0	22.9	26.6	28.7	27.2	81.2	44.9	36.5
Industry	10.2	10.6	16.1	16.3	12.1	12.4	13.4	16.6	15.7	21.2	38.8
Construction	4.7	3.9	5.6	5.5	1.9	2.7	3.1	4.2	14.1	6.4	11.5
Manufacturing	5.6	6.1	9.8	9.7	9.7	9.2	9.6	12.0	1.5	12.9	21.0
Services	43.7	42.2	45.5	55.3	28.4	29.5	28.0	31.3	47.0	16.9	32.0
Activities not adequately described	—	—			6.6	5.5	8.2	6.2	− 11.0	28.8	− 1.6

—, not applicable.
Totals may not add up to 100 because there is a residual for "activities not adequately described."
Sources: GDP data, CBC, *Annual Report*, various issues; employment data, Department of Census and Statistics, *Population Sri Lanka*, 1974, and *Statistical Pocket Book*, 1983 (based on census reports of 1953, 1963, 1971, and 1981)

of the left-wing parties in the 1977 election and the generally tough stand of the new government against unions. In turn the unions, faced with a government with such a large majority, responded with moderation (Nelson, 1984). Table 2.5 presents data on the number of registered unions, union membership, strikes, workers involved, and mandays lost. The data show a general pattern of a higher number of strikes and manday losses before 1978 when the left-wing parties were not in power.

The data available on wage differences are patchy. Information compiled by the Department of Labour shows that wages in agriculture in rupees tend to be somewhat less than in other sectors where wages (adjusted for exchange rate) are typically about US$1.00 per day (table 2.6).

Table 2.5 Trade unions and strikes

	Unions		Strikes[a]		
Year	Number[b]	Membership (thousands)	Number	No. of workers involved (thousands)	No. of mandays lost (thousands)
1960	900	n.a.	160	47.4	175.1
1961	930	n.a.	129	67.2	488.2
1962	1,031	n.a.	189	68.3	995.7
1963	1,034	n.a.	232	92.3	839.6
1964	1,213	n.a.	304	89.4	885.7
1965	1,209	n.a.	230	81.0	572.2
1966	1,256	n.a.	164	142.9	1,151.6
1967	1,283	n.a.	230	89.9	699.3
1968	n.a.	n.a.	197	77.2	998.4
1969	n.a.	n.a.	189	65.2	464.2
1970	n.a.	n.a.	340	149.0	1,311.6
1971	n.a.	n.a.	157	90.8	513.3
1972	n.a.	n.a.	187	55.0	298.9
1973	n.a.	n.a.	238	93.7	390.7
1974	n.a.	n.a.	91	27.1	105.1
1975	n.a.	n.a.	69	21.9	79.2
1976	1,578	1,066	157	56.0	161.1
1977	1,636	1,400	119	38.7	211.0
1978	1,450	968	134	62.7	265.1
1979	1,309	1,441	107	28.5	99.9
1980	1,213	1,338	227	78.6	335.2
1981	1,180	1,010	301	124.2	440.8
1982	1,155	1,008	217	83.0	388.7
1983	1,135	9,785	146	53.1	218.7
1984	1,125	9,782	230	87.3	507.3

n.a., not available.
[a] The number of strikes that ended during the year. Strikes involving fewer than five workers or lasting less than one day are excluded from the statistics except in cases where the aggregate number of mandays lost exceeds 50.
[b] Number of registered unions as at the end of the year.
Source: Department of Census and Statistics, Statistical Abstract, various issues

Table 2.6 Minimum average daily wages of workers in wages boards' trades

Class of worker	Unit[a]	1976	1977	1978	1979	1980	1981
Workers in agriculture	R	6.03	6.03	5.84	11.21	13.99	13.95
	I	370.51	321.43	451.02	571.94	713.56	711.91
Workers in trade other	R	5.17	8.96	10.83	12.65	15.39	17.34
than agriculture	I	282.30	306.90	370.91	433.14	526.95	593.86
Combined rate	R	6.28	6.51	8.99	11.31	14.08	14.19
	I	306.25	319.12	441.20	554.41	690.19	695.35

[a] R, wage rate in rupees; I, index number (1952 = 100).
Source: Department of Labour, Sri Lanka Labour Gazette, various issues

Like education, social security in Sri Lanka has long been relatively widely available. Until 1977 there was no unemployment insurance *per se*, but there was a wide variety of other social security measures. There are free health and education services, along with various schemes organized by the ministries of industry, agriculture, fishing, housing, and trade, such as university scholarships, crop insurance, housing projects, and so on. In 1978, the government introduced an unemployment relief payment of Rs 50 per month. In the organized – typically government – sector, there is a range of pension schemes and provident funds. A workers' compensation scheme covers unemployment due to accidents, but to date this is restricted to the lowest earning group.

Growth and Welfare

In 1948 Sri Lanka entered Independence well placed for continuing economic achievements (Jennings, 1951; Corea, 1965; Snodgrass, 1966). A level of national income higher than that of many Asian countries, a healthy balance of payments backed by large foreign exchange reserves, a sound budgetary position,[1] a prosperous export crop sector organized on commercial lines, a literate and well-fed population, a relatively well-developed economic and social infrastructure, and a competent public administration – all these initial conditions had provided the setting for the expectation that, of all post-colonial nations, Sri Lanka would prove "the best bet in Asia" (Sir Oliver Gunatileke, quoted by Jiggins, 1976).

[1] Both the domestic and external financial positions of the economy were so sound that Mr D. S. Senanayake, the first prime minister of the country, in an interview with *Newsweek* in 1948 stated that Sri Lanka "wanted neither grants nor loans from the United States or any other country" (Wijesinghe, 1976).

Achievements are generally considered to have fallen short of these expectations. Between 1950 and 1983 Sri Lanka's real gross national product (GNP) increased at an annual average rate of about 3.7 percent (table 2.7, and Cuthbertson and Athukorala, 1988, appendix table A.1). This growth has not been uniformly sustained: when the post-1977 policy reform years are excluded, the average GNP growth rate for the remaining period turns out to be 3 percent. Examination of per capita income growth (table 2.7) suggests that, since Independence, Sri Lanka has just managed to keep its head above water in the face of population growth. Table 2.8

Table 2.7 Gross national product, mid-year population, per capita gross national product, and their growth rates, 1950–1983 (annual averages, in 1970 prices)

Period	GNP (million Rs)	Mid-year population (thousands)	Per capita GNP (Rs)	Growth rate (%)		
				GNP	Mid-year population	Per capita GNP
1950–5	7,204	8,089	890	3.8	2.6	1.2
1955–60	8,362	9,165	912	2.5	2.4	0.2
1960–5	9,515	10,411	914	3.3	2.5	0.8
1965–70	11,530	11,710	985	4.5	2.4	2.1
1970–5	13,586	12,884	1,076	1.9	1.6	0.3
1975–7	15,246	13,717	1,112	3.3	1.6	1.7
1977–83	19,778	14,834	1,333	5.8	1.7	4.1
1950–83	n.a.	n.a.	n.a.	3.7	2.1	1.6

n.a., not available.
Source: Cuthbertson and Athukorala, 1988, appendix table A.1

Table 2.8 Selected Asian countries: levels and growth rates of per capita gross domestic product, 1960–1978

Country	GDP per capita (US$)				Growth rates, 1960–78[b]	
	Unadjusted[a]		Kravis-adjusted			
	1960	1978	1960	1978	Unadjusted	Kravis-adjusted
Bangladesh	59	66	355	432	– 0.4	1.1
India	73	96	428	514	1.4	1.0
Indonesia	92	177	370	636	4.1	3.1
Korea	153	488	631	2,053	6.9	6.8
Malaysia	280	588	888	1,856	3.9	4.2
Pakistan	81	134	404	629	2.8	2.5
Philippines	254	409	644	983	2.6	2.4
Sri Lanka	152	226	961	798	2.0	– 1.2
Thailand	95	219	446	1,921	4.6	5.3

[a] At 1960 prices and exchange rates.
[b] Annual averages.
Sources: Bhalla, 1984a; Kravis et al., 1983

compares Sri Lanka's growth with that of ten other Asian developing countries in terms of both "conventional" real per capita GNP (expressed in US dollars) and "Kravis-adjusted" per capita GNP (adjusted in terms of purchasing power parity).

In 1960, Sri Lanka's per capita income ranked much higher than that of neighboring south Asian countries, and compared favorably with middle income countries in southeast Asia. However, by the late 1970s it was at a level comparable with neighboring south Asian countries. When Kravis-adjusted data are used, Sri Lanka's annual average per capita GNP growth rate for the period 1960–78 is − 1.2 percent[2] (as against the 2.0 percent unadjusted growth rate) – the lowest among the Asian countries listed in table 2.8.

Though growth performance has been uneven, Sri Lanka has a good reputation for providing its people with a high standard of living compared with many other developing countries. By most criteria the quality of life in Sri Lanka has continued to be "exceptionally good in relation to her per capita income" (Isenman, 1980). Estimates of income distribution consistency show the poorest 40 percent of the population as having an income share of at least 15 percent. This share increased from 14.6 percent in 1953 to 19 percent in 1973 (table 2.9) and fell to 15.3 percent in 1981–2. Because of these "achievements," with the shift of emphasis in development thinking from growth maximization to basic need fulfillment since the late 1970s, Sri Lanka has been held up by some writers as a model (Streeten and Burki, 1978; Sen, 1981). Their story, though, comes from a single-period cross-country analysis. It is a story which turns out to be rather less persuasive in time series comparisons which take into account Sri Lanka's initial relative position and the capability shown to improve upon (or at least to maintain) that position.

Table 2.9 Relative income distribution of spending units 1963, 1973, 1978–1979, and 1981–1982

Distribution	1963	1973	1978–9	1981–2
Percentage of income received by:				
lowest 10%	1.50	2.79	2.12	2.18
lowest 20%	5.45	7.17	5.73	5.73
lowest 40%	14.66	19.29	16.06	15.32
Gini coefficient	0.45	0.35	0.44	0.45

Source: CBC, *Consumer Finance and Socio-economic Survey*, 1963, 1973, 1978–9, 1981–2

[2] Given the fact that over this period Sri Lanka's ratio of exports to GDP declined (from 44 percent in 1960 to 27 percent in 1978), Myint (1985) argues that even this figure might be an overestimate of its growth rate. Other things being equal, a decline in this ratio may lead to an upward bias in the Kravis-adjusted growth rate by increasing the ratio of nontraded to traded goods in GDP.

At Independence and over the next 20 years Sri Lanka's living standards, measured by most indicators of quality of life, remained well above those of other Asian and other developing countries. However, in recent years Sri Lanka has slipped in this ranking (table 2.10). For instance, in 1950 the infant mortality rate (number of deaths per 1,000 live births) was 77 compared with 102 for the Philippines, 84 for Thailand and 91 for Malaysia. By 1983, Sri Lanka, at 37, ranked behind Malaysia, while both Thailand and the Philippines had improved more rapidly than Sri Lanka. This slippage occurred at a time when direct redistribution expenditures were around 6 percent of GNP and were nearly half of all government expenditure. Since the early 1960s, and notably since the 1970s, in the face

Table 2.10 Measures of levels of living in selected Asian countries, 1950, 1960, and 1983

Indicator	1950	1960	1982–3
School enrollment ratio (%)			
Sri Lanka	54	n.a	103
Thailand	n.a.	n.a.	96
Malaysia	n.a.	n.a.	92
Korea	43	n.a.	100
India	19	n.a.	79
Philippines	59	n.a.	106
Adult literacy ratio (%)			
Sri Lanka	n.a.	75	85
Thailand	n.a.	68	84
Malaysia	n.a.	53	n.a.
Korea	n.a.	71	n.a.
India	n.a.	28	36
Philippines	n.a.	72	75
Life expectancy at birth (years)			
Sri Lanka	54	62	69
Thailand	n.a.	51	63
Malaysia	n.a.	57	67
Korea	n.a.	54	67
India	n.a.	43	55
Philippines	n.a.	51	64
Infant mortality (per 1,000 live births)			
Sri Lanka	77	63	37
Thailand	84	n.a.	50
Malaysia	91	n.a.	29
Korea	n.a.	62	29
India	n.a.	n.a.	93
Philippines	102	98	49

n.a., not available.
Sources: World Bank, World Bank Development Report, 1982, 1984, 1985; Bhalla, 1984a, p. 16

of slow expansion in the overall economy, providing direct welfare to the poor at these levels has become increasingly difficult to sustain. Viewed in this light, the Sri Lankan experience appears equally to illustrate the limitations of a direct approach to achieving social equity and to demonstrate its effectiveness. In the context of slower economic expansion, maintaining the income share of the poor at a relatively higher level than that of other developing countries has little meaning from the viewpoint of absolute poverty. Bhalla (1984b) has recently argued that, though there was little absolute poverty in the mid-1970s, poverty had nonetheless most likely increased since the early 1960s.

Production Structure

Sri Lanka inherited a "dualistic export economy" from the colonial past. A well-organized and productive plantation sector together with service activities had little direct impact on the traditional sector. This was a semisubsistence rural economy based on traditional peasant agriculture and centered around paddy (rice) and a few other subsidiary food crops grown solely for domestic consumption.[3] There was virtually no manufacturing apart from the processing activities associated with export products. The disruption of import trade with the outbreak of World War II led to the setting up of manufacturing units, mainly by the government, to produce a wide range of consumer and intermediate goods. However, the resumption of imports after the war put a sudden stop to this "war-generated manufacturing boom" without leaving any significant lasting effect on the structure of the classical export economy (Karunaratne, 1978).

In 1948, the earliest year for which some form of national account data are available, the contribution of the three plantation crops (including processing of their produce) total GNP was 32 percent. Local produce for domestic use accounted for 25 percent while the balance, 43 percent, was the share of the services sector. The role of the plantation sector was no doubt greater than is suggested by the above figure. For instance, a host of activities in the services sector embracing commerce and distribution, transport, and finance, not to mention government activities themselves, was intimately bound up with the tempo of plantation activities.

Table 2.11 presents data on sectoral growth and changing composition of the gross domestic product (GDP) from 1950 to 1983. The production pattern exhibited only limited structural changes during the immediate post-Independence period up to the early 1950s. The shares of domestic agriculture and industry remained virtually unchanged.

[3] The linkage between these two sectors was substantial. Since the 1930s Sri Lanka had been able to maintain a high level of welfare through the redistribution of export sector wealth.

Table 2.11 Gross domestic product of Sri Lanka, 1950–1983: sectoral composition and growth rates at constant factor cost[a] *(annual averages)*

Sector	1950–4	1955–9	1960–4	1965–9	1970–7	1978–83
Agriculture, forestry, fishing,	46.6	45.5	46.1	41.4	36.8)	24.8
and hunting	(3.9)	(2.5)	(2.5)	(2.4)	(2.1)	(4.1)
Export agriculture	29.8	27.7	26.7	22.7	17.0	10.2
(including export	(2.8)	(1.4)	(1.5)	(0.5)	(− 1.7)	(0.5)
processing)						
Domestic agriculture	14.1	14.6	8.3	15.6	17.5	11.8
	(10.2)	(4.2)	(7.0)	(5.6)	(3.5)	(5.3)
Industry	11.2	11.0	10.3	12.9	16.5	19.0
	(3.4)	(1.7)	(7.6)	(12.0)	(1.0)	(4.2)
Construction	4.2	4.9	2.4	4.7	4.9	4.8
	(11.8)	(2.4)	(5.0)	(13.1)	(− 2.6)	(8.8)
Manufacturing (excluding	5.0	5.1	5.6	7.5	9.1	9.7
export processing)	(− 1.4)	(1.6)	(10.1)	(11.6)	(2.3)	(6.4)
Services	42.3	43.8	43.6	45.6	46.7	56.2
	(6.5)	(2.5)	(3.7)	(3.8)	(3.7)	(7.2)
Total GDP	100	100	100	100	100	100
	(4.5)	(2.5)	(4.1)	(4.8)	(2.9)	(6.0)

[a] Estimates for 1950–70 inclusive are based on data at 1959 factor cost while those for the rest of the period are based on data at 1970 factor cost. For each item, the first row indicates the average GDP share and the second row (numbers in parentheses) indicates average growth rate.
Sources: For 1950–8, Savundranayagam, 1983; for the rest of the period, CBC, *Annual Report*, supplemented with national account files of the bank

Structural changes since the early 1960s are profound and distinct. The GDP share of agriculture has continuously declined from 46 percent in 1960–4 to 37 percent in 1970–7 and to 25 percent in 1978–83. The share of export agriculture in total GDP had more than halved by the late 1970s, while the share of domestic agriculture had come to exceed that of export agriculture. Import substitution attempts in domestic food production, agriculture, and manufacturing probably contributed to the decline in the share of agricultural exports (Athukorala, 1981). The plantation sector suffered from the anti-export bias embodied in commercial policy from the late 1950s. This sector also suffered from a continuing fear of nationalization from about the same time, and from mismanagement following the nationalizations that did occur in 1973 and 1975 (Fernando, 1980; Gooneratne and Wesumperuma, 1984). Since the late 1960s the annual growth rate of the plantation sector has been negative or near zero.

The share of the industrial sector, which was steady at around 10 percent up to about the mid-1960s, expanded thereafter, reaching nearly 20 percent by the early 1980s. The share of the manufacturing subsector (excluding the processing of plantation produce) increased from about 6 percent in the early 1960s to about 9 percent in the early 1970s with little change since.[4] The share of the services sector increased steadily until the mid-1970s when, following the 1977 policy reform, it expanded very rapidly, reaching about 55 percent by the early 1980s.

Sri Lanka's manufacturing sector is new; few firms are more than 20 years old. Early on, the structure of manufacturing was overwhelmingly dominated by consumer goods. For instance, in 1965, the food, beverages, and tobacco sector (International Standard Industrial Classification (ISIC) 31), and the textiles, wearing apparel, and leather products sector (ISIC 32) accounted for over 70 percent of total manufacturing output (table 2.12). By 1982 this share had declined to about 38 percent, mainly because of increased state participation in manufacturing, oriented toward intermediate and, to a lesser extent, investment goods.

Table 2.13 compares the value added-to-output and capital-to-labor ratios of two-digit ISIC industries in 1974 and 1981. For total manufacturing, value added as a share of total output was 36 percent in 1974, falling to about 30 percent in 1981. This decline in the share of value added in output can be observed across all two-digit ISIC sectors. For all industries the capital-to-labor ratio was 26 percent in 1981, rising from less than 10 percent in 1974. This increase is particularly well marked with regard to large-scale industries. The highest capital-to-labor ratios are in the food and beverages sector and in the chemicals, petroleum, and plastics sector, where ratios were more than 40 percent in 1981. It is worth noting that in recent years the public corporations that dominate these sectors have been persistently criticized for politically sponsored overmanning.

By most measures, Sri Lanka's relatively small manufacturing sector would show a high degree of industrial concentration. The 20 or so public corporations are dominant – a legacy of licensing and other protective policies in their respective sectors (for instance, tires, paper, ceramics, steel, chemicals, plywood, fertilizer, and petroleum). In those sectors where private firms are dominant (for instance, soap, bicycles, garments, textiles, rubber goods, and coir matting), the various committees that control the establishment of new firms have typically taken into account the competitive impact of new domestic firms on the domestic market. In some sectors, for instance food and beverages (150 firms), wood products (28 firms), and fabricated metals (250 firms), there are many small (one- or two-person) firms, but even there the bulk of output is concentrated. In 1980, the Ministry of Industries had just over 1,500 firms registered in its 20-sector industry survey. Typically three or four of the largest firms covered 80 percent of output (table 2.14).

---

[4] Throughout this study, departing from the usual national accounting practice, manufacturing is defined *exclusive* of the processing of plantation crops. For a meaningful analysis of industrialization, this data adjustment is needed because the growth of the latter subsector is mostly determined by factors external to the general industrialization policy.

Table 2.12 Composition and growth of gross output of manufacturing industry by industry group, 1965–1982 (at constant 1974 prices)

ISIC sector	Percentage composition				Average annual growth[a]		
	1965	1970	1977	1982	1965–70	1970–7	1977–82
31 Food, beverages, and tobacco	37.31	26.69	26.91	23.83	24.34	7.43	3.95
32 Textile, wearing apparel, and leather products	34.41	23.08	6.80	14.99	26.72	– 2.36	29.33
33 Wood and wood products	0.37	0.71	1.77	1.50	33.50	24.09	7.33
34 Paper and paper products	3.30	3.22	3.78	3.01	12.22	12.54	3.75
35 Chemical, petroleum, rubber, and plastic	14.66	22.33	45.91	45.82	14.88	28.71	3.68
36 Nonmetallic mineral products	5.01	7.56	3.91	3.69	34.97	5.37	3.22
37 Basic metal products	–	2.03	2.28	1.37	11.25	15.55	2.57
38 Fabricated metal products, machinery, and transport equipment	6.72	12.64	8.25	5.53	35.97	3.28	0.45
39 Manufactured products not elsewhere specified	0.21	1.72	0.38	0.23	73.89	2.36	– 1.01
Total gross manufacturing output (value million Rs)	(1,876)	(3,544)	(6,048)	(8,341)	14.05	8.64	5.85

–, negligible.

Current values have been converted into constant values using wholesale price indices for commodities. These indices, which date back only to 1974, were extended backward to 1965. This was done using the Central Bank *Annual Report* for 1974, which gives both constant and current price sectoral output estimates for the years 1970–3. The indices were extended backward to 1970 on the basis of implicit deflators calculated from these data.

[a] Increase in output in each industry between the two years as a percentage of increase in total manufacturing output.

Source: CBC, *Annual Report and Review of the Economy*, various issues

Table 2.13 Manufacturing industry: capital-to-labor and value added-to-output ratios, 1974 and 1981

	Capital-to-labor ratio		Value added-to-gross output ratio	
Major group	1974	1981	1974	1981
1 Manufacture of food, beverages	9.23	32.35	53.32	42.10
2 Textile, wearing apparel, and leather industries	9.32	20.45	45.00	32.62
3 Manufacture of wood and wood products	8.20	18.35	60.37	53.65
4 Manufacture of paper and paper products, printing, and publishing	9.27	9.01	34.30	32.62
5 Manufacture of chemicals and chemical petroleum, coal, rubber, and plastic products	14.12	35.73	18.03	17.46
6 Manufacture of nonmetallic mineral products except petroleum products	6.72	22.35	21.85	47.44
7 Basic metal industries	28.32	32.35	16.15	18.70
8 Manufacture of fabricated metal products, machinery, and equipment	5.12	17.35	39.20	26.30
9 Other manufacturing industries	9.01	35.32	32.5	27.52
Total manufacturing	9.21	26.32	35.91	29.31

Sources: compiled using data from Ministry of Industries and Scientific Affairs, *Second Report on the Field Survey of Manufacturing Industry in Sri Lanka*, 1975–6, and Department of Census and Statistics, *Survey of Manufacturing Industry*, 1981

Table 2.14 Industrial concentration[a], 1979 and 1981

Industry	1979	1981
Meat, fish, and dairy products	81.0	92.2
Fruit and vegetable products	63.5	99.3
Confectionery, bakery, and cereal products	74.5	88.9
Spirits and alcoholic beverages	84.6	85.1
Other food products and tobacco	99.6	99.0
Textiles	41.7	54.4
Made-up garments	54.5	43.1
Petroleum and petroleum products	43.1	64.3
Salt and salt-based chemicals	98.1	99.4
Other chemicals	58.8	72.5
Pharmaceuticals and cosmetics	69.3	62.5
Soap, vegetable and animal oils and fats	99.5	86.7
Leather and rubber products	64.2	61.6
Wood, paper, and pulp products	51.7	43.6
Clay, sand, and cement products	80.6	88.3
Basic metal industries and machinery	58.7	59.1
Ferrous and nonferrous metal products	41.7	41.2
Transport equipment and spares	66.5	88.8
Electrical goods	47.5	80.1
Optical and photographic goods	77.8	79.2

[a] The share of the three major firms in total gross output of each sector.
Source: Department of Census and Statistics, *Survey of Manufacturing Industry*, 1979, 1981

In response to the stringent import controls of the 1960s, foreign firms, which up to then had been exporting goods to Sri Lanka, established subsidiaries and/or joint ventures with local partners for production for a largely captive domestic market (Fernando, 1980). Table 2.15 shows shares of relative output held by firms with direct foreign capital participation ("foreign firms" for short) in 1966–7. At this time these firms accounted for about 35 percent of total output in the organized manufacturing sector, and their role was important in sectors such as food, beverages, and tobacco, chemicals, and machinery and equipment. More recent comparable estimates are not available but, with more firms entering, especially after 1977, it may reasonably be surmised that foreign firms play a more important role in manufacturing now than in 1967 (Cuthbertson and Athukorala, 1988, appendix table A.2).

Table 2.15 Manufacturing industry: the importance of the foreign sector by value of production, 1966–1967

Industry category	Number of foreign firms	Output share of foreign firms (%)
Food, beverages, and tobacco	6	48.5
Textiles and wearing apparel	3	6.3
Paper and paper products	0	0
Wood and wood products	0	0
Leather and rubber	2	24.3
Chemicals and chemical products	28	61.0
Nonmetallic mineral products	3	20.8
Basic metal	0	0
Fabricated metal products	10	21.6
Machinery (except electrical) and transport equipment	5	46.1
Electrical machinery	3	34.0
Miscellaneous	1	11.0
Total manufacturing	61	35.1

Source: Fernando, 1971, table II–6 (estimates are based on unpublished records at the Ministry of Industries)

Consumption, Savings, and Investment

Aggregate consumption as a percentage of GNP has tended to range between 80 and 90 percent (table 2.16). The share of government consumption ranged between 10 and 15 percent until 1977. Since then it has fallen, and was 8 percent in 1983. This decline has been more than offset by expansion in private consumption. The share of gross domestic investment varied in a narrow range of about 15 percent until 1977, and shifted upward markedly after that. By comparison, the domestic saving ratio has remained between 11 and 13 percent ever since Independence,

Table 2.16 Consumption, investment, and savings (based on current price data)

Item	1950–4	1955–9	1960–5	1966–70	1971–7	1978–82	1983
As a percentage of GDP							
Consumption	86.7	86.8	86.5	87.1	84.8	86.9	88.6
of which public consumption is	(9.0)	(12.3)	(14.2)	(13.7)	(12.3)	(8.7)	(8.4)
Investment	13.8	14.4	14.7	16.5	15.8	27.1	28.6
of which public investment[a] is	(5.3)	(6.3)	(7.6)	(7.3)	(8.2)	(14.8)	(15.2)
Savings	11.8	12.2	13.1	13.2	13.4	13.0	13.6
of which public savings are	(0.2)	(0.3)	(0.3)	(0.3)	(0.3)	(0.9)	(0.8)
Savings-to-investment ratio (%)	85.5	84.7	89.1	80.0	84.8	48.0	47.5
Marginal propensity to save	12.8	13.2	13.3	13.6	12.8	12.9	13.0

[a] Including investment by public corporations.
Sources: Snodgrass, 1966, for the period 1950–9; CBC, Annual Report, various issues

consistent with the important role of foreign finance in capital formation. The savings-to-investment ratio, which varied in the range 80–90 percent up to 1977, has dropped below 50 percent since then. Since the early 1960s the public sector has accounted for about half of total annual gross capital formation. Public savings, however, have remained below 1 percent of GNP throughout.

The Role of the State

Since the late 1950s, state-sponsored activities have steadily expanded to become the predominant force in most sectors. In manufacturing and plantation industries the state is now the major producer and employer through a network of public sector enterprises. Direct government involvement through public enterprises has become firmly rooted in the service sector – in transport, banking, and insurance.

More than 60 percent of the tea acreage, over 30 percent of rubber acreage, and about 10 percent of coconut acreage is now owned and managed by the state. The state's share of total value-added production in the plantation sector was about 65 percent in 1981. In manufacturing, the state operates 26 public enterprises, many of them well-protected monopolies, which in 1981 accounted for about 40 percent of total value-added manufacturing (including cottage industries and other production units in the unorganized sector). In the organized manufacturing sector, the state share in gross output increased from about 30 percent in the early 1970s to over 60 percent by the early 1980s (table 2.17). In the service sectors (items 6–9 in table 2.18), shares of the value added of public ventures in 1981 varied from 20 to 40 percent – before 1977 these would undoubtedly have

Table **2.17** Percentage contribution of state industrial corporations to production and incremental production by industry group, 1970–1983

Category	Share in production (%)					Contribution to incremental production (%)	
	1970	1974	1977	1980	1983	1970–7	1977–83
Food, beverages, and tobacco	23.67	41.94	31.22	29.11	19.15	34.42	9.75
Textile, wearing apparel, and leather industries	11.0	37.12	49.28	19.84	17.26	78.84	7.27
Wood and wood products	72.73	92.15	93.51	99.13	95.41	80.18	125.21
Paper and paper products	42.98	69.34	44.35	77.77	58.96	44.87	67.91
Chemical, petroleum, rubber, and plastic products	45.58	70.12	92.41	92.39	95.90	102.56	96.31
Nonmetallic mineral products	72.01	82.35	53.78	76.76	79.22	57.35	89.98
Basic metal products	100.00	100.00	100.00	100.00	100.00	100.00	100.00
Fabricated metal products	2.01	3.43	3.78	7.37	4.77	5.40	6.61
Total industrial production[a]	29.60	65.73	65.48	66.65	63.42	67.78	65.99

[a] Percentage contribution to the total output of the above eight sectors plus "other manufacturing." There is no state participation in the latter sector.
Source: CBC, Review of the Economy, various issues

Table 2.18 Relative shares of public and private sectors in sectoral and total gross domestic product, 1981 (percent)

Sector	Private	Public
Agriculture, forestry, and fishing	88	12
Plantation agriculture	35	65
Other	97	63
Mining and quarrying	81	19
Manufacturing	71	39
Construction	38	61
Electricity, gas, water, and sanitary services	–	100
Transport, storage, and communication	65	35
Wholesale and retail trade	80	20
Banking, insurance, and real estate	59	41
Services not elsewhere specified	71	29
GDP	71	29

–, zero.

Source: Arthur D. Little International Inc., *Developing Sri Lanka's Private Sector and Its Investment Opportunities*, Final report to the Ministry of Finance and Planning, volume 2, August 1983 (based on Central Bank data)

been much higher. When all sectors are taken together, the state share in total GDP works out at about 30 percent.

Fiscal Operations

Table 2.19 summarizes basic data relating to fiscal operations. The most striking feature throughout the post-Independence period has been the almost spectacular expansion in the budget deficit. As a ratio of GNP, government expenditure increased from 23 percent in 1950–1 to about 30 percent in the early 1970s and to about 40 percent in the early 1980s – the jump to 40 percent was partly a reflection of large aid flows channeled through government in these years. The revenue-to-GNP ratio has been varied within a narrow margin of around 20 percent. From the mid-1960s up to about mid-1970, on average about 25 percent of government expenditure was met through deficit financing, and since the late 1970s this share has shot up to about 50 percent.

Throughout the 1950s, taxes on foreign trade dominated revenue (table 2.20). The combined share of export and import taxes in revenue averaged about 60 percent. Since the early 1960s the share of trade taxes in revenue has declined, and by 1977 it was about 20 percent. This mainly reflects slow export growth, stringent import controls which limited imports mostly to those defined as essential categories, and expansion in revenue from taxes on domestic economic activities. This last was a consequence both of a

Table 2.19 Government finance: selected data, 1950–1951 to 1983 (million rupees)

	1950–1	1954–5	1958–9	1964–5	1967–8	1970–1	1977	1980	1983
Revenue	910	1,159	1,330	1,816	2,156	2,815	6,686	14,068	225,310
Percentage of GNP	21.8	21.5	22.5	24.2	21.8	23.8	18.4	21.1	20.7
Expenditure	969	1,031	1,744	2,247	2,871	3,899	9,760	30,343	46,816
Percentage of GNP	23.2	18.9	29.6	30.0	29.0	32.9	26.8	45.5	38.6
Ratio of net cash deficit to surplus	−59	128	−414	−431	715	−1,084	−3,074	−16,275	−21,606
Percentage of expenditure	−6.1	12.4	−23.7	−19.2	−24.9	−27.8	−31.5	−53.6	−46.2
Social welfare expenditures	313	350	582	1,011	1,269	1,464	2,971	2,522	3,837
Education	n.a.	153	255	355	410	532	976	1,846	2,951
Health	n.a.	110	149	167	221	266	498	1,342	1,735
Food subsidy	n.a.	36	146	447	579	514	1,124	305	81
Percentage of total expenditure	32.2	33.9	33.3	44.9	44.2	37.5	30.4	8.3	8.1
Percentage of GNP	9.5	6.4	9.8	13.5	12.8	12.4	8.1	3.8	3.2
Public debt outstanding[a]							22,434	46,779	86,423
Percentage of GNP							61.6	70.2	71.3

n.a., not available.

[a] Public debt figures as a percentage of GNP are not available on a comparable basis until 1977.

Source: CBC, *Review of the Economy* and *Annual Report*, various issues

Table 2.20 Composition of government revenue, 1950–1983 (average annual percentage shares)

Revenues	1950–2	1956–8	1962–4	1968–70	1974–6	1980–2	1983
Export duties	30.3	28.2	16.3	14.6	11.6	20.3	9.7
Import duties	31.1	25.7	33.2	21.8	7.1	19.5	19.2
Other taxes	35.2	41.4	9.6	52.8	50.2	52.0	63.9
Nontax revenue	3.4	4.7		10.8[a]	31.1[a]	8.2	7.2
Total (%)	100	100	100	100	100	100	100
Rs (millions)	829	1,266	1,657	2,463	7,040	16,035	25,210

[a] Including receipts from Foreign Exchange Entitlement Certificates.
Source: CBC, Review of the Economy and Annual Report, various issues

widening in the tax base and of attempts by the government to catch new expanding economic activities in the tax net (sales and turnover taxes were introduced in the 1964 budget). Import tax revenue became somewhat more important in 1978 as tariffs rather than quotas became the main effective barrier. Indeed, as will be seen, short-term revenue considerations were the driving force for many subsequent revisions to the tariff.

During the first two decades or so since Independence, the share of social welfare expenditure expanded steadily as a proportion of total expenditure, passing the 40 percent mark by 1970 (table 2.19). Since then this share has declined because of measures to curtail welfare expenditure, a decline particularly marked since 1977 after the food subsidy scheme was replaced by a selective food coupon scheme targeted at poorer people.

Money Supply and Price Level

The money supply for 1950–83 is shown in table 2.21. Whatever the definition used, an almost exponential growth in money supply can be observed. For instance, between 1960 and 1970 the narrow money supply increased by about 110 percent. This was followed by an increase of about 400 percent between 1970 and 1980.

From Independence to about the mid-1950s, variations in external banking assets were the main determinant of money supply, with government budgetary operations a secondary factor. Since then the order has been reversed and expansionary financing of the budget deficit has dominated. Only in five years (1973, 1974, 1978, 1979, and 1984) has budgetary performance generated anything like a contractionary effect on money supply over the preceding year. Since about the mid-1970s, bank borrowings by public enterprises have been important in the expanding money supply.

Table 2.21 Money supply, 1950–1983 (million rupees)

Year	M1	M2	M3
1950	911	n.a.	n.a.
1955	1,073	n.a.	n.a.
1960	1,209	1,260	1,711
1965	1,716	2,283	2,838
1970	1,967	3,115	3,896
1975	3,088	4,757	6,527
1977	5,366	8,807	11,403
1978	5,936	10,962	14,128
1979	7,669	15,058	19,339
1980	9,428	19,860	24,704
1981	10,025	24,447	29,872
1982	11,760	30,510	38,163
1983	14,748	37,257	46,740

n.a., not available.
M1, currency and demand deposits held by the public.
M2, M1 + time and savings deposits held by the public with commercial banks.
M3, M2 + time and savings deposits held by the public with other savings institutions.
Source: Cuthbertson and Athukorala, 1988, appendix table A.3

Following the monetary reforms in 1978, the expansion of domestic credit to the private sector has also become important. In the four years from 1980 to 1983, this factor had more effect on money supply than government budgetary operations, borrowings by public enterprises, and changes in external banking assets (Central Bank of Ceylon (CBC), *Review of the Economy*, 1984).

Table 2.22 indicates variations in general price levels in terms of four price indices: the Colombo consumer price index (CCPI), the Central Bank consumer price index (CNCPI), the wholesale price index (WPI), and the GNP deflator (GNPD).[5] In the 1950s, price increases were moderate. Both the CCPI and the GNPD indicate an annual average increase of only about 1 percent. The main explanation for this price stability, in the face of practically unabated monetary expansion in the

[5] Of the four indicators, the CCPI is probably the least reliable. It is designed to measure changes in the cost of living of an average working-class family in Colombo town only; the weights have not been revised since 1952 despite changes in patterns of consumption, and the prices in the index are the official subsidized or controlled prices, a practice the invariably tends to underestimate inflation. The implicit GNPD also has its limitations, emanating mainly from deficiencies in the data base of the national accounting system (Shourie, 1974). However, its coverage is better than that of the CCPI. The WPI and CNCPI are compiled by the Central Bank. They are better indicators (both in terms of the coverage and the effort taken to incorporate open-market price changes) but unfortunately they date only from 1974.

Table 2.22 Basic indicators of general price levels

Year	CCPI (1952 = 100)	Increase (%)	CNCPI (1974 = 100)	Increase (%)	WPI (1974 = 100)	Increase (%)	GNPD (1970 = 100)	Increase (%)
1955	102	–	n.a.	n.a.	n.a.	n.a.	79	–
1960	103	0.8[a]	–	–	–	–	81	1.1[a]
1965	113	1.8[a]	–	–	–	–	84	1.7[a]
1970	138	4.2[a]	–	–	–	–	100	3.8[a]
1971	142	2.7	–	–	–	–	104	3.5
1972	151	6.7	–	–	–	–	108	4.3
1973	164	9.7	–	–	–	–	127	17.4
1974	186	12.3	100	–	100	–	160	26.0
1975	198	6.7	100	– 0.5	103	3.4	171	7.3
1976	201	1.2	107	6.7	112	8.2	182	6.0
1977	203	1.3	123	15.2	135	20.9	216	18.7
1978	228	12.1	134	9.1	157	15.8	233	7.8
1979	252	10.8	159	18.9	172	9.5	270	15.7
1980	318	26.1	218	37.1	230	33.8	318	18.2
1981	375	18.0	270	23.7	269	17.0	383	20.5
1982	416	10.1	300	11.0	283	5.6	421	9.9
1983	474	14.0	334	11.4	354	25.0	488	15.8

n.a., not available; –, negligible.
[a] Average growth rate of the five years including the given year.
Source: CCPI, WPI, and GNPD, CBC, Annual Report, various issues (except for the GNPD for 1955–70 for which the source is Savundranayagam, 1983)

domestic economy, is that the economy was able to meet the resultant additional demand through an increased supply of imported goods, drawing upon previously accumulated foreign reserves (Gunasekara, 1963). However, by the end of the 1950s this well had run dry, and by the 1960s, when stringent import controls came into being, the continuing monetary expansion began to bring about increases in the price level. Increased import prices after the onset of the oil price shock in 1973 and the depreciation of the external value of the rupee since 1977 aggravated this inflationary pressure.

Foreign Trade and the Balance of Payments

Trade Dependence

At Independence the trade coefficient (imports and exports as a percentage of GDP) was as high as 70 percent and remained at this level throughout the 1950s (table 2.23). From then, and up to 1977, there was a steady reduction, which can be related to relatively low export prices and the steadily rising import barriers over the period. From 1978 the trade coefficient returned to the level of the 1950s.

The share of imported raw material in total raw material usage typically varies between 60 percent and 85 percent (table 2.24); increases in recent years are partly due to increased oil prices. However, even when the petroleum processing industry is excluded, the ratio remains around 65 percent. Out of the total real output (real value added) in this sector, about

Table 2.23 Trade coefficients[a]: imports and exports as a percentage of gross domestic product, 1950–1983 (selected years)

Year	Ratio of imports to GDP	Ratio of exports to GDP	Ratio of imports plus exports to GDP
1950	31.8	38.3	70.1
1955	35.7	35.5	71.2
1960	31.5	28.2	59.7
1965	25.6	25.5	51.1
1970	17.6	15.3	32.9
1975	20.7	15.2	35.9
1977	18.1	19.1	37.2
1980	54.5	28.3	82.8
1983	45.2	23.0	67.1

[a] Estimated using current values.
Source: Cuthbertson and Athukorala, 1988, appendix table A.4

Table 2.24 The dependence of domestic industry on imported raw materials, 1961–1983

Years[a]	Ratio of imported raw materials to total raw materials (%)	Ratio of imported raw materials to total value added[b] (%)
1961–4		
1967–9	62	39
1970–2	68	48
1973–5	74	56
1976–8	68	59
1979–	76	62
81	85	60
1981–3	82	63

[a] Three-year averages.
[b] Calculations are made in real terms. The deflators used are as follows: (i) for value added, the implicit deflator of manufacturing value added; (ii) for raw materials, the intermediate import price index.
Source: CBC, *Review of the Economy* and *Annual Report*, various issues

Table 2.25 Direct import content of gross domestic fixed capital formation, 1970–1984 (selected years)

Year	1970	1972	1974	1976	1978	1982	1984
Import content (%)	32.8	27.9	23.1	25.8	40.0	36.8	29.8

Source: CBC, *Review of the Economy* and *Annual Report*, various issues

60 percent is directly related to use of imported inputs. The direct import content of gross domestic fixed capital formation in the economy varied between 30 and 40 percent over the period 1970–84 (table 2.25).

Balance of Payments[6]

A striking feature of Sri Lanka's balance of payments has been the persistent and widening deficit in the merchandise account since 1956 – except for a small surplus recorded in 1977 (table 2.26). After the waning of the 1954–55 tea boom, earnings from merchandise exports seem to follow a near-zero growth path.

Table 2.26 Balance of payments, 1950–1983 (million US dollars)

Year	Export f.o.b.	Import c.i.f.	Trade balance	Total goods and services	Total current account	Nonmonetary capital[a]	Basic balance[b]	Import-month equivalent of reserves[c]
1950	296	246	50	43	28	−5	23	11.1
1951	374	324	50	24	18	−9	9	9.0
1952	296	358	−62	−71	−93	5	−88	5.7
1953	314	343	−28	−23	−33	−8	−41	4.2
1954	362	290	71	73	64	4	68	7.8
1955	397	310	87	80	67	−10	57	9.4
1956	372	331	41	29	17	−2	15	9.1
1957	350	370	−19	−33	−40	−3	−37	6.6
1958	341	359	−18	−27	−32	4	−28	5.9
1959	372	411	−38	−41	−43	4	−39	4.0
1960	377	421	−44	−51	−46	3	−43	2.7
1961	358	376	−18	−22	−19	8	−11	3.0
1962	370	400	−30	−31	−29	8	−21	2.6
1963	358	392	−33	−38	−35	18	−17	2.3
1964	371	411	−40	−42	−33	—	−33	1.9
1965	401	403	−2	4	12	3	15	2.6
1966	351	423	−72	−69	−60	25	−35	1.7
1967	346	417	−70	−52	−60	28	−32	2.5
1968	332	395	−63	−62	−59	36	−23	2.1
1969	320	446	−125	−140	−133	44	−89	1.5
1970	338	391	−52	−70	−58	30	−28	1.9
1971	327	375	−48	−51	−36	64	28	2.5
1972	316	358	−42	−45	−33	42	9	3.8
1973	388	438	−49	−41	−27	30	3	3.6
1974	512	702	−190	−179	−137	43	−94	2.2
1975	555	757	−201	−189	−102	83	−19	1.9
1976	556	640	−84	−71	−6	71	65	3.1
1977	726	687	38	71	138	68	206	10.6
1978	853	1,007	−154	−147	−67	203	136	5.9
1979	990	1,463	−472	−424·	−230	200	−30	5.1
1980	979	1,886	−907	−859	−607	405	−202	2.4
1981	999	1,759	−760	−757	−414	356	−58	3.1
1982	989	1,943	−953	−972	−555	284	−271	3.3
1983	1,002	1,809	−807	−868	−445	401	−44	3.5

—, negligible; f.o.b., free on board; c.i.f., cost, insurance, and freight.
[a] Nonmonetary capital is the direct investment and other private investment (long and short) plus central government loans received.
[b] Total current account plus nonmonetary capital.
[c] Calculated as (end-of-year reserves net of sterling loans sinking funds divided by total imports for the year) multiplied by 12.

[6] Foreign trade and the balance-of-payments experience of Sri Lanka has been extensively studied and reported (see, for example, Hewavitharana, 1975; Gunasekara, 1977; Kappagoda and Paine, 1981; Athukorala, 1984b).

The peak export level, 397 million special drawing rights (SDR), in 1955 was not reached again until 1965. Thereafter there was a downward trend until the so-called commodity boom in late 1972. Export volumes of both tea and rubber, the two major export items which consistently accounted for nearly 70 percent of total export earnings (table 2.27), increased continuously through the two decades since Independence. However, world prices of both commodities consistently fell, and these falls exceeded volume expansion in most years (Cuthbertson and Athukorala, 1988, appendix table A.5). Policies to promote nontraditional exports were not introduced until the late 1960s and, because of the heavy anti-export bias embodied in the commercial policy mix, had little impact.

Despite the decline in export earnings, imports increased unabated throughout the 1950s. As mentioned earlier, the resultant balance-of-payments deficit was at first almost totally financed from foreign exchange reserves which had been accumulated during the World War II and Korean War commodity booms and the 1954–5 tea boom. By the end of 1955, foreign reserves were equal to about nine months' import equivalence measured by the rate of import expansion then prevailing (table 2.28). These reserves were depleted at an annual rate of about 18 percent during the second half of the decade.

The eventual depletion of foreign reserves to critically low levels brought about the first really stringent import controls at the beginning of the 1960s. The import controls did reduce import volume: the import volume index declined from 125 in 1959–61 to 107 in 1965–7, and then to 67 in 1974–6. The percentage of compressible imports (nonfood consumer goods) in the import structure declined continuously from 22 at the beginning of the 1960s to seven by the beginning of the 1970s (table 2.28).

Still the balance of payments continued in the red. On the one hand, sharp increases in import prices, notably since the onset of the oil crisis in 1973, far outweighed decreases in import volume. On the other hand, uncertainty generated by the land reform movements in 1972 and 1975 and dislocation in the management of plantations following nationalization

Table 2.27 Exports: commodity composition and annual average growth rates (at current SDR prices)

Category	Shares (%)				Annual average growth (%)		
	1974	1977	1980	1984	1974–7	1978–80	1981–4
Major agricultural products (tea, rubber, and coconut)	71.6	72.8	54.4	57.4	21.5	– 4.5	16.2
Minor agricultural products	8.5	7.7	7.1	5.1	18.7	9.8	16.5
Minerals	3.9	5.0	4.6	2.5	24.6	6.3	3.1
Industrial products (excluding petroleum)	3.6	5.6	14.4	25.5	52.6	51.8	32.7
Garments	0.8	2.2	10.4	20.5	90.4	53.3	37.1
Seafoods	0.8	1.5	1.4	1.8	80.9	11.5	20.7
Processed food (other than seafood)	0.3	0.4	0.4	0.2	33.8	15.7	13.6
Other manufactures	1.7	1.5	2.2	3.0	11.0	23.4	29.0
Petroleum products	10.1	9.1	17.8	8.9	9.6	44.7	– 2.2
Total exports (SDR million)	433.0	628.5	812.0	1,412.6			

Source: CBC, Review of the Economy and Sri Lanka Customs Returns, various issues

Table 2.28 Import structure, 1950–1983 (percentage shares)

	Consumer goods			Intermediate goods			
Year	Total	Food	Other	Total	Oil	Investment	Final goods[a]
1950	72.2	45.0	23.2	15.2	5.2	12.6	84.8
1955	66.6	45.7	20.5	18.4	8.7	15.0	81.6
1960	61.0	38.3	22.6	20.1	6.3	18.1	79.1
1965	52.9	41.0	11.9	28.1	7.4	17.7	70.6
1970	56.0	46.3	9.7	20.0	2.5	23.6	79.6
1975	50.5	48.9	2.5	36.0	16.6	12.4	62.9
1980	29.9	18.9	11.0	47.7	23.8	24.0	53.9
1983	25.6	11.8	13.8	47.7	24.2	26.5	52.1

[a] Total consumer goods plus investment.
Source: Cuthbertson and Athukorala, 1988, appendix table A.6

resulted in a continued decline in export volume of plantation crops, reducing potential gains from improved world prices of primary commodities in the early 1970s.

Reliance on foreign financing increased. The establishment by the United States, the United Kingdom, France, Japan, West Germany, and Canada of the "Aid Ceylon Group" in 1965 appreciably increased the annual inflow of long-term official aid to Sri Lanka (see table 2.26, seventh column). This, however, financed only part of the expanding trade gap. Short-term financing (mostly suppliers' credit and commodity aid) became increasingly important. Continuing reliance on foreign financing sharply increased the pressure of debt servicing on the balance of payments. The debt service ratio, which had remained around 10 percent in the second half of the 1960s, rose to about 23 percent by the mid-1970s (Cuthbertson and Athukorala, 1988, appendix table A.8).

The current account deficit expanded unprecedentedly following the policy reforms of 1977. This reflected the increased use of long-term concessional finance to implement a number of development projects in the country. Despite this heavy reliance on foreign finance, the debt service ratio remained around 20 percent because nearly 75 percent of foreign financial assistance received over this period consisted of grants and long-term loans.

Despite attempts to promote and diversify exports, even by 1983 the three traditional exports – tea, rubber, and coconut products – still accounted for about 55 percent of total merchandise exports (table 2.27). The share of manufactured exports (including processed foods) was about 35 percent, of which 32 percent was accounted for by petroleum products

(12 percent) and garments (20 percent). Since the mid-1970s, the balance-of-payments position has been significantly supported by expanding tourist earnings and migrant worker remittances. In 1982, tourist earnings contributed about 8 percent of total current account receipts; migrant remittances contributed 16 percent. In 1977, the relative shares of these two sources had been only 3 percent and 5 percent respectively. Communal disturbances after July 1983 severely disrupted the expansion in the tourist industry. Tourist arrivals in 1984 showed a 22 percent and 17 percent drop compared with arrivals in 1982 and 1983 respectively. The import structure has traditionally been dominated by consumer goods, mainly essential food items. Recent years have seen relatively higher expansion in the shares of intermediate goods (of which crude petroleum accounts for about 25 percent of total imports) and of investment goods.

3
Changing Governments and Changing Policy

Since Independence from the British in 1948, Sri Lanka has maintained a competitive Westminster-style multiparty democracy. Two main parties – the center-right United National Party (UNP) and the center-left Sri Lankan Freedom Party (SLFP) (sometimes in coalition with Marxist parties) – have alternated in power at six successive general elections (table 3.1) (Wriggins, 1960; Kearney, 1973; Jupp, 1978; Wilson, 1979).

The center-right governments of Sri Lanka can be identified with antipathy to the growing state sector sponsored by the center left, and with an avowed attachment to an open economy and the free play of market forces. The center-left governments, however, are identified with shifting business activity into the public sector, management by control rather than competition, and, if not with a closing up of the economy, certainly wth selective treatment of industry through import controls and other barriers. A convenient way of looking at the swings in trade and commercial policy is therefore according to the government of the day. To do this in the following discussion the period since Independence is broken down into five subperiods.

1948–56   Center right, D. S. Senanayake, UNP government
1956–65   Center left governments led by Mr Bandaranaike to 1960
             and by Mrs Bandaranaike from 1960 to 1965
1965–70   Center right, Dudley Senanayake, son of
             D. S. Senanayake, UNP
1970–7   Center left, Mrs Bandaranaike
1977 onward Center right, J. R. Jayawardene, UNP

1948–1956: Continuation of the Pre-Independence Open Economy

Most of the post-Independence decade turned out to be a time of a liberal trade regime with just a few low taxes on imports and exports to gather revenues. The new government had begun with tight import and exchange

Table 3.1 Sri Lanka: the swings in the political pendulum, 1947–1983

Date	Prime Minister and his/her party affiliation	Percentage of votes		Percentage of seats		Turnout at the election
		UNP	SLFP	UNP	SLFP	
Sep 1947	D. S. Senanayake (UNP)	39.8	–	44.2	–	61.3
Mar 1952[a]	Dudley Senanayake (UNP)	44.08	15.52	44.2	9.5	70.7
Apr 1956[b]	S. W. R. D. Bandaranaike (MEP)	27.44	39.96[c]	8.4	53.7[c]	69.0
Mar 1960	Dudley Senanayake (UNP)	29.62	21.12	48.4	30.5	77.6
Jul 1960[d]	Sirimavo Bandaranaike (SLFP) (wife of S. W. R. D.)	37.57	33.59	33.1	49.7	75.9
May 1965	Dudley Senanayake (UNP)	38.92	30.24	19.9	27.2	82.1
May 1970[e]	Sirimavo Bandaranaike (SLFP)	37.92	36.63[f]	43.7	60.0[f]	85.2
Jul 1977[g]	J. R. Jayawardene (UNP)	52.10	29.80	84.3	4.8	86.3

–, negligible; UNP, United National Party; CP, Communist Party (Moscow); LSSP, Lanka Sama Samaja Party (Lanka Equal Society Party); SLFP, Sri Lanka Freedom Party; MEP, Mahajana Eksath Peramuna (People's United Front); VLSSP, Viplavakari (Revolutionary) Lanka Sama Samaja Party.

[a] The political upheaval caused by the cut in the price of subsidized rice in July 1953 brought about D. Senanayake's resignation in October of that year. He was replaced by Sir John Kotelawala (his nephew) who remained Prime Minister until April 1956.

[b] Mr Bandaranaike came into power as head of a Sinhalese Buddhist-oriented United Front (MEP) comprising his SLFP, the Marxist VLSSP, the pro-Sinhalese Bhasa Peramuna (Language Front), and a group of independent members of Parliament. After Mr Bandaranaike's assassination in September 1959, W. Dahanayake, the leader of the Bhasa Peramuna, became the Prime Minister.

[c] Includes votes received and seats won by the other parties in the MEP.

[d] In June 1964, Mrs Bandaranaike formed a coalition with the Trotskyist LSSP, the main party of the traditional left.

[e] The SLFP was the main party in a three-party United Front (UF), with the Marxist parties LSSP and CP being the other partners. The LSSP was excluded from the UF in September 1975.

[f] The election results of SLFP only.

[g] In February 1978, a new constitution, modeled on that of the Fifth French Republic, was adopted and Mr Jayawardene was installed in the strong executive Presidency under the constitution. In October 1982, through an amendment to the new constitution, the life of the Parliament elected in 1977 was prolonged until 1989.

Source: Wilson, 1979

controls at the request of the UK government. The object was to control drawing on previously accumulated sterling assets so as to reduce the pressure of post-war dollar shortages on the UK balance of payments. In 1950 and 1951 these restrictions were removed in light of an improved balance of payments associated with the Korean War commodity boom. By 1953 license controls were limited to only a few commodities of which the country had some installed production capacity, and even in these cases, in practice, licenses were freely issued. Consistent with the requirements of virtually free import trade, exchange controls were few.

Economic policy was not completely neutral though: there was a bias towards agriculture, and objectives of self-sufficiency in paddy (rice) and subsidiary food crops were high on the political agenda. The Prime Minister, D. S. Senanayake, was committed to the view that agrarian policies were the ultimate solution to the island's economic and social ills (Oliver, 1957). These policies were to involve opening up the *dry zone*, the heartland of the ancient irrigation civilization of Sri Lanka, with new colonization schemes. A secondary objective of these schemes was to reduce population pressure in the densely populated southwestern quadrant of the island.

There was also a modest program of import substitution industrialization, including plans for revamping wartime factories and establishing factories to produce items such as cement, steel, paper, caustic soda, vegetable oil, textiles, and sugar (Oliver, 1956). However, recommendations by a World Bank mission which visited Sri Lanka in 1951 led to a sharp revision of this industrial policy. The mission, referring to inefficiencies in existing industrial undertakings and to considerations such as the smallness of the domestic market and a judged lack of technical and entrepreneurial skills, recommended that industrial policy be concentrated on the development of small or medium-small industries through private enterprise (World Bank, 1953).

The influence of these recommendations is discernible. In the Six-Year Investment Program (1954–9), 44 percent of planned investment outlay was allocated to industry. The Government Sponsored Corporations Act 19 of 1955 provided for the transfer and management of government factories to semi-autonomous public corporations and their transfer thereafter to private enterprise by the disposal of government shares.[1] The Ceylon Institute of Scientific and Industrial Research and the Development Finance Corporation (with capital participation by the International Finance Corporation) were established in 1955 to provide the private sector with technical and financial support respectively. Short-term tax concessions which were first introduced in 1949 were further extended by successive budgets. A White Paper on foreign investment was issued in 1955 to encourage foreign capital participation in industry.

Despite the six-year plan there was not much interest in development planning. The usual practice was to make funds available for ministers to draw up their own long-term schemes. The six-year plan issued in 1950 was a "tied up version" of the budget speeches for 1947–8 and 1948–9, and was prepared only because the launching of the Colombo Plan in that year required the government to submit a development plan. The plan as such was "purely a pro forma exercise and probably had no influence on policy" (Snodgrass, 1966).

The government inherited from the colonial era the practice of maintaining a heavy commitment to the provision of social welfare services, in

[1] Under this Act, in 1955, state-owned plywood, leather, cement, paper, and ceramic factories were vested in public corporations. However, the second stage of transition (that is, transfer of ownership to the private sector) was aborted because of the change in government in 1956.

particular free health services, free public education, and the supply of subsidized food. Of these the rice subsidy was the largest drain on the budget, accounting for between 30 and 40 percent of annual expenditure. In 1953 the world price for rice rose sharply and the government, which was locked into welfare rice distribution programs, was confronted by a large balance-of-payments deficit. When the government sought to increase the price of subsidized rice, civil disturbances broke out, leading to the resignation of the Prime Minister, Dudley Senanayake. Although the UNP recovered from this incident and ruled for another three years, with Sir John Kotelawala as Prime Minister, this event marked the first of a series of similar occurrences which have continued to influence Sri Lanka's trade policy during the last 30 years.[2]

1956–1965: Closing Up

The government changed in 1956 to a center-left-based coalition (MEP) led by Mr S. W. R. D. Bandaranaike's SLFP. Commentators variously attribute the fall of the UNP to austerity measures, in particular the attempt to increase the price of subsidized rice, as well as to such things as Sir John Kotelawala's abrasive style, change for change's sake, and the promises of the MEP, including institution of Sinhalese as the official language, a policy which held great appeal for a growing Sinhalese revival movement.

Unlike the previous UNP governments, the new MEP government placed heavy emphasis on macroplanning with long-term perspectives. In 1956 a National Planning Council was set up under the chairmanship of the prime minister. The council prepared a ten-year plan covering the period 1959–68. The development strategy embodied in the plan was a clear departure from the UNP's approach to industrialization – an approach which was definitely negative rather than just neutral or noninterventionist.

In line with much of the development thinking of the time and the policy orientation in almost all other contemporary developing countries, a lead proposal in the ten-year plan was deliberate import substitution industrialization. The plan mentioned long-term possibilities for expanding manufactured exports, but this was considered an objective to be achieved as an outgrowth of import substitution industrialization and was not a specific objective. In this program, the state sector was assigned the key role on the grounds that "when it is essential to the economy that a new enterprise has

[2] In 1963 the Minister of Finance – from a different party – resigned over attempts by the government to reduce the rice ration. In 1973, Dr N. M. Perera, a Marxist Minister of Finance, also proposed a reduction in the rice ration; although his government did not support him, he did not resign.

to be established, it is not possible to wait or depend upon the initiative of the private sector" (National Planning Council, 1959). In 1957 a policy statement by the Minister of Industries laid down the spheres in which the state would (a) involve itself, (b) join hands with private enterprise, and (c) leave the operation wholly to the private sector.

The political crisis that followed (culminating in the assassination of Mr Bandaranaike in September 1959) and the worsening balance-of-payments situation more or less stopped implementation of the ten-year plan. However, the new policy of "state capitalism" found its expression in a sharp increase in government industrial investment. In the three years 1957–60 the construction of several state industrial corporations was inaugurated, mostly with technical and financial support from Communist bloc countries, to produce shoes and leather goods, caustic soda, chlorine, cotton yarn, sugar, bricks, tiles, and hardboard.

Nationalization of foreign-owned plantations again became a major policy issue in the early 1970s. While this had been discussed even before 1948, the UNP was firmly against it; in Mr D. S. Senanayake's words: "it would be foolish to kill the goose that laid the golden eggs" (Wilson, 1979). In contrast, nationalization of foreign-owned plantations became an accepted policy of the Bandaranaike government. In 1958, the Ministry of Agriculture and Food (which was under the Marxist minister Mr Philip Gunawardene) issued as a part of its agricultural plan a memorandum entitled "A Scheme for the Nationalization of Foreign-owned Tea and Rubber Plantations," which suggested a phased program of nationalization extended over ten years to cover altogether about half the tea and rubber land (Fernando, 1982). Commenting on this proposed nationalization move, Nicholas Kaldor, who visited Sri Lanka in 1958, warned that "the continuance of the present state of uncertainty is bound to have unfavorable effects on the efficiency of tea plantations, since the British plantation companies are not likely to sink fresh capital . . . as they are left in the dark of their future status" (Kaldor, 1959). In 1959 the government issued a statement postponing the nationalization plan indefinitely, but the state of uncertainty it generated continued.

From about 1957, the balance of payments was persistently in deficit (chapter 2). The import trade regime remained relatively liberal for the rest of the 1950s because the government could still fall back on previously accumulated reserves. Nonetheless, the late 1950s saw a growing tendency to use import duties as a protective device. Starting with the fiscal year 1957–8, steps were taken to protect selected local industry by increasing import duties on certain consumer goods and lowering duties on capital equipment and industrial raw material.

The external reserve position had become critical by the beginning of the 1960s (table 2.26). Prospects for exports seemed dim, and shifts in the terms of trade continued to be unfavorable. The government responded by imposing import duties and exchange controls. The 1960 budget sharply increased duties on cars, petrol, liquor, and tobacco. In the following year a 5 percent duty surcharge was imposed, and cars, watches, clocks, radios, and high-priced textiles were banned from import. Import controls were soon all-encompassing: "luxury" items were banned completely and, by the end of 1964, almost everything except essential foodstuffs, fuel, fertilizers, and drugs was subject to import licensing. The Foreign Exchange Budget Committee at the Ministry of Finance had become the supreme authority for allocating foreign exchange on the basis of national priorities. Since public corporations had been assigned monopolies in these areas, virtually all imports went into the hands of the state. In 1964 further foreign exchange controls were applied with a moratorium on repatriation of profits and dividends, and cuts were made in education abroad and on foreign travel. By 1965 the Sri Lankan economy was nearly closed off from the rest of the world (Kappagoda, 1967; Motha, 1971).

The response to this controlled regime was a vigorous expansion in private sector involvement in the manufacturing sector. To supplement the impetus given by import controls, government industrial policy also provided the nascent industrial sector with added support by introducing tax concessions, including a five-year tax holiday for approved projects and, in some cases, regulating import quotas and duties in line with the availability of supplies from these industries. In a context where industrialization was a byproduct of across-the-board import controls, industries invariably tended to concentrate on those very items which were controlled or banned as nonessential imports. Confectionery, air-conditioning assembly, cosmetics, and even motor vehicle assembly are example of activities incidentally fostered during this period.

Direct involvement of the public sector continued to increase in the first half of the 1960s. By 1965, 15 state industrial ventures were in operation and ten more were under construction. The new trend in this sphere was the emphasis on basic and heavy industries with potential for promoting linkages in the industrial structure (Lakshman, 1979). In January 1961 Parliament created the Ceylon Petroleum Corporation with the aim of nationalizing the import and distribution of petroleum products, a trade which had previously been dominated by British and American oil companies.

The initial seizures occurred in 1962, with the Corporation assuming control of 20 percent of the island's gas and oil outlets. On January 1, 1964, all remaining petroleum outlets were seized and the import of petroleum became a government monopoly.[3] In 1961 control of the banking system

---

[3] By nationalizing the oil trade, Sri Lanka became the first (and so far the only) country against which the Hickenlooper Amendment, requiring the suspension of American aid to any country expropriating American property without compensation, has ever been formally applied. This nationalization also had adverse repercussions on aid flows to Sri Lanka from other market-oriented countries as well as from international organizations, in particular the World Bank (Olson, 1977).

was consolidated through three important policy steps. First, the People's Bank was established with the specific aim of providing commercial banking facilities to the rural sector and the cooperative system of the country. Second, the Bank of Ceylon, the largest commercial bank on the island, was brought under complete government ownership. Third, the opening of new branches by foreign commercial banks and the opening of accounts with foreign banks by Sri Lanka citizens was prohibited.

A stylized story for the first period would run as follows. There is a plantation export sector which picks up the cost of an extensive food subsidy program, and the total import bill is dominated by imports of essential foodstuffs for this program. When export revenues fall, the government has tended to take the softest short-term option – cutting back on expenditures is difficult and so is devaluation, and so successive governments have opted for selective controls on imports as a balancing measure, controls which were not intended in the first instance as protective measures but which ended up encouraging and protecting particular industries and firms.

1965-1970: A Partial Departure from the Closed Economy

Although language and religion were again underlying issues, the island's economic difficulties, in particular the scarcity of day-to-day essentials to which the closed economy had subjected the people, were especially prominent in the victory of the UNP in March 1965. The new government headed by Dudley Senanayake was a coalition including the Federal Party, the principal party of the two that represent the Tamil community, and several of the key players from the previous government led by Mrs Bandaranaike. The regime can be classified as center right, but only just.

Gradual efforts to relax the previous government's controls followed. In the area of external economic relations, an early action of the new government was to enter into an agreement (in July 1965) with oil companies to pay compensation (Olson, 1977). A gradual relaxation of the moratorium (introduced in 1964) on profit and divided repatriation by foreign investors began in August 1965. In March 1966 a White Paper on the treatment of private foreign investment in Sri Lanka was issued. The White Paper assured relaxation of restrictions on foreign remittances as the balance-of-payments position improved and that no moratorium would apply to newly approved investment, provided that the capital was supplied by inward remittances of funds, delivery of goods, or debit to a moratorium account.

The first liberalization episode began at about this time. With a view to redressing the inherent anti-export bias in commercial policy, a Bonus

Voucher Scheme for certain nontraditional exports was introduced in December 1966 followed by a 20 percent devaluation of the rupee in November 1967. These steps were followed by the Foreign Exchange Entitlement Certificate (FEEC) scheme in May 1968, under which a significant proportion of imports (about 22 percent in value terms) were freed from quantitative restrictions. This liberalization episode is described and analyzed in detail in chapter 4.

It seems that the new government sought assistance from the World Bank, but perhaps because of Mr Senanayake's downfall over rice subsidies in 1953, he was not interested in apparent Bank preconditions for aid, namely reducing expenditure on food and welfare and devaluing the rupee. Nevertheless, foreign loans were to become extremely important over the next five years (Corea, 1971). In response to the market-oriented policy reforms of the new government, the major aid-giving nations of the West created the Aid Ceylon Club in 1965 to provide financial support for the implementation of these reforms.

Like previous UNP governments, the Dudley Senanayake government emphasized agriculture to produce food for the domestic market. With bleak prospects for export products and the newly established industrial sector under strain apparently because of foreign exchange shortage, the government envisaged import substitution in agriculture as the best possible way out of what it saw as a balance-of-payments crisis. Policy measures taken in this sphere included giving absolute priority to the food drive under the direct supervision of the prime minister, developing agricultural extension services (including subsidized fertilizer and agricultural credit), and steps to boost prices received by farmers. These last included drastically curtailing subsidiary food imports, increasing government guaranteed prices, and curtailing the subsidized rice ration to make agricultural production more profitable. These agriculture-oriented policies culminated in the proposal for the Mahaweli development program, which was a major element in the government platform for the 1965 election.

The government had a declared policy of not commencing any new public industrial enterprise. However, the industrial ventures that were under construction during the previous regime were commissioned, and attempts were made to rationalize the operation of existing ventures.

The approach to development planning during this period was sectoral, in contrast with the overall (aggregative) planning of the previous regime. The intention was that individual programs prepared for selected priority sectors would be combined into one-year programs and gradually extended into a coordinated national plan around a moving five-year period. The hope was that this rolling plan would be more adaptable to change and easier to keep on track with limited financial and human resources.

1970–1977: Back to a Closed Economy

At the general election of May 1970, the SLFP-led United Front (UF) scored a resounding success. Why the Senanayake government lost this election is not easily explained. Production of food, especially rice, had increased rapidly, while the economy had become relatively more open, with a 5 percent rate of economic growth. The climate should have been right for further efforts at opening up, yet with apparent material growth at hand the electorate opted for closing. This rejection has several possible explanations. Was it, as suggested by Myrdal (1968), because the benefits of growth had gone to only a few? Or was it because of the explosiveness of the rice issue? Was it simply because Sri Lankan people like to vote against the government of the day? Whatever the reason, the election results clearly illustrated "the fragility and sensitivity of developing economies to political forces" (Jiggins, 1976, p. 91).

The new government quickly undid the tentative liberalization started in 1968; all import items that had been placed under the Open General License (OGL) scheme were brought back under individual licensing, while only the dual exchange rate element in the FEEC scheme was retained. The import of certain minor agricultural foods items, such as chilies and Bombay onions, which might potentially be cultivated locally, was banned.

The government, in compliance with its election promise of "the establishment of a socialist society," acted to consolidate the dominance of the public sector in the economy. In April 1971, it promulgated the Business Undertaking Acquisition Bill which allowed the takeover of any business enterprise. By 1976, 26 industrial undertakings had been acquired under this Act. Several new industrial corporations were also established under the 1957 State Industrial Corporation Act; by 1976, 31 altogether were in operation. Under the State Trading Corporation Act of 1971, state trading corporations took over the import trade and domestic wholesale trade in all essential commodities. The expanded share of the state in export trade was intended to eliminate perceived foreign exchange abuses. By 1976, the state sector directly accounted for about 88 percent of the total import trade and for about 30 percent of the export trade (Lakshman and Athukorala, 1985). The government-run Paddy Marketing Board (PMB) was made the sole buyer of paddy from farmers. Direct government interventions apart, there were other controls on the operation of the private sector. For instance, there was a capital levy, a compulsory savings levy, and a ceiling of Rs 2,000 on personal expendable income (a most unusual measure indeed). All in all, from 1970 to 1977 the economy was riddled with controls and interventions.

The faith of Mrs Bandaranaike's government in macroplanning was attested to by a five-year plan issued in 1972. Its principal objective was to achieve an annual growth rate of 6 percent, to raise domestic savings from the current level of 12.5 percent of GNP to 17 percent, and to improve the living standards of some 40 percent of the population who earned incomes that barely averaged Rs 200 a month. To accomplish this, the private sector was expected to contribute approximately 52 percent of the total planned investment of Rs 15,000 million. The rationale for expecting this massive contribution in the context of a highly intervened economy was unstated (Fitter, 1973).

Alongside this policy of nationalization of industry the government showed some interest in promoting foreign investment. In 1972 a White Paper reiterated that "private foreign investment has an important role to play in the economic development of the country." According to the criteria laid down in the White Paper, approval of investment proposals in import substitution industries was to be highly selective, while proposals that had the "ability to export a greater part of output" were accorded preferential treatment. Another feature of the new policy was the interest shown in establishing export-oriented joint ventures with capital participation of state industrial corporations and foreign manufacturing firms. However, the unfavorable atmosphere for private sector activities generated by widespread nationalization attempts deterred foreign investment flows. In 1976, the finance minister proposed a Foreign Investment Authority Law aimed at overcoming this problem, but it was not enacted (Weeraratne, 1982). The five-year plan contained a proposal to set up an export-processing zone in Trincomalee to attract foreign capital to export-oriented industries such as shipbuilding, ship repair, and petrochemicals. However, internal opposition within the coalition prevented this proposal from being enacted.

Export promotion managed to stay on the policy agenda in the early 1970s. The dual exchange rate element of the former FEEC scheme was continued with periodic upward adjustments in the premium rate. In 1971, the import duty rebate scheme, which since its introduction in 1964 had been virtually inactive owing to rigid operational rules, was thoroughly reviewed. In the same year, a new import entitlement scheme – the Convertible Rupee Account Scheme – for nontraditional exports was introduced. There were also several fiscal incentives including an eight-year tax holiday on export profits of approved projects. Institutional measures to promote exports excluded the establishment of a multiministerial Export Promotion Council directly under the prime minister, a State Gem Corporation, and a Minor Export Crop Department. Yet despite these measures, the trade policy mix was, on balance, anti-export throughout (Pyatt and Roe, 1977, pp. 104–6).

The food drive initiated by the previous government continued under the new label "cultivation war." Despite election promises, the rice subsidy was not restored, significant upward adjustments in guaranteed prices of paddy and other subsidiary crops were announced from time to time, and, as previously mentioned, import of several subsidiary crops was banned. However, various restrictions on marketing these products (for instance, the PMB's monopoly on the purchase of paddy, and restrictions on the transport of paddy and rice from one district to another) and the distribution of agricultural inputs largely offset the impact of these price incentives.

The government continued to borrow from overseas, having inherited a significant short-term debt which was due for repayment in the early 1970s. Early on it had contracted a large long-term loan from China. Significant borrowing from the International Monetary Fund (IMF), which had declined at first, resumed as oil prices increased in 1973–4.

1977: Opening Up Again

At the general election of July 1977 the UNP, led by Mr J. R. Jayawardene, scored an unprecedented and sweeping victory on a platform of opening up the economy and revitalizing the private sector. Among other things its election manifesto stated the following:

> The political philosophy and the economic and social objectives of the UNP visualize that bureaucratic controls will be replaced with monetary and economic levers. . . . When the economy is opened and unlimited opportunities for growth are made available to all, then the preconditions will be laid for full employment. Without so opening the economy there is no way out for Sri Lanka from its permanent state of siege. (UNP, 1977, *Election Manifesto*, quoted by Wickramasinghe, 1981, p. 47)

On looking at the reasons why the electorate so roundly rejected the previous government, one explanation is that it had failed to deliver in terms of material progress. Perhaps, as in 1965, the electorate had grown tired of the shortages and queues, and of the consequences of being locked into a small domestic market. The aid package linked to the liberalization proposals may also have helped to separate the contestants in the minds of the electorate. Again, rice was an issue: in 1974, rice output had fallen significantly as a result of five bad harvests in a row, while world rice prices were up; rice imports were some 6 percent of the value of GDP at one stage. Finally, the government had maintained power with extended emergency rule and with repeated attempts to muzzle the press, none of which provided a good platform for going to the people.

In November 1977, only a few months after its election, the new UNP government announced a sweeping set of liberalization measures. Most quantitative restrictions were replaced by tariffs – for the most part involving both a change of instrument and a lowering of nominal protection. The exchange rate was floated against an initial unified and substantially devalued rate. Food subsidies were much reduced and were linked to income via a food stamp scheme. The government also announced its plans for several other measures. Foreign investment was to be encouraged, there was to be special assistance for exports, and some government-owned industry and services were to be privatized.

Three large public investment projects were begun. These were the Mahaweli program, and urban development and public housing projects. These projects were largely aid sponsored but were eventually to make large demands on government and private resources.

The promising start to removing the biases in trade incentives soon lost momentum. Instead of further rounds of across-the-board reductions in duties, the government made mainly *ad hoc* changes to import duties on the basis of appeals from local manufacturers. Such across-the-board changes as there were came from Ministry of Finance pressures to meet the revenue demands of the government's ambitious public investment program. Export promotion policy was selective in that the export activities that were encouraged reflected administrative sponsorship by the Export Development Board (EDB) rather than response to an increasingly neutral price regime. The export promotion policies came to include the establishment of free-trade zones which were mainly confined to setting up garment manufacturers for the quota-protected US market.

The Sri Lankan experience with liberalization ran into difficulties on several fronts (chapter 5). Terms-of-trade movements were not helpful although tea prices were good in 1978 and again in 1984. The first round of reforms was not followed up, and indeed was undone in many ways. Macromanagement, particularly ambitious public investment programs, had implications for the real exchange rate and therefore for the gains from liberalization (Lal and Rajapatirana, 1985). Finally, the simmering political tensions between the minority Tamil people and the Sinhalese erupted in extensive civil violence in July 1983. This violence escalated into a small guerrilla war in subsequent years as government-backed armed forces fought to control armed civilian guerrillas whose objective is secession for the north of the island. Coping with this violence has been a prime preoccupation of the government. Many people have sought to leave the country, private foreign investment has dwindled and so has tourism which until 1983 had been an increasingly important source of income for Sri Lanka.

Table 3.2 Summary of the liberalization episodes

Characteristic	1968 episode	1977 episode
Broad nature	FEECs, OGL devaluation	Licensing to tariff almost completely; devaluation, liberalization of foreign investment workers, banking services, free-trade zone
Size, duration	Small, short	Large, long
Stages and targets	Intent to broaden OGL list	No
Economic circumstances before		
Balance of payments, continuing deficits	Yes	Yes
Prices of major exports	Falling	Recovering
Rate of inflation	Low (2%)	High (20%)
Rate of growth	Low (3%)	Low
Almost closed economy	Yes	Yes
Shocks	No	No
Agricultural output	Poor	Recovering
Political circumstances		
Strong stable government	Coalition government/strong opposition	Huge majority
Ideological shift	Yes	Yes – very large
Public perception and debate	Seems not much	Not much before, some after
Administering arm of government	Mainly Central Bank	Ministry of Finance plus trade
International influence	Unclear – possibly large	Unclear – possibly very large
Accompanying policies		
Exchange rate	Dual managed–controlled, large black market	Unified – crawling peg, small black market
Export promotion	Mainly FEECs, soon undermined by export taxes	Typical set of measures: EDB; revised duty rebate; export finance; special tax treatment

Export taxes	Increased	At first very high profile; reduced at first
Monetary policy	Contraction from previous years	Dismantling of controls
Fiscal policy	Continuing deficits	Cutback on consumer subsidies but continuing deficits; housing schemes; Mahaweli scheme
Capital movement	Relaxed slightly	Relaxed substantially
Implementation		
Stages; departures	Small; did not continue; reversed within two years	Large first step: slow thereafter but little reversal
Economic performance		
Employment	Hard to say; limited data; short time	Up; helped by migration, migrant workers, etc.
Inflation	Up quickly from 2% to 5%	Fell from 18% to 8%; then increased to 20% or so
Growth	Jumped to 8%	Again jumped to 8% for 1979–80, falling slightly to 4% in 1983; mainly service sector growth
Imports and exports	Deficit widened	Deficits widened; no large trends in export diversification
Wages	Unclear	Real wages falling

A Liberalization Index

The story of the swings in Sri Lanka's commercial policy since Independence begins with a relatively open economy which persisted for some ten
years. Initial closing up was associated with dwindling foreign reserves,
falling output of main export crops, and an ambitious food subsidy
program with a large import content. Punitive taxes on the main export
commodities and impediments to management of their production gave
rise to a long series of low export years, which in turn saw a relentless
tightening of the import noose. Respites were small and short lived until
1977, when the big break came. An index describing these events is
presented in figure 3.1. It is a subjective compression of these events.
Table 3.2 summarizes the nature, circumstances, and outcomes of the two
episodes identified in Sri Lanka, and the chronology of events is summarized in table 3.3.

A substantial part of this case study is about the circumstances and
methods of opening the economy to foreign trade. A mirror set of
questions and issues concerns the circumstances and reasons for closing up.
The 1953–65 period can be linked to the personalities of the alternative
party leaders, attempts to raise the price of the subsidized rice ration, and
the single-language policy. Moreover, under the center-right government's
eight years of rule in which the economy had not exactly boomed, an
alternative government which promised industrialization, planning, and

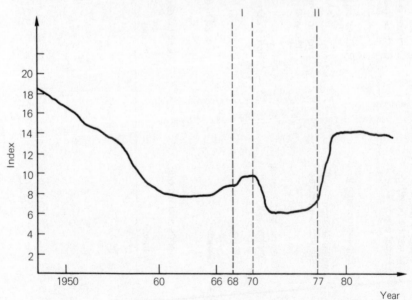

Figure 3.1 Liberalization index: Sri Lanka

Table 3.3 Chronological summary table: Sri Lanka

Date	Policy change
January 1961	Quantitative restriction through licensing on luxury imports
May 1963	Foreign Exchange Budget Committee established
December 1964	Import Duty Rebate Scheme introduced
December 1966	Bonus Voucher Scheme
November 1967	Devaluation of 20%
May 1968	FEECs OGL
August 1969	Export taxes on minor agricultural products
May 1970	Licensing of imports
December 1970	Convertible Rupee Account Scheme for exports
July 1971	Import Duty Rebate Scheme revised
November 1977	Abolition of FEEC scheme
	Devaluation and unified exchange rate
	Removal of most licensing
	Raised tariffs
	Raised export taxes
	Restrictions on movements of capital relaxed
	Embarked on three lead projects
June 1978	Opening of first free-trade zone
October 1980	10% surcharge on highly dutied imports for Export Development Fund
July 1981	Widespread small increases in duty for revenue reasons
September 1981	Turnover tax applied to imports
February 1983	Widespread across-the-board duty increases
December 1984	Widespread revisions in tariff with upward and downward movements designed to set effective protection within a narrower band

state capitalism presumably had some attractions. The second closing-up period is more of a mystery. In this case the economy was performing well, rice was not an issue, and it seems that Mr Senanayake was a popular and respected prime minister. Yet just when all should have been right for more growth and more liberalization, the electorate opted for a party which had controls and state management as explicit policies.

4

The 1968–1970 Episode

Beginnings

Nature and Targets

The early 1960s saw the end of the open-economy phase of Sri Lanka's development. By 1965, the economy was tightly controlled, practically closed to imports, and operating with a highly overvalued rupee and a significant black market in foreign exchange. Against this background the FEEC scheme – a multiple exchange rate cum partial import liberalization policy package – was introduced in May 1968.

Under the FEEC scheme external transactions were divided into two categories. On the export side, category A included earnings from the major (traditional) exports – tea, rubber, and major coconut products – and certain service transactions such as expenditure in Sri Lanka by foreign embassies and official capital receipts. Category A imports included the Food Commissioner's imports of rice, flour, sugar, and certain other essential consumer items (drugs, fertilizers, petroleum); imports of government departments and certain government nonindustrial corporations; and imports necessary for cottage industries, cooperatives, and other small-scale producers. Transactions relating to all other exports (nontraditional exports)[1] and imports were included under category B.

Transactions in category A took place at the official (par value) rate of exchange through the official market, and those in category B were channeled through a newly created certificate market at a premium rate. The intention was that the premium rate (FEEC rate), set initially at 44 percent, would be adjusted weekly by the Central Bank in line with the developments in the certificate market. Exporters of all goods and services in category B were entitled to receive these certificates with a face value in

---

[1] In Sri Lanka all exports other than tea, rubber, and coconut are referred to as "nontraditional." Some of these (for instance, gems and spices) go back a long way in Sri Lanka's history and in that sense are traditional.

Sri Lankan rupees equal to the free on board (f.o.b.) value of exports upon surrender to an authorized bank of the foreign exchange actually earned. Similarly, applicants for foreign exchange for payments in this group were also required to surrender certificates with a par value equal to the exchange applied for. Exporters could use their certificates to buy foreign exchange to pay for imports. Certificates were freely transferable within 30 days from the date of issue to exporters and could also be surrendered to monetary authorities for encashment at the premium inclusive rate.[2] Additional certificates were sold by the Central Bank to importers through tenders. Such certificates were not transferable, but they remained valid for seven months.

The scheme provided for substantial import liberalization. Of category B imports, a few items such as spare parts (except for motor vehicles), certain dairy products, and so on were kept under the former system of import licensing and quotas, but all other items – over a thousand items falling into intermediate and investments goods categories – were placed under OGL. In 1969, the first full year of operation of the scheme, these items accounted for about 15 percent of the total import bill in value terms (Hewavitharana, 1975, p. 9). The plan was to expand the list gradually as the balance-of-payments position improved.

A new tariff structure was introduced as part of the scheme, and all imports of food items, chemicals, essential consumer goods, industrial machinery, and raw materials were allowed in duty free. A preferential rate of 10 percent and a general rate of 20 percent were imposed on nonessential items. Penal rates ranging from 50 to 300 percent were imposed on semiluxury and luxury goods.

The changes were somewhat technical – in contrast with a more direct reduction of import barriers such as, for instance, a lowering of tariffs, they were selective and hard to follow. As reported earlier, the government had set up a Ministry of Planning and Economic Affairs under the prime minister. It acquired the control of the foreign exchange budget and the government capital budget. However, it seems that the implementation of policy took place at the Ministry of Planning and Plan Implementation and the Ministry of Industries, again in contrast with 1977 when the Ministry of Finance was the prime mover.

As a point of perspective, recall that these policy changes in 1968 have been classed as a liberalization episode because they followed on what had been largely a closed economy. However, the structure of incentives to industry remained very discriminatory and was subject to much administrative control. Traditional exports continued to be taxed and import

---

[2] The certificates were not transferable thereafter, but holders could use them when making foreign exchange payments within seven months of the date of issue. Exporters of precious stones received, in addition to certificates, licenses to import raw materials (other than gold) for the jewelry industry corresponding to 25 percent of their export receipts.

licensing and quotas continued to apply to those imports which were imported at official (non-FEEC) rates of exchange – rice, flour, petroleum, drugs, fertilizers, and cottage industry inputs (textiles and yarns).

Policymakers were pessimistic about market prospects for traditional exports and the chances of diversifying exports into more product lines. Import substitution continued to be a basic tenet of development strategy. The following quotation from a paper on policy orientation during this period by Gamani Corea, then the head of the Ministry of Planning and Economic Affairs, exemplifies the general policy stance:

> increasing of export earnings was particularly difficult since these earnings were not entirely the outcome of Ceylon's own efforts. In the case of tea, for example, an increase in production might even aggravate the problem by further dampening world prices. In the case of other items, both traditional and new, earnings could be increased by production, but this takes time calling as it does for the establishment of new capacity. Such an objective must necessarily loom large in any development programme for Ceylon but it does not constitute an overnight solution to the payments problem. . . . The main opportunity for relatively short term gains lay in import substitution. (Corea, 1971, p. 31)

In this context, import liberalization seems to have been perceived largely as an aid to import substitution by way of ensuring the availability of imported inputs and machinery for domestic industry and agriculture, thus overcoming the rigidities and delays which were associated with individual licensing of imports.

Initial Economic Circumstances

As Corea (1971) put it, "the handling of the foreign exchange situation was the major preoccupation of economic policy" from about the early 1960s. During 1956–60 Sri Lanka's export earnings in US dollar terms increased at an average annual rate of only 0.4 percent, and during 1960–5 actually fell by 1 percent per annum. Despite drastic import curtailments since 1962, the balance of payments continued in the red; the trade deficit between 1960 and 1965 was about 7 percent of average annual export earnings. Foreign reserves varied between one and two months' "import equivalent" during these five years, and because of animosities generated by nationalization of foreign-owned companies the relative contribution of foreign finance to Sri Lanka's import capacity remained insignificant. In the early 1960s external capital flows financed 22 percent of total imports of Asian countries, but for Sri Lanka the corresponding proportion averaged little more than 4 percent (Corea, 1971). A major reason for this was the leftward drift of Mrs Bandaranaike's government and, in particular, the dispute over the expropriation of oil companies (Olson, 1977, p. 211). The import restrictions from 1962 virtually eliminated imports of what were defined as luxuries and nonessential consumer goods, and the scope for local production in this field had been well exploited. The inevitable outcome of continual export stagnation was therefore the curtailment of raw material and machinery imports, with adverse repercussions on existing production levels. In 1964, the Central Bank reported that

> Ceylon encountered shortages of supplies in respect of various categories of goods. Foreign exchange difficulties have begun to limit Ceylon's ability to meet her full requirements of raw materials, machinery and spares, not only for accelerating development, but also for the full utilization of existing capacity. (CBC, *Annual Report*, 1969, p. 15).

The first policy document of the Senanayake government, "The Development Programme – 1966–67," commenting on the economic legacy it inherited from the previous regime, noted

> Foreign exchange shortages over a period of years had resulted in a severely depleted level of supplies throughout the country. Agriculture, industry and transportation were hampered by a deterioration of capital stock. (Ministry of Planning and Economic Affairs, 1967, p. 2)

A widening budget deficit has been a feature of Sri Lanka's fiscal operation since the mid-1950s. Government revenue increased only marginally as there were hardly any changes in the tax structure, while expenditure increased rapidly mainly because of the commitments to food subsidies and other social welfare services. Over the period 1960–5 about 28 percent of government expenditure was met through deficit financing, compared with 17 percent during 1955–60. Most of this budget deficit was financed by domestic expansionary borrowing.

Inflation was low during the 1950s – below 1 percent. The reason for this remarkable price stability in the face of unabated monetary expansion seems to be the liberal import policy. The additional demand from the monetary expansion was satisfied by increased supply of imported goods. With the stringent import controls of the early 1960s, the continuing monetary expansion began to have inflationary effects of around 2 percent.

Estimates of unemployment at the time come from several sources and vary widely. Jones and Selvaratnam (1971) tentatively estimate employment increases at 2.6 percent per year in the period 1963–8 and at 1.3 percent per year for the period 1953–68. An ILO survey of 1959–60 gives a low estimate of 10.5 percent and a high estimate of 12.8 percent unemployment for that year. A 1968 labor force survey, considered by Jones and Selvaratnam to be comparable with the ILO work, estimates unemployment to be 11.0 percent. A rural employment survey of 1964 also shows unemployment at 12.5 percent – although this may not be a comparable estimate. Although the estimates are not strictly comparable, by the time of the first liberalization episode it would seem that between 10 and 13 percent of the total labor force in Sri Lanka was unemployed.

Political Circumstances

Was the political structure stable? The Senanayake government did not have a majority and governed with the aid of the Federal Party, whose policy was a Federal Constitution guaranteeing Tamils freedom to manage their own affairs. The coalition was difficult, with Sinhalese interests somewhat suspicious of the separatist demands of the Sri Lankan Tamils.

The UNP had campaigned to undo such measures as nationalization, printing of textbooks by the government, the Sinhala-only Act, takeovers of denominational schools, and Chinese aid; however, it failed to bite the bullet on most of these issues, thereby apparently disenchanting supporters without attracting any new adherents. Reports of the events of that time suggest a government juggling a number of social and economic pressures with little direction and purpose. There is little evidence that its policies toward liberalization were widely regarded as likely to be implemented. Also, the chances are that the electorate simply did not understand what the FEEC scheme entailed.

Nonetheless, there had been an ideological shift in 1965; the Senanayake government was a center-right group whose rhetoric, at least, advocated market solutions with little intervention. The rhetoric was a marked shift from that of the two preceding Bandaranaike governments. While the new government once in power apparently found it difficult to introduce many of the policies it had advocated while in opposition, the ones it did apply – such as the liberalization effort – were consistent with its ideological position.

In March 1968 the SLFP and its Marxist allies, the Lanka Sama Samaja Party (LSSP) and the Communist Party (CP), formed a Samagi Peramuna (UF). The Twenty-Five Point Program of Work on which the alliance was forged suggested a decision by the SLFP to move to the left (Wilson, 1979). This program contained promises such as the nationalization of foreign and local private commercial banks and foreign trade in essential commodities, land reform, and the renegotiation of the terms imposed by the World Bank for the Mahaweli Diversion Project[3] so as, among other things, to

---

[3] The Mahaweli Diversion Project was a river basin development scheme to provide irrigation and power. The area envisaged for irrigation was large, involving about two thirds of the cultivable land in the North Central Province, the heartland of the ancient irrigation civilization of Sri Lanka. Detailed plans were prepared in 1966 for this scheme on the basis of a 30-year program of development and construction. Work started in 1968 and continued on this 30-year completion basis under Mrs Bandaranaike's government. The UNP government in 1977 was to adopt the so-called accelerated Mahaweli program with the intention of competing the project in seven years.

have the raised water tax lowered and to provide employment for 750,000 people without jobs, including 15,000 graduates. This strengthening of the UF was undoubtedly a major constraint for the Senanayake government in implementing its market-oriented election promises, in particular privatization of public corporations and curtailment of consumer subsidies.

Commercial policy does not seem to have been of major importance as a public issue. Unlike the events in 1977, there was little immediate action from the government on assuming power; further, the government was to serve only one term before there was a return to a party with a track record of closing the economy (although it is true that the 1965 Senanayake government was the first to run its full term). In much the same way, and again in contrast with 1977, the changes lacked public attention. The balance of discussion between Parliament and the bureaucracy probably lay in the bureaucracy.

The presence of international organizations was significant, although Mr Senanayake was cautious in accepting World Bank and IMF policy advocacy.[4] The following quotation from a 1985 speech by Gamani Corea to the 1985 Annual Session of the Sri Lanka Association of Economists indicates a close and cooperative relationship between the government and the two agencies:

> At that time [1968] too we embarked upon an exercise in liberalization – not total but partial . . . We did this after negotiation with the IMF and although, I can say, that the Fund was never happy with the concept of a dual exchange rate, it agreed to our decision, with its officials saying to themselves that it was, after all, 'a wrong step in the right direction'! (Sri Lanka Association of Economists, 1986, p. 11)

Foreign aid was a much more likely option for the Senanayake government, which was at least market oriented, than it had been for Mrs Bandaranaike. Indeed, aid did become a cornerstone of economic policy and action. A sharp upturn in aid flows to Sri Lanka took place after the UNP won the 1965 election and compensated the oil companies. In 1965 the major aid-giving Western countries formed an Aid Ceylon Club (under the chairmanship of the World Bank)[5] to support the new government's market-oriented policy reforms. From 1965 to 1970 five meetings of the club were held and a total of Rs 1568.2 million of commodity and project aid was pledged. During the same period Sri Lanka obtained a total credit of Rs 723.4 million from the IMF.

The opposition argued that dependence on foreign aid led to a tailoring of internal policies to suit the prescriptions of the World Bank, the IMF,

---

[4] Recall that in 1953, as Minister of Finance, he had sought to remove the rice ration on World Bank advice and had seen his government lose power in 1955.
[5] In 1964 the World Bank deemed Sri Lanka "no longer creditworthy" and from then until 1965 was not involved in providing financial support to Sri Lanka (Mason and Asher, 1973).

and the donor countries. Some economic commentators saw this as nonsense: "an emotive disapproval of institutions which the Left saw as elements in the imperialist and capitalist network" (Marga Institute, 1974). In these commentators' views, although the international agencies diagnosed the problems of the economy and prescribed remedies, both diagnosis and remedy were rather obvious and were recognized by Sri Lanka's own advisers and economists as desirable and necessary. By this interpretation the aid enabled the government to take steps which may have been otherwise difficult politically, but the measures taken, rather than being preconditions of aid, represented the best possible use of that aid as judged by the Sri Lanka government. It is interesting that Wilson (1979) contends that conditions included in the original and 1968 agreement for the Mahaweli scheme (a water tax plus some conditionality about the construction program) were a central issue in the 1970 elections to the eventual electoral disadvantage of the UNP. One of Mrs Bandaranaike's election campaign promises was renegotiation of these Mahaweli loan conditions with the World Bank. Wilson's interpretation is that Mrs Bandaranaike had little success in these subsequent negotiations.

Accompanying Policies

Exchange Rate Policy

When Sri Lanka joined the IMF in 1952, the initial par value of the rupee was established at the rate of Rs 4.7619 per US dollar (Rs 13.3 = 1). Despite a widening deficit in the balance of payments starting in the mid-1950s, this par value was maintained until 1967.

Following the devaluation of the pound sterling by 14.3 percent, the rupee was devalued against that currency by 20 percent on November 22, 1967. Compared with mounting domestic demand pressure on imports generated by an expansionary budgetary policy and the size of the balance-of-payments disequilibrium which had developed over the past decade, this 5.7 percent net devaluation (that is, allowing for the sterling devaluation) was not enough to bring domestic prices into line with the scarcity value of foreign exchange.

When the government decided to liberalize imports in 1968, further devaluation of the rupee was essential. Perhaps because of a presumption of structural rigidities in demand for and supply of the dominant traditional exports, or perhaps because of anticipated unfavorable sociopolitical repercussions of an overall increase in import prices, authorities at that time did not seem to favor an overall devaluation (Rasaputrum, 1973). The operation of a Bonus Voucher Scheme introduced in 1966 had convinced policymakers that selective incentives would be more effective; therefore they chose the FEEC scheme which was, in effect, a dual exchange rate system.

In the original FEEC proposal the premium rate on transactions relating to category A imports and exports was meant to be a floating rate. The Central Bank was to adjust the premium, taking into account variations in the demand for and supply of certificates, when selling certificates to importers under a weekly tender system. The hope was that this method of exchange rate determination would ensure a more realistic external value for the rupee.

Export Promotion Policy

Up to the mid-1960s, attempts to increase export earnings had been confined to the traditional export sector. A subsidy scheme aimed at replanting the existing rubber acreage with new improved varieties was introduced in 1953. The Tea Rehabilitation Scheme for smallholders and the Tea Replanting Subsidy Scheme for the plantation sector were inaugurated in 1958. Steps toward providing production subsidies for the coconut industry were taken under the Coconut Rehabilitation Scheme introduced in 1956. Besides these direct production incentives, interest was shown in improving cultivation practices through the operation of tea, rubber, and coconut research institutes. These supply-side measures had little impact in a context of falling profitability of plantation production –a result of increases in export tax rates (since the late 1950s) juxtaposed with declining world market prices.

Since the late 1960s, policy has gradually shifted toward the promotion of nontraditional exports. Import substitution attempts, pursued since the late 1950s, had reached a crisis point by this time, mainly because of the shortages of imported raw materials and other inputs. Policymakers appeared to think that the world-market prospects for tea and rubber were poor, and they wanted to restructure the export sector so as to lessen the dependence on these traditional products.

In December 1966, following the examples of Pakistan and Indonesia, a Bonus Voucher Scheme was introduced. Under this scheme, exporters of all manufactured goods with a local content of 25 percent or more of the f.o.b. value and exporters of some specified minor primary products were granted transferable vouchers equal to 20 percent of their export earnings. The vouchers entitled the holder to import licenses of the same face value for the import of any trade quota items, industrial raw materials, and essential spare parts. Licenses were transferable to other parties in an open market. According to estimates by the Ceylon Chamber of Commerce, in 1967 the total foreign exchange earnings of eligible exports and the value of licenses issued were Rs 5.1 million (3.2 percent of total domestic exports) and Rs 0.8 million respectively. In the open market some vouchers fetched prices as much as 33 percent higher than their face value.

With the liberalization of May 1968, it seems that policymakers thought that the FEEC premium itself would be a powerful enough incentive for new exporters, and so no specific promotion scheme was included in the policy package. An exception was the active interest shown in promoting tourism. Steps were taken to set up an organizational framework for expanding the tourist industry. In May 1966 the Ceylon Tourist Board and the Ceylon Hotel Corporation were formed. The Tourist Development Act was enacted in 1968 to provide for the establishment of national holiday resorts, protection of highways and places of scenic beauty, and the promotion of hotel development projects.

The FEEC scheme left the bias against traditional exports (tea, rubber, coconut) intact and instead was pitched at raising incentives for nontraditional agricultural crops – spices, oil, and so on – and manufactured goods for export. The apparent target on this front was export expansion for these nontraditional crops and manufactured goods that were mainly processed agricultural goods – coconut, including fiber products, and rubber goods. Thus continued the paradox found in much of Sri Lanka's so-called export promotion – that significant export incentives are applied to small export items and very large export taxes are applied to the large traditional export earners, apparently with little thought about the long-run elasticities of export demand.

Table 4.1 shows estimates of nominal and effective protection for 1970. It is based on tariffs and export taxes. While controls on private sector imports had tightened by 1970 owing to steady increases in government imports and falling terms of trade, the table points to a few important aspects of the incentive environment. It illustrates the export taxes on tea, rubber, coconut, oils, and fats of between 20 and 35 percent (column 1). The positive effect of FEECs of between 5 and 40 percent on other agriculture, mining and quarrying, coconut fiber, and services is also shown. There are a number of items for which the assistance effects are large. Despite the FEEC scheme, biases against exports apparently remained for many nontraditional products. According to the table (columns 4 and 5), there was a bias against exporting for 14 of the 28 sectors which had recorded exports, despite the 55 percent FEEC subsidy. Biases against exporting, or only a small bias in favor, can be seen in several sectors where a country of Sri Lanka's level of development might have some hope of achieving success, such as textile, rubber products, ceramics, and "other" (miscellaneous) manufacturing.

Capital Movement Policy

From Independence to the early 1960s, Sri Lanka maintained a fairly liberal stance on capital outflows. Capital transfers due to persons residing

Table 4.1 Estimates of nominal and effective protection and the bias against exporting: 1970 (coefficients)

	1	2	3	4	5
Industry	Nominal protection	Effective protection[a]	Net effective protection[b]	Bias against exporting[c]	Export earnings (million Rs)
1 Tea	− 0.23	− 0.31	− 0.40	+ 0.31	1036
2 Rubber	− 0.21	− 0.21	− 0.31	+ 0.06	411
3 Coconuts	− 0.35	− 0.04	− 0.16	+ 0.54	3
4 Paddy	0	− 0.01	0	−	−
5 Livestock	0.09	0.02	− 0.11	− 0.34	−
6 Fishing	0	− 0.01	− 0.01	−	−
7 Logging and firewood	0	− 0.01	0.01	−	−
8 Other agriculture	0.14	0.15	0	− 0.29	66
9 Mining and quarrying	0.10	0.09	− 0.05	+ 0.31	12
10 Milling	0.02	0.01	− 0.12	− 0.92	2
11 Dairy products	0.24	2.57	2.03	− 0.69	−
12 Bread	0	− 0.25	0.05	−	−
13 Other bakery products	0	− 0.32	− 0.41	− 0.59	1
14 Carbonated beverages	0	− 0.06	0.01	. −	−
15 Desiccated coconut	− 0.13	− 0.94	− 0.95	*	109
16 Other processing food	0.24	− 0.50	− 0.72	− 0.57	4
17 Distilling	2.91	7.57	6.37	*	1
18 Tobacco	1.00	1.93	1.55	+ 0.50	1
19 Textiles	0.51	1.07	0.80	− 0.06	6
20 Wood products	0.68	0.95	0.80	+ 0.20	−
21 Paper	0.43	0.34	0.16	− 0.14	−
22 Leather	0.45	0.85	0.61	− 0.18	4
23 Rubber	0.88	2.23	14.81	+ 0.64	1
24 Chemicals	0.27	0.02	− 0.11	− 0.35	7
25 Oils and fats	0.41	*	*	*	101
26 Coconut fiber and yarn	0.44	0.21	0.05	− 0.53	33
27 Petroleum and coal	0.74	1.40	1.12	+ 0.60	34
28 Structural clay products	0.54	0.64	0.43	− 0.01	−
29 Ceramics	0.87	1.27	0.98	+ 0.45	−
30 Cement	0.67	0.96	0.80	+ 0.33	−
31 Basic metals	0.56	0.43	0.24	+ 0.02	−
32 Light engineering	0.72	1.08	0.81	+ 0.32	1
33 Transport equipment	0.89	*	*	*	−
34 Machinery, other equipment	0.83	1.64	4.79	+ 0.59	−
35 Other manufacturing	0.85	2.39	3.00	+ 0.49	1
36 Construction	0	− 0.20	− 0.15	−	−
37 Electricity	0	− 0.04	− 0.02	−	−
38 Road passenger transport	0	− 0.18	− 0.14	−	−
39 Rail transport	0	− 0.01	− 0.05	−	1
40 Trade and other transport	0.20	0.15	0	− 0.25	190
41 Services	0.11	0.05	− 0.06	− 0.35	223

−, negligible; *, estimates are not possible owing to data deficiency.

[a] Cordon definition, that is, the ratio of value added under the existing tariff structure to that in the absence of tariff.

[b] Effective protection coefficients adjusted for exchange rate overvaluation. An overvaluation of 15 percent of the official value of the rupee has been assumed. For details on the methodology see Pyatt and Roe (1977, p. 105).

[c] Domestic value added in production for domestic market over that obtainable in exporting.

Source: Pyatt and Roe, 1977

in other parts of the Sterling Area were freely authorized. Most capital payments due to persons outside the Sterling Area were also allowed if they were related to investment in approved securities. The proceeds of investment in approved projects could be repatriated, along with capital appreciation, upon sale or liquidation. The proceeds from the sale or liquidation of investments not approved by the government did not receive approval for repatriation, but they could be invested in securities in Sri Lanka and the current income from them was eligible for repatriation.

With the rapid worsening of the balance-of-payments position, the policy turned out to be increasingly restrictive, culminating in 1962 in the imposition of a moratorium on foreign remittances. Under this decision, nonresident firms and persons were no longer permitted to remit abroad investment income or the proceeds of the sales of their movable or immovable property in Sri Lanka.

In the three years preceding the 1968 liberalization attempt, restrictions gradually began to be removed. In August 1965 remittances equivalent to Rs 2 million, corresponding to about 10 percent of profits and dividends accumulated up to June of that year, were authorized. In March 1966 a policy statement on the treatment of private foreign investment in Sri Lanka assured that the restrictions on foreign remittances would be relaxed as the balance-of-payments position improved, and that the moratorium would not apply to new approved investment provided that the capital was supplied by inward remittances of funds, delivery of goods, or debit to a moratorium account. By 1970 all the profits and dividends belong to foreign parties accumulated during the period of moratorium had been repatriated.

Monetary and Fiscal Policy

With the introduction of the import liberalization measures in May 1968, the Central Bank immediately raised the bank rate from 5 to 5.5 percent, apparently expecting a sharp increase in demand for credit with the liberalization of imports. At the same time the bank fixed ceilings on commercial bank lending to limit the increase in specified forms of commercial bank advances. These limits applied to loans, overdrafts, import bills and local bills, agricultural loans, advances to government corporations, and loans under the tea factory modernization project.

The lending and deposit rates of commercial banks responded to the bank rate increase. Rates on fixed deposits rose from 3.25 percent in 1968 to 3.5 percent in 1969, and on savings deposits the increase was from 4.5 to 5.5 percent. The maximum rates for most categories of loans moved up from about 9–9.5 to 10–11 percent. The annual increase in total credit to the private sector also tended to be lower in 1968–70 (Karunatilake, 1974). Nonetheless, the Central Bank was unable to maintain monetary stability because of expansionary financing of government expenditure. Commenting on these developments, the bank noted:

> it is pertinent to add that the reversal of the trend of monetary expansion, which has been persistent over a decade, cannot be achieved in the short period of a year. It must however be mentioned that policies adopted towards this end met with obstacles in the field of fiscal management and foreign exchange budgeting. (CBC, *Annual Report*, 1969, p. 17)

While the need for fiscal and monetary discipline was formally recognized by policymakers, no significant move was made and the budget deficit continued to expand at an increasing rate.

Implementation

While the intention had been for the premium exchange rate applicable to category B transactions to be adjusted weekly by the Central Bank in line with variations in demand for and supply of FEECs, this only happened for about a month (Tilakaratne, 1970, pp. 15–32). In June 1968 the weekly tender system operated by the Central Bank was stopped. Henceforth FEECs were sold by commercial banks on demand to bona fide users at a premium determined by the Central Bank from time to time. Thus the premium rate came to be fixed at 44 percent until June 1969 when it was adjusted to a new fixed rate of 55 percent.

The introduction of the FEEC scheme was followed shortly afterward by revisions in export duties. These revisions led to a significant reduction in the envisaged incentives of the scheme for nontraditional agricultural exports. In August 1969 cinnamon, citronella oil, graphite, cocoa, cardamom, and coir fiber, which up to then had remained either free of export duty or subject to nominal specific duties, were brought under *ad valorem* export duties ranging from 10 to 40 percent of the f.o.b. value. These duties would have absorbed a significant portion of the benefit of the premium rate to exporters because of Sri Lanka's insignificant world-market position in these commodities, perhaps with the exception of cinnamon.

In 1968 the imports under category A amounted to about 77 percent of total imports in terms of value, with the balance under category B. Of the category B items, imports which were allowed under OGLs amounted to only 12 percent of total imports. In 1969 the category A imports had fallen to 68 percent of total imports, and the imports under OGL had increased to about 14.6 percent of total imports (Dahanayake, 1977, p. 128).

The policymakers who formulated the FEEC scheme expected to bring a larger proportion of imports gradually under the OGL system. However, the continuous deterioration in the balance of payments stopped this happening. In April 1970, on the eve of the general election, the OGL system was temporarily suspended to avoid balance-of-payments pressure due to speculative import demand. The newly elected SLFP coalition completely abolished the OGL system – bringing all imports under individual licensing – in May 1970, retaining only the dual exchange rate element in the FEEC scheme. Thus the first Sri Lankan liberalization episode was aborted two years after its initiation.

Economic Performance

Major Prices

In the three years of the 1968–70 episode inflation was higher than in the immediate pre-liberalization period (table 4.2, item 2(a)). Two supplementary elements of the policy package – upward adjustment of wages in December 1967 to cushion wage earners against the impact of devaluation, and increased turnover taxes on certain manufactured goods in August 1969 – exerted some pressure on prices (CBC, *Annual Report*, 1986, p. 238).

A three-year period is too short for analysis of the impact of trade liberalization on the rate of inflation. However, quarterly figures of the CCPI (CBC, *Annual report*, 1970, table 54) show that the sudden increase in prices recorded in the first two to four quarters following the liberalization tended to slow down gradually thereafter. This accords with the view that the impact of trade policy reform on price levels is mostly a one-time phenomenon (Krueger, 1978).

There was no noticeable change in the pattern of real effective exchange rates (REERs) for traditional exports (table 4.2, item 2(c)) compared with preceding years. This is to be expected since the trade policy measures included in that package were limited only to nontraditional exports. For nontraditional exports the nominal effective exchange rate (NEER) for manufacturing exports shows a noticeable increase during 1968–70 compared with the average level of the three preceding years (see Cuthbertson and Athukorala, 1988, appendix B, for data definitions and methods of calculating REERs). However, the increase in NEER for nontraditional agricultural exports is small. This is because the favorable impact of the FEECs on exporters' current receipts was almost offset by the upward adjustments in export duties introduced almost concurrently. In real terms (all four definitions of the REER), even for manufactured exports the increase in price incentive appears to be much less than that indicated by the NEER. It seems that most of the exchange rate depreciation brought about by the FEEC scheme was absorbed by domestic inflation. Since the early 1960s there was a thriving black market for foreign exchange in Sri Lanka. Up to about 1967 the black-market rate was well above twice the official exchange rate. The import liberalization and exchange rate reform under the FEEC scheme was capable of achieving only a marginal reduction in the black-market premium.

With the measures of May 1968, the Central Bank immediately raised the bank rate from 5 to 5.5 percent, anticipating that there would be a sharp increase in demand for credit as an outcome of the expansion of domestic economic activity and increase in import flows. This increase in the bank rate led to an increase in interest rates charged by the commercial banks on their short-term and long-term lending (table 4.2, item 2(b)). However, when allowance is made for inflationary expectations (table 4.2, footnote a), these increases seem marginal. Throughout 1966–70 short- and long-term real interest rates varied in the narrow ranges of 7.5 – 8.6 percent and 9.0–9.7 percent respectively.

Economic Growth

In 1968 and 1969 GNP grew markedly (table 4.2, item 1). Commenting on this recovery of the economy, the Central Bank noted that "the expansion in the preceding two years was sustained to a large extent by the availability of a wide range of imports, mainly for industry and transport and communication and construction" (CBC, *Annual Report*, 1970, p. 2).

The policy reform soon affected the manufacturing sector. Central Bank data show that gross manufacturing output increased from Rs 954 million in 1967 to Rs 1,399 million in 1968 and Rs 1,627 million in 1969. Value added in manufacturing in constant prices increased by 8 percent in 1968 and 30 percent in 1969. The contribution of manufacturing (excluding plantation crop processing) to total GNP increased from 7.5 percent in 1967 to 9 percent in 1969. This immediate increase in manufacturing output can be considered as the outcome first of the immediate release of stocks of imported intermediate goods built up earlier by the trader in view of uncertainty about the future, and then of the increase in intermediate goods imports. The intermediate goods volume index (1967 = 100) increased to 112 in 1968.

There are no data on capacity utilization in manufacturing prior to 1968. According to a survey conducted by the Ministry of Industries and Scientific Affairs (1971) utilization of existing capacity in 1968 and 1969 was 44.4 percent and 45.6 percent respectively. This level of capacity utilization appears to be very low indeed. It might be taken as a sign of how much the economy had been closed through the 1960s. It is also a sign of the mistakes made by earlier protection policies as industries were established under the protective umbrella of quantitative restrictions with little thought of the availability of factors of production and economic

Table 4.2 Movement of major economic variables before and during the 1968–1970 liberalization episode

Economic variable	Annual average 1960–5	1966	1967	1968	1969	1970
1 Economic growth (annual %)						
(a) Real GNP	3.3	3.3	3.8	8.4	4.5	4.1
(b) Real per capita GNP	0.8	0.8	2.7	5.9	2.3	2.7
(c) Sectoral growth (real)						
Plantation agriculture	3.2	0.1	6.8	2.1	−6.5	1.0
Agriculture (other)	5.4	8.3	5.5	13.0	10.9	5.1
Industry	6.3	6.9	8.8	19.6	24.4	17.5
Manufacturing	9.0	−1.3	4.1	8.4	30.7	17.5
Services	5.2	−7.5	13.7	5.6	2.2	2.4
2 Major prices						
(a) General price level (% change)						
CCPI (1952 = 100)	1.7	−1.0	2.7	10.2	4.0	3.6
GNPD (1970 = 100)	1.5	−0.1	2.2	5.8	7.4	5.9
(b) Real interest rate[a]						
Short term	7.4	7.5	8.0	8.3	7.8	8.6
Long term	9.0	9.0	9.7	9.8	9.2	9.6
(c) Exchange rates (Rs per US$)						
Official	4.76	5.95	5.95	5.95	5.95	5.95
Including FEECs	4.76	5.95	5.95	8.57	9.23	9.23
Black market	8.39	13.00	14.15	11.35	12.00	15.20
REER – total exports	7.55	7.15	6.55	6.92	5.92	6.59
REER – traditional exports	7.65	7.23	6.45	6.77	5.88	6.51
REER – nontraditional exports	5.48	5.43	6.38	6.72	5.98	7.00
(d) Real wage index (1980 = 100)						
Private sector[b]	48.2	48.5	49.1	53.6	50.0	47.7
Public sector	100.2	100.7	102.1	112.1	107.8	110.7
3 Savings and investment (%)						
Investment/GNP	14.9	14.3	15.2	16.1	19.3	19.4
Savings/GNP	13.2	10.9	12.1	12.7	12.5	16.7

4 Trade and balance of payments (million US$)

(a)	Exports	372	351	346	332	320	338
(b)	Imports	400	423	417	395	446	391
(c)	Current account balance	−25	−60	−60	−59	−13	−58
(d)	Basic balance	−18	−35	−32	−23	−89	−28
(e)	Foreign reserves	83.2	59.0	86.0	70.0	55.0	62.0
	In import-month equivalent	2.5	1.7	2.5	2.1	1.5	1.9
(f)	Foreign debts (% of exports)	2.1	4.0	4.5	11.2	16.0	10.0
	Debt service ratio	5.2	7.2	6.0	11.8	15.3	22.5
(g)	Trade indices (1960 = 100)						
	Export volume	115	110	114	117	112	116
	Import volume	80	82	75	76	81	76
	Terms of trade	86	72	62	65	60	56
	Import purchasing power of exports	91	76	70	72	63	62

5 Fiscal operation and money supply

(a)	Budget deficit as percentage of total expenditure	28	31	31	33	32	34
(b)	Expansionary effect of the budget[c] (%)	33	15	44	17	30	12
(c)	Money base, growth (%)	7.6	7.2	16.2	10.3	2.0	− 2.6
(d)	Money supply M1, growth (%)	9.2	−1.8	11.2	9.2	4.7	9.2
(e)	Money supply M2, growth (%)	8.6	−0.1	10.1	8.7	4.1	10.5

6 Employment (manufacturing sector) (thousands)

1,876	2,081	2,236	3,011	3,103	3,544

[a] Nominal interest rate deflated by the expected rate of inflation. The estimates are based on the assumption that the expected rate of inflation is equal to the last period's rate of inflation. The measure of inflation used is the GNPD. Short-term interest rate, commercial bank's discount rate; long-term interest rate, commercial bank's interest on secured loans.

[b] Workers in Wages Board Trades.

[c] The portion of the budget deficit which was filled through commercial bank borrowing and money creation.

Source: related tables in the text and in Cuthbertson and Athukorala, 1988 (except for black-market exchange rate which is from *Pick's Currency Yearbook*, 1976)

scales of production. The system also sponsored the setting up of large-capacity units since allocations for raw materials and so on were granted on the basis of the installed capacity, or of a percentage thereof, depending on the availability of exchange.

Gross domestic fixed capital formation as a ratio of GNP remained at an average annual level of about 15 percent during the 1960s up to 1967. This ratio increased to 16 percent in 1968 and to 19 percent in 1969. However, the domestic saving ratio continued at the historical level of about 12 percent, indicating that the increment in capital formation was due almost totally to capital inflow.

Employment

Even though there are no comprehensive statistics on unemployment, the available evidence points to expansion. The number of employees registered under the Employees' Provident Fund (EPF) increased from 1.3 million in 1964 to 1.8 million in 1969. Even if allowance is made for increases due to expanded coverage under the EPF, the increase reflected by these figures remains significant. According to the Central Bank's annual survey of the manufacturing sector, employment in the organized manufacturing sector increased from 2.01 million in 1967 to 3 million in 1968 and 3.1 million in 1969.

External Transactions

One of the major objectives of the FEEC scheme was the promotion of nontraditional exports. Between 1967 and 1970 nontraditional exports increased (table 4.3). This partly reflected diversification of the export sector, which had always been dominated by the three traditional crops. The share of nontraditional exports in total commodity exports increased from 6 percent during 1960–6 to 9 percent during 1967–70. The volume

Table 4.3 Exports of nontraditional products (million US dollars)

Product	1967	1968	1969	1970	1971
Minerals	1.4	1.7	2.1	5.5	3.7
Minor agricultural products	15.4	19.5	20.4	20.1	20.0
Manufactures	1.7	2.4	2.0	3.5	5.1
Clothing and textiles	n.a.	0.7	0.6	1.3	1.2
Total nontraditional	19.3	25.6	27.1	33.3	34.0
Total merchandise	284.3	342.0	322.0	341.7	327.2
Nontraditional exports share (%) of the total	6.8	7.4	8.4	9.7	10.3
Nontraditional export volume index	100	116	118	122	125

n.a., not available.
Source: CBC, Annual Report, various issues

index of nontraditional exports increased from 100 in 1967 to an average
level of 119 in 1968–70.

Table 4.4 indicates the production and exports of manufactures during
the period 1965–72. With the increase in the value of production, there was
some increase in manufactured exports. However, the exported share of
total production remained negligible. This suggests the view that the rupee
premium granted to exporters through the FEEC scheme were apparently
insufficient to shift sales to export markets.

Table 4.4 Production and export of manufactured goods,
1965–1971 (million rupees)

Year	Value of industrial production	Value of industrial exports	Column 2 as a percentage of of column 1
1965	847.0	6.1	0.07
1966	580.3	7.0	0.08
1967	954.2	7.8	0.08
1968	1,398.9	12.0	0.09
1969	1,626.8	10.7	0.07
1970	1,945.0	18.0	0.09
1971	2,239.4	17.5	0.08

Source: CBC, Annual Report, various issues

The placing of tourist expenditure (that is, foreign currency which
tourists cashed in Sri Lanka) under the FEEC rate and institutional steps
taken to promote tourism paved the way for a large expansion in foreign
exchange earnings from tourism. Total receipts from this source increased
from US$1.2 million in 1967 to US$2.8 million in 1969.

Despite these developments relating to nontraditional exports, total
export earnings (in US dollar terms) continued to decline during the period
(table 4.2, item 4). This was because of the continuous decline in the
world-market prices of tea and rubber which together accounted for about
85 percent of Sri Lanka's total export earnings. The terms of trade
continued to deteriorate, reaching the lowest level ever recorded in 1970.
The export volume index did not increase to counterbalance these adverse
movements. The unavoidable outcome was a drastic decline in the import
purchasing power of exports (table 4.2, item 4(g)).

The unfavorable developments for exports, coupled with increased
imports under the OGL system, resulted in a widening trade deficit. This
deficit was about 7 percent of total export earnings in 1960–5 and rose to
about 22 percent of export earnings by 1968–70. The external resource
gap – the difference between total foreign exchange receipts and payments – as a ratio of GDP rose from 5 percent in 1967 to 11 percent in
1969. Official debt outstanding, which increased at an average annual rate

of 12 percent in the first half of the 1960s, expanded at an average annual rate of 22 percent from 1965 to 1968 and by 30 percent in 1969. The debt service ratio increased from the average level of 6.2 percent in 1960–7 to 15.3 percent in 1969 and then to 22.2 percent in 1970. The import-month equivalent of foreign reserves fell to 1.5 by the end of 1969. It was this precarious external payment situation which led to the suspension of the OGL system in April 1970.

5

The 1977 Episode

Beginnings

Nature and Targets

The 1977 episode began with a marked shift from licensing and quantitative restrictions to tariffs. While many of the tariff changes involved a gazetted increase in the rate, for the most part protection was much lower than that previously provided by way of licensing. In making the switch there was no real attempt to set tariffs at a level equivalent to the protection provided by licensing controls. Instead, the government devised a cascading six-band duty structure, and items were forced into bands as appropriate.

There was significant devaluation, and the exchange rate was unified and allowed to float. Forthcoming export promotion measures were announced, as were moves to free capital and labor markets and to hand government-owned and government-run activities back to the private sector. The proposals for further reducing import barriers were vaguely phrased and referred to such policies as removing anomalies and considering appeals against the 1977 changes. The prospective targets all had a strong liberal competitive flavor, with an open economy particularly in capital, services, and labor markets. These were explicitly linked with growth, full employment, and improved economic welfare.

The Mahaweli irrigation and power scheme was accelerated with a view to attaining virtually full hydroelectric power by 1985. The irrigation schemes were intended to expand and diversify output of food crops. Traditional crops remained unfavored sectors with export taxes on them remaining high and even increasing in several significant cases. Domestic agriculture, mainly paddy (rice), was boosted with fertilizer subsidies and pricing policies. Tourism became a glamor sector with the freeing of the economy, and perhaps facilitated by selective encouragement of foreign investment and the wide availability of tax holidays.

Export encouragement was a large part of the announced policy. An export-processing zone was established, as was an EDB responsible to the Export Development Council of Ministers headed by the President. Revisions of export incentives schemes were foreshadowed and policy statements repeatedly emphasized the importance of exports.

Intended and Actual Sequence

Instead of setting the scene for a multistage policy, the policymakers apparently felt that the policy shift was radical enough for the time being and that too much talk of further steps or stages was either unnecessary or likely to prejudice acceptance of the measures already in process. Indeed the subsequent measures were of a defensive and reassuring kind – modifications to the strategy rather than follow-up measures. For instance, in mid-1978, a body to hear appeals against the new tariffs was established more as a response to protests from manufacturers about the changes than as part of a planned sequence. This appeals body, the Tariff Review Committee (TRC), was made up of half a dozen government officials whose job was to hear appeals from manufacturers who felt that they had been disadvantaged by the liberalization.

From 1978 a proposed next step was the setting up of a Presidential Tariff Commission (PTC) which, by "open and objective inquiry," would revise the tariff structure. Guidelines for this body were prepared in 1978 and among other things referred to "an appropriate tariff structure based on the concept of the effective rate of protection." While the intention of these guidelines was to impose a much needed discipline on the appeals system, the guidelines themselves were a mixed bag. The instructions were vague and, if followed, would have been unlikely to result in further liberalization. For instance, the PTC would take into account "the need to encourage local industry through protection." This proposed charter and the PTC were adopted and appointed in 1980.

Initial Economic Circumstances

The period 1970–7 has been called the time of a closed economy. The government had met sharp increases in oil and fertilizer prices with successive squeezes on imports and with some help from foreign aid. In 1975 the World Bank observed that "Sri Lanka is among those countries worst hit by the recent adverse developments in the world economy" (World Bank, 1975). The World Bank report went on to back external support for a well-conceived agricultural development program. External finance was to play a major and increasingly important role over the period 1974–6 and subsequently.

By July 1977, when the UNP government was elected, economic circumstances were somewhat brighter. There had been some recovery from the oil price shock of the early 1970s, and commodity prices had also recovered somewhat. Although imports remained absolutely restricted in 1976, the actual overall balance of payments had surpluses of over Rs 500 million on both current and trade account. Reserves were up in both absolute terms and as a ratio to imports. There had been a small but significant improvement in the balance of services and private transfers owing to rising remittances and receipts from tourism.

However, unemployment had worsened between 1973 and 1977, particularly in the cities. The 1973 labor force survey had estimated unemployment at almost 800,000, or about 17.6 percent of the total island workforce (Kappagoda and Paine, 1981). Kappagoda and Paine cite a 1976 study which found just over a million people unemployed and a 1977 urban budget survey which found unemployment of 27.8 percent for the survey area and 29.4 percent for Colombo. When the UNP assumed office in July 1977 the unemployed could have totalled as many as a million of the 14 million people in the country and about a quarter of the workforce.

Inflation had become an issue from about 1972 and was about 6 percent through the mid-1970s. Inflation was to jump markedly in 1976 when the WPI rose by 41 percent and the Central Bank's unpublished consumer price index rose by 25 percent. As described in chapter 2, the money supply, however measured, rose sharply in 1960. This reflected efforts to stimulate the economy by a government in trouble plus demand pressures generated by a rising export surplus.

Political Circumstances

Beginning with the suppression of a youth insurgency movement in April 1971, Mrs Bandaranaike's government ruled under a state of emergency until February 1977. It had extended the life of Parliament by two years by changing the constitution as one of its first acts after taking office; it only held elections in 1977 when faced with open threats of civil disobedience from the opposition.

The 1977 elections saw an opposition UNP landslide win. The Bandaranaike government (the SLFP and its coalition partners), which had a three-quarters majority in 1970, was defeated when the UNP won 139 seats, 83 percent of the seats in the Assembly (table 3.1). By almost any standard, it can be said that the new government was very secure and the political structure was very stable.

The new government's statements suggested strong attachment to a market-oriented open economy and indicated a marked ideological shift from that of the previous government. The new Finance Minister, Ronnie de Mel, in an address to the British press in October 1977 outlined the economic policies of the UNP government as follows:

> My government welcomes trade, aid and foreign investment. These are the cornerstones, the very foundations of our economic policy. It is our objective to maximize foreign investment in Sri Lanka by giving foreign investors the necessary incentives and the necessary guarantees and safeguards consistent, of course, with our national sovereignty and economic goals. We expect aid and support from the World Bank and the I.M.F. and also from the countries of the Aid-Group. . . . We shall give the private sector its due place in our economy. . . . The basis of a free and just society, in my opinion, is a free and just economy. We will accordingly move away from restrictive policies and controls of the last seven years to a more liberal economic policy. (*Ceylon News*, October 20, 1977)

To what extent were these policy shifts pragmatic moves as compared with an ideological commitment? Presumably the UNP proposed these capitalist open market-oriented policies because that was its perception of what the electorate wanted. The experience with a closed economic policy had not been good, and perhaps even a reelected Bandaranaike government would have moved toward liberalization. Whatever the interpretation, the UNP government persisted with its rhetoric, and after reelection in 1983 the President and senior ministers continued issuing statements similar to that of Mr de Mel quoted here.

The manufacturing sector had become increasingly centralized and state owned under Mrs Bandaranaike's government. Nearly 70 percent of the registered manufacturing establishments in 1974 were located in and around Colombo, and these establishments accounted for 90 percent of the total value of output. The number of public corporations had reached 24 by 1970, and the first half of the 1970s saw increased state participation in the trading and service sectors. Although not many new public corporations had been created, capital investment in public sector enterprises had doubled. The bulk of this new investment went into new capacity in cement, textiles, plywood, paper, and caustic soda and chlorine.

By 1977 commercial policy was seen by the public to be of major importance – it was the focus of debate and attracted a lot of attention. Liberalization was at the center of the new government's election platform. The cabinet, which first met in August 1977, had introduced the new measures by November of that year. The speed with which it acted and the momentum of events appear to have overridden arguments about whether the policy should be introduced. The debate came later, as disaffected parties regrouped to marshal their arguments and resources and put pressure on the government.

The ministry most in charge of policy was the Ministry of Finance and Planning, with the Central Bank responsible for foreign exchange. Following the dismantling of licensing, the Ministry and the Bank jointly ran the Ministry of Industries. The Ministry of Finance and Planning and to some extent the Ministry of Trade and the EDB handled negotiations with the World Bank and the IMF and managed much of the advice and funds coming from these organizations.

How significant was the influence of outside advice on policy? We conclude that outside influence did not affect the first episode much; the 1977 episode is hard to interpret. One judgment sometimes made by Sri Lankan government officials is that the advice and policies coming from outside did not differ much from that offered by local officials. However, from time to time newspapers interpreted the policies as a positioning for receipt of Western aid, and contended that in 1977 the IMF and the World Bank became Sri Lanka's "new masters." For example, these commentators would attribute the changes in rice rationing to IMF pressure. Adjudicating this difference of opinion is not easy: on the one hand it seems almost certain that the advice offered was to remove the rice ration; on the other hand, such removal had been attempted several times by various governments since 1953 without outside advice. What does seem clear is that the UNP told the electorate that it would be seeking aid support, and that with the kinds of policies it was advocating such aid would be forthcoming.

A statement by President Jayawardene to Parliament during the debate on the 1978 budget is quite open about the important role of the international agencies in policy development:

> the World Bank and the IMF came to our aid. They said, You go ahead; we will give you cover. Under the money we are giving you, you can free both import controls and exchange controls. If you take certain decisions with regard to giving food free, then we will help you by giving you money for development but not for eating. (Jayawardene, 1978, p. 67)

One interpretation of this statement is that conditionality was overriding. Another is that the President was using the international agencies and their loans to absorb some of the backlash from policies that were expected to be unpopular. While the extent of influence on actual policy is difficult to assess, there is little doubt that from 1978 onwards the presence of other countries and international agencies increased significantly (Levy, 1985). Very large loans were mobilized for the Mahaweli program and other projects, and outside advisers and managers were employed on a large scale to manage these projects. Nonetheless, all this happened after the main liberalization actions had been taken. As will be seen, changes in commercial policy from 1978 onward were only marginal.

The World Bank did sponsor a project in 1979 which was intended to be a basis for encouraging further reform of the tariff. This project, completed in 1981, was to estimate the levels of an effective protection regime for manufacturing industry evolving from the 1977 changes in import barriers, and to assist in training and establishing a secretariat for the proposed PTC. In February 1985 the PTC submitted a report to the government proposing a new tariff regime which, among other things, was designed to reduce disparities in effective protection.

Implementation

The Sri Lankan experience supports the proposition that a government has the best chance of introducing substantial reform in the early days of its life. The 1977 episode was dominated by moves made by the government in the first three months – in the so-called 100 days of grace. The general impression of planning at that time is that there was a policy stance of liberalization but that there was no delineation of subsequent stages. The time taken to implement the main elements of the episode, as far as it went, was quite short. As far as commercial policy was concerned, much of what went on afterwards was a holding action. Within three months the import-licensing system was substantially dismantled and supplanted by a revised system of tariffs, establishment of a free-trade zone was started, the basis of what was to be the EDB was set up, the dual exchange rate system was abandoned along with most currency exchange restrictions, restrictions on movement of workers were lifted, and entry into banking, tourism and other sectors was made much freer. Indeed, a striking characteristic of Sri Lanka's 1977 episode is the speed at which all these things happened. It is true that even the revised system of duties provided substantial and distorting import barriers, and it is also true that physical and legislative implementation of some of these early policies took time to introduce, but nonetheless the first stage can be considered as having been far reaching, short, and much more important than any later stages.

The New Tariff

A six-band system was used by a committee of officials to design the initial tariff. The band system yielded an escalating set of duties, with low rates on raw materials and so-called essentials and high rates – 100 percent – on final goods and goods produced locally. A large proportion of imports in subsequent years was to enter duty free: these were mainly government and public corporation imports of petroleum, flour, rice, sugar, and the like. The average duty – duty revenue as a percentage of total import value – resulting from this six-band system was between 10 and 15 percent.

The November 1977 changes removed most quantitative restrictions. Still, some 280 items were listed to remain under license. Import of most industrial investment goods and spare parts, railway vehicles, aircraft, and ships still required approval from an investment advisory committee if the cost, insurance, and freight (c.i.f.) value of the consignment was significant. Items left under license included weapons, explosives, poisonous compounds, nuclear devices, radio transmitting devices, vehicles, jewelry, minerals, fuels and oils, pharmaceutical products, chemicals, artificial resins and plastic materials, textile yarns and fabric, and tobacco and alcohol. Licenses were not transferable and the basis for allocation varied. For the most part licenses were issued freely and the license system does not seem to have been much of a protective barrier (Cuthbertson and Khan, 1981). It seems as if it may have been politically easier to leave some sensitive items under license and to have these licenses freely available than to tackle the job of making the nominated list of items smaller.

The escalating duty system yielded a wide range of effective rates. As part of a tentative next stage, the World Bank supported a study of the trade regime in order to find levels of effective protection (Cuthbertson and Khan, 1981). That study focused on 1979 data and the 1979 regime – which was little changed from 1977 and 1978 – and found, predictably enough, that for many products effective protection was very high whereas for others it was quite low. Activities which received relatively little assistance included most food processing, pharmaceuticals, basic metal-fabricating industries, and transport equipment and spares. Highly protected industries included many products of the public corporations, for example tires, steel, chemicals, apparently luxury items such as jams and cosmetics, and protected manufacturing activities such as processed rubber goods and electrical products.

Revisions

A PTC whose charter included, among other things, further reform of the 1977 system, drawing on measures of effective production, was set up in 1980. It replaced the Tariff Review Committee – a group of officials appointed in 1978 to hear appeals for duty changes. Between 1978 and 1983 the appeals bodies allowed some 700 duty changes. Many duties were lowered, often to assist the local user of a raw material or intermediate product that was not then manufactured locally. Many of these changes can be traced to fine tuning of particular tariff items to resolve administrative problems. These problems often resulted from attempting to vary duty rates within a single class of items on the basis of criteria such as style, size, or value. Motor vehicles are a good example. There, duty rates differed according to value, size, and body style of car. These differences encouraged importers to select those vehicles for import that would technically qualify for lower duty rates. This response in turn encouraged the appeals body to insert yet another definition into the tariff.

How much reform went on during those six years is a moot point. A 1983 World Bank mission report concluded that over that time the tariff had probably become a little more complicated, a little more protective, and a little more capable of raising revenue (World Bank, 1983). An important issue is the scope for appeals bodies to improve a given protection regime. In Sri Lanka it does seem that the best that could be expected in the appeal process would be for the commission to have just held things as they were. Appeals systems, even with public scrutiny, are stacked toward escalating assistance because appellants are usually industries in some kind of difficulty from competition of one sort or another. Recommendations tend to be biased toward adding protection for the industries concerned.

How likely is it that the use of the concept of effective protection as a basis for formulating a new tariff regime will yield a lower and less biased assistance structure? One view is that measures of effective protection are a useful descriptive tool but are not much good for forcing positive across-the-board changes. Proponents of this view would press for across-the-board reductions in nominal protection, which they say would automatically lower and compress effective protection anyway. The other view, and the one which has apparently held sway in Sri Lanka, is that across-the-board reductions are not politically practical and that fine tuning using an apparently scientific measure such as effective protection is the next best bet. As it turned out, much of the fine tuning of duties after November 1977 was aimed at saving the monopoly position of certain public corporations, for example, tires, chemicals, paper, and pharmaceuticals.

Other than the small amount of modification of tariffs initiated by the appeals system, the main changes in duty structure between 1978 and 1982 arose from the Ministry of Finance. However, an across-the-board levy of 10 percent applied on all items duties at over 50 percent was introduced by the government in 1980. This was ostensibly in order to gather funds to promote exports and was a marked setback in progress toward liberalization. Expectations about the timing of further rounds of tariff reform were couched in the most general of terms.

The changes that did occur were initiated at budget time for revenue-raising purposes. At first, unlike the export levy, they usually involved widespread small increases of low duties. In the escalating system of tariff rates that prevailed, these revenue-oriented changes would have reduced the variance of effective protection. However, in November 1982 the Ministry of Finance applied some large selective increments of duty on items already duties at high rates. These changes had a marked impact on the protective structure, for the most part increasing assistance to already highly assisted goods – for example, carpets, toothpaste, cosmetics, batteries, paints, tires, and plastic pipes and fittings.

Table 5.1 shows license status as of 1977 and adjustments made up to 1984 for the 20-sector manufacturing industry classification. The table shows a conventional swapping of license control for high tariffs for most sectors. However, a few capital goods sectors were taken off licensing and put on low duties.

After an initial flurry of license dismantling, a few items returned to the licensing list from about 1979 on – matches, plywood, and caustic soda. The decision on matches was a straight-out special protective move, but the plywood argument had dimensions other than price: mainly that Sri Lanka's tea exports were being harmed because the quality of tea packing cases varied so much. Licensing of imports was rationalized on the grounds that it would control this variability. However, the licensing had definite protective effects, since the government-owned plywood corporations which provided a small part of the tea exporters' requirements also had sole rights of distribution of all plywood. It used profits from import plywood to subsidize domestic output, with the added costs being borne by tea exporters. Other items put back under license included newsprint, chilies, some chemicals, textile fabrics, cotton yarn, vegetables, resins, plastics, and some iron and steel items. The steel licensing reflected the not uncommon objective of protecting a public corporation – in this case the Steel Corporation. Similarly, the control on newsprint was designed to protect the paper corporation.

Whether or not these returns to the licensing list signified a significant transformation of the licensing system is difficult to judge. One clue is that the trends in imports of goods under license and goods placed under license since 1977 generally show a steady increase in imports of nearly all licensed items – there are no instances of a cutback in imports in a year following recall of that item to the licensed list. However, this may not mean much. Within any particular class of item public corporations were able to import the particular goods not produced by them without paying duty. For example, the steel corporation could import certain dimensions of steel rod and the paper corporation could import certain kinds of paper. Imports could thus have grown within a class of items, while locally produced goods remained well protected.

Until 1980 artificial resins and plastic materials were under license to protect traditional local industries – clay, wood, and metal fabrication – which it was felt would be affected by competition from plastic goods. There were also restrictions on molds and extrusion machines for much the same reasons. In 1980 most plastic items were freed from licensing, although several very finely specified raw materials and some machinery continued to be licensed.

Table 5.2 presents estimates of effective protection for the 20-sector categories of the Ministry of Industries. The figures suggest little change over this five-year period in terms of a reduction in level and variation of effective protection. This is consistent with the diagnosis of the fine tuning that went on over those years. Despite a great many tariff changes, there

Table 5.1 Nontariff protection to industry

Industry	Before 1977	1977–84
Meat, fish, and dairy products	Licensing with high duty	Liberalized with moderate duties; milk powder and fish preparations under license in 1984
Fruit and vegetable products	Licensing with high duty	Liberalized with high duties
Confectionery, bakery, and cereal products	Licensing with high duty	Liberalized with high duties
Spirits, alcoholic beverages, and aerated water	Licensing with high duty	Liberalized with high duties except molasses and alcoholic spirits which were under license and subject to a moderate duty rate in 1984
Other food products and tobacco	Licensing with high duty	Liberalized with very high specific duty; unmanufactured tobacco is still under license
Textiles	Licensing with high duty	Still under license, although not clear how significant licensing is; several attempts made to liberalize but failed due to resistance from public and private sector interested parties; some progress with privatization; recommendations made by the Tariff Commission in 1984 for dismantling of licensing
Made-up garments	Licensing with high duty	Liberalized with duties of 100% in 1977; in 1984, a 25% tariff reduction was made covering all garments
Petroleum, petroleum products	Licensing with high duty	Petroleum oils, some petroleum products such as bitumen under license to 1984; many plastic items taken off license in 1980
Chemicals	Licensing with high duty	About 30 chemicals and a number of agricultural insecticides under license in 1984

	Licensing with high duty	Pharmaceuticals under license in 1984; imports of cosmetics liberalized in 1977; subject to very high duties
Pharmaceuticals	Licensing with high duty	
Soap, vegetable and animal oils and fats	Licensing with high duty	Liberalized with high duties
Leather and rubber products	Licensing with high duty	Liberalized with high duties
Wood, paper, and pulp products	Licensing with high duty	Liberalized with high duty for wood and paper products and low duty for pulp; plywood panels left under license
Clay, sand and cement products	Licensing with high duty	Liberalized with low duties
Basic metal industries and machinery (excluding transport machinery)	Licensing with low duty	Most imports liberalized with moderate duties in 1977; iron and steel wire remained under license
Ferrous and nonferrous metal products (other than machinery)	Licensing with low duty	Liberalized with moderate duty except for a few items such as hand tools
Transport equipment and spares	Licensing with moderate duty	Liberalized with low duties
Electrical goods	Licensing with high duty	Liberalized with high duties
Optical and photographic goods	Licensing with high duty	Liberalized with high duties

All imports of basic raw materials were subject to a quota system which was abolished completely in 1977.

Table 5.2 Estimates of effective protection

Industry	Effective protection coefficient		
	1979	1981	1983
Meat, fish, and dairy products	0.81	0.54	0.57
Fruit and vegetable products	0.97	1.86	1.61
Confectionery and bakery products	0.87	0.88	0.46
Spirits, alcoholic beverages, and aerated water	0.32	1.11	1.00
Other food products and tobacco	0.82	1.34	1.40
Textiles and woven textile products	1.20	1.38	1.81
Made-up garments	2.48	2.38	2.17
Petroleum products	2.94	1.24	1.27
Salt and salt-based chemicals	2.01	1.56	2.53
Other chemicals	2.98	1.07	1.06
Pharmaceuticals, medical supplies, and cosmetics	1.26	1.30	1.26
Soap, vegetable and animal oils and fats	1.03	10.07	7.64
Leather and rubber products	1.14	2.35	1.70
Manufacturing of wood, paper, pulp	1.79	1.53	1.32
Clay, sand, and cement products	0.69	0.91	1.00
Basic metal industries and machinery	1.22	1.28	1.34
Ferrous and nonferrous metal products (other than machinery)	2.22	2.07	2.22
Transport equipment and spares	1.10	0.87	0.93
Electrical goods	3.66	2.42	3.01
Optical and photographic goods	1.19	1.96	2.13
Total manufacturing	1.37	1.90	1.50

Sources: Cuthbertson and Kahn, 1981; *Report of the Presidential Tariff Commission*, 1985 (for 1981, 1983)

was little advance from the first steps taken in 1977, but nor was there a significant retreat into protectionism.

Accompanying Policies

Macromanagement

A massive public investment program was launched in 1978. The so-called three lead projects – the accelerated Mahaweli program, a public housing program, and an urban development program – were all largely financed by foreign aid (see chapter 4, n. 3). Between 1978 and 1982 the three projects accounted for about 75 percent of public investment; the Mahaweli scheme alone accounted for about 45 percent. Public investment, which was about 8 percent of GDP in 1970, jumped to about 15 percent of

GDP through 1978–83 (see table 2.16). Increases in public savings were inconsequential and the expanded public investments were funded by foreign capital (mainly aid) inflows and Central Bank borrowing (Lal and Rajapatirana, 1985). Total external debt outstanding quadrupled between 1977 and 1984 (table 5.3). With this aid-funded public investment the current account deficit rose from 5.5 percent of GDP in 1977 to 20 percent of GDP in 1980.

The pressures on the government's capacity to keep its macromanagement house in order came from several sources. To begin with, the three lead projects were all long term and no revenue was generated in those early years. Despite substantial pruning in 1979, 1980, and 1981 of the projects as they were originally envisaged in 1978, the pressures on the government for continued huge expenditures on them were unrelenting. The President and the Prime Minister had staked themselves politically on the Mahaweli scheme and the housing program respectively, and more backing off from either project was politically very difficult. Moreover, even though aid donors might have been urging stringency on the government they also had an interest in seeing that local resources and manpower were allocated to the projects. The external environment did not help: tea prices fell in 1979 and 1980 and Sri Lanka's terms of trade fell markedly (Stern, 1984). Rising world interest rates raised the cost of foreign borrowing. The impact of the combined shock of these pressures – export demand, terms of trade, and rising interest rates – has been estimated to be equal to 25 percent of GDP (Balassa and McCarthy, 1984).

By 1980 the government was finding it increasingly difficult to keep spending at a level which could be financed by aid-backed borrowing and domestic revenue. The lead projects took on a life of their own, absorbing an ever increasing share of public investment. Public enterprises, despite all the rhetoric about privatization, continued to be a drain on public funds. During 1978–83 the annual share of transfers to public enterprises in total capital payments was constantly about 30–40 percent. Budget deficits in the years around 1980 were large. In 1978 the food subsidy was withdrawn from nearly half the population, and in 1979 a food stamp scheme was introduced. This scheme was only available to families with less than a specified minimum monthly income, initially set at Rs 300. However, this expenditure cut was more than offset by the transfers to loss-making public enterprises. The government spent heavily on fertilizer subsidies, the airline (Air Lanka), and state-run domestic transport industries. Rottenberg (1983), in a review of Sri Lanka's public expenditure, observed that with government expenditure at about 35 percent of GDP in 1982 this Sri Lankan government was attempting more tasks than almost any other Asian country.

With hindsight, the early and largely irreversible commitment to the accelerated Mahaweli scheme can be understood in that the plans and

Table 5.3 External debt outstanding, 1976–1984

SDR million

Item	1976	1977	1978	1979	1980	1981	1982	1983	1984[a]
Long-term debt	484.4	560.3	721.9	778.6	973.5	1,219.6	1,471.1	1,758.4	2,083.9
Project loans	n.a.	n.a.	243.3	248.8	296.5	386.0	529.5	746.2	1,008.2
Nonproject loans	n.a.	n.a.	449.0	462.4	581.5	728.8	831.1	875.5	962.9
IMF Trust Fund loans	n.a.	n.a.	38.6	67.4	95.6	104.8	110.5	114.7	112.8
Suppliers, credits	61.7	51.0	49.1	40.7	36.6	46.6	42.4	34.0	22.8
IMF drawings	89.4	64.1	76.5	126.3	112.6	241.9	217.8	196.0	191.8
Bank borrowing	30.1	29.2	7.7	3.4	18.7	11.2	78.7	71.6	0.5
Other[b]	n.a.	n.a.	n.a.	n.a.	180.2	270.5	457.8	546.1	581.8
Total	665.6	704.8	855.2	949.0	1,321.7	1,789.2	2,267.8	2,606.1	2,880.8

n.a., not available.
[a] Provisional.
[b] Comprises commercial borrowing of public corporations, Air Lanka, Greater Colombo Economic Commission enterprises, and other for private foreign borrowings and trade credit.
Source: CBC, Review of the Economy, various issues

proposals were complete in 1978 so that the project could absorb the aid funds which were available to the newly elected government at that time (Levy, 1985). In addition, the government grasped at the Mahaweli project as a way of generating employment quickly – for reducing the pool of unemployed it had inherited and possibly for people expected to be displaced by liberalization measures. However, the projects placed huge economic strains on the economy. Lal (1985) has explained how the capital inflow to finance the projects caused an appreciation of the real exchange rate (the domestic relative price of nontraded to traded goods). Demand for construction and other nontradeable goods related to the projects bid their prices up and drew resources into nontraded sectors and away from the traded sectors.

Exchange Rates

In November 1977 the dual exchange rate system which had operated since May 1968 was abandoned and a unified exchange rate was established. The initial par value was fixed at Rs 16 per US dollar. Compared with the official (FEEC exclusive) exchange rate which existed at the time of policy reform (Rs 8.70 per US dollar) this was nearly a 100 percent devaluation (Cuthbertson and Athukorala, 1988, appendix table A.9).

With the introduction of a unified exchange rate, the value of the rupee against the US dollar, the pound sterling, the deutsche mark, the French franc, the Japanese yen, and the Indian rupee was determined at daily meetings of representatives of commercial banks and officials of the Central Bank. The rate fixed at this meeting was intended to reflect the demand for and supply of foreign currencies in Sri Lanka and exchange rates in international foreign currency markets. The Central Bank intervened in the exchange market through buying and selling of foreign currencies.

In November 1982 procedures for fixing exchange rates were changed. Under the new system, the Central Bank carried out its exchange operations only through the US dollar, which became the intervention currency. The procedure involved the bank announcing the rate at which it would spot buy and sell US dollars against Sri Lankan rupees.

The government maintained throughout the policy position that maintenance of a realistic exchange rate was a must. For instance, in the 1984 Budget Speech the Minister of Finance, Mr de Mel, stated that

> it seems legitimate to assert that given the limited options and the narrowly circumscribed room for maneuver confronting countries like Sri Lanka, expot-led economic diversification and an open economy provide the best possible framework for economic policy. A flexible exchange rate policy is a sine qua non for such a development strategy. (Budget Speech, November 1983)

However, inspection of exchange rate movements (both in current and real terms) over this period suggests that in practice the Central Bank had gradually intensified its intervention in the exchange market to support the exchange rate of the rupee (table 5.4). In real terms the rupee gradually appreciated against both the SDR and the US dollar. It seems that, from about 1983, a street market for US dollars had evolved with quotes well above the official rate of exchange – Rs 28.00 per US dollar compared with the official rate of Rs 24.00 per US dollar.

Monetary Policy

Significant changes in interest rate policy were introduced in August and September 1977. The low interest rate regime or "cheap money" policy came to an end in 1977. The bank rate was raised from 8.5 to 10 percent and the National Savings Bank (NSB) was induced to raise deposit rates from 7.2 to 8.4 percent. This was followed by an increase in the commercial bank fixed deposit rate for a 12-month deposit from 7–7.5 percent to 14–15 percent.

In the four months ending December 1977, total monthly savings and fixed deposits of the nonbank private sector rose by Rs 583 million compared with an increase of Rs 613 million during the first eight months of the year (Cuthbertson and Athukorala, 1988, appendix table A.3). Over the same four months, savings and fixed deposits of the NSB increased by Rs 342 million compared with the increase of Rs 190 million for the first eight months. In 1978 and 1979 total narrow money (M1) grew by about 35 percent, whereas time and savings deposits of the NSB and commercial banks increased by about 150 percent. The percentage of narrow money (M1) in total broad money (M3) declined from 47 percent in January 1978 to 40 percent in December 1979, and then dropped to 32 percent in December 1981.

The commercial banks maintained reasonable growth of credit expansion, including some increased investment in long-term financing, although the expansion of narrow money supply was later brought down to about 12 percent compared with rates of well over 30 percent in the immediate pre-liberalization period.

With the liberalization of trade and exchange, the tax base, particularly that relating to foreign trade, expanded and led to increased revenue. However, the revenue-to-GDP ratio continued to decline after 1978. The overall budget deficit as a ratio of GDP increased in all years except in 1983 when this ratio indicated a slight decline (table 5.4). Thus the government had to rely on bank borrowing, leading to far-reaching consequences for prices and the balance of payments.

Export Promotion

The Export Development Act 40 was enacted by the national State Assembly in 1979. The Act provided for the establishment of the EDB. The EDB was to prove to be an energetic body with a good deal of local and institutional support. It set in train a wide range of schemes, all pitched at export promotion.

Despite all the activity the effectiveness of the export drive effort must be questioned if only because of the manner of funding it. This was – after October 1980 – by a 10 percent levy (cess) on imports dutied at more than 50 percent and by a smaller cess on certain nontraditional export items. This meant that export development measures were financed by conferring higher protection to activities likely to be already highly assisted, which was hardly an effective way of redressing the imbalance of incentives against exports. The same might be said for the small cess on certain nontraditional exports invoked in 1980 for the purposes of funding export development.

In 1980 the existing duty rebate scheme was substantially revised and implementation was placed under EDB management. The number of products receiving duty drawback expanded rapidly. By 1984 the scheme had come to cover almost all the nontraditional products using imported material and to include sales to the investment promotion zones (IPZs) (provided that the sale proceeds were realized in foreign exchange). Payments grew rapidly, reflecting both increased cover and the expansion of manufactured exports. Average annual payment during 1980–2 was SDR 25.6 million compared with an average of SDR 9.4 million for 1978–9.

While the duty rebate scheme was to become the vanguard of export promotion many other measures were also tried. A scheme of manufacture-in-bond for exporters importing material for reexport as part of a finished good (for example, labels and tags for the production of tea bags) was introduced in 1980. An export grants scheme was set up in 1981, as were various special credit measures for exports.

Financial assistance from the EDB to selected export-oriented projects took two forms: equity participation, and the provision of short-term financing to projects with potential for expansion of exports in the short run. The objective was to promote private sector activities in export production by providing seed capital, leaving the management of the project in the hands of the investor. Projects in such product areas as gloves, resin, rubber soling sheets, and medical aid were selected by the EDB as worthy projects. By the end of 1982 some seven projects involving direct investment of Rs 154 million by the EDB had been established. Although this was small in the total scheme of things, it was still a relatively simple measure. A scheme for short-run credit for industrial exports was

Table 5.4 Movement of major economic variables before and during the 1977 liberalization

Indicator	1970–7	1978	1979	1980	1981	1982	1983
Economic growth (%)							
Real GNP	2.8	8.7	6.2	5.5	4.7	4.8	4.7
Real per capita GNP	1.3	6.9	4.3	3.6	3.1	3.5	3.2
Sectoral growth (real)							
Plantation agriculture	−1.7	4.1	4.1	−10.0	7.5	−1.5	–
Agriculture (other)	3.5	4.7	0.6	7.3	6.3	2.8	3.5
Industry	1.0	13.5	8.4	4.0	3.5	3.4	3.1
Manufacturing	2.3	10.8	4.8	6.1	4.2	9.1	2.8
Services	3.7	7.1	5.9	9.1	6.3	6.5	5.8
Major prices							
General price level (% change)							
CCPI (1952 = 100)	5.6	12.1	10.8	26.1	18.0	10.1	14.6
GNPD (1970 = 100)	11.8	7.8	15.7	18.2	20.5	9.9	15.8
WPI (1974 = 100)	10.8	15.8	9.5	33.8	17.0	5.6	25.0
Real interest rate							
Short term	8.6	9.8	9.1	9.3	7.9	7.3	6.6
Long term	10.3	9.3	8.6	10.4	9.5	7.8	8.7
Exchange rates (Rs per US$)							
Official	6.9	15.6	15.6	16.5	19.2	20.8	23.6
Including FEECs	11.3	n.a.	n.a.	n.a.	n.a.	n.a.	n.a.
Black market	14.7	21.3	21.3	22.4	n.a.	n.a.	n.a.
REER – total imports	6.0	14.5	16.6	18.0	18.2	18.7	18.7
REER – total exports	5.5	9.7	10.3	12.8	16.6	19.3	21.2
REER – traditional exports	5.5	8.1	7.9	10.1	13.0	15.4	17.5
REER – nontraditional exports	12.1	16.4	17.2	19.5	23.8	24.7	26.4
Real wage index (1980 = 100)							
Private sector	51.6	89.4	101.6	100	87.4	91.0	86.0
Public sector	103.5	108.1	114.3	100	95.8	111.0	112.1

Savings and investment (%)							
Investment/GNP	15.7	19.7	27.1	36.1	27.3	30.3	28.6
Savings/GNP	13.4	14.5	14.4	11.9	12.5	12.9	13.6
Trade and balance of payments (million US$)							
Exports	465	853	990	979	999	989	1,002
Imports	543	1,007	1,463	1,886	1,759	1,943	1,809
Current account balance	−26	−67	−230	−607	−414	−555	−445
Basic balance	21	136	−30	−202	−58	−271	−44
Foreign reserves in import months	3.7	5.9	5.1	2.4	3.1	3.3	3.5
Debt service ratio	17.8	15.5	13.0	12.4	16.8	18.6	21.6
Trade indices (1960 = 100)							
Export volume	110	109	110	108	111	122	118
Import volume	62	99	122	139	144	148	178
Terms of trade	46	53	38	31	24	20	23
Import purchasing power of exports	53	65	49	40	35	34	30
Fiscal operation and money supply							
Budget deficit as percentage of total expenditure	27.5	38.0	40.8	53.6	47.8	54.1	46.2
Expansionary effect of the budget	5.2	2.9	6.7	74.5	38.3	31.2	9.2
Money supply M1, growth (%)	14.7	10.6	29.1	22.9	6.3	17.3	25.4
Money supply M2, growth (%)	14.5	24.4	33.2	31.8	23.1	24.8	22.1
Employment							
Manufacturing sector	110,059	136,168	146,260	154,563	164,440	170,577	n.a.
Organized sector	414,845	446,085	470,188	476,086	481,475	484,802	489,472

−, negligible; n.a., not available.

Source: related tables in the text and Cuthbertson and Athukorala, 1988 (except for the black-market exchange rate which is from *Pick's Currency Yearbook,* 1976)

introduced in 1982 with the stated objective of helping existing export ventures to expand production and to improve product quality. Under the scheme the EDB financed up to 50 percent of total expenditure. Export market potential, expected net foreign exchange gain, and the period of payback were the major criteria used in selecting projects for financing.

A pre-shipment refinancing scheme for nontraditional exports introduced by the Central Bank in December 1977 became operational from about the second half of 1978. Under this scheme the Central Bank provided refinance at a concessional rate in respect of loans granted by the commercial banks to exporters at or below a predetermined concessionary rate. In February 1979 the Sri Lanka Export Credit Insurance Corporation (SLECIC) was established with provisions for (a) issuing bank guarantees on both pre-shipment and post-shipment credits and (b) issuing insurance policies to exporters to cover the risk of nonpayment or delayed payment by the buyers. Bank guarantees issued by the SLECIC meant that exporters could obtain credit from banks on liberal terms. The protection given by insurance policies was said to be to encourage exporters to export to new markets and to new buyers, as well as to increase exports to existing clients on easy credit terms.

A five-year tax holiday was introduced in the 1978 Budget Speech for all export-oriented companies incorporated on or after November 15, 1978. In addition, costs of advertising and other sales promotion activities and traveling in connection with the export trade were made deductible in calculating taxable income. Up to March 1983, the tax holiday was not completely limited to exports. Some import-substituting production and construction also enjoyed similar, or even more attractive tax concessions. This situation changed with the declaration, in the 1983 budget, of March 31, 1983, as the cutoff date for approval of projects in nonexport activities.

Capital Movement Policy

The promotion of foreign investment was a central element in the new policy introduced in 1977. Relaxation of controls on exchange transactions, including those on capital and profit repatriation, was an explicit complement to other parts of the liberalization package that included introduction of a unified sliding peg exchange rate system, reforms in the money and banking system including the removal of the prohibition that had existed since 1963 on opening of branches by foreign banks in the country, the introduction of a Foreign Currency Banking Unit Scheme, and the relaxation of government control on private sector activities.

Outflow of capital was relatively liberalized. From November 1977, remittance of profits of foreign companies and nonresident partnerships operating in Sri Lanka and dividends accruing to nonresident shareholders of rupee companies was permitted without prior approval of the Controller of Exchange. Some 12 months later remittance controls were virtually lifted, with companies being allowed to remit on the basis of their reported interim profits and dividends.

Foreign investors were allowed by the Controller of Exchange to repatriate their capital contribution in the equity of a company on the sale or liquidation of the investment, after settlement of local liabilities such as taxes. Transfer of shares was freely permitted provided that such transfer would not lead to an increase in the prevailing ratio of nonresident shareholding originally approved.

One of the largest single efforts at promoting export-oriented foreign investment was the setting up of the Greater Colombo Economic Commission (GCEC) in 1978. The incentive package offered by the GCEC to investors included allowing 100 percent foreign ownership in investment projects; a tax holiday for up to ten years with complete tax exemption for remuneration of foreign personnel employed, royalties, and dividends of shareholders during that period; and duty exemption for the import of equipment, construction material, and production inputs. The first IPZ, at Katunayake near the Colombo International Airport (henceforth KIPZ), was opened in June 1978. Construction activities started in November 1983 on the second IPZ, which was devoted to heavy industry and was located at a Biagama site (BIPZ) which covers an area of 450 acres.

The Foreign Investment Advisory Committee (FIAC) continued its operation in approving and monitoring foreign investment outside the non-GCEC areas. Unlike the GCEC, which approved only export-oriented projects, the FIAC was empowered to approve import substitution projects also, on the basis of criteria such as employment generation, net import saving, and contribution to domestic technology. However, the potential contribution toward export development was usually taken as the major criterion. With regard to existing production and export incentives, FIAC-approved projects were treated equally with locally owned firms.

Economic Performance

Selected indicators of economic performance following the 1977 episode are presented in table 5.4. For purposes of comparison the average figure for 1970–7 is also reported.

Major Prices

General Price Level
The first 12 months under the UNP government saw a sharp increase in the price level. The CCPI rose by 12 percent (from 203 to 227). Increases in the

GNPD and the WPI of the Central Bank between 1978 and 1979 were 16 percent (from 135 to 157) and 8 percent (216 to 233) respectively (see table 2.22). The average annual increase in the CCPI during 1978–83 was 15.3 percent compared with 5.7 percent during 1970–7. Inflation was highest in 1980 and 1981. While the sharp increases in import prices following the third oil price hike would not have helped contain inflation, the main pressures for it can be traced to the expansion associated with public investment programs – Mahaweli, public housing and urban development, and the related current account deficits and exchange rate differentials (Lal, 1985).

Real Rate of Foreign Exchange

Estimates of effective rates of exchange and the method of calculation are reported by Cuthbertson and Athukorala (1988, appendix B). That analysis illustrates the extent to which nontraditional exports have been favored over the three traditional exports and how this discrimination was reduced by the exchange rate unification in 1977. Within the broad category of nontraditional exports, manufactured exports have generally been favored over nontraditional primary exports, a pattern which shows up more in the data since 1977.

The NEER on imports increased continuously after 1977 – an outcome of exchange rate depreciation coupled with upward adjustments in tariff. The index of the nominal local currency price of imports increased even faster, reflecting increases in world-market prices of imports. However, the REER has not changed much, and it seems that throughout the period the cumulative impacts of exchange rate depreciation and increases in import tariffs and world-market prices were almost counterbalanced by the rate of domestic inflation.

Estimates of trade bias (table 5.5) suggest that the trade regime continued to favor import substitution over export production after 1977. The policy package can be viewed as having a marginal bias toward export promotion if the focus is only on nontraditional exports. A comparison of estimates of nontraditional agricultural products and manufacturing suggests that this was mostly a reflection of favored treatment accorded to manufacturing; for the former the trade bias index remained below unity throughout this period.

Wages

The two wage indices are the wage rate index of workers in Wages Board trade and the wage rate index of government employees. There are several limitations in these wage data. First, both indices completely leave out wage changes in the unorganized sector and the small cottage firms that make up about 65 percent of the total workforce. Second, even for the organized sector the indices only pick up information for industries

Table 5.5 Trade bias index[a], 1965–1983

Year	Total exports	Traditional exports	Nontraditional exports		
			Total	Agriculture	Manufacturing
1965	0.64	0.64	0.74	0.71	0.80
1966	0.68	0.68	0.75	0.74	0.84
1967	0.63	0.62	0.78	0.77	0.85
1968	0.66	0.63	0.89	0.87	0.98
1969	0.65	0.63	1.05	10.3	1.19
1970	0.66	0.64	1.03	0.97	1.24
1971	0.65	0.62	1.01	0.95	1.28
1972	0.66	0.62	1.14	1.05	1.36
1973	0.72	0.61	1.48	1.23	1.44
1974	0.70	0.57	1.45	1.19	1.51
1975	0.83	0.70	1.66	1.36	1.69
1976	0.79	0.62	1.23	1.26	1.50
1977	0.76	0.59	1.55	1.34	1.59
1978	0.56	0.47	0.96	0.85	1.08
1979	0.59	0.46	1.01	0.86	1.11
1980	0.71	0.56	1.08	0.86	1.20
1981	0.79	0.62	1.13	0.89	1.22
1982	0.85	0.68	1.09	0.91	1.19
1983	0.83	0.66	1.08	0.89	1.16

[a] Ratio of NEER for exports to NEER for imports.
Source: Cuthbertson and Athukorala, 1988, appendix tables B.1 and B.2

covered by Wages Boards. These industries are tea; rubber and coconut growing and manufacture; engineering; printing; match manufacturing; motor transport; building; cinemas; and dock, harbor, and wharf transport. Third, the surveys are made at irregular intervals. Finally, the indices available to deflate such wage data as there are, are not well regarded even by the Central Bank which generates them (Field, 1986).

Table 5.6 presents two wage indices, one in nominal terms and the other adjusted to give indices of real wages. The nominal series track together after 1977, but after indexing for price movements only it appears that government sector wages have increased.

Looking across the four different bases for estimating the real wage movements of workers covered by the Wages Board, the series (d) based on the index of prices of imported inputs falls relative to the other three series which all rely on domestic price movements. It seems that the real price of labor increased more slowly than the cost of imported inputs over this period.

A little information on wage levels in the unorganized sector exists in the form of wage rates collected under the Country-wide Data Collection Scheme of the Central Bank. The data are available for the years since 1980 and relate ony to wage rates prevailing in smallholding cultivation of

Table 5.6 Wage rate indices, 1965–1983 (base, 1980)

	Workers in Wages Board trade[a]					Government employees	
	Nominal wage	Real wage rate index[b]				Nominal wage	Real wage[b]
		(a)	(b)	(c)	(d)		
1965	17.09	48.2	n.a.	n.a.	743.0	34.8	100.2
1970	20.8	47.7	n.a.	n.a.	611.7	47.8	110.7
1975	35.6	56.9	78.2	60.5	374.7	62.8	101.2
1977	44.9	70.1	75.5	69.5	275.5	67.2	105.7
1978	64.3	89.4	94.0	85.7	189.1	77.0	108.1
1979	81.2	101.6	107.5	100.4	121.9	90.2	114.3
1980	100.0	100.0	100.0	100.0	100.0	100.0	100.0
1981	103.3	87.4	87.5	85.0	77.1	112.5	95.8
1982	119.4	91.0	96.2	89.0	78.4	144.6	111.0
1983	128.2	86.0	90.8	98.8	66.8	166.1	112.1

n.a., not available.

[a] Refers to minimum wage rates of tea growing and manufacturing, rubber growing and manufacturing, coconut growing and manufacturing, engineering, printing, transport, match manufacturing, and the building, dock, tea, rubber, and cinnamon trades.

[b] Real wage rate index: (a) real wage rate received by employees (deflator, CCPI); (b) nominal wage rate index deflated by WPI, availabe from 1974 onwards; (c) nominal wage rate index deflated by producer price level in the industry (proxy index used, WPI of the domestic subgroup); (d) nominal wage rate index deflated by price level of imported inputs (proxy index used, intermediate import price index).

Source: CBC, Annual Report, various issues

tea, rubber, coconut, and paddy, and wage rates in building construction activities in the private sector (excluding large construction firms). On the basis of these data the Central Bank has concluded that unorganized sector wages increased (both in nominal and real terms) between 1980 and 1984.

Field (1986) has reviewed real wage movements and the significance of different deflators for conclusions about these movements. He contends that the CCPI understates price movements and thus overstates real wages. Using a consumer price index derived by Bhalla and Glewwe, Field concludes that "the workers of Sri Lanka received at best marginal real wage increases in the last twenty or so years." Field's adjusted data also show small average real wage declines between 1978 and 1982.

The available wage data are too thin to allow a strong conclusion. Perhaps the most robust statement that can be made is that over the six years after 1977 real wages just about held their own.

Rates of Interest

Table 5.7 shows the variations in interest rates on short- and long-term borrowing, in both current and real terms, during 1965–83. In the absence of any composite interest rate index, the methodology adopted is to bring together interest rate figures pertaining to the lending institutions for which data are readily available. There were sharp increases in nominal interest rates, both short and long term. However, in real terms, the increases were much smaller. It seems that the real rates increased only up to about 1980; since then a decline in real rates can be observed.

External Transactions

Imports

Between 1978 and 1983 the value of commodity imports varied between US$1,000 million and US$1,900 million with signs of a fall in the actual rate of increase (table 5.4). In the first half of the 1970s the import-to-GDP ratio was about 20 percent. Since 1977 it has been consistently more than 40 percent, peaking at 55 percent in 1980 and falling to 40 percent in 1983. The import volume index shows an almost trebling of investment goods imports in the five years after 1977, a doubling of intermediate imports, and an almost stable level of consumer goods imports over the same five years (Cuthbertson and Athukorala, 1988, appendix table A.5).

The share of investment goods in the value of total imports over the same five years was consistently around 25 percent (Cuthbertson and Athukorala, 1988, appendix table A.6). Consumer goods in the first couple of years were about 40 percent of imports but this share dropped to around 25 percent in later post-liberalization years. Interestingly, in the closed period before 1977 consumer goods, principally food items, typically made up about half of all imports. In post-liberalization years the food import share fell away markedly, and also fell in volume terms. Similarly, in the 1970s petroleum as a share of the import bill rose from a typical 5 percent to a consistent 25 percent.

The major import items in post-liberalization years were mainly petroleum, machinery, essential food items, fertilizers, and raw materials for garment and textile manufacturers. There was a strong aid project connection, with surges in machinery and petroleum imports. The total import demand generated by the housing program has been estimated to be about equivalent to 35 percent of the cost of that program. For the Mahaweli Project, import demands were about 80 percent of costs (Stern, 1984). For manufacturing, the effect of liberalization showed up in easier access to essential inputs. Manufacturing as a whole had an import dependence ratio of 55 percent – mainly due to petroleum and steel billets. For garments and textiles the import dependence in 1980 was about 70 percent.

The protective impact of the six-band cascading tariff regime is reflectd in the very small share of imports entering in the so-called competitive duty band. Most adjustment took place in the garments and textiles sector.

Table 5.7 Interest rate variation, 1965–1983

| | Nominal rate of interest | | | | | | |
| | Short-term borrowing | | | Long-term borrowing | | | |
Year	Interbank call loans	Bills discounted	Commercial banks – secured	Commercial banks – unsecured	State mortgage and investment bank[b]	Development Finance Corporation	National Developme Bank
1965	3	4.5–8	5–10	7–9	–	–	–
1966	3	4.5–8	5–10	7–9	–	–	–
1967	3	4.5–8	5–10	7–9	–	–	–
1968	3.5	5.5–8.5	5.5–11	7–10	–	–	–
1969	4	5.5–9	6–11	7.5–11	–	–	–
1970	4.5	6.5–10	6.5–12	8.5–12	–	–	–
1971	5	6.5–10	6.5–12	8.5–12	–	–	–
1972	5	6.5–10	6.5–12	8.5–12	5–12	9.5–10.5	–
1973	5	6.5–10	6.5–12	8.5–12	5–12	9.5–10.5	–
1974	5	6.5–10	6.5–12.5	8.5–13.5	5–12	9.5–10.5	–
1975	5–8	8.5–12	6.5–13	9.5–14	5–12	9.5–12.5	–
1976	5–8	8.5–13	6.5–14	9.5–14	5–12	9.5–12.5	–
1977	7–9.5	11–21	10–20	18–20	5–15	9.5–12.5	–
1978	7–9.5	11–21	10–20	18–20	5–14	9.5–13	–
1979	9–11	13–21	10–20	18–21	5–18	9.5–16	10–12
1980	21.5–25	15–25	11–28	19–30	5–20	10.5–17	10–17
1981	15–25	15–25	10–30	19–32	12–24	13–17	10–17
1982	14–28	14–28	10–30	14–30	12–24	12–17	10–17
1983	18–28	13–28	11–28	11–30	12–24	11–14	9–14

—. negligible.

[a] Nominal exchange rate deflated by the expected rate of inflation. The estimates are based on the assumption that the expected rate of inflation is equal to the last period's rate of inflation. The measure of inflation used is the GNPD.

[b] Interest rates given for the period prior to 1979 relate to lending by both the State Mortgage Bank and the Agricultural and Industrial Credit Corporation (these two institutions were amalgamated in 1979 to form the State Mortgage and Investment Bank).

Source: CBC. Review of the Economy, various issues

Real rate of interest[a]

Short-term borrowing			Long-term borrowing			
Interbank call loans	Bills discounted	Commercial banks – secured	Commercial banks – unsecured	State mortgage and investment bank	Development Finance Corporation	National Development Bank
3.7	5.4–9.7	6.2–12	8.5–10.9			
3.6	5.4–9.6	6.0–12.0	8.4–10.8			
3.6	5.4–14.5	8.5–10.9	8.5–10.9			
4.2	6.5–10.1	6.5–13.0	8.3–11.9			
4.3	5.9–9.7	6.5–11.8	8.1–11.8			
4.6	6.7–10.4	6.7–12.4	8.8–12.4			
5.0	6.5–10.0	6.5–10.0	8.5–12.0			
4.8	6.3–9.7	6.3–11.6	8.2–11.7	4.8–11.6	9.2–10.2	
4.6	6.0–9.3	6.0–11.2	7.8–11.1	4.6–11.1	8.8–9.7	
4.0	5.1–7.8	5.1–9.9	6.7–10.6	3.9–9.5	7.5–8.3	
3.1–5.0	5.3–7.5	4.1–8.1	5.9–8.7	3.1–7.5	5.9–7.8	
2.9–4.7	5.0–7.6	3.8–8.2	5.5–8.2	2.9–7.0	5.5–7.3	
3.8–4.4	3.8–7.2	5.5–11.0	9.9–11.0	2.8–8.3	5.2–6.9	
3.3–4.4	5.1–9.8	4.6–9.3	8.4–9.3	2.3–6.5	4.4–6.0	
3.9–4.7	5.6–9.1	4.3–8.6	7.7–9.0	2.1–7.7	4.1–6.9	4.3–5.2
8.0–9.3	5.6–9.3	4.1–10.4	7.1–11.1	1.9–7.4	3.9–6.3	3.7–6.3
4.7–7.9	4.7–7.9	3.1–9.5	6.0–10.6	3.7–7.5	4.1–5.3	3.1–5.3
3.6–7.3	3.7–7.3	2.6–7.8	3.7–7.3	3.1–4.3	3.1–4.3	2.6–4.3
3.4–6.6	5.1–6.6	3.1–8.7	3.1–7.1	4.1–8.7	2.6–3.3	2.1–3.3

Import competition was important for small handloom textile firms but the employment losses there seem to have been swamped sector-wide by the rapid growth of exports.

Exports

Despite the expansion in services receipts (an outcome of expanding tourism) and private transfers (mainly remittances by migrant workers), merchandise exports still dominate total foreign exchange earnings – accounting for over 80 percent in all years since 1977 (Cuthbertson and Athukorala, 1988, appendix table 11). Escalation of import prices (notably since the onset of the oil crisis in 1972) in the face of declining or slow-moving export prices has meant deterioration in the terms of trade. With only slow growth of export volume, the cumulative outcome was a significant erosion of the import purchasing power of the economy (table 5.4). The index of import purchasing power of Sri Lankan export earnings has declined over most of the years under study, with the annual rate of decline acclerating in recent years. Import purchasing power in 1983 was only 30 percent of that of 1960 (Stern, 1984).

The slow growth of total exports during the period under study reflects not so much a failure to develop new export items as the stagnation in the traditional "triple" – tea, rubber, and coconut products. The main exception to this observed overall pattern was the sudden upturn in the current value of tea exports around 1983 as an outcome of a jump in tea prices.

Estimates of Sri Lanka's share in total world exports of these three traditional items (table 5.8) suggest that, for these commodities, external demand was not a real constraint. Market shares are erratic but general downward trend is discernible.

Table 5.8 Tea, rubber, and coconut kernel products – Sri Lanka's share of total export volume of producing countries (percent)

Year	Tea	Rubber	Coconut – desiccated coconut	Copra	Coconut oil
1974	31.8	4.2	38.5	0.08	2.5
1975	34.9	5.5	45.5	0.13	6.5
1976	31.8	4.4	35.3	0.11	5.7
1977	29.6	4.3	23.0	0.03	10.0
1978	31.6	4.3	38.1	0.34	2.3
1979	29.0	3.9	30.5	0.19	3.0
1980	28.2	3.8	25.2	0.06	0.3
1981	27.5	4.3	23.7	0.03	1.3
1982	26.7	3.7	22.3	0.02	1.4

Sources: FAO, International Trade Yearbook, various issues supplemented by World Bank, Commodity Trade and Price Trends, various issues

For rubber and coconut products there seems to be no systematic relationship between REER and output (table 5.9). The overall level of REER for both products was relatively higher during 1978–84 than during 1974–7, but the real export series continued to decline. In the case of rubber, two public sector corporations, the Sri Lankan State Plantation Corporation (SLSPC) and the Janatha Estates Development Board (JEDB), account for about 30 percent of total registered acreage and about 35 percent of total production. Unlike rubber – of which only about 8 percent is absorbed locally – nearly 75 percent of total coconut production is consumed in Sri Lanka. Therefore domestic demand is important in determining export levels. Throughout the period under study, coconut output expanded at a slower rate than the rate of expansion in local demand. This reflects the policy conflict between keeping prices for domestic consumers low and raising export returns; it seems that, in setting rates of export tax, greater policy weight was given to keeping consumers' costs low.

As noted earlier, although the private sector accounts for only about 25 percent of the total registered tea acreage, its output share has increased from about 20 percent in 1980 to over 30 percent in 1983, possibly in response to clearer signals about relative returns for different kinds of tea. According to the agricultural census of 1973 and 1982, the area under tea cultivation declined from 233,987 to 211,865 hectares. This is consistent with the low producer prices and the increasingly higher export taxes that applied in these years. The acreage decline was more clearly marked for mid-country private sector tea growers who were apparently able to diversify easily into other more profitable crops (Bandaranaike, 1984). Field surveys show similar contractions in total estimated rubber land. Profitability considerations are usually considered less important for investment decisions of state plantations, since revenue shortfalls are usually met by Treasury grants. However, experience in the tea sector in the late 1970s and early 1980s shows that higher producer margins brought about by a favorable REER also encourage planting and output of state plantations. An improved liquidity position and associated improved financial independence from the Treasury saw both the JEDB and the SLSPC implement their capital expenditure programs as scheduled (CBC, *Annual Report*, 1984).

The relative contribution of manufactured exports to total commodity exports in 1974, 1977, and 1984 was 4 percent, 6 percent, and 42 percent respectively (see table 2.27). However, as noted, growth was rather lopsided and has emanated from a single commodity – garments. The overall export orientation of manufacturing appears to have increased from 1976 (Cuthbertson and Athukorala, 1988, appendix table A.12). In 1976 the export coefficient – the ratio of exports to total gross manufacturing output – was 12 percent. This increased to 18 percent in 1978 and then to 24 percent in 1980. Yet sectoral estimates indicate that export coefficients increased for only a few product categories (at the three-digit ISIC level), namely wearing apparel, leather goods, rubber and plastic goods, and ceramic ware.

Export earnings from garments continued to expand despite a consistent and sharp decline in the REER in the early 1980s. Total exports in 1977 were SDR 14 million, increasing to 85 million in 1980 and 289 million in 1984. From 1979 until 1984, the share of KIPZ firms in total garments exports continuously increased. The incentive package available to KIPZ producers is quite different from that available to non-KIPZ producers, and the REER series reflects mainly the incentive available to the latter. Non-KIPZ firms do have the option of selling in a protected domestic market but exports by these firms have also expanded spectacularly.[1]

Textiles and garments were the major attraction for both KIPZ investors and FIAC investors. There are two reasons for this: (a) the imposition of stringent quota restrictions by major consuming countries on garment imports from traditional developing country producers in order to generate a potential market for newcomers; (b) the comparative advantage of Sri Lanka in the production of garments and other light manufactured goods in the face of increases in the cost of labor in other major garment-producing countries in Asia. The importance of the getting-round-the-quota motive for the upsurge in foreign investment in the garment sector is reflected in the involvement of a large number of Hong Kong owned firms (Athukorala, 1984a). Since the mid-1970s, the strictest US quotas have been those against Hong Kong – the major developing country garment exporter. Apart from garments, the other areas of production in the KIPZ, in the order of the number of firms, are nonmetallic minerals (lapidary and jewelry), rubber goods, and other labor-intensive products such as footwear, toys, and electrical appliances.

Agricultural exports other than tea, rubber, and coconut kernel products have increased steadily since about the late 1960s, when export diversification became an issue in trade policy. The rate of expansion increased in the three or four years following the 1977 policy reforms but growth has been slow since. The observed overall pattern is generally supportive of the hypothesis that the exchange rate matters.

For the category of coconut products, charcoal, fiber-bristle, fiber mattress, and coir yarn there is a positive relationship between real export

---

[1] Part of this increase may comprise fictitious exports. In 1983 customs authorities discovered that garments exporters, with the help of buyers abroad, had overinvoiced exports with a view to obtaining duty rebate benefits and becoming eligible for the import of textiles which could be sold in the open market at attractive prices. Eighteen factories were identified as being involved in this practice. From this evidence alone it was found that the Treasury had paid duty rebates of some Rs 80 million on fictitious exports (converted at a relevant rate of duty rebate, the value of fictitious exports related to this practice is about Rs 250 million).

earnings and the REER (table 5.9). Acreage under cocoa cultivation increased from the late 1960s, and later declines in export volume were due to expansion in domestic absorption. From 1977 the biscuit and confectionery industry expanded rapidly, benefiting from the availability of imported inputs and relatively higher protection for final products ensured through successive upward adjustments in tariffs. A captive local market for cocoa generated by the expansion of biscuit and confectionery production and the gradual erosion in real incentives for cocoa exports have made selling that product on the domestic market relatively more profitable than exporting. A continuous expansion in coffee exports was an outcome of replanting and new plantings undertaken since about the early 1970s which reflected favorable prices in the world coffee market. Exports of spices (pepper, cinnamon, cloves, nutmeg, and cardamom) have increased steadily, with no apparent tracking of variations in REER.

Apparent export growth of mineral products has been slow since about 1978 (table 5.9) – the average annual growth rate in 1978–80 was 6.3 percent compared with 25 percent for 1974–7. The rate of growth declined even more in 1981–4, falling to 3 percent per year. This apparent contraction could be due to the slow expansion in recorded gem exports which make up about 80 percent of Sri Lanka's total recorded mineral exports. Gems, more than most traded goods, allow scope for illicit trade and, in Sri Lanka, recorded trade in gems has varied with the taxes, implicit or explicit, imposed on them. The Convertible Rupee Account (CRA) scheme introduced in 1972 was an attempt to bring the foreign exchange earnings from gem exports into official channels. In the restricted trade regime of the time, CRA credits (first 25 percent and later 20 percent of f.o.b. exports) allowed to gem exporters for financing scarce imports fetched a premium of 150–200 percent in the market. The result was a substantial enhancement of the REER and the bringing of more gem exports into the open market.

The CRA scheme was abolished in November 1977 and there was no replacement incentive for gem exports. In 1980 profits from gem exports were made tax exempt, but there were apparently ample avenues for tax evasion anyway so that this did not seem to be a significant incentive. A 5 percent business turnover tax (BTT) on gem sales, introduced originally on November 15, 1977, and retroactive from January 1, 1976, was withdrawn temporarily on March 31, 1978, reintroduced on June 19, 1980, and abolished again in 1983. On the control side, policing has proved difficult and it seems that smuggling has continued unabated. The gem export series according to customs data indicates an average annual growth rate of only 0.7 percent and a negative growth rate of 1.7 percent in current and real SDR terms respectively during the period 1978–84. When this series is adjusted by deducting cut-and-polished diamond exports the two figures turn out to be − 1.2 percent and − 3.4 percent respectively.

Table 5.9 Real effective exchange rate and export performance[a] (million constant 1980 SDR)

		1974	1975	1976	1977	1978	1979	1980	1981	1982	1983	1984	r[b]
Tea	REER	58	57	72	103	100	92	95	84	80	89	132	− 0.097
	Exports	262	320	302	280	295	282	288	285	283	253	324	
Rubber	REER	74	65	95	72	100	124	98	87	78	73	67	− 0.282
	Exports	126	157	133	132	134	128	120	128	128	129	126	
Coconut kernel products	REER	65	55	69	117	100	96	111	89	63	66	89	− 0.341
	Exports	80	138	119	56	96	88	35	72	102	95	58	
Coconut byproducts	REER	104	84	101	116	100	107	111	100	86	65	58	− 0.192
	Exports	21	19	23	22	21	24	22	19	20	22	20	
Spices	REER	78	82	114	99	100	111	102	94	78	52	40	+ 0.064
	Exports	18	14	16	22	17	21	24	31	22	28	28	
Other agriculture	REER	78	64	94	118	100	106	77	65	63	59	57	+ 0.297
	Exports	14	13	16	8	22	22	17	31	41	31	21	
Gems[c]	REER	140	136	156	150	100	94	98	78	80	70	53	+ 0.292
	Exports	16	26	32	30	27	26	29	25	24	29	22	
Garments	REER	52	61	98	105	100	84	82	82	85	73	65	− 0.258
	Exports	4	4	9	15	27	63	85	112	116	149	251	
Seafood	REER	91	97	88	105	100	94	91	92	102	75	57	− 0.220
	Exports	6	5	9	10	10	14	12	14	14	13	17	
Other manufactures	REER	61	77	94	80	100	105	93	94	98	80	67	+ 0.086
	Exports	13	14	15	26	21	18	14	22	39	35	38	

[a] Base year 1978
[b] Pearson's correlation coefficient
[c] In customs returns gem exports are recorded under BTN 71.02 ('Precious and semi-precious stones') together with diamonds. In recent years exports of cut and polished diamonds of Blue Peacock Diamond Ltd (a joint venture with a Belgian firm) have contributed a significant portion of the value of this category. Export figures (obtained from EDB records) of this company for the period 1979-84 are as follows (in SDR million): 1979: 0.8. 1980: 0.9; 1981: 2.09; 1982: 8.58; 1983: 15.3; 1984: 10.1

However, production has continued to expand (Cuthbertson and Athukorala, 1988, appendix table A.13) and the decline in exports must reflect a growing illicit trade.

Up to about 1979 the series of real seafood exports followed the time pattern of the REER series closely. After that the real seafood exports continued to increase despite an apparent overall REER decline. This could reflect developments in supply. By 1983 there were about 12 regular seafood exporters and, of these, about five firms accounted for about 80 percent of the total export volume. Benefitting from generous financial assistance provided under the Export Expansion Grant Scheme, these firms had launched extensive investment plans to expand production. The steady expansion in exports despite a falling REER in recent years mainly reflects these earlier investments.

Real export earnings of food, beverages, and tobacco – mainly margarine, confectionery, fruit juice, canned fruit, and tobacco products (mainly cigarettes) – are erratic, but the general pattern roughly follows the corresponding REER series. For most of the firms involved in the export of these products, the proceeds of exports account for a relatively small proportion of total turnover compared with their domestic sales. Therefore the relative profitability of selling in the domestic market compared with exporting is an important factor in determining the behavior of export earnings from these products.

Income and Product

Recall that the lowest average growth recorded in Sri Lanka occurred during 1970–7 – the period preceding the second episode. The fastest recorded growth came in 1965–9, encompassing the first episode. Growth was also rapid in the period 1978–82 after the economic reforms of the second episode. This rapid growth is attributed to both the reforms and the slack economy to which they were initially applied (Cuthbertson and Athukorala, 1988, appendix table A.1). The relative contributions made by each sector in GDP and their average growth rates are shown in table 2.11. Agriculture continued to be important throughout the period. Services, the second most important sector, increased slightly, while manufacturing including export processing, has grown rather slowly. Throughout, the share of manufacturing in GDP is relatively constant and small at about 10 percent. Probably the most noticeable feature is the rapid growth that has occurred in the trade, construction, utilities, and transport sectors.

Table 2.17 shows that, despite the policy rhetoric about transferring economic activity back to the private sector, the aggregate share of public enterprises in manufacturing sector output has been maintained in the post-liberalization period, being as high as 63 percent even in 1983. This continuing dominance, coupled with an apparent inability of the public sector to meet the challenges of trade liberalization as observed above, provides one explanation for the relatively slow growth performance of manufacturing over the period. As noted later, however, the private sector still accounted for most employment growth.

The falling off in long-run trends of production in export agriculture which started in the late 1960s continued after 1977. Export agriculture's share of total GDP fell from 9 percent in 1970 to 5 percent in 1983. Domestic agriculture expanded from 1977 and in the post-policy reform period has grown at about 7 percent per year. Its share of GDP is steady at about 20 percent (table 2.11).

The changing composition of manufacturing is reported in table 2.12. The chemical, petroleum, rubber, and plastic product category has the largest share of total manufacturing, with petroleum products playing the major role (32 percent and 28 percent of total manufacturing in 1977 and 1982 respectively). The significance of food, beverages, and tobacco products fell away in 1977 and 1982. The relative contribution of textile, wearing apparel, and leather industries increased markedly after 1977, from 7 percent in 1977 to 14 percent in 1982. The responses of the different sectors to liberalization in light of sector characteristics and the beginning of protection is summarized in table 5.10 and the remainder of this section.

Table 5.10 provides no basis for linking together sector disruption and degree of liberalization. Production in each of the sectors has grown in all cases except one, and much the same story applies to employment. In the case of textiles and wearing apparel, protection from imports continued to be high but output and employment grew as a result of access to preferred export markets. This meant that sector output and employment were maintained despite an estimated very large contraction in the handloom sector, where by one estimate 30,000 of the 110,000 handlooms operating in 1977 had gone out of production by 1980. Textile output shifted to the larger mills, but attempts to put more competitive pressure on them by opening up licensing barriers met with stiff opposition. Interestingly, though, textile mills are one of the few areas of industry where the much talked of privatization program made some headway.

Opinions differ on the significance of continued license controls in maintaining output and production. One view is that through the early 1980s licensing was not an important barrier and that the applied 35 percent duty was the relevant barrier. It does seem that the textile industry was given a new lease of life by the rapid export growth of garments. The scheme for rebating garment exporters for import duty imposts is relevant here. This was a standard rebate scheme which did not discriminate against the use of domestically produced inputs in export production.

Some other sectors continued to receive high effective protection after 1977. For example, wood and wood products, where the major employer was the Plywood Corporation (85 percent of sector output), benefited from continued licensing of plywood imports. However, as with many of the public corporations, there were also implicit and explicit taxes on the Plywood Corporation. Included here might be the price controls on materials sold to the Tea Corporation, the hiring obligations, and regional production objectives. A similar story applies to the paper and paper products sector. After 1977 this sector remained small, grew slowly, and continued to be dominated by a public corporation which had output selectively protected at high levels.

Employment Disruption and Trade Liberalization

In some models of trade liberalization some disruption and economic dislocation, if only in the short term, is regarded as an inevitable consequence of the adjustment process. This disruption is seen as a price that has to be paid for the longer-term and economy-wide gains to be had as resources move to new and higher return activities. How much of this economic dislocation and actual unemployment will occur depends upon such things as the state of the macroeconomy and how well the labor market works. In some circumstances growing unemployment and disruption need not be accompaniments to a trade liberalization effort. According to this view of the world, if factors of production are able to adjust quickly to new prices and opportunities the positive opportunities created by trade expansion will soon pick up people displaced by pressures from import competition on particular economic activities.

The Sri Lanka evidence supports the second view of trade liberalization. The data are not good, and there are many other phenomena and policies at work. Even so, detailed searches of firms and worker behavior at the industry level which deliberately set out to establish links between unemployment, business failure, and liberalization were unsuccessful in every case.

In 1980 the Ministry of Industries and Scientific Affairs and the Industrial Development Board each conducted an industry survey for the express purpose of showing the disruptive effects of liberalization on industry. These survey results were expected to provide a basis for requests for increased protection for many industries. The larger survey of the two – conducted by the Ministry of Industries and Scientific Affairs – found that some 20 percent of the firms on its list were actually inoperative at the time of the survey (Cuthbertson and Athukorala, 1988, appendix table A.14). However, this finding can be explained easily enough. To begin with, interest in being on the ministry list of approved firms had fallen away in 1978 and 1979 as the dismantling of licensing did away with the need to be in the Ministry's good books, as it were. Thus by 1980 the listing was not comprehensive anyway. Also, the focus on apparent

Table 5.10 Summary of sector attributes by degree of liberalization for food, beverages, and tobacco, garments, textiles, and chemicals, petroleum, and plastic products[a]

Indicator	Food, beverages, and tobacco	Garment
Sector description	Not dominated by public corporations	Export oriented, mainly privately owned in GCEC and outside; significant foreign investment
Initial protection	Moderate	Very high
Degree of implementation	Significant but variable	Despite continued licensing, significant rationalization and adjustment
Size	Large	At about 60,000 people, the largest organized sector
Geographic concentration	Relatively scattered	Free-trade zone and around Colombo
Industrial concentration	Very high	Relatively low with three firms comprising about half of production
Production	About a quarter of manufacturing output; becoming relatively more important	Growing rapidly
Employment	Second-largest sector	Growing rapidly
Profit rates	Little known	Implicitly quite high
Business failures	Few	Infrequent
Exports	Mainly processed seafoods and fruit	Substantial growth of exports – about 80% of output exported

[a] Organized sector only.

Textiles	Petroleum and chemicals
Formerly government owned, significantly privatized	Dominated by the Petroleum Corporation plus a mix of smaller public corporations, large foreign firms, and small local firms
Very high	High
Free entry and liberal regime for export market – domestic remains sheltered	Neither exceptionally full nor exceptionally deficient
About 35,000 people; one of the large employers	Large – even without the Petroleum Corporation about 20% of manufacturing output
Scattered	Slightly more decentralized than most manufacturing
Scattered	Much the same as other sectors; relatively strong foreign ownership
Stable	Rapid growth even aside from petroleum; mainly paints, toilet products, pesticides, drugs, medicines, etc.
Stable	Stable
Not much known; confused by privatization and adjustment	Little known
Frequent	Number of small firm closures in 1978
About 7% of output	Mainly rubber goods and petroleum refining byproducts

business closures took no account of new openings. That there were new entrants is shown by FIAC and Local Investment Advisory Committee (LIAC) approvals for new projects and, more importantly, the increased output which can be found for nearly all sectors.

Table 5.11 summarizes the available estimates on unemployment, obtained from scattered sources. Owing to the differences in sample coverage, sample definition, and methods of data collection, unemployment rates reported by these surveys are not strictly comparable. That said, all the data consistently point to significant reductions in unemployment from 1977.

Central Bank data on employment in the organized manufacturing sector during 1974–82 are reported in table 5.12. Despite rapid expansion in import flows in almost all import categories following trade liberalization in 1977, the number employed in manufacturing continued to increase, if anything faster than before liberalization. The data show that the major part of this increase in employment originated in private sector industries, although the output shares have remained very much the same. From 1979, the public sector share in total employment declined continuously. Of the increase in total employment (52,000 between 1977 and 1982), about 80 percent (42,400) originated in the private sector.

A comparison of output and employment since 1971 for the nine manufacturing industry sectors reveals that only the fabricated metal and machinery and transport equipment sectors show a post-liberalization decline in employment (Cuthbertson and Athukorala, 1988, appendix table A.15). All others indicate increases in employment, though at

Table 5.11 Estimates of unemployment

Year	Source[a]	Unemployment as a percentage of labor force
1953	Population census (DCS)	0.8
1959–60	Survey on employment (ILO)	10.5
1963	Population census (DCS)	10.8
1964	Consumer finance survey (CBC)	13.8
1968	Labor force survey (CBC)	11.0
1969–70	Socioeconomic survey (DCS)	14.0
1971	Population census (DCS)	18.7
1973	Labor force participation survey (CBC)	18.1
1973	Consumer finance survey (CBC)	24.0
1975	Land and labor utilization survey (DCS)	19.8
1978–9	Consumer finance survey (DCS)	14.7
1980–1	Socioeconomic survey (DCS)	13.6
1981–2	Consumer finance survey (CBC)	11.7

[a]DCS, Department of Census and Statistics; ILO, International Labor Organization; CBC, Central Bank of Ceylon.

Table 5.12 Employment in the organized sector, 1974–1983

| | Public sector | | | Organized private sector | | | | Private sector |
Year	Government	Semigovernment[a]	Total	GCEC	Other[b]	Total	Total	contribution (%)
1974	412,284	247,001	659,285	—	220,830	220,830	880,115	25.09
1975	425,865	259,184	685,049	—	229,100	229,100	914,149	25.06
1976	406,381	541,044	947,425	—	235,810	235,810	1,183,235	19.93
1977	422,647	617,033	1,039,680	—	283,427	283,427	1,323,107	21.42
1978	446,085	681,034	1,127,119	261	321,690	321,951	1,449,070	22.18
1979	470,188	749,034	1,219,222	5,876	310,096	315,972	1,535,194	20.58
1980	476,086	769,122	1,245,208	10,538	348,597	359,135	1,604,343	22.38
1981	481,475	778,199	2,259,674	19,729	348,365	368,094	1,627,768	22.61
1982	484,802	784,370	1,269,172	24,926	320,753	345,679	1,614,851	21.41
1983	489,472	785,717	1,275,189	28,705	—	—	—	—

—, not applicable.
[a] Public corporations, universities, boards, banks, etc.
[b] Based on Employees' Provident Fund (EPF) data (number of active accounts, that is, accounts which have received at least one contribution during the course of the year, with the EPF).
Source: CBC, Review of the Economy, various issues

varying rates. The wearing apparel and leather products sector accounted for 44 percent of the total employment increase in manufacturing between 1977 and 1980, despite the evidence that this sector (especially its spinning and weaving subsector) was among the most affected by import competition with substantial contraction of the cottage-style output.

Cuthbertson and Athukorala (1988, appendix table A.16) show production, imports, and employment at a four-digit ISIC level for selected import-competing sectors for 1978, 1979, and 1980. For those small sectors where production and employment did not appear to grow, for example tobacco, cutlery, handtools and general hardware, there was no link with imports, which were virtually zero in the period concerned. Employment actually did fall and imports actually increased in glass products, footwear, and metal furniture and fixtures. The employment numbers are small in each case as were the increases in imports in real terms. Glass and glass products is an example of a sector in which a deliberately low duty was applied, despite a small established local manufacturing presence, for consumption objectives – to keep packaging charges down for the Pharmaceutical Corporation. The contractions in footwear employment did match the production cutback and the import figures. The Leather Corporation, a public corporation, employs about half the people in the organized sector. Import duties remained high throughout (100 percent), and with export taxes or bans applying to leather and rubber and low duties for inputs, effective protection post-liberalization was high for both leather and nonleather shoes. There were also some small exports of nonleather shoes. The State Hardware Corporation, a public corporation which in 1979 employed about 1,500 people, dominates the cutlery and handtools sector. However, the cutback in employment in the sector did not match output reductions, even though the ratio of imports to production did increase somewhat.

Metal furniture and fixtures is about the only area where there was a relatively large increase in imports and a relatively large consistent cutback in employment. Even here the story is confusing, as there was a strong recovery in output if not employment in 1980, and in any event the figures are small.

Thus the Sri Lankan experience immediately after liberalization was not one where a surge of imports brought about unemployment either in aggregate or in major individual sectors. Instead, the initial response was widespread growth of output and employment. There are several possible explanations for this. Two factors outside the trade policy reforms may have contributed to the post-liberalization falls in unemployment. First, a large number of skilled, semiskilled, and unskilled workers migrated temporarily to Middle Eastern and west Asian countries. This began in small numbers in about 1975, with the number of migrant workers rising to an estimate of more than 70,000 at the end of 1982 (chapter 2). Second, since about 1975 about 20,000 persons have been repatriated to India each year under the Sirima–Shastri Agreement on plantation workers of Indian origin.

It might also be argued that the liberalization's first step, large as it was, was still quite selective, and that this is a reason why pockets of unemployment cannot be identified for individual sectors. In the organized sector public corporations remained relatively secure and they followed liberal hiring practices from 1978 onwards. The new tariff bands began with at least 100 percent nominal protection for established industries (with low duties on inputs), and measures of effective protection show as much variation within sectors as across sectors.

In garments and textiles the export growth appears to have swamped the unemployment effects of small textile firms that went out of business immediately following liberalization. There were other small sectors where, following liberalization, the initial protective duty for local firms was substantially reduced for specific consumption objectives. For example, safety helmets, sporting goods, cycles, and motorcycles were dutied at lower rates as consumption objectives took precedence over protection of local industry.

A wage flexibility theory could explain why employment in some manufacturing sectors apparently did not fall with liberalization. Unemployment was high when the episode started and unions did not have much influence with the new government. However, demand for labor in nonmanufacturing sectors was very strong. Construction activity soon boomed owing to the quick start on aid-financed projects and the impact of liberalization on the hotel and banking sectors, and labor demand was further boosted by demand for Sri Lankan workers from overseas. The wage data that are available (table 5.6) indicate general increases in wages, although this observation depends on price index data about which no one is really confident.

Another hypothesis is that moving to a tariff, even a high protective one, and away from administered systems of allocating foreign exchange for imported inputs could have given rise to dynamic growth effects. This could have happened as domestic manufacturers became better able to take advantage of economies of scale. Another source of dynamic gains might have been the increased competition on the domestic market engendered by license removal. This explanation fits the results of the Ministry of Industries' 1980 survey on the effects of liberalization. The ministry concluded that, though there had been a significant number of business failures, they had been more than offset by employment opportunities elsewhere either in the same sector or in construction or services.

When considering employment effects it also needs to be remembered that the population of Sri Lanka is overwhelmingly rural and that nearly half the workforce is engaged in agriculture. Smallholder agriculture, mainly paddy, has benefited since 1977 first from the raising of price controls and second from the irrigation development flowing from the accelerated Mahaweli program.

Income Distribution and Socioeconomic Attributes

Sri Lanka was for many years regarded as a relatively rich Asian country with a high level of quality of life indicators. In 1960 available measures of income, life expectancy, and school enrollments put it ahead of most Asian countries, a state of affairs which, it is generally held, did not persist over the next 25 years. Some writers contend that after 1960, when UNP governments more disposed to easing controls and opening up trade were in power, both growth and quality of life improved (Lal and Rajapatirana, 1985). Some data on per capita real consumption expenditures even point to a diminution in these expenditures, especially between 1970 and 1977 when the SLFP coalition ran generally a closed controlled economy (Bhalla, 1984a).

On the face of it some elements of the 1977 episode appeared to erode benefits important to lower income people. The producer price for rice was raised and some food subsidies were removed, including the rice subsidy. A food stamp program was set up in 1979. These moves cut both the number of subsidy recipients and the total cost of subsidies. Moreover, the food stamp policy fixed the nominal value of the stamps and the high inflation of the 1980s quickly eroded their real value (Edirisinghe, 1986).

According to the factor share data, labor's share seems to have fallen after 1977 while the share of property incomes appears to have risen (Lakshman, 1985). Expected inflation, expansionary demand, easing of building restrictions, and expectations that widespread government acqui-sition of property was unlikely would all have had a positive impact on the rapid increase in property values that occurred from 1978. Higher rates of inflation, government borrowing, and reduced interest rate controls would all have made for increased observed nominal interest rates. Lakshman (1985) says that noninstitutional lending increased and did so at higher interest rates than institutional lending. This is surprising, as reduction of institutional controls would ordinarily have been expected to encourage funds into the institutional lending sector. Interestingly, it seems that the proportion of interest-free loans raised from friends and relatives did fall.

Thus the facts in Sri Lanka's case give rise to some dispute about the conventional wisdom that times of closed controlled economies bring equalizing redistributions of income, and vice versa as economies are opened to trade. Conclusions about whether or not the pre-1977 period relatively enhanced the lot of the poor depend on whether income or consumption measures are used in comparisons. Bhalla and Glewwe (1986), using real consumption expenditures, found a fall in living stan-dards immediately post-liberalization but concluded that by 1980–1 there had been a recovery to 1977 levels. Lakshman's income data display the same general post-1977 fall and subsequent recovery (Lakshman, 1985). He has arranged the Central Bank Consumer Finances Survey data into income deciles and derived rates of income growth by decile for the periods from 1973 to 1978–9 and from 1978–9 to 1981–2 (Cuthbertson and Athukorala, 1988, appendix table A.17). While these data show income growth to be concentrated in high income groups, the overlapping of the data for the period from 1973 to 1978–9 confuses the comparisons. For example, the growth of income for the very highest decile was highest and for the lowest decile was lowest in the first period. This could reflect the impact of 1978 data, especially removal of food subsidies. Between 1978–9 and 1981–2 income growth in the two highest and two lowest deciles exceeded income growth of other deciles with that of the highest decile being greatest, but not by much. According to these various data, then, the process seems to be one that begins with a definite increase in income dispersion and then settles down to income growth for lower deciles that is not much different from that for higher deciles.

In two recent papers, Glewwe (1986, 1988a) has extended his previous work with Bhalla to shed further light on the trade liberalization–growth controversy. In this new work he examines the extent to which the means-tested food stamp scheme introduced in 1979 encouraged under-reporting of incomes by low and middle income groups. Glewwe based these analyses on household expenditure data. In the 1986 paper he compared household expenditure patterns of 1969–70 and 1980–1 (using data from a socioeconomic survey conducted by the Department of Census and Statistics) and concluded that inequality of expenditure distribution had declined over the period.

This analysis was extended by Glewwe (1988b) to cover three more data sets – the 1973, 1978–9 and 1981–2 Consumer Finance Surveys conducted by the Central Bank. In this study a distinction was made between inequality "before transfers" (that is, excluding food rations) and "after transfers." The results showed that the distribution of expenditures before transfers was smaller in 1981–2 than in 1978–9 and 1973. When transfers were added, the degree of inequality was roughly the same for 1981–2 and 1978–9. This result is inconsistent with the fact that the equalizing impact of food coupons declined over this period owing to high inflation. In light of these results, Glewwe concluded that, according to the Sri Lankan experience, "economic liberalization policies do not necessarily bring about greater inequality."

Glewwe (1986, 1988a) does not deny that available survey results, based on household income data, generally indicate an increase in income inequality after reform. Rather, he disputes the income data and presents alternative results on the basis of expenditure data which he perceives to be more appropriate for the purpose. Glewwe's data choice is, of course, open to criticism (Ravallion and Jayasuriya, 1988). However, officials in Sri Lankan statistical agencies generally seem to accept household expenditure figures as being more reliable than the corresponding figures on household income (Glewwe, 1988b).

Other indicators are mixed. The food stamp program was better directed at poor people than the general subsidies it replaced, job opportunities were substantially increased (see the section on employment), and the availability of both essentials and luxury consumer goods was much more comprehensive. However, there are reports of increased morbidity, reduced calorie consumption, and increased malnutrition in lower income families (Shan, 1987). The 1984 Central Bank *Annual Report* refers to increasing avoidance of school at the high school level. The latter may be linked to such influences as the quality of education, the returns expected from it, and perhaps rising opportunity costs of education reflecting improving wage and employment opportunities.

Budgetary Impact

The switch from licensing controls to tariffs had immediate positive impacts on revenue. Revenue from import duties rose from an average of about 10 percent of tax revenue to about 20 percent. However, the dismantling of the FEEC system in 1977 closed that source of revenue and overall the relative importance of import levies as a revenue earner did not increase post-liberalization. Revenue from export duties, which was about

10 percent of government revenue before 1977, jumped to around 30 percent (reflecting the unification of the exchange rate) in 1979, 1980, and 1981 before falling to between 10 and 15 percent of revenue after 1982 (Cuthbertson and Athukorala, 1988, appendix table A.10).

Duty revenue as a proportion of the value of imports is relatively low – consistently around 10 percent in post-liberalization years. Immediately following liberalization a striking feature of the composition of imports was the very large share which came in free of duty – typically about 50 percent. Prior to 1982, about a third of the imports which entered free of duty were items actually classified as duty free; the rest were government department inputs which were exempted from duty and imports into the GCEC. Petroleum for refining, wheat, rice, and other basic consumer items, agricultural inputs, and textile inputs dominated these duty-free items.

Despite the fine tuning of the tariff, the broad composition of revenues from import duties remained stable. About three quarters of total import duties seem to be collected from five main groups: prepared foods, textiles, metal products, machinery and appliances, and vehicles and transport equipment.

An instance in which revenue considerations were inconsistent with liberalization was the levy on imports duty at more than 50 percent imposed in 1980 in order to finance the export development fund. The contrariness of this step has been discussed earlier; suffice it to say here that it provides an example of how misunderstanding, institutional determination, and the budget difficulties of raising monies for effective export assistance can erode liberalization objectives.

In 1978 the new government had taken a number of accompanying subsidy removal steps: this should have reduced pressures to raise revenue, as well as removing the distortions that the subsidies involved. A food subsidy, which by 1977 had grown to account for 24 percent of revenue and 6 percent of GDP, was the first to be tackled. Early in 1978 a substantial proportion of higher income groups was made ineligible for the rice ration and in September 1979 the rice ration was replaced by a food stamp scheme. Similarly, the losses on subsidizing petroleum items were reduced substantially. While these parts of the package have not been undone, other commitments have as their most important objective the assurance that public corporations would survive on the basis of performance. This has proved impossible, and regular compensation for losses has been common with attendant serious effects on industry and fiscal policy.

6

Inferences and Conclusions

Sri Lanka provides two quite different episodes as bases for inferring what makes and breaks attempts to liberalize trade. In 1968 a small first step in what might have become a multistage program was aborted within two years. In 1977 a large first step, involving widespread switches of quotas to tariffs, occurred in what might then have been expected to be a multistage program. While that program suffered a number of significant setbacks, even after some eight years it was not reversed.

The multicountry study of which these Sri Lanka episodes make up one part identifies ten issues about which inferences should be drawn for the timing and sequencing of a trade liberalization episode. In the case of two of these issues the Sri Lankan experience offered little basis for drawing inferences and these matters are not taken further here. These issues related to the nature of discrimination among activities and the choice among forms of a uniform process. In the Sri Lankan case the apparent link between unemployment and liberalization is treated as an issue in its own right. Thus the list of issues for drawing inferences in the Sri Lanka study is as follows:

1 preference of one-stage versus gradual multistage liberalization;
2 appropriate speed of liberalization;
3 trade liberalization and unemployment;
4 desirability of a separate stage of replacement of quantitative restrictions by tariffs;
5 desirability of a separate stage of export promotion;
6 uniform versus discriminatory treatment of sectors;
7 appropriate circumstances for the introduction of liberalization policy;
8 sustainability of liberalization under alternative accompanying policies.

Table 6.1 summarizes the key issues for each Sri Lankan episode. At the beginning of this case study we offered some preliminary propositions as to what the Sri Lankan experience suggested about these issues. These preliminary propositions reflected several influences: impressionistic evidence from Sri Lanka, general observations about liberalization, economic

Table 6.1 Sri Lankan liberalization episodes and summary of issues

Issues	1968	1977
One-stage or multistage	Further expansion of OGL foreshadowed but not achieved	First step relatively large; next stages vague and mainly fine tuning holding action
Speed and length	Started with small step and aborted within 2 years	Pace implied by first step not sustained
Quantity restrictions to tariffs	Selective replacement of licensing by free entry at higher rates of exchange	Deliberate and explicit switch – main feature of liberalization
Export promotion	Dual exchange rate by way of FEEC scheme favored non-traditional exports and taxed traditional exports	Separate follow-up component – visible large institutional content; contradictory financing by import duty levy
Alternative forms of industry protection	Process not uniform; forms indirect and not easily related to actual incentive afforded sectors	First-step switching to tariffs amenable to uniform treatment but indirect fine tuning forms persisted
Appropriate circumstances	Government 2 years after a closed regime	New government immediately following a closed regime
Sustainability	Failed as exports did not take off; wrongly priced imported essentials reasserted dominance	Persisted, sustained by reasonable opportunity for exports, tenacity of government supported by aid
Implications for desirable path	Small and selective steps seem to gain more detractors than supporters	In hindsight first step could have been bolder or else government should have locked itself into credible gradual program of continuing liberalization

theory, and almost certainly personal bias. A systematic collection of all the evidence from Sri Lanka changed the story. The Sri Lankan experience is reviewed below with a view to drawing inferences on the basis of just two episodes and also to providing a summary for use in the synthesis document.

Preference of One-stage versus Gradual Multistage Liberalization

One way of tackling the question of one-stage or gradual liberalization is to use hindsight to ask how liberalization might have been conducted better in Sri Lanka. Among the options facing policymakers in 1977 three stand out:

1 a very large, almost one-shot, opening up of trade barriers;
2 announcing a nonnegotiable gradual phasing out of trade barriers over, say, five years;
3 taking a significant first step and following up as appropriate.

As has been documented in this case study, policymakers laid the basis for the third option. It is understood that the one-shot option was seriously contemplated, and the preliminary proposition of the case study is that it would have been better to have done that. After review, the conclusion is that either the first or the second option would have been better. The links between the trade liberalization that did occur and disruption, whether in terms of unemployment or business failures, are virtually untraceable. Thus it seems that the government could have come down much harder with trade barrier dismantling and not caused much, if any, economic dislocation.

Similarly, if the government had been able to establish in the minds of the electorate a credible gradual program of license removal and tariff reduction, the end result might well have been much the same as with a "one large shot" approach. Even a very slow pace of adjustment, with a definite target, would have been more likely to produce results than the heavily managed defensive fine tuning that did occur. By allowing industry policy to be formulated on an industry-by-industry basis after the first broad measures the Sri Lankan government found itself enmeshed in detail and without direction.

The arguments about these propositions turn very much on judgments about what is politically possible. Sri Lankan policymakers can argue that, despite great difficulties, at least the 1977 episode has not been reversed and that reversal would have been a real danger if more rapid or definitely targeted change had been attempted. Perhaps so, but it could just as well be argued that the exciting and successful days of growth and prosperity happened soon after the first turnabout of trade policy and it might be asked where the political obstacles were to adopting a policy which seemed to have such early and general rewards.

Both Sri Lankan episodes provide an example of a first step in trade liberalization. Neither episode is a good example of one-stage or multistage liberalization. For this reason the lessons from Sri Lanka about the desirability of a one-stage versus a multistage liberalization are limited.

What can be said with the benefit of hindsight, particularly for the 1977 episode, is as follows: first, the initial changes could have been larger; second, a credible follow-up program of general but gradual reductions would have been desirable; third, the fine tuning defensive actions turned debate and policymaking interest away from a long-run target of further reductions and toward managing and sustaining the existing system of protection and structure of industry.

Appropriate Speed of Implementation

The 1977 episode tends to support the notion that governments have "100 days of grace" to secure significant and durable policy change. The story from 1968 is less clear. What liberalizing actions there were took place some 18 months after the government took office. However, these actions were relatively small and fizzled out quickly. At first glance this tentative evidence for quick action raises a question of whether transparency of policy and consequent public understanding and appreciation of the need for change are prerequisites for durable change. However, in 1977 the government had campaigned on a program of reversing the closed economy. To this extent an election campaign can be seen as the forum for public understanding and persuasion. Once a decision or commitment has been made, the question of speed of implementation is bound up with the question of one-stage versus multistage processing. On this matter the previous conclusion can be restated. Credibility and commitment may be good substitutes for quick implementation, and indeed without these qualities any liberalization effort is bound to come unstuck.

Liberalization and Unemployment

Sri Lanka does not seem to be a stylized case where some activities suffered visible cutbacks in output and employment as a result of direct effects of import competition arising from liberalization. With few exceptions, capacity utilization, employment, and output rose during the postliberalization period. By and large in the Sri Lankan experience there is little disruption that might be attributed to liberalization. There are several possible explanations for this:

1 specific labor and capital resources in manufacturing industry adjusted quickly to lower returns;
2 the tariff regime in the first stage of the 1977 episode was, in fact, carefully pitched to ensure continued survival of local production;
3 possibly the losses in the textile and wearing apparel sector were offset by the growing garment export industry which expanded because of the coincidental emergence of favorable market opportunities;
4 the demand for labor shifted because of the expansion of economic activity due to swapping tariffs for quotas, the aid development program, and expansionary budgets;
5 liberalization policies which encouraged construction for tourism and banking, and the opportunities for overseas work and worker remittances, overwhelmed what might have been negative individual industry employment effects due to increased exposure to imports;
6 the data are inadequate.

Whether the apparently small unemployment effects in Sri Lanka can be explained in terms of flexible wages is not clear. Union power does not seem to have been strong in the post-liberalization period, and in the relatively large unorganized sector both wages and job classifications are likely to be subject to frequent renegotiation. The wages data available show little increase in post-liberalization real wages but the data on wage adjustments in particular sectors are not detailed enough to test a flexible wages argument. It could be that wages were flexible enough to prevent unemployment and output reductions, but that nonetheless individuals with specific skills or who owned specific factors of production faced losses in accommodating to the new price regime. The business failures reported in the 1980 special survey by the Ministry of Industries could be used as an example of losses borne by individual physical plant owners, but not necessarily of social losses if the social value of the firm was in fact negligible.

In examining the second explanation for such apparently small disruption, recall that the revised tariff structure incorporated a protective band of 100 percent for established local production. Combined with the low duties on material inputs this meant continuing very high effective protection for much of established industry, as the available measures show. Certainly for the public sector corporations – tires, hardware, steel, chemicals, and paper – tariff policy was largely concerned with specifying duties which would protect the usually restricted items made by the public corporations but which would let in similar items not made locally at a much lower rate. Needless to say, a tariff industry all its own was created as the opportunities for taking advantage of these lower-duties items were seized by consumers, for example using steel rod when wire would do, putting heavy-duty truck-size tires on passenger vehicles, or rewinding industrial sewing thread for domestic use. This led in turn to the introduction of redressing duties to stop these obviously socially wasteful activities.

One proposition is that the expansion in the export garment sector that occurred in the aftermath of the 1977 episode would have happened anyway owing to the preferential market access which became available to Sri Lanka at that time. This argument would hold that the main ingredient of industry growth and exports in Sri Lanka had little if anything to do with the liberalization episode of 1977. However, this argument goes too far. To begin with, a lead project of the episode was the establishment of the free-trade zone. Second, there were several other measures which, although of marginal importance, together with the free-trade zone must have increased the relative attractiveness of exporting garments from Sri Lanka. The general opening up that occurred with liberalization, expectations about stability and conditions for foreign investment, taxation holidays, and treatment of the incomes of foreign experts would have made post-liberalization Sri Lanka a much better bet for establishing a garment export industry than a number of countries with similar natural endowments, and certainly a better bet than pre-1977 Sri Lanka.

Whether at the country study level or in the synthesis of country studies, the objective of drawing inferences about liberalization and responses to it requires sorting through the other things that have impinged on the economy. Principal among the factors which complicated the isolation of the net effects of liberalization in Sri Lanka was the huge program of public investment, most of which was aid financed but which made substantial demands on domestic resources. Related to this have been large budget deficits, high rates of inflation relative to past Sri Lankan experiences, and high rates of interest, all manifestations of the claim for resources from the public sector.

One of the most difficult interactions to untangle is the impact of the substantially aid-backed lead projects for irrigation, hydroelectric power, and housing. In the immediate post-liberalization period, these projects generated no revenues but drew heavily on domestic resources. They generated growth in economic activity and in demand, particularly perhaps the output of the still protected manufacturing industry, but at the same time would have drawn resources away from local export- and import-substituting industries. They also put considerable strain on the balance of payments, and in the late 1970s and early 1980s a large part of the import bill was attributable to aid projects. The enormous expansion of public investment created pressure for the exchange rate to appreciate as the added demand for nontradeables caused their prices to rise relative to prices of traded goods. The rapid expansion of the construction sector and concurrent rapid increases in construction costs are indicative of these effects at work.

The data do present problems. One set of figures – from the organized sector – shows steady growth in most of the manufacturing sector following the start of the episode. This growth, while dominated by the organized garment sector, has nonetheless been steady in all except the very small fabricated metals sector and shows little evidence of being knocked by import competition. There are reports of closures of firms, but the entry of new firms is documented as widespread. The data for the large unorganized sector are much less satisfacotry. Some of them suggest that there were cutbacks of output and employment in that sector but that there was also some increase in real wages. There are several possible interpretations. One is that the data are inadequate. Another is that the protective regime was much less finely balanced in sustaining production in this unorganized sector of small confectionery firms, metal fabricators, makers of handlooms, and so forth. A third explanation is that labor from this sector could have been diverted into construction activities in Sri Lanka and to join the flow of labor to the Middle East. A fourth interpretation is that some firms coped well with the competition in resources from other sectors and others did not.

Desirability of a Quantitative Restriction to Tariff Stage

The 1977 episode was very much a switching of quantitative restriction to tariff barriers, and the experience is consistent with the advantages usually held to flow from making that switch. The breakdown of barriers to entry into some domestic activities, such as plastics packaging materials, was significant and could explain why liberalization led to increased domestic output in some manufacturing sectors. In addition to this boost to performance from greater domestic competition in the early days of the episode, the much freer access to imported inputs enabled slack capacity to be taken up, thereby giving an early and easy push for growth.

It is interesting that in the Sri Lanka exercise there was no effort to guess at the protective tariff equivalent provided by the license control. Instead, goods were classified according to stage of production and duties were applied accordingly. Goods produced locally under license received instead a duty of 100 percent. Thus for some goods the adjustment may have meant a substantial increase in protection while for others it probably meant a decrease. The Sri Lankan experience therefore highlights the importance, in making the switch to tariff-only protection, of locking in a program of reductions across the board. If that were to be done it would not matter if the initial switching to tariffs were to err on the high side. There was no locking in of next steps in Sri Lanka and such adjustments as were done were carried out on a piecemeal fine tuning basis.

Desirability of a Separate Stage of Export Promotion

This predilection to fine tuning was particularly apparent in export promotion efforts. Presented almost as the second stage of liberalization, export promotion in Sri Lanka was an important part of the policy platform from 1978. However, the program was not effective. To begin with, it was not driven by the rationale that liberalization was about neutrality. It was not even as if export development was seen to be concerned with encouraging exports; rather, it came to be directed to selected exports, particularly new exports and manufactured exports. Thus taxes on traditional exports – whether directly or indirectly in the form of a levy on highly dutied imports – were invoked to support an export drive. The partly deregulated finance system was manipulated so that special discount windows were made available to selected exporters who were frequently chosen on criteria that bore little relationship to efficiency or neutrality. In the case of Sri Lanka, therefore, the evidence does not disprove the proposition that the direct approach to trade liberalization, with direct reductions of high protection, is preferable. The indirect approach to neutrality by way of increasing assistance for lightly protected activities (incuding exports) tended to founder for two important reasons. First, the information and administrative requirements for achieving neutrality proved to be too much. It was not possible to identify and measure the taxes on different export activities, let alone to design, administer, and pay for offsetting instruments. Second, the ploy of selective export encouragement can become an end in itself and thereby distract policymakers from neutrality, the objective of liberalization in the first place.

Uniform versus Discriminatory Treatment of Sectors

The initial step in Sri Lanka with the six-band duty structure was at first neutral across sectors, although it discriminated among classes of goods. Where there was a local production to protect, a 100 percent duty replaced licensing. Only in a few cases did licensing stay on to protect local industry. With hindsight the greatest policy failure was not to apply a program of gradual (even very gradual) overall reductions to this new set of tariff-only barriers. Instead, the government fine tuned the tariffs on a discriminatory basis. It would have been much better to have taken further across-the-board measures. This was apparently judged to be politically impossible. The fine tuning did not secure much progress in trade, and it distracted attention from the need for across-the-board measures; however, it did not lead to a wholesale return to protectionism.

Appropriate Circumstances and Sustainability of Liberalization

Political circumstances were similar in both liberalization cases: a newly elected center-right government took up the reins from center-left administrations that had run largely closed regimes which had brought low growth and high unemployment. In both episodes the Sri Lankan experience points to a willingness to try liberalization after a disillusioning experience with a closed economy. In each case growth was low, unemployment was up, and rationing queues and restrictions were widespread. Inflation was not a major issue. Outside circumstances were propitious in 1977. Tea prices had recovered, aid commitments were on standby, opportunities for Sri Lankans to work abroad were available, and there was even a chance of access to the preferred garment markets of the United States and Europe. Table 6.2 summarizes the behavior of major economic variables leading up to the episode.

In 1977, initial policy actions was rapid while later changes were more about fine tuning existing arrangements than continuing sweeping reform. This continuing adjustment left many distortions intact. Public corporations continued to drain the economy and the lead projects to which the government committed itself in the early liberalization days became sources of substantial macroimbalance. Commodity prices, while favorable at first, were not encouraging for much of the post-liberalization period, and violence on a wide scale has beset the island since 1983. The 1968 episode did not last for several reasons. There were continuing balance-of-payments difficulties, slow export growth, low commodity prices, and finally a change to a government with a completely different ideology. By comparison, the 1977 episode was extended despite the setbacks from communal disturbances, low tea prices in the late 1970s, continuing high public sector claims on resources, and some inconsistent fine tuning of trade measures. Working in its favor have been such things as continuing aid flows, a recovery of tea prices in 1983, remittances from people working abroad, and a government firmly entrenched in power.

Sustainability of Liberalization under Alternative Accompanying Policies

A stylized story for Sri Lanka since 1948 has been one of successive governments locked into import-dependent expenditure programs, which to be sustained in times of balance-of-payments crises required a squeeze on other import goods. Thus the pressure for import controls and rationing of foreign exchange has been persistent in Sri Lanka.

Table 6.2 Summary of the behavior of major economic variables before liberalization episodes

Variable	1968	1977
Aggregate production	Growth variable between 3 and 6%	Very low growth rates
Unemployment	About 15%	About 20%
Business failures	Closed economy – limits on domestic competition; data poor; probably few starts and few failures	Same as in 1968
Exports	Falling real exports and widening trade balance over the past 10 years, apart from a mild improvement in 1965	A small positive trade balance in 1977, partly due to a recovery in tea prices and very low economic activity
Imports	Tightly controlled; pressure on import bill eased by excellent paddy harvest	Same as in 1968
Foreign exchange reserves	Lowest since 1940	Reserves well up in 1976 and 1977
Debt service position	Low relative to exports and GDP	Steady increases in debt through mid-1970s
International prices for exports	Large falls in tea prices over decade; rubber prices down in 1965, recovering in 1967; coconut prices up but production down	Tea prices recovered in 1977; value of exports increased by 20% between 1966 and 1977
Import prices	Stable	Petroleum prices rise in 1973; also high grain prices
Terms of trade	Continuous deterioration over previous 10 years; worsened in 1966 and 1967	Continuous deterioration over the previous 20 years; a slight improvement in 1977 owing to tea price hike and falling sugar and flour prices
Real rates of exchange	Steadily declining for traditional exports; for minor agricultural exports stable until late 1960s; for imports relatively stable from 1965 to 1967	For exports declining to mid-1970s; then an upturn reinforced by exchange rate unification in 1977
Inflation	About 3% in mid-1960s	About 6% through mid-1970s
Real rate of interest	Heavily controlled – rates apparently low and stable	Controls meant that measured or apparent nominal and real rates were quite low and stable

In the 1977 episode the Sri Lankan government became locked into a demanding program of public investment. Large capital inflows and deficit financing paid for this public investment in the initial years. By 1980 the budget deficit was some 20 percent of GDP, as was the current account deficit. Part of the problem was the nature of the projects in that, once committed, adjustment of scale was difficult. However, the government did manage to bring things back under some control. By 1983 deficits were reduced substantially, partly by government success in scaling down the projects. Also, the natural demands of the large projects tapered off as they neared completion, with some savings as hydroelectricity came on stream.

Fiscal management was not helped by the persistent demands made by the public corporations on the government, nor by the worsening external situation. The projects had yet to yield revenues and the mounting capital inflow put upward pressure on the real exchange rate. This real exchange rate appreciation occurred by way of an inflationary increase in the prices of nontraded goods, thereby checking the earlier progress of liberalization.

The government managed to avoid a retreat to import barriers as a way out of the balance-of-payments deficit pressures. While many changes in tariffs were of a fine tuning protective nature, some were driven by revenue objectives. There was no recourse to the very high shut-out duty increases that might be applied to bring the balance of payments into line but which erode a government's revenue collection base. Moreover, while tourism revenue fell after the disturbances of July 1983, tea prices did recover briefly and revenues from migrant workers and garment exports were maintained, as were aid flows.

The government won another six-year term in October 1982. Despite some pressures to the contrary, the rhetoric of liberalization, privatization, and deregulation survived. The key personalities in the government had remained in position for the five years from the beginning of the episode, and they were committed by both personal conviction and their past actions and statements to liberalization. Despite mistakes that are easily spotted with hindsight, the debilitating communal disturbances, and a measure of plain bad luck, their policies had had sufficient successes to be a better bet than closing the economy up again.

Indeed, in the course of the 1986 budget debate, the leader of the opposition said that the basic elements of the 1977 liberalization package – tariffs and not quotas, and a larger role for the private sector – would be retained even with a change in government.

References

Athukorala, Premachandra (1981) "Import substitution, structural transformation and trade dependence: a case study of Sri Lanka." *Developing Economies*, 24 (2), 119–42.

Athukorala, Premachandra (1984a) "Direct foreign investment and manufactured export expansion: the case of Sri Lanka." *Vidyodaya Journal of Arts Science and Letters*, 12, 21–41.

Athukorala, Premachandra (1984b) "Export development policies and achievements." *Economic Review, Peoples' Bank, Colombo*, 10 (3), 4–20.

Athukorala, Premachandra (1986) "Sri Lanka's experience with international contract migration and the reintegration of return migrants." In *International Migration for Employment*. Geneva: International Labor Organization, Working Paper (International) no. 26, pp. 1–51.

Balassa, Bela and Desmond McCarthy (1984) "Adjustment policies in developing countries." Mimeo, July. Washington, DC: World Bank.

Bandaranaike, R. Dias (1984) *Tea Production in Sri Lanka: Future Outlook and Mechanisms for Enhancing Sectoral Performance*. Colombo: Central Bank of Ceylon, Occasional Papers, no. 7.

Bhalla, Surjit (1984a) "Is Sri Lanka an exception? A comparative study of living standards." Mimeo. Washington, DC: World Bank.

Bhalla, Surjit (1984b) "Living standards in Sri Lanka 1970–1980 – an interpretation." Mimeo. Washington, DC: World Bank.

Bhalla, Surjit S. and Paul Glewwe (1986) "Growth and equity in developing countries: a reinterpretation of the Sri Lankan experience." *World Bank Economic Review*, 1 (1), 35–64.

CBC (Central Bank of Ceylon) *Annual Report*, various issues.

CBC (Central Bank of Ceylon) *Review of the Economy*, various issues.

CBC (Central Bank of Ceylon) (1963, 1973, 1978–9, 1981–2) *Consumer Finance and Socio-economic Survey*.

Corea, Gamani (1965) "Ceylon." In Cranley Onslow, ed., *Asian Economic Development*. London: Wiedenfeld and Nicolson.

Corea, Gamani (1971) "Aid and the economy." *Marga Quarterly Journal*, 1 (1), 19–54.

Cuthbertson, Andrew G. and Premachandra Athukorala (1988) "The timing and sequencing of trade liberalization policies: Sri Lanka, statistical appendices." Available from the Brazil Department, World Bank, Washington, DC.

Cuthbertson, Andrew G. and M. Z. Khan (1981) *Effective Protection to Manufacturing Industry in Sri Lanka*. Mimeo. Colombo: Ministry of Planning and Finance.

Dahanayake, P. A. S. (1977) *Economic Policies and their Implications for the Foreign Exchange Resource Availability in Sri Lanka 1956–72*. Colombo: Central Bank of Ceylon.

Department of Census and Statistics, Ministry of Plan Implementation (1974) *Population, Sri Lanka*. Colombo: Printing Division, Department of Census and Statistics.

Department of Census and Statistics, (1979, 1981) *Survey of Manufacturing Industry*. Colombo: Printing Division, Department of Census and Statistics.

Department of Census and Statistics (1983) *Statistical Pocket Book – 1983*. Colombo: Government Publication Bureau.

Department of Census and Statistics, *Statistical Abstract*, various issues.

Department of Labour, *Sri Lanka Labour Gazette*, various issues.

Dutta, Amita (1973) *International Migration, Trade and Real Income: a Case Study of Ceylon, 1920–38*. Calcutta: World Press.

Edirisinghe, Neville (1986) *The Food Stamp Program in Sri Lanka: Costs, Benefits and Policy Implications*. Washington, DC: International Food Policy Research Institute.

FAO, *International Trade Yearbook*, various issues.

Fernando, L. E. N. (1971) "Some aspects of private foreign enterprises in Ceylon." PhD dissertation, University of Hull.

Fernando, N. A. (1980) "A study of the impact of the land reform laws of 1972 and 1975 on tea production in Sri Lanka." *Central Bank of Ceylon, Staff Studies*, 10 (142) 54–85.

Fernando, N. A. (1982) "Some socio-economic aspects of tea plantations in Sri Lanka during the post-independence period." *Central Bank of Ceylon, Staff Studies*, 12 (2), 25–63.

Field, G. S. (1986) "Public policy and the evolution of the labor market in Sri Lanka." Mimeo. Washington, DC: World Bank.

Fitter, Jorn Carstern (1973) "Ceylon on the road to long-term decline." *Intereconomics*, 1, 25–7.

Glewwe, Paul (1986) "The distribution of income in Sri Lanka: a decomposition analysis." *Journal of Development Economics*, 24 (3), 255–74.

Glewwe, Paul (1988a) "Economic liberalization and income inequality: further evidence on the Sri Lankan experience." *Journal of Development Economics*, 28 (2), 233–46.

Glewwe, Paul (1988b) "Response to Ravallion and Jayasuriya." *Journal of Development Economics*, 28 (2), 257–60.

Gooneratne, Wilbert and D. Wesumperuma, eds (1984) *Plantation Agriculture in Sri Lanka Issues in Employment and Development*. Bangkok: International Labour Organisation, Asian Employment Programme.

Gunasekara, H. A. de S. (1963) "Ceylon." In Wilfred Frank Crick, ed., *Commonwealth Banking Systems*. Oxford: Clarendon.

Gunasekara, H. M. (1974) "The economy of Sri Lanka 1948–73." *The Ceylon Journal of Historical and Social Studies*, New Series, 4 (142), 73–92.

Gunasekara, H. M. (1977) "Foreign trade of Sri Lanka." In K. M. de Silva, ed., *Sri Lanka – a Survey*. London: C. Hurst.

Hewavitharana, B. (1975) "Recent trends in the management of external and internal finance in Sri Lanka." *Marga Quarterly Journal*, 2 (4), 1–37.

ILO (International Labor Organization) (1971) *Matching Employment Opportunities and Expectations: a Programme of Action for Ceylon*. Geneva: International Labor Organization.

Isenman, Paul (1980) "Basic needs: the case of Sri Lanka." *World Development*, 8, 237–58.

Jayawardene, J. R. (1978) *A New Path*. Colombo: Government Publication Bureau.

Jennings, Sir Ivor (1951) *The Economy of Ceylon*, 2nd ed. Madras: Oxford University Press.

Jiggins, Janice (1976) "Dismantling of welfarism in Sri Lanka." *ODI Review*, no. 2. Overseas Development Institute.

Jones, Gavin W. and S. Selvaratnam (1971) "Some problems of employment creation in Ceylon." *Marga Quarterly Journal*, 1 (1), 72–91.

Jupp, James (1978) *Sri Lanka: Third World Democracy*. Totowa, NJ: Cass.

Kaldor, Nicholas (1959) "Observations on the problem of economic development in Ceylon." In *Papers by Visiting Economists*. Colombo: National Planning Council.

Kappagoda, Nihal M. (1967) "Foreign exchange budgeting – Ceylon's experience." *Monthly Bulletin of the Central Bank of Ceylon*, September, 23–31.

Kappagoda, Nihal and Suzanne Paine (1981) *The Balance of Payments Adjustment Process: the Experience of Sri Lanka.* Colombo: Marga Institute.

Karunatilake, H. N. S. (1974) *Central Banking and Monetary Policy in Sri Lanka.* Colombo: Lake House.

Karunaratne, Neil Dias (1978) "A historical review of industrial development policy in Sri Lanka." *Asian Profile*, 7 (1), 49–62.

Kearney, Robert N. (1973) *The Politics of Ceylon (Sri Lanka).* Ithaca, NY: Cornell University Press.

Kravis, Irving B., Alan Heston, and Robert Summers (1983) *World Product and Income – International Comparison of Real Gross Product.* Baltimore, MD: The John Hopkins University Press.

Krueger, Anne and National Bureau of Economic Research (1978) *Foreign Trade Regimes and Economic Development: Liberalization Attempts and Consequences.* Cambridge, MA: Ballinger.

Lakshman, W. D. (1979) *Public Enterprises in the Economic Development of Sri Lanka.* Colombo: National Institute of Business Management.

Lakshman, W. D. (1985) "Income distribution impact of adjustment policies." Unpublished paper.

Lakshman, W. D. and Premachandra Athukorala (1985) "Analysis of trading channels for the foreign trade of Sri Lanka." In ESCAP/UNCTC Joint Unit on Transnational Corporations, *Transnational Trading Corporations in Selected Asian and Pacific Countries.* Bangkok: United Nations.

Lal, Deepak (1985) "The real exchange rate, capital inflows and inflation: Sri Lanka 1970–82." *Weltwirtschaftliches Archiv*, 121 (4).

Lal, Deepak and Sarath Rajapatirana (1985) "Trade liberalization in Sri Lanka." Paper prepared for the Research Meeting on Participation of Developing Countries in the International Trading System convened by the Trade Policy Research Centre, October 22–25, 1984. To be published as *Impediments to Trade Liberalization in Sri Lanka*, Thames Essay 51. London: Gower, for the Trade Policy Research Centre.

Levy, B. (1985) "Economic aid in the making of economic policy in Sri Lanka." Mimeo. Washington, DC: World Bank.

Manor, James (1984) *Sri Lanka in Change and Crisis.* London: Croom Helm.

Marga Institute (1974) "Welfare and growth in Sri Lanka." Colombo, Marga Research Studies no. 2.

Mason, Edward Sagendorph and Robert E. Asher (1973) *The World Bank since Bretton Woods; the Origins, Policies, Operations, and Impact of the International Bank for Reconstruction and Development and the Other Members of the World Bank Group: the International Finance Corporation, the International Development Association, the International Centre for Settlement of Investment Disputes.* Washington, DC: Brookings Institution.

Mathews, B. (1981) "President Jayawardene: half-term report" *Round Table*, 282, 149–62.

Ministry of Industries and Scientific Affairs (1971) *Capacity Utilization Survey.* Colombo: Ministry of Industries and Scientific Affairs.

Ministry of Planning and Economic Affairs (1967) *Development Program – 1966–7.* Colombo: Government Public Bureau.

Motha, J. G. G. (1971) "The impact of import policies on the economy of Ceylon." PhD dissertation, Stanford University.

Myint, Hla (1985) "Growth notices and income distribution." Washington, DC: World Bank, Development Policy Issues Series.

Myrdal, Gunnar and Twentieth Century Fund (1968) *Asian Drama – an Inquiry into the Poverty of Nations*, Part 3. New York: Twentieth Century Fund.

National Planning Council (1959) *The Ten-Year Plan (1958–68).* Colombo: The Planning Secretariat.

Nelson, Joan (1984) "The political economy of stabilization." *World Economy*, 12 October (10) 983–1006.

Oliver, Henry Madison (1956) "Industrialization of Ceylon's opinions and policies." *Ceylon Economist*, 3, 178–225.

Oliver, Henry Madison (1957) *Economic Opinion and Policy in Ceylon*. Durham, NC: Duke University Press.

Olson, R. S. (1977) "Expropriation and international economic coercion: Ceylon and the 'West' 1961–65." *Journal of Developing Areas*, 11 (2), 205–26.

Pick Publishing Corporation (1976) *Pick's Currency Yearbook*. New York: Pick's World Currency Report.

Pyatt, F. Graham and Alan Roe (1977) *Social Accounting for Development Planning with Special Reference to Sri Lanka*. Cambridge: Cambridge University Press.

Rasaputrum, W. (1973) "Exchange rate experience and policy in Sri Lanka since World War II." In Herbert G. Grubel and Theodore Morgan, eds, *Exchange Rate Policy in Southeast Asia*. Lexington, MA: Lexington Books.

Ravallion, Martin and Sisira Jayasuriya (1988) "Liberalization and inequality in Sri Lanka: a comment." *Journal of Development Economics*, 28 (2), 247–55.

Robinson, J. (1959) "Economic possibilities of Ceylon." *Papers by Visiting Economists*. Colombo: Planning Secretariat.

Rottenberg, Simon (1983) "Sri Lanka: public finances." Mimeo. Washington, DC: World Bank.

Savundranayagam, T. (1983) "Estimates of Sri Lanka's gross national product from 1950 to 1981." *Central Bank of Ceylon, Staff Studies*, 1–2, 70–202.

Sen, Amartya Kumar (1981) "Public action and quality of life in developing countries." *Oxford Bulletin of Economics and Statistics*, 43 (4) November, 287–320.

Shan, David E. (1987) "Changes in the living standards of the poor in Sri Lanka during a period of macroeconomic restructuring." *World Development*, 15 (6), 809–30.

Shourie, Arun (1974) "Growth, poverty and inequalities." *Foreign Affairs*, 340–52.

Snodgrass, Donald R. (1966) *Ceylon: An Export Economy in Transition*. Homewood, IL: Richard D. Irwin.

Sri Lanka Association of Economists (SLAE) (1986) *Proceedings of the Annual Sessions – 1985*. Colombo: SLAE.

Stern, J. (1984) "Liberalization in Sri Lanka: a preliminary assessment." Mimeo. Colombo: Ministry of Finance and Planning.

Streeten, Paul and Shahid Javed Burki (1978) "Basic needs: some issues." *World Development*, 6 (5), 268–80.

Tilakaratna, W. M. (1970) "How the FEEC Scheme came to be introduced." In *Research and Industry*. Colombo: Industrial Development Board.

United National Party (1977) "Election Manifesto."

Weeraratne, S. (1982) *The Proposed Foreign Investment Authority Law of Sri Lanka (1976)*. Colombo: Lake House.

Wickramasinghe, E. (1981) "The policies of the U.N.P." *Insight into the Sri Lanka Economy 1970–1983*. Colombo: Centre for Society and Religion, pp. 45–53.

Wijesinghe, Mallory E. (1976) *The Economy of Sri Lanka, 1948–1975*. Colombo: Ranco Printers.

Wilson, Jeyaratnam (1979) *Politics in Sri Lanka: 1947–1979*, 2nd ed. London: Macmillan.

World Bank (1953) *The Economic Development of Ceylon*. Baltimore, MD: The Johns Hopkins University Press.

World Bank (1975) "Recent economic development and current prospects." Mimeo. Washington, DC: World Bank.

World Bank (1982, 1984, 1985) *World Development Report*. Washington, DC: World Bank.

World Bank (1983) "Report of a World Bank Industry Policy Mission to Sri Lanka." Mimeo. Washington, DC: World Bank.

World Bank, *Commodity Trade and Price Trends*, various issues. Washington, DC: World Bank.

Wriggins, William Howard (1960) *Ceylon: Dilemmas of a New Nation*. Princeton, NJ: Princeton University Press.

Index

biases against, 346
under liberalization (1968–70),
354–6
Export tax
Indonesia, 24
Pungutan Ekspor: PUEK, 55–6,
60–1
Pakistan, 257

Federal Party, Sri Lanka, 328, 342
FEEC.*See* Foreign Exchange Entitle-
ment Certificate (FEEC), Sri
Lanka
Feith, Herbert, 28, 29, 30, 36, 42n, 46,
49n, 52, 69
Fernando, N. A., 305, 309, 326
FIAC.*See* Foreign Investment Advi-
sory Commission (FIAC)
Field, G. S., 379, 380
Fiscal deficit.*See* Deficit, domestic
Fiscal policy
Indonesia
before and after liberalization,
125–9
Pakistan, 210–11, 254
Sri Lanka, 312, 314
with 1968 liberalization, 348–9
with 1977 liberalization, 372
See also Deficit, domestic; Reve-
nues; Spending, government;
Taxation
Fitter, Jorn C., 331
Food stamp scheme, Sri Lanka, 314,
369, 397, 399
Food subsidy program, Sri Lanka,
314, 336, 397, 400
Foreign aid.*See* Economic assistance
Foreign Currency Banking Unit
Scheme, Sri Lanka, 376
Foreign exchange
Indonesia
allocation among industrial firms
of, 57–60, 78
government intervention in, 22–5,
86–8
Pakistan
allocation of, 245
dependence for liberalization on
reserves, 268–80
Sri Lanka
allocation of, 327
See also Overprice system

Foreign Exchange Bourse, Indonesia,
87
Foreign Exchange Budget Committee,
Sri Lanka, 327
Foreign Exchange Certificate system,
Indonesia, 13, 31–3, 37, 56, 63–4
Foreign Exchange Committee
Pakistan, 245
Foreign Exchange Entitlement Certifi-
cate (FEEC), Sri Lanka, 329, 330,
338, 342, 346, 349
Foreign Exchange Entitlement Certifi-
cates (FEEC), Sri Lanka
effect of, 350–1, 354–6
imports and exports under scheme
for, 338–9, 344–5, 349–50
Foreign Exchange Institute
(LAAPLN), Indonesia, 43, 58
Foreign exchange right (*Bukti Induse-
men*), Indonesia, 25, 33–4, 37,
38–9, 42–3
Foreign Investment Advisory Commis-
sion (FIAC), Sri Lanka, 377, 386,
394
Foreign Investment Law (1967), Indonesia, 116, 129–31, 185
Foundation for Raw Material Stocks
(Jajasan Persidiaan Bahan Perindustrian: JBP), 58
Furnivall, John S., 18, 30n

Garment industry, Sri Lanka, 390,
406–7
GESTAPU, Indonesia, 70
Glassburner, Bruce, 28, 42, 71
Glewwe, Paul, 380, 398–9
Gooneratne, Wilbert, 305
Government intervention
Indonesia, 14, 21–2, 30, 33–4, 58–9,
68–9
in banking system, 119
in foreign exchange market, 86–8
Pakistan, 223, 271
in international trade, 224
Sri Lanka, 310, 327–8
in economy, 330
during period of closed economy,
360
See also Bukti Indusemen; Export
Bonus Scheme (EBS); Import
control; Import licenses
Government Sponsored Corporations
Act 19 (1955), Sri Lanka, 324